新医科英语系列教材

ENGLISH-CHINESE MEDICAL
CONFERENCE INTERPRETING

英汉医学会议口译教程

主　编◎李　俊　郭靓靓
副主编◎陈　庆　王　晶
编　者◎陈　庆　丁羽翔
　　　　郭靓靓　黄久佐
　　　　李　俊　王华树
　　　　肖　月　杨丰源
　　　　赵　威
（按姓氏拼音排序）

清华大学出版社
北京

内 容 简 介

本书以医学卫生健康国际会议翻译为教学目标,选材覆盖医学学科中的多个子学科及其下设方向:预防医学(如流行病学)、基础医学(如免疫学)、临床医学(如内科、外科)等。语料选择上,本书兼顾科普性语料和专业性语料,既有完整讲话实录,又有讲话选编。语料既有中文,又有英文,英汉、汉英翻译的讲解和练习材料基本平衡。此外,本书还向读者补充介绍物理、化学、生物、统计、数学等医学相关学科的基本词汇和表达的译法,以夯实医学会议口译学习者的知识和语言基础。

根据编写团队医学会议口译实践经验,本书还提供了大量附录和词汇拓展,分别置于本书末尾和一些章节末尾,可供读者拓展学习。此外,本书将技术紧密地融合到医学会议口译的教学中,在上篇专门编写了两个章节,分别讨论术语和语料库使用问题。

版权所有,侵权必究。举报:010-62782989,beiqinquan@tup.tsinghua.edu.cn。

图书在版编目(CIP)数据

英汉医学会议口译教程 / 李俊,郭靓靓主编. —北京:清华大学出版社,2023.9(2025.1重印)
新医科英语系列教材
ISBN 978-7-302-64695-2

Ⅰ.①英… Ⅱ.①李… ②郭… Ⅲ.①医学—英语—口译—教材 Ⅳ.① H315.9

中国国家版本馆 CIP 数据核字(2023)第 185726 号

责任编辑:白周兵
封面设计:张伯阳
责任校对:王凤芝
责任印制:刘海龙

出版发行:清华大学出版社
网　　址:https://www.tup.com.cn,https://www.wqxuetang.com
地　　址:北京清华大学学研大厦 A 座　　　　邮　编:100084
社 总 机:010-83470000　　　　　　　　　　 邮　购:010-62786544
投稿与读者服务:010-62776969,c-service@tup.tsinghua.edu.cn
质量反馈:010-62772015,zhiliang@tup.tsinghua.edu.cn

印 装 者:天津鑫丰华印务有限公司
经　　销:全国新华书店
开　　本:185mm×260mm　　印　张:18.5　　字　数:446 千字
版　　次:2023 年 10 月第 1 版　　　　　　　 印　次:2025 年 1 月第 2 次印刷
定　　价:78.00 元

产品编号:094941-01

前　言

在习近平总书记提出构建人类卫生健康共同体的倡议以后，国际医学学术会议、全球卫生治理会议、多边和双边医疗卫生交流会议等变得更加频繁，准确高效的会议口译服务变得愈发重要。有鉴于此，我们组织了一批在一线从事医学会议口译实践和教学的教师、医生、科学家，共同合作编写了本书。跨学科的编写团队成员从各自的视角和专长出发，贡献了自己的力量，同时相互协作，确保本书的科学性和实用性。

英汉医学会议口译以国际医学会议、国际卫生管理会议为主要场景，因此我们在选材上侧重择取与这两类会议相关的常见主题。选取的练习材料既包括科普性语料，又包括专业性语料。这主要是缘于编写团队在受邀到外语院校系部开展医学口译教学时发现，外语院校师生对缝合、棉签、灭菌等卫生健康业内的基础性日常词汇都比较陌生，遑论行业专业术语。鉴于医学会议术语和行话较多，我们希望这些科普性语料能够帮助读者逐步补足卫生健康日常词汇和表达，促进他们在学习中不断积累，最终能够胜任术语繁多、专业技术性很强的医学学术和卫生管理会议的口译。本书既择取了中文讲话，又择取了英文讲话作为原文，且针对英汉、汉英翻译的讲解和练习材料保持基本平衡。

此外，医学本身除了囊括解剖、生理等临床医学基础课程，还涉及物理、化学、生物、统计、数学等多个学科，因此我们向读者介绍了这些相关学科的基本词汇和表达的译法。再者，广义的医学可进一步细分为预防、基础、临床、药学、护理等诸多子学科，我们的选材也尽量关照到上述各子学科。

本书的目标读者群体大约有三个：（1）对医学口译感兴趣的英语专业师生及研究者；（2）对会议口译感兴趣的护士、医生、药师、公共卫生专家等医疗卫生工作者及这些专业的学生；（3）医学英语专业、翻译专业等直接相关专业的师生。第一个群体在使用本书时，可重点关注下篇，补充医学词汇与知识；第二个群体在使用本书时，可重点关注上篇，补齐口译知识和技能；对于第三个群体，我们建议可以由上篇开始，循序渐进过渡到下篇，然而由于各院校医学英语专业、翻译专业课程设置中，医学、英语、口译的课程比重各有不同，需由师生结合自身实际酌情使用。

在编排顺序上，我们试图根据目标读者的背景知识和技能情况，从易到难地安排教学内容。上篇分七章，详细介绍医学会议口译的基本原理和技巧；下篇分五章，主要为实践案例。实践案例部分从专家和机构介绍、会议仪式性话语出发，逐渐过渡到公共卫生和临床医学（内科和外科），最后是基础医学。我们考虑到目标读者中，有不少人可能没有接受过系统性的医疗卫生教育，但接受过人文社科、英语、翻译等专业的教育，因此选择从与文科更接近的医疗卫生相关话题开始。已有的英汉医学口译教材，对于临床话题覆盖较好，但对于基础医学话题收录较少，这也许是因为它们的重点不在会议上，所以不会大量涉及基础医学话题。此外，与临床医学口译相比，基础医学口译更多涉及生物、化学、物理知识和词汇，口译时，译员还需要结合大量的基础医学知识，因此我们也将基础医学内容收入其中，放在下篇的最后一章。我们根据医学会议口译实践经验提供了一些附录和词汇拓展，分别置于本书末尾和一些章节末尾，补充了大量的词汇和表达，可供读者拓展学习。此外，我们还将技术紧密地融入医学会议口译的教学当中，在上篇专门编写了两个章节，分别讨论术语和语料库使用问题。

在本书编写过程中，我们得到了多位领导、同事、学生（包括代雨函、杜思钰、段骁睿、龙天音、马望尧、陶思晴、王睿、王羿博、张薇、赵朗、邹佳函等）及清华大学出版社的帮助，在此，向他们表示诚挚的谢意，也感谢北京信息科技大学贾红霞老师的引荐。感谢董晨院士、Jean-Paul Schmid 教授、王汉萍教授等专家学者慷慨地允许我们使用他们的讲话作为练习材料。董晨院士还专门帮助我们校正了讲话原稿，在此对他表示深深的谢意。此外，还要感谢郭莉萍教授、吴朝霞教授帮忙审读书稿。

编写一本跨学科的口译教材实属不易，编写团队虽尽其所能，但仍难免有诸多疏漏错误之处，敬请广大读者不吝赐教，期待未来可以继续发展、完善。

编者
2023 年 2 月

目 录

上 篇
理论与技巧

第 1 章 医学口译概况..................3
1.1 医学口译定义与分类 3
1.2 医学口译教育与培训................5
1.3 我国医学口译行业现状 7
1.4 国外医学口译行业现状 11
1.5 医学口译相关学术机构、行业协会和学术刊物 13
参考文献................................13

第 2 章 医学会议交替传译实现过程和训练方法 15
2.1 口译中的听解............................15
2.2 语块理论与交传中信息的提取和压缩 16
2.3 交替传译中的记忆 17
2.4 口译笔记....................................21
2.5 临场应变....................................32
2.6 交替传译的训练方法 32
2.7 笔记和复述练习 33
参考文献................................34

第 3 章　医学会议口译质量与译员素养培养……36
3.1 医学语言的特点……36
3.2 医学会议口译质量标准……38
3.3 提高口译质量的途径……39
3.4 医学会议口译译者素养培养……44
3.5 文化因素对口译质量的影响……45
3.6 英汉医学语言中的文化问题……48
3.7 称呼语的文化差异……49
参考文献……50

第 4 章　数学、物理、化学、统计学名词及变化趋势相关表达译法……51
4.1 数字……51
4.2 物理学、化学……54
4.3 统计学……56
4.4 描述变化趋势的常用表达……58
4.5 句型练习……62
参考文献……64

第 5 章　医学会议口译译前准备……65
5.1 了解会议目的和传译要求……65
5.2 查阅相关资料……65
5.3 整理资料并建立词汇表……66
5.4 了解发言人的口音特点……67
5.5 了解工作环境、工作方式并准备相关物料……69

第 6 章　语料库在医学会议口译中的应用 70

- 6.1 语料库设计 70
- 6.2 语料收集 71
- 6.3 语料数字化 71
- 6.4 语料清洗 73
- 6.5 语料对齐 75
- 6.6 语料格式转换 81
- 6.7 语料应用 82
- **参考文献** 88

第 7 章　术语库在医学会议口译中的应用 89

- 7.1 术语与术语库 89
- 7.2 术语收集 89
- 7.3 术语提取 90
- 7.4 术语格式转换 94
- 7.5 建立术语库 100
- 7.6 术语库应用 103
- 7.7 术语综合技术应用 107
- **参考文献** 116

下 篇　案例实践

第 8 章　人物和机构简介及仪式性讲话 119

- 8.1 人物和机构介绍 119
- 8.2 仪式性讲话 132
- **参考文献** 139

第 9 章　公共卫生 140

- 9.1 流感大流行预警级别提升通告 140

9.2 艾滋病防控 147
9.3 烟草控制 160
参考文献 165

第 10 章 内科 166
10.1 肺癌靶向治疗 166
10.2 多发性骨髓瘤 170
10.3 心脏康复 174
参考文献 188

第 11 章 外科 191
11.1 残胃癌治疗研究 191
11.2 乳腺肿瘤的外科手术治疗 201
11.3 脓肿切开引流 205
11.4 提上睑肌腱膜缩短术 216
参考文献 220

第 12 章 基础医学 221
12.1 艾滋病和流感的疫苗策略 221
12.2 慢性疲劳综合征 231
12.3 免疫疾病及免疫治疗 245
参考文献 255

附录 I 常见物理学和化学单位及公式英汉对照表 256
附录 II 医疗卫生翻译中难译的非专业词汇 262
附录 III 常见医学词汇英汉对照 265
参考文献 270

目录

附录Ⅳ 国家卫生健康委员会及其内设机构名称汉英对照 271

附录Ⅴ 中国疾病预防控制中心及其内设机构名称汉英对照 276

附录Ⅵ 国家医疗保障局及其内设机构名称汉英对照 279

附录Ⅶ 国家药品监督管理局及其内设机构名称汉英对照 280

附录Ⅷ 常见药物英汉对照 283

上 篇
理论与技巧

第 1 章

研究目的

第1章

医学口译概况

本章简要介绍医学口译的定义与分类、我国大陆和台湾地区及国外部分院校的医学口译教学与培训情况、我国医学口译行业现状、国外医学口译行业现状及医学口译相关学术机构、行业协会和学术刊物。

1.1 医学口译定义与分类

早在2 000多年前,我国就有了专司翻译的人员,被称作"象寄之才""狄鞮""通译""通事"等(周密,2012)。《礼记·王制》中记载,东西南北中五方的人民,虽然言语不通,嗜好不同,但当他们要表达心意、互相交流的时候,需要有懂得双方语言的人帮助沟通。这种人在东夷叫寄,在南蛮叫象,在西戎叫狄鞮,在北狄叫译(钱歌川,2013)。《后汉书·和帝纪》提到了当时对译者的需求:"偏师出塞,匈奴逃去,漠北地空;都护远征西域,降五十余国,语言通译四万里。"(王子今、乔松林,2013:10)

从现代的翻译实践来看,翻译(translation)是把源语言(source language)承载的信息转换并传递到目标语言(target language)的交际活动,既包括笔头翻译(笔译,written translation / translation),也包括口头传译(口译,interpretation/interpreting)。按翻译主题,口译可细分为法律口译、金融口译、医疗卫生口译、旅游口译、商务口译、媒体口译等;按口译场合,它可细分为法庭口译、医院口译、会议口译等;按口译实现形式,它又可细分为现场口译、电话口译、在线视频口译等方式。

会议口译的两大基本形式是交替传译(consecutive interpretation)和同声传译(simultaneous interpretation)。同声传译可在同传厢(booth)内完成,也可在同传厢外[1]通过耳语同传(whispering)完成。耳语同传时,译员一般坐到某一个或几个听众身旁小声耳语翻译,有时也会为译员配置带麦克风的耳机和无线电信号发射装置等的简易同传设备。有时,由于现场使用语言较多,甚至需要接力同传。陪同翻译(liaison interpretation)也是口译的一种形式,参观、非正式会见和小型谈判常用此种方式。如使用英汉两种语言沟通的听众双方只有一位译员,则该译员需负责双向传译。有时,该译员甚至需要协助交流双方完成简单的文秘工作。

医学口译是以医疗卫生为主题或发生在医疗卫生场景下,涉及医疗、医药、卫生、健康的口译,包括医学学术口译和医疗口译。广义的医学包括基础医学、临床医学、预防医学、药学、护理学、社会医学、人文医学,还有传统医学[2]和现代医学并存的现象。国内外用以描述医学相关口译的术语较多,包括医学口译、医疗口译、卫生口译、医疗卫生口译、medical interpreting、interpreting in health care、health care interpreting等。

1　即在会场内做同传,英文用on the floor表达"在会场内"之意。

2　又称补充和替代医学(complementary and alternative medicine),包括中医、阿育吠陀医学、阿拉伯传统医学及其他民族医学。

在美国等移民国家,常见的医学口译形式是医疗口译(interpreting in health care),即"发生在医生办公室、诊所、医院、医生上门访视、面向公众的医疗知识宣讲等医疗相关场景下的口译,尤其是发生在医患对话过程中的口译"。在美国,医疗口译的形式除了传统的口语翻译,还包括手语翻译(何静,2010)。

对医学口译进行分类时,考虑到交际目的、交际场合、交流方式、翻译方向等因素,我们可根据医学口译发生的场合、内容、参与口译协助下的沟通双方(或多方)所处空间、译员工作模式、目的等对医学口译进行细分。医学口译可分为医学会议口译、医院参观考察评鉴口译、医疗产品展览口译、医疗投融资洽谈口译和诊疗口译等。

按场合,医学口译可分为会议口译和社区口译(包括在医院、诊所、康复中心、养老院等广义的社区);按内容,它可根据不同医学专科进行细分;按参与口译协助下的沟通双方(或多方)所处空间,它可分为面对面口译、远程音视频口译等;按译员工作模式,它可分为联络翻译、交替传译和同声传译等;按交流目的,它可分为学术类口译(如医学会议/讲座口译)、涉及医疗和医学的洽谈合作类口译(如医药公司等洽谈合作陪同口译)、医疗口译(如诊疗中的口译服务)等(于苏甫,2016)。

在我国,医学往往指广义医学,专科和亚专业繁多,故医学口译涉及的话题和亚专业也较多,突破了在美国、澳大利亚等国家的"医学翻译以医患会话口译为主"的模式。我国典型的西医院校学科分类详见图1.1。在我国,大量医学口译发生在会议中,尤其是医学会议中。值得注意的是,我国医学中还存在中医药及其他民族医学[1],这使得医学口译的话题更加繁多。

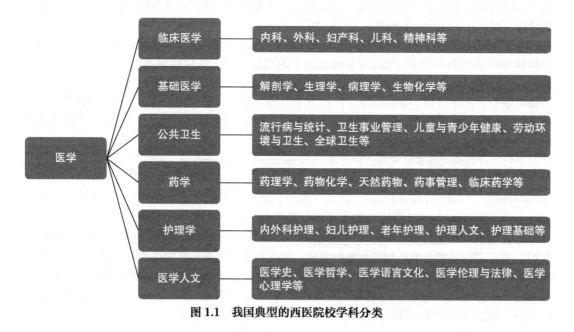

图 1.1 我国典型的西医院校学科分类

---

1 国外也将这些医学形式称为传统医学、补充和替代医学或民族医学(ethnomedicine)。

1.2 医学口译教育与培训

中华人民共和国成立后，较为系统的译员培训始于1979年，联合国在当时的北京外国语学院（现北京外国语大学）设立了译员培训班，在40多年的办学过程中，为中国培养了大批高级译员，译训班现已发展为北京外国语大学高级翻译学院。目前，国内大多数综合大学和外国语大学都兴办了翻译硕士专业学位（Master of Translation and Interpreting，MTI）专业型硕士项目，比较著名的院校包括上海外国语大学、广东外语外贸大学、西安外国语大学、四川外国语大学、厦门大学、同济大学、复旦大学、对外经济贸易大学、外交学院等；在台湾地区，开设翻译硕士项目的有辅仁大学和台湾师范大学等；在香港，开设该项目的有香港中文大学、香港城市大学等。在国外，比较有名的院校如英国的巴斯大学、纽卡斯尔大学，美国的蒙特雷国际研究院等也都开设了该项目。口译专业在细分发展，如科技口译人才培养、医学口译人才培养已经进入学界视野。

我国开展医学口译培训硕士项目的学校有西安交通大学、台湾辅仁大学、南京中医药大学、河南中医药大学、重庆医科大学等。广东外语外贸大学前后开展了三期医学口译工作坊，吸引了大批学生和爱好者；北京大学医学部、北京协和医学院等均建有医学翻译社，面向学生开展医学翻译培训活动。西安交通大学和北京大学医学人文学院开展了较为系统的医学口译教学。西安交通大学开设了医学方向MTI，要求学生口笔译融合发展，给学生开设一般性MTI课程[1]，并辅以医学方向翻译课程。此外，该校在翻译硕士教学阶段，不重复本科课程，学生以实践为导向进行学习，教师以实践为基础进行教学。师资力量既包括早前西安医科大学科技英语专业培养的人才，也包括部分医学知识相对缺乏的教师（聂文信等，2013）。

北京大学医学部举办了医学英语专业5年制本科项目，并在招生简章中明确提出将培养合格的医学翻译员作为其培养目标之一。它同时开设医学和英语课程，其教学强度基本相当（医学课程大约占30%的学分）。此外，它还设有部分医学与语言融合课程，如医学文献编辑、医学英语词汇等。医学课程由医学专业教师讲授，英语和翻译课程由该系英语教师及有丰富医学口译经验的教师讲授。该校医学英语专业课程设置参见图1.2，学生从二年级下学期开始接触口笔译。开设翻译理论课一门，实践课6.5门，包括英汉笔译、汉英笔译、医学文献翻译、口译基础、医学同声传译、医学交替传译等。

- 大一：有机化学、高等数学、计算机、中国近现代史、英语听说读写课、通识课程等
- 大二：生物统计、解剖、生化、组胚、生理、英语听说读写课、口译基础1等
- 大三：免疫、病理、微生物、寄生虫、全球卫生史、生物伦理、卫生法、翻译理论与实践、口译基础2、医学交替传译1、英汉笔译、英语医学词汇、英语医学文献阅读等
- 大四：药理、流行病与社会医学、预防、病理生理、临床医学医学交替传译等，进入医院见习（下学期）
- 大五：医学文献翻译、实习和毕业论文撰写等

图1.2 北京大学医学部医学英语专业课程设置概况

---

[1] 该校生源中，约三分之一的本科生就读的是医学英语专业。

北京大学医学部医学英语专业医学口译课程设置分基础口译和医学口译、工作坊和口译实习三个阶段。基础口译阶段主要介绍口译的基本技巧，并提高学生的英汉双语能力，练习材料主题覆盖传统口译练习话题，如政治、经济、文化、社会、外交、科技、教育等。医学口译阶段教学从社会和人文医学入手，逐步过渡到临床医学和生物医学，以学术会议现场录音录像为主要教学材料，辅以部分科普节目。医学方向练习材料主题包括流行病学、全球健康、医学社会学、医学伦理学、内科疾病治疗、外科疾病治疗、肿瘤靶向治疗、基因编辑技术。由于教学时间有限，只能从各个主题中选取一两个案例进行教学。例如，内科疾病，选择慢阻肺的治疗进行教学。这个阶段的教学重点包括六个方面：强化双语术语听说、会议语言及英汉会议文化对比、医学各专科和疾病专题知识、生物统计学、流行病知识、医学科研方法。之所以重视统计学知识和医学科研方法，是因为北大医学部的口译培养主要是为各医学国际会议输送高级口译人才，而这些国际会议大多学术性较强，交流过程常常涉及统计学知识、医学科研方法。在教学过程中，教师注意强化交传、视译、同传技巧、课堂口译练习和课后笔译、口译练习结合，并按认知模块和知识结构梳理词汇和表达。医学口译工作坊和口译实习等实践教学项目为高水平和对医学口译感兴趣的学生开放。工作坊主要是采取讲座形式，由本校翻译教师针对一些专题为感兴趣的学生提供讲座。口译实习则是学生在教师的带领和监督下完成真实的口译工作，并由教师进行事后的总结和点评，以帮助学生将课堂学习内容与实际工作相结合。

在医疗口译人才培养模式和课程设置方面比较有代表性的是我国台湾辅仁大学国际医疗口译学程（硕士学位项目）和美国国际医疗口译员协会（International Medical Interpreters Association，IMIA）的医疗口译员认证课程。

辅仁大学外语学院/跨文化研究所国际医疗口译学程为两年制硕士研究生课程，包括汉英、汉日两个方向，其必修课程包括笔译、文件管理等，共8学分；还有汉英、汉日共同选修课程7门：医疗服务礼仪、国际医疗概论、医疗程序与医务概论、医疗口笔译与医院评鉴、国际医疗保单与核保、医院文件管理、医疗名词解释（共17学分，要求学生选够8学分课程即可）。针对汉英方向，要求学生在1—2学分/门、共计17学分的选修课程中选够4学分，课程包括中英医疗对话口译、中英医疗文件视译、中英医疗逐步口译[1]、中英医疗进阶口译（1学分）、医疗科技翻译（一）：英译中、医疗科技翻译（二）：中译英、中英字幕翻译。

美国的医疗口译员培训课程共包括2个阶段。孟菲斯大学公共卫生学院开设的课程是美国国际医疗口译员协会第一个认证的项目，面向双语或多个语言熟练者开放，至少凑齐10人才可开班；每年集中授课一次，集中学习60个小时。学习内容包括医疗口译角色和模式、医疗口译操作规程、文化胜任力、医学术语、解剖学和生理学基础、疾病、伦理原则、实践标准、相关法律法规、源语言信息口头转达至目标语言练习等。完成60个小时的课堂学习以及至少10个小时实习的人才可获得迈阿密大学颁发的结业证书。开始第二个阶段的学习前，学习者需要完成第一阶段课程，第二阶段的学习内容包括急诊、重症监护室（ICU）、肿瘤科、缓和医疗科口译等，同时进一步学习解剖、生理、医学术语。在师资上，比起辅仁大学，它有明显不足，目前只有一名精通英语和西班牙语的资深医疗口译员负责讲授所有课程。据课程网站介绍，

---

[1] 即"交传"。

这位教师拥有30年的教学经验，也同时拥有医疗口译员资格证，并在圣裘德儿童研究医院（St. Jude Children's Research Hospital）执业。

在教材建设方面，1978年至今，国内有两本公开出版的医学口译教材：复旦大学出版社于2012年出版的《当代医学英汉笔译与口译教程》、外语教育与研究出版社于2015年出版的《医学口译》。《当代医学英汉笔译与口译教程》选材广泛覆盖了医学的各门子学科，主题包括医学教育、青霉素的发现、癌症的血液诊断、病毒、健康生活方式、饮食与糖尿病、健康是可传染的、父母定制婴儿、代价昂贵的医疗差错、明日的医院等。可谓是从临床医学、基础医学、预防医学、药学、护理学、医疗制度、医学人才培养等学科视角出发编写的一本广义上的医学口译教材。《医学口译》则主要关注疾病临床诊疗口译；该书共有15章，内容囊括心血管内/外科、神经内/外科、消化科、血液内科、内分泌科、口腔科、神经病科、眼科、肿瘤科、呼吸内科、普外科、妇产科、矫形外科（骨科）、儿科和耳鼻喉科常见疾病诊疗。

1.3 我国医学口译行业现状

医学口译市场的需求可以从医学国际会议口译需求、医疗口译和医疗产品展会三方面来说明。与美国不同，中国医学口译主要是医学会议口译和医学洽谈类口译（于苏甫，2016），近年来，我国医疗口译的需求量逐渐出现增长。

在医学国际会议口译需求方面，据国际大会与会议协会（ICCA）数据，2017年，北京接待会议数量21.5万个，其中高规格国际会议81个（北京日报，2018）。据笔者的不完全统计[1]，2018年，我国至少召开了62场国际医学会议，详见表1.1。2019年后，线下会议减少，但线上医学卫生会议数量保持稳定，甚至有所增长。

表1.1 2018年我国部分机构举办的国际医学会议统计

渠道	个数
中华医学会	12
正保医学教育网	10+
MedSci 梅斯网	10+
中国医师协会	20+
北大医学系统	10+
总计	62+

在分布特点上，国际医学会议召开有地域集中、季节性强的特点。召开地域上，以北京为主（北京日报，2018），其次是上海和广州，再次是各省和直辖市中心城市。召开季节上，九、十月份是医学会议召开高峰期，此外，三月份会议也较多，冬季会议较少，这主要是因为气候条件影响了会议的召开时机选择。

---

[1] 在医院系统方面，我们仅仅调查了北大医学系统（包括医学部本部和九家附属医院）的情况。上海、广州、深圳及其他省会城市未调查。

此外，由于世界经济全球化，越来越多的外国药企在中国运营，越来越多的中国药企也可能在不久的将来进入国际化运营的阶段。在中国境内召开的医学会议，常常由药厂赞助，虽然从医学伦理学的角度，可能存在利益冲突，但事实上促进了医学国际会议的召开，客观上推动了医学口译的需求量增加。

近年来，中外医疗投融资合作不断增加，环球医疗等国内大型国企下的医疗投资部门大力吸引外资；2018 年 11 月，泰康仙林鼓楼医院与美国西奈山医院达成长期合作，成为西奈山医院附属医院。这些对医学口译的蓬勃发展也起到了促进作用。

此外，医疗口译也在蓬勃发展，以著名的跨国医疗服务公司盛诺一家为例，该公司总部位于北京，国内子公司设在上海、广州、杭州、深圳，国外子公司下设的办事处位于波士顿、休斯敦、罗彻斯特、纽约、克利夫兰、巴尔的摩、伦敦、柏林、东京。当前员工数在 200 人左右，主要提供出国看病、远程咨询、海外体检等服务。据我们了解，他们也需要数量可观的医学口译和笔译人才。

医药产品会展方面，以中国医药保健品进出口商会为例，该商会每年均在境内外举办几十场大型展会。例如，2018 年，它在国内外举办国际医药/化工原料类展会 13 场、营养保健品类展会 12 场、食品配料类 7 场、医疗器械/耗材敷料类 15 场、制药设备/包装类 11 场。再如 2022 年，它举办会议论坛活动 51 场、境内展览 12 场、境外医药/化工原料类展会 8 场、境外健康产品类展会 9 场、境外食品配料类展会 6 场、境外医疗器械类展会 7 场、境外制药设备/包装类展会 4 场。

当今，中国在不断参考和学习西方在医学、医疗方面的经验：临床操作、新药研发、医疗体系改革等，国人都希望能借他山之石，因此医疗界的翻译工作量（包括笔译和口译）一定会增加。

目前，从事医学口译的五类典型译员为：医药院校教师、翻译院校教师、自由职业者（医学背景、翻译背景）、医疗卫生机构在职人士、出国看病中介机构翻译者。对无医学背景或不在医学院校任教者而言，为一次医学会议做精心准备很是耗时费力，他们往往认为这样的业务不划算；对于极少数无翻译专业背景、自学成才的医师，由于其医学知识坚实，翻译质量较为可靠，业内认可度反而更高。

译员从业形态分为固定职位译员（in-house interpreter/translator/staff）与自由职业者/兼职者（free-lance/part-time）两类。图 1.3 至图 1.9 是几则医学口译招聘广告，从中可见市场对医学口译从业者的资质要求及相应的薪资报酬情况。

国内某大型集团招聘

岗位 1：
- 男性，3—7 年工作经验，专八 & CATTI 口 3+
- 医学英语专业毕业或毕业后从事医院英语翻译工作
- 能陪同男性领导全国出差
- 年薪税后 40 万—60 万元

岗位 2：
- 护理背景，着重口译，年薪税后 40 万元

图 1.3　国内某大型集团医学口译招聘广告

通用环球医疗招聘翻译（职责）
翻译助理（北京总部，国际医疗合作部）
- 陪同公司领导进行出国业务考察，担任相关口笔译工作
- 出席各大商务会议，并负责在公司与外商的商务谈判中进行口译工作
- 在公司与外商的联络和接待中担任翻译工作
- 协助进行公司外事活动的组织管理工作
- 负责公司各项英文材料的审核、校订和修改工作
- 负责公司日常资料、商务材料及相关产品和服务信息的英文翻译、撰写工作
- 负责部门和公司安排的其他工作

图1.4　通用环球医疗翻译助理招聘广告

通用环球医疗招聘翻译（要求）
- 英语口译、医学英语、英语语言文学、科技英语等相关专业硕士研究生学历，具有英语专业8级证书
- 优秀的中英文口头和书面表达能力
- 有丰富的笔译和口译工作经历，能独立完成商务方面的口译和笔译任务
- 接受过外事礼仪等相关培训，能很好地完成外事活动的接待、翻译和组织工作
- 形象气质佳，举止得体大方
- 具有很强的应变能力，优秀的计划、组织、管控、协调沟通、人际交往能力
- 具备大型会议做会经验者和具备经济、金融、医学等知识背景者优先考虑

图1.5　通用环球医疗翻译招聘广告

某翻译公司招聘（兼职译员）
- 寻医学领域口译两名
- 行业：康复医学认证
- 地点：上海
- 性质：兼职口译（中英＋英中）
- 内容：协助认证考察现场翻译，涉及行政和康复医学临床内容
- 时间：2023年5月14日至16日
- 周期：视情况可长期合作
- 待遇：根据个人能力和水平可谈
- 要求：熟悉医学领域知识及术语，接受电话测试

图1.6　某翻译公司康复医学现场口译员招聘广告

某翻译公司招聘（兼职译员）
- 时间：2021年10月底至11月初，共需4天
- 地点：南京一家整形医院
- 口译内容：美国JCI专家组前来检查，需要对医学、医院管理都了解一些的英语交传翻译，先检查，再会议汇报

图1.7　某翻译公司医院认证口译员招聘广告

```
某翻译公司招聘（兼职译员）
• 时间：2022年4月24日
• 地点：长春
• 日语陪同翻译（医学领域）
• 要求：有留学经历、陪同翻译经验，熟悉日本商务礼仪，口语流利，形象气质佳
```

图 1.8　某翻译公司日语陪同医学口译招聘广告

```
某翻译公司招聘（兼职译员）
• 语种：中德互译
• 类型：同声传译
• 时间：2020年5月4日上午9：00—12：00
• 行业：口腔医学（齿科）
• 会议规模：40—50人
• 招聘人数：1人
• 地点：北京，国家会议中心
```

图 1.9　某翻译公司德汉口腔医学同声传译译员招聘广告

通过以上招聘广告可见，固定译员一般需要具备"一专多能"的素质。英语兼职翻译往往要求医学背景；而小语种兼职翻译对医学背景要求不高。在薪酬方面，大型企业集团普遍给出了较高的薪酬，年薪高达40万—60万元；兼职译员薪资水平在5千元/天—1.2万元/天。

医学口译员首先需要具备一般口译员必备的素质，包括能够熟练掌握和使用外语和汉语语法、能够精确和广泛使用外语和汉语词汇、纯正的英语和汉语发音、良好的双语听力理解能力、了解翻译相关国家和中国的基本情况、了解笔译等。此外，由于医学话题的复杂性，译员还需要了解医学的基本知识，如各国医疗制度、医学分科情况、常见疾病、基础医学知识、治疗方法和药物、统计知识、临床试验设计和数据分析。上述条件可能会让大多数入门译员望而生畏，但是入门译员不应该因此而不敢开始训练，毕竟译员和其他专业人士一样，都应该是活到老学到老的终身学习者，哪方面不足就在哪方面下功夫。

表1.2展示了两种场合中常见的译者身份，并比较了各自的优势与劣势。

表 1.2　两种场合中常见的译者身份及其优势、劣势对比

场合	译者身份	优势	劣势
医患间诊疗	病人家属或朋友	与交流的一方关系密切，无须付费	缺乏医学知识或/和翻译技能不足
	有双语能力的医务人员	具有医疗知识，无须付费	翻译技能不足
	普通口译员	翻译技能高	缺乏医学知识
	医疗口译员	具有医疗知识和翻译技能	收费比普通口译员高

（续表）

场合	译者身份	优势	劣势
医学会议	有双语能力的医药卫生专业人员	具有医学知识	翻译技能不足
	专业会议口译员	具备翻译技能	缺乏医学知识，收费较高
	具有医学知识的专业会议口译员	同时具备翻译技能和医学知识	收费较高，较为稀缺

当今中国，医学口译从业者数量有限。出现这个现象的原因有以下几点：第一，医学知识系统庞杂，术语较多、较复杂，医学文本和话语佶屈聱牙。第二，医学界对于非医学背景专业人士从事医学相关翻译的质量持一定的保留或怀疑态度。第三，虽然有少数医生、药师、护士等具有医药背景的人士也在兼职从事医学口译，但不少人总是感觉自己缺乏系统的翻译技能培训，底气不足。第四，医学领域收入普遍较高，职业上升渠道较多、空间较大，医学专业人士不愿意发展为医学口译员。

没有受过医学教育培训的人士如果想要从事医学口译工作，需要重点学习医学翻译所必需的医学知识、医学术语，了解医学和医疗行业内部组织、管理、制度等信息。没有受过翻译专业教育培训的人士如果想要从事医学口译工作，必须要加强英汉双语基本功的学习，以及翻译技巧和理论的学习。理想的人才培养模式是要培训医生、药师，乃至护士、医院管理者中有兴趣的人和实践者。总而言之，一切医疗界中要用到翻译的地方就应该有受过训练的专业人士。

此外，我们还要注意，在中国以外召开的国际会议一般使用国际通用学术语言，并默认所有参会者可以运用该语言交流。中国无任何法律要求医学学术会议不应由语言障碍而对任何人构成歧视。从另一个角度看，甚至可以说，医务人员有义务学好外语，毕竟要求外国医学同道学好中文暂时不太实际。

在译员培养上，我们可借鉴美国一些地区和我国台湾地区的医疗口译员培训方案。在认证制度方面，我们可借鉴美国国家医疗口译员认证协会的经验，建立中国医学口译员认证制度。我们可首先确立会议口译和医疗口译两个方向，展会方向后续再确立。

1.4 国外医学口译行业现状

国外的医学翻译往往是指社区翻译大类别下的医患交流过程中的翻译，美国和加拿大两国移民数量较多的大型医院开展免费的口译服务，由医院提供。它们主要覆盖的语言是西班牙语，因为美国讲西班牙语的非母语者居多。许多去海外工作、学习、生活的人士都反映在国外看病很难，因为与医疗相关的沟通实属不易。甚至，美国本国人对于一些医学词汇说法也不甚明了，以至美国国立卫生研究院（NIH）专门开设了网站，教人们如何听懂医生的话。诚然，医生在诊疗过程中应尽量避免使用术语，但对术语的了解和熟悉的确可以在很大程度上便利医患交流。

相较于别国,美国的医疗口译比较普遍和规范,其原因主要有二:

其一,联邦法律保护所有人(不论种族和语言)均有权接受同样的医疗卫生服务。1964年,《民权法案》规定在美国不得以种族、肤色或民族血统为由将任何人排除在联邦资助的项目以外,剥夺其利益或以其他方式使其受到歧视。民权办公室将这种保护扩大到语言领域,规定"所有接受联邦资金的医疗机构都应通过双语工作人员或专业口译人员为英语水平有限的患者免费提供适当的口译服务"(蔡丽婷,2014:10-11)。然而,部分机构并未提供语言服务,或至少提供的语言服务质量欠缺(Jacobs et al., 2006)。

其二,美国有大量移民,尤其以拉丁裔居多。有学者(Flores, 2006)在《新英格兰医学杂志》(New England Journal of Medicine)撰文指出:按照调查对象自报的数据,约4960万美国人(占美国居民的18.7%)在家里说英语以外的语言;2230万人(占8.4%)的英语水平有限,说英语的程度低于"非常好"。1990—2000年,美国人在家里说英语以外的语言的人数增加了151万(增长了47%),英语能力有限的人数增加了730万(增长了53%)。在某些地方,这一数字尤其高:2000年,40%的加利福尼亚人和75%的迈阿密居民在家里说的不是英语,20%的加利福尼亚人和47%的迈阿密居民的英语水平有限。美国联邦调查局数据显示,2019年,近6800万人在家说英语以外的语言。与此同时,只说英语的人数也有所增加,从1980年的1.872亿增长到2019年的2.41亿,增长了约1/4。医疗口译因而也得到了学界的足够重视,连医学类期刊上都常常见到以消除语言障碍为题发表的论文(Karliner et al., 2007)。有学者在对总计涉及84 750名参与者的15篇研究论文进行综述后发现,如果医患双方语言不匹配会影响健康结果(Cano-Ibáñez et al., 2021)。

此外,职业化的发展,也保障了美国医疗口译的质量,获得了医疗界的信任。美国医疗口译的职业化发展历程可以从职业协会的建立和行业标准的制定发展两个维度来观察。

在职业协会的建立方面,1986年,马萨诸塞州医疗口译员协会(Massachusetts Medical Interpreter Association, MMIA)成立;1996年,加利福尼亚医疗口译协会(California Healthcare Interpreting Association, CHIA)成立;1998年,全国医疗口译委员会(National Council on Interpreting in Health Care, NCIHC)成立(Arocha & Joyce, 2013)。

在行业标准的发展方面,美国早在1986年就出台了首部地方性的《医疗口译伦理守则》;1995年,又出台了首部地方性的《医疗口译实践规范》。美国全国医疗口译委员会在2004年出台了《伦理守则》(IMIA Guide on Medical Interpreter Ethical Conduct),并在2005年制定、出台了《国家从业规范》。国际医疗口译员协会于2010年颁布了第一版的《伦理守则》。

此外,美国医疗口译国家认证委员会于2009年建立国家认证体系。考核过程分口试和笔试两步(2018年,收费标准分别为175美元和325美元),考察内容包括医疗知识和语言、翻译能力、职业操守。美国国内有其认可的培训项目,但委员会不参与各培训项目的教学设计。目前,美国有两个国家级认证机构:(1)医疗口译员认证委员会(Certification Commission for Healthcare Interpreters, CCHI),该委员会是一个国家级非营利组织,通过有效、可信、供应商中立的测试对医疗口译员进行认证。该委员会通过笔试和口试对英语—西班牙语、英语—阿拉伯语和英语—普通话等语言组合的医疗口译员进行认证。(2)国家医疗口译员认证委员会(National Board for Certification of Medical Interpreters, NBCMI),该委员会则通过笔试和口试，对英语—西班牙语、英语—俄语、英语—粤语、英语—普通话、英语—韩语和英语—越南语等语言组合的医疗口译员进行认证。

网络上，有医院口译服务的使用者对服务质量进行了反馈（盛诺一家，2022）："医院（指的是美国麻省总医院）提供中文翻译，有两种——现场翻译和电话翻译，陪同翻译比较好。现场翻译非常忙，好像不能百分之百满足预约。而电话翻译由于不在现场，有些翻译并不准确，所以还是陪同翻译比较放心。"

美国医疗口译如此发达有诸多历史和文化的原因，但不可忽视的是，其通过法律赋予了各个语族人群的平等医疗权利。而在我国，医疗口译尚处于发展阶段，医疗口译员主要依靠医疗机构和医疗中介机构自行培养。近年来，极个别高等翻译院校开始意识到医疗口译的重要性，逐步开始培养相关人才。医学会议口译人才主要靠口碑及同行、熟人推荐才能找到口译工作和机会（于苏甫，2016）。从这个层面来讲，中国的医学口译市场还处在起步阶段。

1.5 医学口译相关学术机构、行业协会和学术刊物

国内外与医学口译相关的专业协会与学会包括国际会议口译员协会、国际医疗口译员协会[1]、世界翻译教育联盟医学翻译与教学研究会、中国翻译协会医学翻译分会、中科院科技翻译工作者协会、中国中医药学会传统文化翻译与国际传播专业委员会、中国中医药学会中医药翻译与国际传播专业委员会等。

国内出版的与医学口译相关的主要翻译类学术刊物有《中国翻译》《上海翻译》《中国科技翻译》《医学语言与文化研究》以及《英国医学杂志中文版》。其他外语类核心期刊也先后发表了不少医学口译相关论文。发表医学口译相关论文的英文翻译类刊物有《专门用途笔译和口译杂志》(*Journal of Specialized Translation and Interpreting*)等。值得注意的是，《普通内科医学杂志》(*Journal of General Internal Medicine*)先后发表了多篇医疗口译相关论文。世界顶级的高影响因子医学刊物，如《美国医学会杂志》(*JAMA*)、《新英格兰医学杂志》等，也偶有发表医疗口译相关论文。

参考文献

北京日报. 2018. 北京接待国际会议数量全国居首. 来自中华人民共和国中央人民政府官方网站.
蔡丽婷. 2014. 病人视角下的专业医疗口译员与朋友译员之对比研究. 厦门：厦门大学硕士学位论文.
雷天放, 陈菁. 2006. 口译教程（学生用书）. 上海：上海外语教育出版社.
何静. 2010. 医疗口译的发展及现状. 河南医学高等专科学校学报, 22（3）: 261–263.

---

[1] 我们根据该协会官方网站上对 medical interpreting 的界定可以看出，其主要关注医疗口译，因此改变既往国内学界的翻译方法，不再称其为"国际医学口译协会"。

李小艳, 毛红. 2012. 释意理论对中医药国际会议口译的启示. 海外英语,（1）: 153–154.

玛依努尔·于苏甫. 2016. 医学领域口译市场现状及行业分析——基于问卷调查和访谈的实证研究. 北京: 对外经济贸易大学硕士学位论文.

聂文信, 陈向京, 白永权. 2013. MTI医学口笔译方向人才培养模式探讨. 外文研究,（2）: 89–94, 108.

钱歌川. 2013. 翻译的基本知识: 第2版. 北京: 世界图书出版公司北京公司.

盛诺一家. 2022. 肺癌患者出国看病为何被拒? 来自北京盛诺一家医院管理咨询有限公司网站.

王桂珍. 2013. 新编汉英/英汉口译教程. 北京: 高等教育出版社.

王子今, 乔松林. 2013. "译人"与汉代西域民族关系. 西域研究,（1）: 9–15, 140.

薛英利. 2012. 医学国际会议口译员综合素养与学科素养分析. 语文学刊,（12）: 71–73.

余倩菲. 2017. 中日两国医疗口译的职业化研究初探. 广州: 广东外语外贸大学硕士学位论文.

詹成, 严敏宾. 2013. 国内医疗口译的现状、问题及发展——一项针对广州地区医疗口译活动的实证研究. 广东外语外贸大学学报,（3）: 47–50.

朱珊, 刘艳芹, 冯鸿燕. 2015. 医学口译的行业现状及执业原则. 中国翻译,（2）: 111–114.

周密. 2012. 癸辛杂识. 上海: 上海古籍出版社.

Arocha, I. S. & Joyce, L. 2013. Patient safety, professionalization, and reimbursement as primary drivers for national medical interpreter certification in the United States. *Translation and Interpreting*, 5(1): 127–142.

Cano-Ibáñez, N. et al. 2021. Physician–patient language discordance and poor health outcomes: A systematic scoping review. *Frontiers in Public Health*, (9): 629.

Flores, G. 2006. Language barriers to health care in the United States. *New England Journal of Medicine*, 355(3): 229–231.

Jacobs, E. et al. 2006. The need for more research on language barriers in health care: A proposed research agenda. *Milbank Quarterly*, 84(1): 111–133.

Karliner, L. S. et al. 2007. Do professional interpreters improve clinical care for patients with limited English proficiency? A systematic review of the literature. *Health Services Research*, 42(2): 727–754.

Ngo-Metzger, Q. et al. 2007. Providing high-quality care for limited English proficient patients: The importance of language concordance and interpreter use. *Journal of General Internal Medicine*, 22(S2): 324–330.

Woloshin, S. et al. 1995. Language barriers in medicine in the United States. *JAMA*, 273(9): 724.

第2章

医学会议交替传译实现过程和训练方法

医学会议的交替传译与一般会议的交替传译一样,大致可以分为三个步骤:(1)听解;(2)短时记忆与笔记;(3)根据笔记和记忆产出译文。每两个步骤之间存在部分重叠。对于初学者来说,三个步骤一般是依次完成的[1]。本章介绍交传的三个步骤及具体操作要点和训练方法,并提供交传笔记和原语复述的练习材料。

2.1 口译中的听解

2.1.1 听解的两个方面

口译中的听解过程,包括两个方面:是否听见与是否听懂。

1)是否听见:指的是译员有没有听到源语言,包括源语言的句子、短语、单词、音节、音素,这个阶段主要是语音信号的捕捉和接收。因此,我们希望口译现场没有构成干扰的噪声,译员有良好的听力。

2)是否听懂:指的是译员是否听懂源语言,并依据背景知识、语言知识,对语音信号构成的语流所代表的语义进行解读。译员只有结合长期记忆中的背景知识和当下讲话的环境或上下文才能准确解读语音信号。例如"běiyī"[2],在北京大学的师生听来,它可以表示北京大学医学部;而"běiyīnǚ"[3]虽然只比"běiyī"多了一个音节"nǚ",但在台北人听来,"běiyīnǚ"可以表示台北第一女子高中。如果用学术话语来阐述,听力理解实际上是人依靠语音刺激产生的信号,刺激大脑搜索长期记忆,结合讲话的环境,解码语音信号意义的过程。借助心理学的术语,这个部分可以被视作口译听解过程中的编码活动,具体来讲,包括划分层次、提取信息、压缩信息三个过程。

1　对经验丰富的译员来说,也有边听解边在心中默默翻译,同时进行记忆并做笔记,然后依据笔记产出译文的情况。

2　北医。

3　北一女。

2.1.2 划分层次

口译的听解，不是无意识地听到，而是聚精会神并带着分析的听，是积极的听（active listening）。

译员必须要跟上发言人的逻辑，要学会一边听，一边在心里为讲话制作"思维导图"，划分逻辑层次（chunking）[1]，最好不要遗留任何细节。为了加深记忆，译员还应该边听边联想，以调动长期记忆辅助短期和瞬间记忆。

为什么我们需要对发言人所讲的内容进行意群划分呢？认知科学早已证实，只有听者加以分析和思考并进行认知层面整理加工的内容才更容易在大脑中留下印迹、进入记忆（雷中华，2007）。

划分层次的方法和小学语文里划分段落层次的方法类似，只不过在口译过程中，信息往往是通过听觉的方式从发言人传递到译员[2]，而不是像笔译或阅读过程中，通过视觉的方式从作者传递到译员和读者。

2.2 语块理论与交传中信息的提取和压缩

近年来，语块理论和图式理论在口译教学中受到重视。语块是由连续或非连续的两个或多个词组合而成的、有一定心理现实性的（使用时是整存整取而不经过语法分析生成的）预制语言单位，包括多元词、习俗语、限定性结构短语、句子构造型短语等。如果我们的语言是以单词为单位，翻译的时候，需要一对一地进行转换，记忆的效率就会比较低，但如果我们记住了很多固定的东西，如改革开放政策（reform and opening up policy），我们在翻译的过程中就能够减轻记忆的压力，提高翻译的效率。这就是口译学界所提倡的使用语块来改善口译效果。

例如："I want to talk with you today about the key message you have to convey to your readers when you are writing a report." 如果按音素计，它包含了几十个信息点；如果按单词计，则有二十多个；如果按短语计，则约有七个；如果从需要记忆的关键信息点角度出发，对于一些人，也许只有两三个。由此可见，用不同方法对信息点进行提取和压缩，其数量是不同的。

人类的短期记忆可以处理的信息容量为五到九个组块，平均约为七个。也许，并非每个人都能在短期内记住七个互不相干、没有任何意义的信息点，但是如果我们对信息点进行提取和压缩，甚至加上联想意义，情况就不同了。学者们早已发现，我们在记忆中会把信息压缩成块，能够把前后联系的一组信息条目作为一个信息项目来记忆，如记谚语"小洞不补，大洞吃苦"时，不是一字一字地记，而是把它作为一个整体来记。又如，我们在记英语新闻的六大要素 who、what、why、when、where、how 时，将其记成"5w and 1h"，这样一来，就把原

---

1 常见言语逻辑关系包括并列、列举、概括、分述、对比等。不同的逻辑关系就有不同的记忆要点，如并列关系语义出现时，要梳理并列列举信息的结构数量和特点。
2 有时是听觉与视觉结合，如发言人使用幻灯片辅助讲演。

来的6个信息点缩减成2+2个（5算一个信息点，w算一个信息点；1算一个信息点，h算一个信息点），7个信息点的记忆"内存"空间里还剩下3个点。再如，在我们的记忆中，北京外国语大学电话号码的头四位是8881，而常见的查号台号码是114。在口译中听到88811114后，我们便可将需要记忆的信息处理为"北外+1+查号台"，将原来的8个数字（8个信息单位）变成3个信息单位。当然，也一定有人会记成"3个8+4个1+1个4"，这样也可以。不过，3个8、4个1、1个4是3对信息组合，每对信息组合各由2个信息单位组成，共6个单位，还是不如前一种方法节省记忆空间。

练习：请记住电话号码82801114。（提示：8280是北京大学医学部电话号码的头四位。）

在口译记忆中，不管用笔记，还是用脑记，都强调记住关键的信息（message），而关键的信息并不等同于字词（words）。分析发言人话语的过程就是译员对接收到的语音（有时也辅以视觉）信号进行提取（抓取关键信息），并进一步进行压缩的过程。例如，在现场口译"I want to talk with you today about the key message you have to convey to your readers when you are writing a report."这句话的时候，译员知道这是开场白，于是就从永久记忆中调出中文开场白的句型"今天，我想给大家讲讲……"，所以这个信息点就不用记了。you have to convey to your readers 也不用记忆，这是因为上下文可以互相提醒。所谓 key message，就是译员必须要向听众传递的信息。至于 you are writing，它是对 report 的具体描述。因此，我们的关键性记忆信息点就剩下 key message 和 report 了。

通过提炼发言人话语，提取和压缩信息，译员需要记的东西就变少了，做笔记时也就更从容。有些人以为口译员要先学会速记，像会议现场的速记员一样把发言人说的每个字都记下来，这是错误的。在口译时，逐字记录既不可取，又没必要。作为译员，需要花费精力去构思译入语，若是逐字记录，精力定然不够。对发言人话语逻辑层次的分析能够加深记忆，再辅以口译笔记，口译员就可以顺利地回忆起发言人所讲的内容。

2.3 交替传译中的记忆

交替传译中的记忆及记忆训练与图式理论密切相关，口译员应在图式理论的指导下快速提取和压缩关键信息，并配合使用三种记忆方法来改善记忆效果。

口译中的记忆按事件发生顺序来看，主要是回溯型记忆，而非前瞻性记忆；按照源语言产出后译入语产出间隔长短来看，可分为长期记忆、短期记忆和瞬间记忆，口译员需要快速地从发言人的源语言中提取和压缩信息，同时配合使用瞬间记忆、长期记忆和短期记忆，帮助口译员完成口译工作。在口译训练过程中，我们应该提倡首先进行无笔记记忆训练，这好比肌肉锻炼过程中的孤立练习，只针对某一个肌肉块，而非两个，这样教师和学生才能清楚地了解究竟是否记住了发言人的话。如果一开始就允许学生记笔记，则无法让他们体会如何在听的过程中划分层次、在头脑中构建发言人发言信息的思维导图和图上的细节信息。

图式理论在口译训练中的作用也得到了重视。图式一词早在康德的哲学著作中就已出现。

所谓图式，是指围绕某一主题组织起来的知识的表征和贮存方式。人的一生要学习和掌握大量的知识，这些知识并不是杂乱无章地贮存在人的大脑中，而是围绕某一主题相互联系起来，形成一定的知识单元，这种单元就是图式。人的大脑中有大小、层次不同的图式彼此连通、共同作用，形成一个庞大而有序的网络体系。图式可分为三类：语言图式、内容图式和修饰图式。语言图式是指词汇、短语、语法、句子结构、段落、习惯用法等语言知识；内容图式是指语言的意义和文化背景知识；修饰图式是指篇章结构知识。这三种图式的掌握情况决定了一个人理解语言的能力。

图式具有三种特性：可增长、可调整、可新建。可增长，指人类可以在旧图式上增加新的内容，从而扩展图式；可调整，指在发现旧图式有错误或者不适应新情况时，可修改现有图式；可新建，指在遇到全新的事物或经验后，人类可建构全新的图式。人们在接触新事物时，总是自觉或不自觉地把它和自己大脑中已有的相关或相似的图式作比较，并加以调整，从而不断修改、完善已有的图式或重建新的图式。

在图式理论方面，皮亚杰提出了两个重要概念："同化"和"顺应"（转引自杜领利，2013）。同化就是把外界的信息纳入已有的图式，使图式不断扩大。顺应则是当环境发生变化时，原有的图式不能再同化新信息，必须通过调整改造，建立新的图式。低级的图式通过同化、协调、平衡而逐渐向层次越来越高的图式发展。

2.3.1 瞬间记忆、短期记忆、长期记忆和工作记忆

瞬间记忆：人类记忆模型的最开始阶段就是感觉登记，即瞬时记忆。在信息被认知并转入短期记忆以前，它可以以原来刺激最忠实模写的形式在记录器中保持一个非常短暂的时间。我们的周围有很多信息，但是我们只会选取我们需要的信息进入大脑，也只有这部分经过选取的内容才能成为瞬时记忆。例如，大街上有大喇叭在播放流行歌曲，但是我们和朋友在逛街买衣服，那我们可能完全不会注意到歌曲的内容，而只会注意到衣服的款式、颜色、价格等。

短期记忆（也称短时记忆）：指外界刺激以极短的时间一次呈现后，保持时间在一分钟以内的记忆。短时记忆的容量有限，一般成年人为5—9个单位。

长期记忆：指长期存留在大脑中的一些固定的信息。

工作记忆：这是心理学家和翻译学家提出的一个概念，指在完成口译等语言或认知活动中所暂时需要的瞬时记忆、短期记忆和长期记忆的总和。在一定的时间内，工作记忆的容量是有限的，一旦所需记忆的信息量超过上限，就会出现记忆或回忆困难。

2.3.2 口译中三种记忆的配合

1. 长期记忆与瞬间记忆的配合

在教学中，教师可请学生复述这句话："My favorite piece of music is Handel's water music suite." 其中，Handel 和 suite 对大多数学生来说可能是陌生的，因此构成瞬时记忆的

内容，他们即便是复述出来了，也不知是什么意思，仅仅是简单的模仿发音。而句子本身"My favorite piece of music is something"，可被视为短期记忆的内容。有部分学生可以完整复述，这是因为他们熟悉亨德尔的水上音乐套曲，相当于将其他同学需要利用短期记忆实现回忆的内容利用长期记忆替代了。

2. 长期记忆与短期记忆的配合

要把"5w and 1h"还原成 who、what、why、when、where、how，需要我们从长期记忆（也就是我们学到的知识）里将英语新闻的要素调动出来。如果我们之前就听说过"5w and 1h"的说法，则只需要在长期记忆中调动这个记忆单元，然后将它所代表的具体内容进行解读即可。虽然交替传译中主要涉及短期记忆，但是长期记忆也可以起到极大的辅助作用。这就要求我们在平时要多积累。

美国学者帕尔穆特对儿童、20岁的成人、60岁的老年人的记忆做了对比研究。她发现，老年人记忆衰退，但如果记忆作业不是死记硬背，而是关于现实生活的，则老年人比年轻人完成得更好，因为老年人有一个储备丰富的头脑。这表明：首先，拥有的现实生活信息越多，长期记忆中的连锁网络越密，就越容易抓住一个新事实，将它把握在网络上，就像苍蝇落在蜘蛛网上一样；其次，把我们知道的东西重新安排在一个完善的等级系统框架中需要时间和经验。这也说明了口译员按照认知框架构建口译工作所需的长期记忆的重要性。

为比较对不同熟悉程度话题讲话的记忆效果，可使用不同的话语结构模式（图式）来辅助记忆，并体会三种记忆的配合。自学时，学习者可自行复述讲话材料。若是在教学中，教师可要求学生交叉听录音并互相评分，然后对话题评分进行对比。

复述练习1：清华大学某同学大学生活的一天（归辰，2014）

一般，大一刚来的同学，由于受到军训的良好熏陶，早上会在七点或之前起床，上午上课，中午吃饭，下午上课，傍晚吃饭，晚上上课。一天最多六大节课（当然，如果你搞到了赫敏的时间转换器可以多上两节）。/ 如果没有课，同学们普遍选择去教室或者图书馆上自习。自习内容主要是写作业。/ 到了大二、大三，部分同学已经明确有出国意向，自习的内容除了写作业以外，还有背单词。

这段话体现了汉语的一大特点，那就是关系连词比英语少。但是通过语义分析，我们是可以厘清句子之间的逻辑关系的，厘清逻辑关系有利于记忆和回忆。

"一般，大一刚来的同学，由于受到军训的良好熏陶，早上会在七点或之前起床，上午上课，中午吃饭，下午上课，傍晚吃饭，晚上上课。一天最多六大节课（当然，如果你搞到了赫敏的时间转换器可以多上两节）。"这段话是按照时间先后顺序描述了大一学生"学习日"一天中的作息情况，而内部又可继续划分逻辑层次。

"一般，大一刚来的同学，由于受到军训的良好熏陶，早上会在七点或之前起床，上午上课，中午吃饭，下午上课，傍晚吃饭，晚上上课。"这是讲作息的细节。"一天最多六大节课"是概括。两部分之间，构成总分关系。而"一天最多六大节课（当然，如果你搞到了赫敏的时间转换器可以多上两节）"，构成了让步状语从句，是一种条件关系。

"如果没有课，同学们普遍选择去教室或者图书馆上自习。"跟前面部分形成对照，是一种非此即彼的"选择关系"。

"到了大二、大三，部分同学已经明确有出国意向，自习的内容除了写作业以外，还有背单词。"这是讲大二、大三的自习内容，与前句共同构成并列关系。

复述练习2：马术

古代为了做到战车所用的马匹在战场上移动精确，常对马匹进行各种技巧和协调性的训练，后来就发展成为马术比赛。马术比赛于1900年首次进入奥运会，当时只设障碍赛一个项目。1912年，马术比赛扩大为盛装舞步赛、障碍赛和三日赛三项。从1952年起，女骑师被允许参加奥运会的马术比赛，马术也成为奥运会中唯一一个男女同场竞技的比赛项目。作为一个团队，马匹和选手将共同获得奖牌和名次。

此段也可按照复述练习1的方法进行时间和逻辑的分析。有学生反映，这段话的记忆难点在于如何准确记忆三个年代。能够完整地复述该段内容的学生反映，三个年代他们是这样记忆的：1900、1912、1952都是偶数，且都是4的倍数，因为奥运会每四年召开一次。其次，第二个年代和第三个年代中都包含尾数2，只不过第一个是12，第二个是52。

我们发现，在这些练习中，学生很容易听懂并记住比较熟悉的话题，如大学生活。而对于陌生的词汇和表达，他们则不容易听懂。由此可见，听懂的前提是听过这个词或表达，并且明白它在上下文中的意思。而且，在长期记忆中，与之相关的背景知识充分并在听解过程中被激活。所以，作为口译员，我们应该通过各种途径扩充自己的词汇和背景知识，并且要做到在语音层面的对应，也就是听到一个词就要立刻反应出它在上下文中的意思。换言之，我们要在大脑里形成双语对应的长期记忆"语料库"，形成双语的知识结构图式（长期记忆）。我们让学生听一段关于日常生活的话，不做笔记。听完后，让一位同学来复述，这位同学几乎完整地复述出了所听的内容。但若是接着再听一段关于某方面的高科技发展动向的发言，他们复述起来就很困难。由此可见，记忆熟悉的话题（即有长期记忆的、形成了图式的话题）比记忆不熟悉的话题要容易得多。这也提示译员平时要注意扩大知识面，熟悉各种话题。

2.3.3 口译记忆教学方法建议

杜领利（2013）指出，口译课只教授学生口译技能是不够的，教师还应向学生传授各种话题的背景知识，建立尽可能多的图式。教师在教学过程中，既要重视学生语言基本功的训练和传授口译技巧，又要以图式理论为指导，扩展学生的图式，并指导学生用图式知识来增强记忆能力。首先，教师要注重图式的积累。在口译课上进行口译练习之前，教师可介绍一些与材料主题相关的知识，或者通过提问、讨论等方式激发学生原有的背景知识。在口译练习结束后，教师应指导学生梳理材料中的图式，并把与材料主题相关的知识进行总结，整理出相关话题的图式。这种方式可以帮助学生不断扩大自己的图式群，并养成自觉用图式理论积累背景知识的习惯。其次，教师要用图式来进行记忆训练。在口译教学中，教师应注重培养学生的图式意识，可以在多个层面让学生将口译材料归纳成句子结构的图式、篇章结构的图式、事物之间关系的图式等；训练学生对段落、句子的意义进行分类、分层归纳和处理，使学生养成按图式进行记忆的习惯，提高记忆效率（杨先明、何明霞，2007）。

1. 瞬间记忆的训练法

教师可使用重复电话号码、重复 3—5 个单词等办法；训练的难度逐渐加大，一开始说较短的电话号码，说较少的单词，随着学生的表现改善，逐渐加大难度（雷中华，2007）。

2. 短期记忆的训练法

按照话语结构类型来看，发言人的话语中一般会使用时间、空间、逻辑三类话语结构（李长栓，2013）。具体来看，逻辑结构包括因果关系、层递关系、主次关系、总分关系/分总关系、并列关系等。在实际的话语中，时间、空间、逻辑三类话语结构可交织出现。在口译听解过程中，可按照这些描述类型进行话语分析，加强短期记忆。

对于短期记忆，教师最好用学生熟悉甚至是感兴趣的话题发言或录音来做训练。教师可以使用母语讲话材料，这样做的主要目的是独立训练记忆。如果让学生听外语讲话材料，里面可能存在听不懂的单词和表达，这会干扰记忆（雷中华，2007）。

3. 长期记忆的构建

如今，译员的准备资源已经变得越来越丰富多样，甚至充满趣味性。除了传统的书籍，虚拟化的互联网资源和学术数据库、语料库等也已经被许多译员广泛使用。例如，某译员要为某一家文化演艺公司做关于百老汇音乐剧的翻译，那就可以到网络上搜索相关的中英文介绍，通过文字和多媒体的手段了解音乐剧和百老汇，但要记住不要当作娱乐来看，要当成研究问题来看，记下其中出现的音乐剧、表演艺术等行业的专业术语并查找对应的中文，了解专业术语的搭配（可以用哪些形容词修饰、用哪些动词搭配等）。再如，要为某保健品或健身设备公司的新产品发布做翻译，那可以上国内外的健康网站了解信息。如果要为医院外科做翻译，可以看原版或中英文对照的外科手术教材和视频。译员还需要关注《人民日报》《中国日报》（*China Daily*）、新华网的英文版和中文版新闻，通过双语阅读，了解中国特色词汇的译法和中英文常见的词语搭配方法。最重要的是，译员要对看到的话题和词汇进行归类总结，形成图式，以便日后使用。

2.4 口译笔记

2.4.1 口译笔记的目的、原则和主要内容

口译笔记的目的是辅助译员回忆发言人在上一个片段讲话的逻辑关系和具体细节。因此，口译笔记不等于速记，不需要逐字、逐句转写发言人的所有文字和数字。

如果发言人说一句或两句代表一个意思，这个时候译员就没有必要再划分意群，因为发言人已经把意群划分好了，译员需要做的就是抓住这个意群里的关键信息进行翻译。

但是，如果发言人滔滔不绝，口若悬河，连续讲了几分钟，讲话信息较多，而且其中有很多逻辑关系不同的意群，译员就需要一边依靠大脑分析这些关键信息之间的关系并记忆；另一边再依靠笔记辅助记下关键信息[1]。

此外，在无法记笔记且发言段落较长时，译员一定要注意发言人的逻辑，厘清讲了几个大点，每个大点下面是否有分述的小点，是否有引入和总结等。

口译记忆的原则是脑记与笔记配合，要做到简明扼要。脑记、笔记各占多少比例，需要依据译员的个人习惯（先天记忆能力）和掌握的背景知识（长期记忆、图式）来定，以便在脑记和笔记之间找到合适的平衡，并通过不断练习达到个性化稳定。按照丹尼尔·吉尔（Daniel Gile）的认知负荷模型（Effort Model）理论，一定时间内，人脑能够处理的信息量，或者说是能够驾驭的负荷是有限的。新近的研究发现，大脑处理多线程能力很高，往往是多个脑区同时处理一项任务。

口译笔记的主要内容是源语言的逻辑关系和具体信息点。口译笔记不同于课堂笔记，也不同于现场速记员的速记。不需要每个字都记，记下来的东西也不是为了给别人看。甚至，如果在完成交传工作后较久的时间点，译员被邀请依据口译笔记回忆源语言内容，译员也未必能够顺利回忆起来。

2.4.2 口译笔记的材料和工具

口译中，译员需要准备一定数量的纸张和笔做笔记。一般来说，职业译员倾向于使用上下翻页的笔记本或者装订好的白纸。译员根据个人习惯和现场条件决定白纸和笔记本大小和张数（或厚薄）。白纸中间可以对折，B5大小的笔记本中间可以通过等分画线，将其分割为左右两栏。一般来说，使用普通铅笔（而非自动铅笔）为宜。与签字笔、圆珠笔、钢笔等相比，普通铅笔发生故障的几率较小，但普通铅笔的缺点是消耗速度较快，所以最好多准备几支。

翻译时，译员可以从上往下、从左到右做笔记，记满一张纸后翻页，用手指卡住，以防发言人讲话很长，译员记下很多却不知道是从哪里开始。翻译时，译员翻译完一个片段画一条双横线，以便翻译下一片段时快速找到开头。

---

1 按照黎凤（1985）的理论，帮助改善记忆的方法有四种：一是外部辅助法，如笔记、提示、学习大纲、教科书、参考书、日历、地址本、日记本。二是联想法，如记"1944"这个数字联想到"第二次世界大战快要结束"；又如，许多人背诵八国联军的国家名字时，使用各国的谐音"饿的话，每日熬一鹰"（俄、德、法、美、日、奥、意、英）以进行记忆，即利用联想法将新资讯置入长期记忆中。三是等级系统法，如美国学者鲍威尔等人给两组受试者看26个词的卡片；一组看的是按等级排列的；另一组是随机排列的。第一组受试者记住这些词比第二组快好多倍。四是利用长期记忆中的连锁网络。口译过程中用笔记是外部辅助记忆法。

2.4.3 口译笔记布局特点和操作要点

口译笔记布局特点可概括为：线段分割层次，符号和缩写记录信息。具体来讲，有三个操作要点：（1）递进信息右倾缩进，并列信息垂直；（2）依据发言的层次和意群在笔记中用横线分割；（3）可以在翻译完成的部分下面画双线，或在结尾画一条单线，并用斜线划掉已经翻译完的部分。

1. 垂直发展的笔记

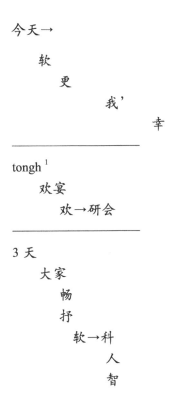

口译的笔记总体来看是垂直的，换句话说，是一行一个信息，并利用缩进体现层次和并列关系。有的学生改不掉横着记的习惯，认为并无大碍，请看下面的例子：

我们的禁烟教育应该进入医学院、医院，让医学生和医生都积极地参与进来。

若横着记，笔记如下：

禁烟→医　院　生　医　参

学生本想用"医"代表"医学院"，"院"代表"医院"，结果合在一起成了"医院"，翻译的时候有可能翻译了 enter the hospitals，而忘了 and the medical schools。

1　表示 tonight。

若竖着记，并使用英文表示医院和医学院，如下所示：

禁烟

→ schl[1] → 生 ⎫
→ hspt[2] → 医 ⎬ 参
                ⎭

这样一来，学生看到 schl，再看到下面正对的 hspt，很容易明白二者是并列的关系；再看到"生"和"医"，很容易提醒自己"让医学生和医生都积极地参与进来"与前面的"进入医学院、医院"是递进的关系。

再来看一个例子：

今天，能够邀请大家参加软件评估和更新研讨会，我们感到非常的荣幸。今晚，我们为大家准备了欢迎晚宴，欢迎大家来参加此次研讨会，希望在未来的三天时间大家畅所欲言、各抒己见，帮助我们把软件设计得更加科学化、人性化、智能化。

某学生横着做笔记，如下所示：

今天→软件 更 我们 幸 tongh 欢宴
欢→研会 3 天 大家 畅 抒 软→科 人 智

该学生将其复述为：今天，我们邀请大家参加软件更新大会。我们很荣幸今晚给大家欢迎晚宴。欢迎大家 3 天的研讨会，欢迎大家畅所欲言、各抒己见。把软件设计得更加科学化、人性化、智能化。

源语言是两层意思，由于该生没有分行记，导致复述时出现错误，扭曲了讲话人的意思。

如果分行记，如下所示：

今天→
　　软
　　　更
　　eval[3]
　　　　我'
　　　　　幸

---

[1] 表示 school。
[2] 表示 hospital。
[3] 表示 evaluation。

```
Tnt¹
    欢宴
        欢→研会
_____

3 天
    大家
        畅
            抒
                软→科
                    人
                        智
```

这样看起来，一个句子是从左到右垂直缩进和并列有机构成的一个单元（一幅立体图），翻译的时候，译员能很快厘清句子间的逻辑关系，不会出现句子间信息错误放置的情况。

2. 并列关系的信息垂直记

并列的信息一定要垂直记录。这样一来，译员就能知道其中的并列关系。请看下面的例子：

今天，妈妈给我买了铅笔、橡皮、尺子和卷笔刀。

笔记如下所示：

```
今
    妈
        买
            我
                铅
                皮
                尺
                刀
```

当然，因为这句话很短，如果发言人讲完可立即翻译，有的译员只需要记：

```
                铅
                皮
                尺
                刀
```

---

1 表示 tonight，英文母语者有用辅音字母表示元音较多的长单词的习惯，例如公路的路牌上 expressway，写作 xprsw。

再如：

到 2003 年，世界旅游组织（World Tourism Organization，WTO）有 300 多个正式会员，100 多个联系会员和 300 多个附属会员，正式会员中 100 个是发展中国家，200 个是发达国家。

笔记：

2003
  WTO
    300 正
      100 ing
      200 ed
  100 联
  300 附

2.4.4 口译笔记操作要点

1. 用源语言记或用目标语言记

译员可以用源语言记，也可以用目标语言记。宗旨是书写笔画越少、书写费时越少，越好。例如，发言人说"如果"，译员就没有必要用中文记下这两个汉字，笔画太多，写起来费时，用英文 if 记，则省时省力。

英语讲话、英语笔记示范如下：

There are 21 members in APEC: Australia; Brunei Darussalam; Canada; Chile; People's Republic of China; Hong Kong, China; Indonesia; Japan; Republic of Korea; Malaysia; Mexico; New Zealand; Papua New Guinea; Peru; the Philippines; Russia; Singapore; Chinese Taipei; Thailand; the United States; and Vietnam.

笔记：

21 APEC	Indo	Peru
Aus	Jp	Phil
Bru	ROK	Ru
Ca	Mal	Sg
Chl（注意：如果写 ch，就会和 China 混淆）	Mex	Ctp/TW
CN	Nz（注意：此处用汉字记"新"不可取，因为后面还有新加坡）	Thai
		US
HK CN	PNG	Vn

在较短的一段笔记中，符号所代表的意义最好要有一致性、排他性。

2. 合理使用笔记符号

以下是一些常用的口译笔记符号，大部分逻辑关系符号均可在口译笔记中使用：

¥	人民币	≈	基本上	○	圆满；成功
$	美元	∨	于是	I	我
!	非常	Σ	总共；总计	I'	我们
@	地址是，地点是	∵	因为	y	你
……	还很多；还不止这些；等等	∴	所以	y'	你们
		⊙	用于替代反复出现的关键概念	ta	她；他；它
=	也就是说			ta'	他们；她们；它们
——	用来划分意群	≠	不等于；不意味着；不代表	↑	增长
{	可以分为几个小点			↓	减少
}	可以归纳为一点	≤	小于等于	org	组织
←	之前	≥	大于等于	口	国家
→	然后	±	左右	口+口	国际
?	疑问	∫	交换	○'	地球；全球；世界
/	或者	⊥	在……基础上；支持		

医学口译中，可以综合使用来自数学（如 Σ）、物理（如 N）、化学（如 Zn、Fe）、生物（如男性符号）和医学（如 CHD，即 coronary heart disease，冠心病；CVD，即 cardiovascular diseases，心血管疾病）等相关学科的符号和缩写，这些学科符号和缩写系统特别发达。

笔记符号不宜太过繁杂，否则会辨认困难。

3. 用汉语记笔记的小窍门

1）没用的字不要记，如"我谨代表某某单位欢迎大家的到来"中的"谨"字。

2）互相重复或者提示的信息只需要记其中之一，如汉语双音节的联绵词"欢迎"就只要记"迎"，"特别"记"特"，"普通"记"普"，"详细"记"详"即可。

3）开头相似的双音节（A+B、A+C）要记不重复的字（B和C），如江苏、江西、河北、河南、湖北、湖南：

不要记：	要记：
江	江苏
江	西
河	河北
河	南
湖	湖北
湖	南

当然，还可以用拼音首字母缩写，如：

Js

Jx

He b

He n

Hu b

Hu n

也可以用双语混合记，如：

江苏

西

河 n（north，北）

　　s（south，南）

湖 n

　　s

还可以用各省别称，但如果用汉字记录，别称的书写笔划太复杂，可考虑用别称的发音来记，如：

Su

Gan

Ji

Yu

E

Xiang

下面是课堂笔记教学实录，为了让学生把精力集中在笔记练习上，源语言是汉语，口译笔记以汉字为主：

女士们，先生们，上午好！

我谨代表北京大学医学部学研公司[1]欢迎大家来到北京大学。我公司成立于1998年，是隶属于北京大学医学部的科研型企业，专门从事医学教育软件的开发。1999年，公司开发了学研临床和基础医学培训软件，投入市场10年来，年销售量不断增长，从1999年的2 000余份，增加到今年的60 000余份。年销售总额从200万元上升到目前的7 000多万元。公司正是在广大用户的支持下才取得了今天的成绩。

今天，能够邀请大家参加软件评估和更新研讨会，我们感到非常的荣幸。今晚，我们为大家准备了欢迎晚宴，欢迎大家来参加此次研讨会，希望在未来的三

---

1 公司名称是作者为教学目的进行的虚拟，如有雷同，纯属巧合。

天时间大家畅所欲言、各抒己见，帮助我们把软件设计得更加科学化、人性化、智能化。我们公司会一如既往地为大家提供周到的设计和跟踪服务。

最后，预祝本次研讨会圆满成功，祝各位代表在京期间生活愉快，万事如意。谢谢大家！

点拨："我谨代表北京大学医学部学研公司欢迎大家来到北京大学。"其中，"谨"不需要记；北京大学医学部用缩写PUHSC（Peking University Health Science Center）；需要记的是"学研"，"公司"用脑记，"欢迎"记"迎"，"北京大学"记PKU（北京大学校名的英文缩写）。

笔记如下所示：

I
PUHSC
　　迎
　　　PKU

点评：如果只有这一句话，它在七个记忆容量单位内，根本不需要记笔记。"我（1）谨（不用记）代表（2）北京大学医学部（3）学研公司（4）欢迎（5）大家（不用记）来到（6）北京大学（7）。"但如果源语言比较长，信息量较大，就需要记。否则翻译时，译员就容易搞错究竟是代表北大还是代表北大医学部，是欢迎来到北大还是北大医学部。

点拨："我公司成立于1998年，是隶属于北京大学医学部的科研型企业，专门从事医学教育软件的开发。"过滤掉不用记的，一部分用心记，落在纸上的笔记就剩下：

est.[1]
1998
under
PUHSC
　　科研
　　　医教软
　　　　发

点拨："1999年，公司开发了学研临床和基础医学培训软件，投入市场10年来，年销售量不断增长，从1999年的2 000余份，增加到今年的60 000余份。年销售总额从200万元上升到了目前的7 000多万元。"

学生笔记如下所示：

99 clin[2] basi[3] 医软

1　表示established。

2　表示clinical。

3　表示basic。

10 年 sv[1] _____ ↑
99 2 000
今 60 000
年 sv
99 200 万
目 7 000+ 万

教师修改如下所示：

99
 Clin
 Basi
  医培软
_____
→市
10—
 年销 ++ ↑
_____
   99 2 000
   今 60 000
_____
年销额
   99 200 万
   目 7 000+ 万

点拨："今天，能够邀请大家参加软件评估和更新研讨会，我们感到非常的荣幸。今晚，我们为大家准备了欢迎晚宴，欢迎大家来参加此次研讨会，希望在未来的三天时间大家畅所欲言、各抒己见，帮助我们把软件设计得更加科学化、人性化、智能化。我们公司会一如既往地为大家提供周到的设计和跟踪服务。"

学生笔记如下所示：

今天→软件更 我们 幸
tongh 欢宴 欢→研会
3 天 大家 畅 舒 软→科 人 智

教师修改如下所示：

---

1 表示 sales volume。

3 天
　大家
　　畅
　　　抒
　　　　软→科
　　　　　人
　　　　　　智

点拨："最后，预祝本次研讨会圆满成功，祝各位代表在京期间生活愉快，万事如意。谢谢大家！"

学生笔记如下所示：

Final may 会 成
代 生 快 万 如 谢

教师修改如下所示：

final
　may
　　会
　　　成
　　代
　　　生☺
　　　　万
tky[1]

4. 关于发言人的语速问题

国家人力资源与社会保障部翻译资格考试口译二级英汉口译部分考试共 30 分钟，要求翻译总量为 1 000 个英文单词的讲话两篇。根据笔者的经验，学生译员翻译时间往往大于源语发言时间，假设按照源语发言共 12 分钟计算，该部分考试语速为每分钟 83 个英文单词。但在实际工作中，每分钟 200 个单词的情况也会常常碰到，所以作为译员，应该不断提高自己的快速听力理解能力，关键是要加强语音和意义层面的联系；作为发言人，应该体谅译员，以沟通为目的，配合译员完成工作。译员可以设法和发言人沟通，请求发言人使用合适的语速。

---

[1] 表示 thank you。

2.5 临场应变

2.5.1 如何有技巧地请求发言人重复

有时，即便准备得很充分，也积累了不少知识和词汇，现场还是会碰到突发情况，例如没听懂、专业术语不会翻译等。若是没听懂，译员可以请求重复和澄清，但要讲究技巧，不要一味地说："Pardon / Could you repeat…"要确切地告诉发言人是什么地方没听懂、怎么没听懂。比如说，"Sorry, but I didn't follow your logic after you talked about XXX.""Sorry, but could you please repeat the three names of the animals?"等，一定要快速、准确地发问，并获取信息。若是专业术语不会翻译，译员可以请现场专家帮忙。

2.5.2 现场学习词汇

会议的内容可能包罗万象，比如国际劳工组织的工作场所艾滋病教育项目的会议，从名字上我们知道肯定会说到与艾滋病、劳工权益相关的词汇，但是由于是一个教育宣传项目，发言人也许会谈到传播学、广告学、电影、电视等相关词汇，译员也不一定都已掌握，可能需要现场学习新词汇。

2.6 交替传译的训练方法

交替传译训练可从听力入手，从熟悉话题过渡到陌生话题，从短意群交传逐渐过渡到长意群交传，三人或两人结伴练习，从慢速发言过渡到快速发言，从用源语言概括到用目标语言概述，利用各种资源获取语料进行练习。

从听力入手，原因在于听懂意思是正确传译的先决条件。从熟悉话题过渡到陌生话题，这是因为听自己熟悉、感兴趣的比较容易入门。从短意群交传逐渐过渡到长意群交传，从一句一句地翻，不记笔记地翻，到两句两句地翻，三句三句地翻，再逐渐过渡到一个小意义段一翻，易产生不断精进的成就感。一开始练习简短的交替传译，除个别数字外，不提倡记笔记，鼓励学习者靠脑记，锻炼翻译时的短期记忆能力。可三人结伴练习，具体做法是练习者A念稿子，练习者B、C记笔记，练习者B翻译，练习者C做监听和点评，练习者A、C也可以提醒练习者B漏译或错译的地方。如果找不到三个人搭档，也可以两人搭档练习。

根据语言学家、心理学家的研究，人的记忆单位为 7 ± 2。根据塞莱斯科维奇和勒代雷的研究，无笔记交替传译作为有笔记交替传译的过渡练习能够达到较好的效果（塞莱斯科维奇等，2007）。无论是课堂教学，还是自主学习，都可以两人搭档训练简短交传，一人在翻译过程中如出现遗漏的情况，另一人可以采取提问的方式提醒。例如，"The trade volume between China and Japan last year totaled 1.4 trillion yuan."一位练习者将其翻译为："中日贸易额达到1.4万亿元。"此时，另一位则可以提问："When? Of what currency?"来提醒他/她回忆。

从慢速发言过渡到快速发言是符合认知规律的练习方法。语速较慢的语料，可以从一些慢速广播节目获取，也可以让同学、友人等帮忙朗读、录音，可练习三次左右，不要超过四次，以免次数太多以后，记住所讲内容，失去口译记忆练习的意义。快速语料也可从多种渠道获取。

从用源语言概述逐步过渡到用目标语概述。在英译中时，用源语概述指：把英文听完以后，用英文讲大意；用目标语概述指：把英文听完后，用中文讲大意。笔者在教学中发现，学生普遍反映在英译中的口译练习中，用源语概述比用目标语概述难。

学生可利用磁带录音、网上资源、电视会议和现场会议、讲座等各种资源进行练习。例如，可将中国国际电视台（CGTN）的对话、访谈类节目录制下来作为练习；可观看由其转播的中央和地方政府各机构配有现场翻译的医疗卫生相关新闻发布会，用笔记本记下陌生词汇和表达的翻译方法。虽然这些新闻发布会大多数时间都是把发言人的中文译为英文，但仍然可以帮助学生积累双语对应的语言资料，等于建立了小型语料库，便于英译中。几大世界顶尖医学杂志（*JAMA*、*NEJM*、*BMJ*、*Lancet*）也有视频、音频节目推出，部分医学英语学习网站、应用、视频公众号也有大量资源可供利用。

2.7 笔记和复述练习

请按照本章所讲方法做下面的笔记练习，如多人同时学习，可交换笔记，互相提出修改意见。练习前，学习者还可以上网搜索相关的中英文材料，以补充该话题涉及的语言外信息，减轻笔记压力，提高复述和翻译质量。

迈阿密大学生命科技园介绍

1. 词汇热身

the University of Miami Life Science & Technology Park（简称 the UM Life Science & Technology Park）：迈阿密大学生命科技园

the University of Miami Leonard M. Miller School of Medicine：迈阿密大学里奥纳多·M. 米勒医学院

iconic symbol：标志性的象征

best-in-class facilities：最好的设施

nurture：培育

commercialization of university-based innovations：大学创新成果的商业化

a diverse, multi-cultural city：一座多元文化的城市

academia：学界

business entrepreneurs：创业者

catalyst：催化剂

foster：培育；促进
commercially viable enterprises：有商业价值的企业
fuel economic growth：推动经济发展
research and development (R&D)：研发

2. 练习正文

The University of Miami Life Science & Technology Park is located in Miami's Health District, which includes the University of Miami Leonard M. Miller School of Medicine, six hospitals and one of the largest health care footprints in the country. / The park will be an iconic symbol[1] with best-in-class facilities that nurture research, development and commercialization of University-based innovations. /

Situated in the heart of a diverse, multi-cultural city, the UM Life Science & Technology Park will bridge academia and industry, bringing faculty, scientists, students, and business entrepreneurs together to encourage collaboration and innovation. /

The UM Life Science & Technology Park will serve as a catalyst[2] that fosters new scientific discoveries, builds commercially viable enterprises and fuels the economic growth of the South Florida community. Construction has begun and the opening of R&D Building One is anticipated for the second quarter of 2011.

3. 参考译文

迈阿密大学生命科技园位于迈阿密的卫生事业区域，该区域有迈阿密大学里奥纳多·M.米勒医学院、六家医院，而且还保留着美国最大的医疗卫生事业的遗迹。该园区设施先进，必将成为促进研发和大学创新成果商业化的领头羊。

位于迈阿密这座拥有多元文化的城市的迈阿密大学生命科技园必将成为链接产业界和学界，链接教研人员、科学家、学生和创业者的纽带，推动其合作和创新。

迈阿密大学生命科技园将会成为推动科学发现、打造成功企业、推动南佛罗里达地区经济发展的摇篮。园区已经开建，1号研发大楼预计在2011年第二季度开放。

参考文献

杜领利. 2013. 英语专业交替传译教学中记忆训练的认知研究. 南昌教育学院学报，28（9）：146–147.

1　此处为意译，见参考译文。
2　同上。

归辰. 2014. 清华北大的学生的一天是如何度过的. 来自知乎网站.

雷中华. 2007. 交替传译教学中的短期记忆训练. 语文学刊,（2）: 53-56.

李长栓. 2013. 理解与表达：英汉口译案例讲评. 北京：外语教学与研究出版社.

黎风. 1985. 记忆的理论和方法. 医学与哲学,（7）: 42, 53-55.

塞莱斯科维奇，等. 2007. 口译训练指南. 北京：中国对外翻译出版公司.

杨先明，何明霞. 2007. 图示理论与口译记忆能力训练. 上海翻译,（3）: 42-44.

第3章
医学会议口译质量与译员素养培养

本章从医学语言特点、会议口译译文质量标准、译员素养、文化因素对口译质量的影响等方面,探讨如何提高医学会议口译质量。

3.1 医学语言的特点

医学语言涉及多种语类,包括描述性(如病例报告、机构和个人简介、综述、临床研究方案介绍、研究结果呈现)、评论性(如论文讨论部分、临床指南专家评论)、会话性(圆桌讨论、问答环节、医患交流、医疗工作者互相交流)语类等,每种语类各有特点。同样,医学会议语言作为医学口头语言的一种形式,也会涉及上述语类。此外,学术型医学会议还涉及大量学术和科研用语[1]。

医学语言,尤其是医学英语,还具有术语庞杂,拉丁文、希腊文来源词汇多,两栖词多,一词多义现象普遍,部分英语词汇的汉语译入语阙如,部分词汇英汉构词角度存在差异等特点。

1. 术语庞杂

以《英汉汉英医学词典》为例,它共收词13万条,但即便有这部工具书作参考,医学译员还是常常需要借助国家名词委员会"在线术语"[2]网站查找术语。以国家卫健委医疗机构医疗服务项目英译为例,它共有1.3万个词条,涉及多个临床专业[3]。

2. 拉丁文、希腊文来源词汇多

在西方科技语言中,包括医学、生物、数学等学科语言,很多词汇以拉丁文、希腊文作为

---

[1] 伯明翰大学的网站 Academic Phrasebank 按交际目的、原创研究文体要件等分类,提供了大量学术语言表达参考。

[2] 详见术语在线官方网站。

[3] 译员可利用专家网络、专家库联系专家、医学生等知情人士来协调解决翻译中的理解和措辞问题。

词源[1]。术语一般由"词根+前缀、后缀"构成。以"卵巢囊肿切除术"（Ophoro-cyst-ectomy）为例，它由三部分组成：前缀"Oophoro-"是拉丁文的"ovary"（卵巢）；词根"cyst"意为囊肿；后缀"-ectomy"含"cutting off"或"removal"（去除、切除）之意。

3. 两栖词多

以 tender 和 murmur 为例。在日常话语"This cake is tender."中，tender 就是"柔软"的意思。但在医学中，tender 可指"有压痛"[2]，如"The patient's abdomen is tender."murmur 一词在日常英语中指叽哩咕噜、说话不清楚的意思，但在医学语境中，"Heart murmurs could be heard among these patients."[3] 中的 murmur 意为"心脏杂音"。

4. 一词多义现象普遍

一词多义现象广泛存在，此处以 medicine、medical、patient 三个词为例。

在"中医""中药""中医药"的英文对应表达中，medicine 一词都会用到。但如何准确翻译这三个中文术语呢？如果是狭义的"中医"，指中医师行医或指中医师开展诊疗，英文可用"the practice of Chinese medicine"表示。当特指"中药"的时候，如果上下文不发生歧义，可以用"Chinese medicine"来表示；但若有歧义，就要使用拉丁文"materia medica"[4] 来表达[5]。但"中医药"——将药物概念与诊疗实践合并作为一个术语呈现的时候，在不发生上下文歧义的时候，可用"traditional Chinese medicine"[6] 来表达。

medical 既有"医学"，又有"内科"的意思。"He is a medical doctor."中的 medical doctor 究竟是指医生，还是指内科医生？这需要根据语境判断。例如，在对话中，A 问 B："Are you from a surgical department?" B 回答道："No, I'm from a medical department." 那么，B 的意思则是："我来自内科。"

---

1. 医学翻译中的协作：医学译员常常需要扮演各个医学专科专家的角色，类似于全科医师，但还需要常常面对专科里面的特定疾病和其最前沿的问题。将民族医药介绍到世界也非常困难。最近，笔者接到一个任务——将中医药、民族医药政策和知识体系通过专著介绍到西方。苗医药文献资料需要用汉字来书写（换言之，音译）苗医的所有诊断、药物、病症名称等。译员若不懂苗医，可能需要邀请民族医药专家合作，协助解读透过汉语苗医文献想表达何意，然后再将其翻译为英文。这种翻译可能需要两个步骤：苗语到汉语、汉语到英语，跟古汉语翻译需要经历古汉语到现代汉语的翻译，再从现代汉语译入英语有些类似。
2. 笔者尝试在某翻译引擎中输入"His abdomen is tender."，该翻译引擎将其译为"他的腹部很软。"，这是错误的翻译；笔者尝试第二个翻译引擎，它将其译为"他的腹部压痛。"第二个机器翻译引擎很准确，毕竟这个句子缺乏充分的语境信息。接下来，笔者把这个句子做了改动，提供了具体语境，将其改为"The patient's abdomen is tender."，表示这是临床医疗话语，再到不同引擎中尝试翻译，结果两个翻译引擎都没有问题，都正确翻译出了"病人腹部压痛。"这说明对语境的正确理解是翻译多义词的基本条件。
3. 某学生将其错译为"这些病人之间可以听到心与心之间的私语。"
4. 字面意思是"药材"。
5. 从 medicine 派生出的 medication，则指药物治疗，也可用 pharmaceutical therapy 或 drug therapy 表示。此外，"药物"一词可对应 medicine、pharmaceutical、drug——可谓一中文意，多英文形。
6. 对应中文"传统中国医学"或"中医药"。

新冠疫情期间，微信帖子中出现了配有"Be Positive, Be Patient"字样的图片，意思是"积极向上，要有耐心"，却被网友戏谑地误读为"成为阳性，成为病人"，这也充分体现了医学翻译中的一词多义现象。

5. 部分译入语阙如

比如在 *Patient Involvement in Health Technology Assessment*[1] 一书中出现的三个词组：patient engagement、patient involvement 和 patient participation。在翻译引擎中分别输入这三个词组后，翻译结果都是"病人/患者参与"。但在该书中，这三个词是有区别的，且这三个词贯穿全书反复使用，我们显然不能将其都翻译为"病人/患者参与"。通过专家协商，我们确定将 patient participation 翻译为"主动参与"，将 patient involvement 翻译为"被动参与"，将 patient engagement 翻译为"调动患者"。这些新名词反映出国内外医疗卫生制度和治理上的差异。译员需要做好背景知识的学习以及近义词的辨析和翻译。

6. 英汉构词角度存在差异

按照英国的视角和制度，medical education 指临床医学教育（Walsh，2013）。因此，《牛津医学教育教科书》（*Oxford Textbook of Medical Education*）中不使用 clinical medicine education 来表达这一含义。但在我国，medical education 可指医疗卫生教育（见本书第 1 章图 1.1）。

该书中的 basic medical education 的字面意思是"基础医学教育"，其实是指"本科医学教育"，但在我国基础医学指的是生物学、生物化学等作为临床医学的基础学科，换言之，我国把临床医学所依托的基础科学称为"基础医学"。如果把我国的"基础医学"翻译为 basic medical sciences，这在美国、英国可能会引起误解。

3.2 医学会议口译质量标准

提及译文质量，我们会自然而然地想到耳熟能详的"信达雅""信达切""神似"等翻译标准。判断会议口译的质量好坏可以有两个标准：一是忠实于发言人；二是让听众满意。

这两条标准看似简单，实则不易实现。忠实于发言人就要求译员能够明白发言人讲话的意图，传达发言人想要传达的信息，包括语气、语调、修辞、专业术语、词语的语域等。让听众满意意味着译出语要让听众听得懂，最好能让听众听完译出语后和听源语发言听众得到同样的感受。美国翻译理论家尤金·奈达（Eugene Nida）提出了著名的功能对等理论，认为译入语中信息发挥的功能应和源语中的信息发挥的功能对等。

美国语言学家诺姆·乔姆斯基（Noam Chomsky）所提出的"转换生成语法"（Transformational-

---

[1] 该书主要介绍如何邀请病人参与卫生技术评估，可作为医保报销、国家卫生经济战略制定的参考信息。这种做法体现了医学的人文关怀。

Generative Grammar)的观点之一,体现的就是"表层结构"(surface structure)与"深层结构"(deep structure)的动态关系。他认为,深层结构是人说话之前存在于头脑之中的连贯意念,是抽象的,是人类的思维形式。但人在说话时必须将这种深层结构用表层结构的句子表现出来。而翻译是用译入语语言表层结构体现译出语深层结构的一种过程。

即席会议口译至少应做到准确、通顺、及时。国内外主要行业组织也对口译质量标准提出了各自的要求(详见表3.1)。其中,国际会议口译员协会的标准在译员培训中最具可操作性。

医学会议,特别是医学学术会议,往往有大量专业词汇,并配有演示幻灯片。译员应做到术语翻译准确、完整,并能解读幻灯片中的主要信息,认真考虑译出语如何与幻灯片中的信息配合,实现更佳的交际效果。

表3.1 国内外主要行业组织对口译质量的标准要求(王东志、王立弟,2007)

	国际会议口译员协会	欧盟口译司	联合国	中国翻译协会
质量标准	忠实;清楚;流利度;术语;完整性;语法;音质;口音	忠实、连贯;与听众的交流;表达沉着、稳定;避免直译;译文准确、自然	翻译的完整性、准确性;词汇与声音的运用;句法与风格;话筒的使用习惯[1];源语有关的知识	用清楚、自然的目的语,准确、完整地重新表达源语言的全部信息内容

3.3 提高口译质量的途径

从操作层面来看,提高口译翻译质量可以采取语义优先、对语句结构进行解析、对词语进行简化等策略(同上)。更细致地说,我们还可从词语、句子和交际效果等微观角度来提高译文质量。

从词语的角度来看,我们应做到名从主人、名词化处理、直译和意译的尺度把握。首先是"名从主人",如我们不可按普通话发音将布达拉宫翻译为Budala Palace,而应按藏语发音将其翻译为Potala Palace。不过,关于俄国著名作家Chekhov(契诃夫)名字的翻译,国内能见到的翻译法至少有七种,译员恐怕也只能从众了。会议口译前,译员一定要做好此类名词的译法查证工作。其次,英汉会议口译中,译员常把英文代词处理成名词。英文常用不同的词表达同一个意思,汉语可用同一个词表达,用同一个汉语词汇表达更加符合汉语听众的习惯。再次,要把握好直译和意译的尺度。直译,顾名思义,指字对字翻译、不顾词语深层含义而做简单翻译。有时,直译也无可厚非,如我们可将"We are very happy to see you."直译为"我们很高兴见到你。"因为这句话中的英文单词逐字换成中文,并按顺序排列,并不会导致误解。与直译对应的是意译。例如,谈到戒烟时,英文会用 go cold turkey,于是有人把它直译成"去冷

---

[1] 话筒的使用习惯指的是同声传译员进行口译工作时,往往两到三人坐在同一间同传工作间。他们轮流工作,完成一个会议的同传。由于同传工作间的译员话筒灵敏度极高,翻动文件、喘气等杂音都可能被传出去,所以要训练译员养成良好的麦克风使用习惯。一般来说,不讲话的时候不开麦克风。如需清嗓子、咳嗽,或与工作间里的同伴译员说话时等,要先按下操作台上的静音键。

火鸡"。殊不知这是一个习语，指的是"突然间完全停止做某事"。按照戒烟专业人士的解释，我们应将其意译为"干戒"，即"以不使用任何药物治疗或心理咨询的方式戒烟"。

从句子的角度来看，会议口译中还要注意英汉句型、句式的差异。汉语是流水句，或者说是主题引导的句型，总是先说主题，再加评论，重意合。英语重形合，有很多代词、连词来表达语内的关系，强调语法形式合乎规则。例如，"When I come back, I will tell them."汉语要表达同样的意思，只需说"我回来叫他们"就够了。英汉口译时，如果把代词和连词都译出的话，就会出现满篇"你、我、他、你们、我们、他们"和"当、当、当、当、当"不断的情况。这是初学译员常犯的错误。

此外，将英语中的几种常见句式——被动句、定语从句、状语从句、形式主语从句译入汉语，应把握如下规律[1]。

1）被动句：可翻译出"被"字，也可不用"被"字。例如：

- The man was beaten by the police.
  那人被警察打了。
- Heart murmurs are frequently heard in these patients.（叶子南，2004）
  这些病人中常可听到心脏杂音。
- X-ray examination of the chest and heart should be routinely performed.（同上）
  胸部和心脏 X 线检查应列为常规。
- The problem of refugees should be dealt with in an integrated manner.（张维为，2004）
  难民问题的处理应采用综合的方法。
- The relationship between the two countries was characterized by mutual understanding.（同上）
  两国关系的特点是互相谅解。
- Cultural China can be defined as…（同上）
  文化中国的定义是……
- The Olympic spirit is characterized by…（同上）
  奥林匹克精神的特征是……

可将被动换主动，但需谨慎。例如：

- The house next door has been bought.
  有人已经买了隔壁的房子。
- This sort of advertisement is seen everywhere.
  人们到处都能看到这类广告。
- When he arrived, he was arrested.
  他一回家就被逮捕了。
  他一回家，人们就把他逮捕了。

1　例句译文均是较为口语化的译法。

汉语中的其他被动标志还有"受、遭、挨、叫、让",如"被人欺负了""给人欺负了""让人欺负了""叫人欺负了""遭报应""你等着挨打吧""为情所困""他吓得要死"。

下面的几组句子中,第一句都不符合汉语的表达习惯,第二句或(和)第三句是符合汉语习惯的说法(思果,2004)。

- 他被许可来美。
  他已经获准赴美。
- 最近一件事被注意。
  有一件事情最近已经有人注意到了。
  最近化学家已经注意到……(根据上下文添加"化学家")
- 这地方被称为天堂。
  大家把这地方叫作天堂。
- 他被指定为负责人。
  他成了负责人。
  某某指定他为负责人。
- 这条条文被修改为……
  这条条文已经委员会修改。
  这条条文已经修改为……
- 他被查出贪污。
  他贪污有据,已经查明。

由此可见,在翻译时,被动语态可保留"被"或改变句式(不用"被"字、动词转名词)或补出行为者(被动换主动)。

2)定语从句:基本原则是把从句和主句表达的意思都理解以后分拆开,再按照汉语的语言习惯进行重新组合,有时需要重复主题词。例如:

- ASUS WL-500g Premium is a wireless router that is much cleverer than one might think.
  ASUS WL-500g Premium 是一种无线路由器,这种路由器比想象中还要好用。
- All citizens who have reached the age of eighteen have the right to vote and to stand for election with the exception of persons deprived of the rights by law.
  所有公民,只要年满18岁,都有选举权和被选举权,除非是被依法剥夺选举权和被选举权的人。

3)状语从句:学习英语以后,我们反而容易忘记汉语的简练,有时会翻译出这样的句子:"He is so tired that he can't keep working.(他是如此的累,以致不能再工作下去。)"其实不用这么复杂,可直接译为"他太累了,干不动了。"请看下面的例子(叶子南,2004):

- He stole, not because he wanted the money but because he liked stealing.
  他偷窃,不是因为他想要钱,而是因为他喜欢偷。☹
  他偷窃的目的不是钱,他就是喜欢偷。☺(注意:省掉了一个"他"。)

- The day were short, for it was now December.
  白天短了，因为是十二月。☹
  现在是十二月，白日短了。☺
- When it is rainy, the buses are crowded.
  当天下雨的时候，公共汽车拥挤。☹
  下雨天的公共汽车总是很拥挤。☺
- As the sun rose, the fog dispersed.
  随着太阳升起，雾散了。☹
  太阳一升起，雾就散了。☺
- How can you expect your children to be truthful when you yourself tell lies?
  你如何期待你的孩子讲真话，当你自己说谎的时候？☹
  当你自己说谎的时候，你如何期待你的孩子讲真话呢？☹
  如果你自己讲假话，怎么能期待孩子说真话呢？☺（注意：省掉了一个"你的"。）
- There was so much dust that we couldn't see what was happening.
  尘土如此的多，以至于我们不能够看到正在发生什么。☹
  尘土很大，我们看不清发生了什么事。☺

另外，我们还要注意，汉语中的状语从句位置不像英语中那么灵活。例如：

- I tried to be polite, although I didn't like him.
  我试着表现得礼貌，尽管我不喜欢他。☹
  我虽然不喜欢他，但还是显得很有礼貌。☺

4）It is + adj./n. to do sth. 句型（张维为，2004）。

方法一：将真实主语前移。例如：

- It is exciting to visit your great country.
  访问贵国这个伟大的国家，真令人激动。
- It is certainly useful to hold a seminar devoted exclusively to the role of traditional knowledge in biological diversity.
  召开一个研讨会，专门讨论生物多样性中传统知识的作用肯定是有益的。

方法二：按照顺序翻译。例如：

- It is important to see our shared interest in maintaining regional peace and promoting growth.
  重要的是要看到我们在维护地区和平和促进增长方面的共同利益。
- It is difficult to believe that he could make such an accusation.
  难以想象他会做出这种指控。
- It would be useful to remind all the participants that there would be a reception this evening after this plenary meeting.
  有必要提醒所有与会者本次全会之后今晚还有一个招待会。

方法一和方法二均可。例如：

- It is necessary to guarantee women full equality of rights in social life as a whole.
  有必要充分保障妇女在整个社会生活中的平等权利。
  充分保障妇女在整个社会生活中的平等权利是很有必要的。
- It is common sense that a liquid has no definite shape, yet it has a definite volume.
  众所周知，液体没有一定的形状，但有一定的体积。
  液体没有一定的形状，但有一定的体积，这是常识。

方法三：添加或替换主语。例如：

- It will be very difficult to make a decision without knowing all the facts.
  如果没有全面了解事实的话，我们很难做决定。
- It is not a bad idea to consider our participation in this research project.
  我们可以考虑参加这个研究项目。

有时，方法一、方法二和方法三均可。例如：

- We all know that it is very difficult to reach a consensus on a peaceful solution to this conflict.
  我们都知道很难就和平解决这场冲突的办法达成共识。
  就和平解决这场冲突的办法达成共识很难，这一点我们都知道。
  我们都知道就和平解决这场冲突的办法达成共识很难。
- It is necessary to guarantee women full equality of rights in social life as a whole.
  有必要充分保障妇女在整个社会生活中的平等权利。
  充分保障妇女在整个社会生活中的平等权利是很有必要的。
  我们有必要充分保障妇女在整个社会生活中的平等权利。

5）"It is said that..."（据说……）、"It is reported that..."（据报道……）、"It is confirmed that..."（据证实……）、"It is believed that..."（人们认为……）。

最后，从交际效果的角度来看如何处理会议翻译中较难处理的两种情况：

1）源语发言人说了伤害译入语听众感情的话。这时候，译员要酌情处理，可以过滤掉容易引起双方不快的部分，保证双方继续做该做的事情。例如，有一位译员在陪同外宾参观成都大熊猫繁育基地时，外方说："I don't want to see the damn panda."这时，中方问他外方意向如何，他就婉转地说："他对熊猫没太大兴趣。"当然，也有人反对这种美化策略。

2）源语发言人讲了笑话。例如，源语发言人讲的汉语笑话是在玩同音字的游戏，无法翻译成能起到同样效果的译文。这种情况下，如果时间允许，那就解释这个笑话给听众听，但这样可能会失去笑话的"包袱"。

总之，若要提高译文质量，译员应该在宏观理论的指导下，多进行翻译练习与实践，并从词汇、句式、交际效果层面多加总结。

3.4 医学会议口译译者素养培养

译员应重视译者素养的培养。译者素养至少包括语言、知识、传译能力、交际能力四个方面。作为译者,平日要通过多阅读、多做笔译、口译练习,多看、多听音视频,多开口讲相关话题内容,积极提高语言水平。

笔者建议中高级阶段的学习者学习单词时,要同时学习单词的常见搭配和在句子中的用法,Collins Cobuild 词典在此方面做得非常适合学习者。中国的中高级阶段英语学习者词汇的水平也就大致相当于美国的高中生,所以不要误以为"中高级"就表明自己的语言水平很好,很多专业词汇或与工作和研究过程中使用的相关语言,中高级学习者都未必学过。

当前的大学英语教育中,很多教材的选材偏文学化,学生接触了很多含义丰富的词汇,尤其是大量的形容词,但实际用英语进行口语交流(如国际会议发言和问答)或非口语交流(如论文写作)时很少能够使用或需要使用;而真正需要使用的词汇往往是表达中国情况的基本词汇,可这些学习者又往往没有接触过,或接触得较少。很多学生在用英语沟通的起步阶段都是在翻译自己的话,但往往不知道怎么翻。例如,学生想说:"我们要大力倡导节能减排。"可是没有在大学教材或其他载体上见过这句话怎么说,于是就"失语"了。在大学英语教材和教学中,教师应该尽快补充学生在日后的工作和学习中需要使用的口语和书面内容,尤其是介绍中国情况的内容。

近年来,语言学家提出"语块"(chunk)概念,认为译员应积累大量的语块,以便在语言表达过程中快速调用,提高整体表达速度。如果译员积累的英汉对应词汇很多,那么表达时就可以词汇为单位快速转换;如果译员积累的英汉对应句子很多,就可以句子为单位进行快速转换。口译研究发现,让学生背诵中英文对照的礼仪性场合常见句子后,大部分学生的翻译表现都比较好。如果会议口译译员可以在汉英对照的句子层面多做积累,口译时一定会更加轻松。

用于积累的句库材料可自己收集,与传统的关键句型总结类似,只不过要在其后加上译文。也可购买英汉对照口语书籍和口译、笔译教材等双语对照材料作为素材进行积累。此外,一些主题读物有双语对照的词汇、句子和对话,话题也十分广泛和新颖。

译员平日积累知识和词汇,可采用以下办法:

1) 紧跟时事。会议口译与现实生活关联性很强。发生经济危机时,各行各业都可能受到影响,译员一定要知道相关的背景和对应的说法,如经济危机有如下几种代称:economic downturn、economic slowdown、sluggish economy、tough time、economic winter 等。再比如,受到新冠疫情影响的行业有哪些?制造业、外向型企业[1]用英文如何表达?译员平日可多阅读《新闻周刊》(News Week)、《经济学人》(Economist)、《纽约客》(The New Yorker)、《华盛顿邮报》(Washington Post)、《北京周报》(Beijing Review)、《中国日报》等英文报刊,关注政治、经济、生活、科技、军事等方面的双语信息。

2) 关注几大词汇来源:译员可对外交部和各大国家部委网站上的翻译园地(或叫翻译天地等)提供的一些词汇进行分类整理,如商务部翻译园地、外交部翻译园地、联译网、《中国

---

1 制造业为 manufacturing industry,外向型企业为 export-oriented enterprises。

日报》的"Language Tips"栏目等。

3）购买综合分类词典和行业专业词典，如银行业词典、医学词汇词典、农业词汇词典等。

4）完成口译任务后及时整理、完善、更新词汇表。译员每次完成口译任务后，都会留下一些资料，这时应趁热打铁，及时整理、完善、更新任务开始前做的词汇表。

此外，还有一些质量管理方法也可提高翻译质量：如制作翻译质量反馈表，请求客户填写并收集保存，为日后承接新的翻译工作提供证据，说明客户对自己翻译工作的认可，并了解客户的建议和意见，便于日后提高。执业译员需及时在个人简历上添加翻译任务相关信息，如时间、地点、会议名称、主办单位、话题等，以提高潜在翻译业务和自身翻译经历匹配度，减少译前准备的投入，提高翻译工作的经济效应。

除了提高自己的语言基本功外，由于会议口译是一种社会交际活动，译员还要广泛学习礼仪、文化和交际方面的知识，提高交际能力。会议的语言具有一些特点，可专门进行学习（詹成，2015）。

医学口译中包含大量术语，学习者可自学相关术语，市面上相关教材较多，包括郭莉萍、顾海华主编的《医学词汇学习手册》等，中国大学慕课网也有医学术语学相关课程；此外，还可通过互联网访问美国院校推出的网络课程，如"Medical Terminology"（Des Moines Medical University，需要指出的是，该课程是用英文解释英文，且无对应术语中文译法，初学者可能会感到比较困难）、美国国立卫生研究院（National Institutes of Health）网上医学词汇和医学口语课程、香港大学网上医学术语课程等。医学会议口译译员还应熟悉我国及世界各国主要医学研究机构、医疗机构、医药器械和药物生产商的中英文名称。医学会议口译译员素养还包括带口音英语的听辨能力及计算机辅助翻译技能等。

医学口译员的学习训练资源包括《英国医学杂志》（*BMJ*）官网科研新闻、综合网站Youtube、哔哩哔哩、医学视频网站 medicalvideos[1]、"Johns Hopkins All Children's Hospital Surgical Training Videos"系列《新英格兰医学杂志》多媒体栏目（可下载视频，有文字转写）、世界卫生组织网站多媒体频道等。

3.5 文化因素对口译质量的影响

文化可以指一个人群普遍都做的事，这个"群"（community）可大可小，可以是一个办公室，有办公室文化；也可以是一个地区或国家。例如，在四川，打麻将、坐茶馆是一种文化；在北京，称呼别人用"您"是一种文化；在我国西北地区，宴席上吃鱼时，鱼头对着的客人要喝酒，鱼尾对着的客人也要喝酒，这也是一种文化。外国人吃完东西，有时会用嘴去吮吸手指头，这也是文化。

不同文化的人在一起，会觉得对方的行为动作很奇怪。译员则是消除这种怪异感，甚至是

1　其内容主要是非手术、动画版临床视频；图像清晰、发音标准、语速适中、有成段的字幕；可供交传、同传、视译练习使用。

治疗"文化休克"（cultural shock）的良医。很多外国人都认为中国人吃饭响动太大，往桌上甚至地上吐骨、刺等很不礼貌。中国人则觉得外国人吃得太拘谨。很多美国人不吃动物的内脏、头、爪等。这时，在必要的情况下，译员一定要对双方的行为做出解释，避免误会。

外方宴请时，准备的菜肴并不是太多，常常让中方觉得"寒酸"，也不会给别人夹菜和不断地敬酒。而中方宴请时，菜肴往往过于丰盛，并不断地敬酒，甚至给客人夹菜。外方对中方的敬酒基本上是来者不拒，但如果接连被宴请且总被夹菜，也会觉得难以招架，甚至有外国人向译员表示，只工作，不接受中方宴请。这种情况下，译员一定要委婉地向双方解释，协调沟通，避免误会。

英语国家人士有一些特别的做法，如把食指和中指交叉并说出"Let's cross the fingers / fingers crossed"，表示希望好运降临；说了不吉利的话以后希望能够避免倒霉事的发生，这时会说 touch wood，同时触摸木头制的东西；此外，他们还认为黑猫不吉利。

下文"To Look or Not Look Is the Question"选自《中国日报》，作者从海外华人视角，比较了中外在社会交际中眼神交流上的文化差异。

To Look or Not Look Is the Question

By Raymond Zhou

What is the biggest cultural barrier for a Chinese to overcome when dealing with people from other countries?

For me personally, it is none other than looking into the eye of the other party.

I knew early on while I was still in school that Western people value eye contact. But it is one thing to know something; it is another to be able to practice it.

It took me a good three years living in the United States to completely get over my "handicap". For a while, I invented a fence-sitting strategy whereby I would almost look at the person I was conversing with, but with a slight angle so that our eyes wouldn't be locked together at all times. I would appear to be looking without really looking.

Now you may ask: What's the big fuss about looking at someone in the eye while talking to him? Isn't it the most natural thing to do?

Well, let me tell you: No, not for someone brought up and taught NOT to look that way. Actually, I've never encountered a specific instruction in our textbooks that we should not look directly at someone else while talking. And in school, we also look at the teacher. But when it's a one-on-one conversation, it is simply impolite to gaze, especially at someone of a senior generation or ranking.

This little habit of ours has probably created more misunderstanding than most cultural quirks. In Western culture, it is impolite to look at something other than the eyes of the one you talk to. Besides, you may be interpreted as lacking self-confidence or even lying.

Just imagine how many perfectly competent job candidates fell through this crack when recruiters from multinational companies took their Chinese way of politeness to mean the typical negative things associated with "not looking them in the eye".

Now, you may say that since we have rational knowledge of this behavioral discrepancy, why can't we adopt the Western way while talking to the Westerners? Shouldn't that be easier than speaking a foreign language?

Easier said than done. Because "not looking" is so rooted in our cultural genes, during my transformative years, I constantly went through a process of internal struggle of "looking or not looking". I knew I should look, but just couldn't bring myself to it.

To understand how hard it is, you may have a little role-reversal and for once pretend you're a typical Chinese and look at the translator while talking to your host. If you feel comfortable, you can probably be a good actor.

Now let's take a step back. Suppose you cannot do that with ease just as you cannot take on a new accent at your will. You should pause for a moment when you see your Chinese friends engaging in the "wandering eye" and say to yourself: Hey, this guy may be a little shy, but he is not being discourteous because he grew up in a culture of discouraging such stares.

As for my personal experience, switching between looking and not looking is much harder than switching between two languages. After I came back to China as a "sea turtle", I could refrain from sprinkling my speech with English words, but I simply couldn't go back to looking sideways again.

Later, a friend scolded me for being "thoroughly Americanized" because my intent look was "too aggressive" and made him "nervous". I wish I could return to my "looking yet not looking" mode again, but no amount of theorizing can help me adjust with each occasion.

Habits die hard—good habits or bad. They make us who we are. Maybe we should all install a little mental translating device to remind ourselves of our little differences.

仪式性会议的口译往往需要考虑气氛，译员需要使用合适的语气来协助传达发言人的意图，有时甚至需要重复部分重要信息或需要适度添加润色词语。总之，译员既要表达发言人的意图，又要让听者感到符合自己的"接收"习惯。有些学者可能会认为这样的翻译是"超额翻译"，但是在"不得已而为之"的情况下，会议口译译员不得不采用这样的办法。

在口译工作中，译员还会碰到一些成语、习语，如"new wine in old bottles"（旧瓶装新酒——旧形式不适合新内容）、"to carry/take coals to Newcastle / reinvent the wheel"（多此一举）、"to call a spade a spade"（直言不讳）、"The devil is always in the details."（麻烦在于细节之处。）、"Everybody's business is nobody's business."（众人的事就是无人过问的事。/ 三个和尚没水喝。）、"to grow like mushrooms"（如雨后春笋般迅速发展）等，应注意平日多加积累。

汉字文化圈人名、地名的恰当翻译问题，也是口译乃至笔译工作中需要加以重视的一个问题。汉字文化圈，即曾使用或仍在使用汉字的国家和地区，包括越南、日本、朝鲜、韩国、新加坡、马来西亚等。这些国家的人的名字在英语里是按照罗马字的方法来拼写的，译员不能简单地按照发音来翻译，如 Hiro Nakamura（美剧《英雄》里的角色）翻译过来是中村宽，Lee

Junki 翻译过来是李准基，Ho Chimin 翻译过来是胡志明，新加坡、马来西亚等国知名华人的名字可以参考新加坡译名统一委员会的网站。总之，要看原本的中文是什么。

中国香港人和台湾人的名字同样要注意，这些人的名字是按照粤语、客家话、闽语等发音用旧式的威妥玛拼音拼出来的，如 Lam 是姓"林"，Ng 是姓"吴"，Hsu 是姓"徐"或"许"等，回译时一定要注意查证。

翻译是社会交际行为，在医学会议口译工作中，口译交际能力关系到如何开展协作翻译，如何与主办方沟通，也涉及如何开展协作翻译的问题。陪同口译中，在代表团人数众多的情况下，很可能涉及多个译员参与口译工作；在技术性强、工作时间久的医学培训会的交替传译中，也会有多个译员合作；而同声传译要求至少两人组成同传团队，通过每 15—20 分钟轮换口译的方式共同完成同传任务。对难度普遍较高的医学同传，三人搭档更为常见。这其中除关系到译员如何与主办方和同传搭档沟通外，还涉及术语统一等技术问题。多人协作笔译时，可把书拆成一章章进行分配；多人协作口译时，可将会议按日程划分成若干部分分配给译员。术语的统一依靠基于既往翻译积累的词汇，但在当前翻译任务中碰到的新词汇则需商议定译。此外，利用人工智能翻译管理平台，可在后台制定主控术语表，给予相应人员添加术语的权限，给予专家修改术语、定稿译法等权限，以确保术语的统一性。

3.6 英汉医学语言中的文化问题

医学会议中，中外双方会使用一些文化负载词来表达观点，如救死扶伤、大医精诚、大医治未病、养生、patient care、cancer care、health care 等。翻译时，除注意达意，译员还应注意文化差异，适当做补充解释。

"救死扶伤"按字面意思可被翻译为 saving those dying、helping those injured。美国医师特鲁多墓志铭曰"to cure sometimes, to relieve often, to comfort always"，意为"有时去治愈，常常去缓解，总是去安慰"或"偶尔治愈，常常帮助，总是安慰"。

《大医精诚》出自唐朝孙思邈所著之《备急千金要方》第一卷，乃是中医学典籍中论述医德的一篇极重要的文献，为习医者所必读。《大医精诚》论述了有关医德的两个问题：第一是精，亦即要求医者要有精湛的医术，认为医道是"至精至微之事"，习医之人必须"博极医源，精勤不倦"；第二是诚，亦即要求医者要有高尚的品德修养，"见彼苦恼，若己有之"，常发"大慈恻隐之心"，进而发愿"普救含灵之苦"，且不得"自逞俊快，邀射名誉""恃己所长，经略财物"。西方医学伦理学则强调 medical professionalism，即医师职业精神。

《备急千金要方》中提到"上医医未病之病，中医治欲病之病，下医医已病之病"，认为一名医术高超的医生应把握时机，重视在没有病症前就加以调理防范，而不是在疾病发生后"亡羊补牢"。中医"治未病"理论经过 2 000 多年来医者们的总结、传承与发扬，具备了较深刻的内涵，主要包括四大方面，即未病先防、欲病早治、已病防变及愈后防复。西方则有"预防医学"（preventive medicine），拉丁文中的 prophylaxis 也有预防之意。近年来，我国更是提出大力发展治未病科的目标；若将其解释性地翻译为 preventive medicine department，可能会给西方读者造成一些理解困扰，毕竟西方 preventive medicine 的实质与实践方式与中医的治未病还是存在一定差异的。

养生指通过各种方法颐养生命、增强体质、预防疾病，从而达到延年益寿的一种医事活动。现代意义的"养生"指的是根据人的生命过程规律主动进行物质与精神的身心养护活动。我们可将其解释性地翻译为 preserve one's health、keep in good health，但"养生学院"[1]中的"养生"恐怕要用名词性短语 health preservation 来译更为合适。

《湘雅医学词典》旧版曾将 patient care 翻译为"病人保健"。殊不知，patient care 等于诊断、治疗、康复、心理支持、社会支持等一系列"照顾"病人的医事活动和社会活动。目前，我国港、澳、台地区通行"患者照顾"（陈孝平，2017；王一方，2017）或"患者照护"，并逐步被内地（大陆）医学界所接受。医院评价医师工作，主要分三个方面：科研、教学、医疗，这里的医疗就是 patient care。有人认为应该将 cancer care 翻译为"癌症诊疗"，我们认为应该将其翻译为"癌症照护"。"诊疗"一词似乎暗示将心理、社会的照顾排除在患者照护之外。我们可以依据上下文及中文习惯将 health care 翻译成"医疗卫生"[2]"医疗"[3]等。

此外，patient 中文究竟对应"病人"，还是"患者"，学界也有争论。专家们的争论焦点在于"患者"和"病人"哪个词更礼貌。然而，standard patient 已经固定翻译为"标准化病人"，成为标准术语，在医学界通用。类似的争论还有 dementia 究竟应被翻译为"老年痴呆症"，还是"老年失智症"，这关涉是否存在年龄歧视和弱势者歧视的问题。

3.7 称呼语的文化差异

研究发现，有些患者有将护士称为医生或大夫的现象。这一点在会议交流中也常常发生，如将副教授称为教授等。译员应考虑传译效果合理使用对应译法。

东西方称呼中的头衔习惯用法有差异，如韩启德先生，西方人常常以 Dr.、Professor 来称呼他，而国人习惯称他为委员长[4]、韩校长[5]、韩院士[6]等。西方尊称与爵位、学位、总统、院长、主席等有关，中国则常用党政干部头衔、学术头衔、职务头衔等。联合国会议中常用 your excellency、Mr.、Ms. 表示尊称。翻译头衔称呼时，采用归化与异化方法各有利弊。归化的好处在于可唤起译入语听众与发言人的共鸣，弊端在于会让听众误以为发言人熟悉译入语文化。

此外，中文提及受到重视或得到支持的时候，常说到"领导"（leadership）的重视和支持，

---

1 如成都中医药大学养生康复学院。
2 如 provide health care to local people（为当地人提供医疗卫生服务）。
3 如 health care reform（医疗改革，简称医改）。
4 他曾担任第十一届全国人大常委会副委员长。
5 他曾担任北京大学常务副校长。
6 他是中国科学院院士。

英文更多提及"support from the management"（来自管理层的支持）。我们若按字面意思翻译"学校领导"，则是 leaders of the school，但其实西方人更常用 school managers 来表达这一含义。英文更多强调"leadership"（领导力）和"teamwork spirit"（团队精神）；中文更强调"在……的领导下"（under the leadership of...），更强调"党政领导班子"（leaders of the Party and the administrative departments）和"公司领导班子"（leaders of the management）等。这些都是英汉文化不同在语言表达上造成的差异。这样的文化差异要求译员具有较为敏锐的跨文化交际意识。

参考文献

陈孝平. 2017. 关于将医学教材及医学出版物中"患者"一词统一更改为"病人"的建议. 中国实用外科杂志，37（1）: 5.

思果. 2004. 翻译研究. 北京：中国对外翻译出版公司.

王东志，王立弟. 2007. 口译的质量和控制. 中国翻译，（4）: 54–57.

王一方. 2017. 与陈孝平院士商榷：请留住"患者". 来自知识分子网站.

叶子南. 2004. 高级英汉翻译理论与实践. 北京：清华大学出版社.

詹成. 2015. 会议口译常用语手册. 北京：外语教育与研究出版社.

张维为. 2004. 英汉同声传译. 北京：中国对外翻译出版公司.

Nida, E. 2004. Principles of Correspondence. In L. Venuti (Ed.), *The Translation Studies Reader*. New York: Routledge, 153–167.

Walsh, K. 2013. *Oxford Textbook of Medical Education*. Oxford: Oxford University Press.

第4章

数学、物理、化学、统计学名词及变化趋势相关表达译法

在医学会议中,由于涉及较多学术交流,故发言人常使用数字、物理、化学、统计学名词及变化趋势相关表达。本章对这些表达的译法进行概括,医学会议口译员应熟悉这些表达。

4.1 数字

4.1.1 数位的表达

数位相关表达在医学会议中十分常见。译员应经常按百、千、万、十万、百万、亿、十亿、百亿、千亿、万亿顺序进行英汉、汉英两个方向的对照口译练习。

表 4.1 常用数位中英文对照

中文	英文	中文	英文
百	one hundred	亿	100 million
千	one thousand	十亿	1 billion
万	10 thousand	百亿	10 billion
十万	100 thousand	千亿	100 billion
百万	1 million	万亿	1 trillion
千万	10 million		

在会议口译工作过程中,译员往往是通过听觉而非视觉,来获取待翻译数字信息,故应在平时的训练中,着重练习通过听觉辅以笔记进行口译的能力。例如,听到960万,应抓住主要单位百万,然后将其换算为9.6 million;听到4 000万,应想到千万在英文里对应10 million,4 000万则对应40 million。

对一些常用数字,译员要熟悉其翻译法。例如,"中国人口有14亿"中,14亿对应1.4 billion;"中国贸易总额达上万亿"中,万亿对应英文trillion;"精子总数达数千万,乃至上亿"

中，千万对应 10 million，亿对应 100 million。

一些数字很大，译员精力有限，有时可能无法逐个数位完整翻译，但至少应保证主要位数的准确翻译，如 43 987.16，译员至少应该翻译出 forty-three thousand，还可加上 about，表示大约，而 forty-three thousand 之后的数字，可根据实际情况处理。

4.1.2 运算（calculation）的表达

加法（addition）："四加五等于九"可被译为"If you add 4 to 5, you get 9"或 " 4 and 5 equals 9"；"1 + 1 = 2"可被译为"One and/plus one equals two"。sum 意为"和"；"The sum of 5 and 3 is 8"意为"五加三的总和是八"。

减法（subtraction）：minus 意为"减"；"Six minus two equals four"意为"六减去二等于四"。subtract 意为"减"；"If you subtract 2 from 8, you get 6"意为"8 减去 2 是 6"。"2 – 1 = 1"可被译为"Two minus one equals one"。

乘法（multiplication）：multiplied by 意为"乘"；"Four multiplied by seven is twenty-eight"意为"7 乘 4 等于 28"。"2 × 1 = 2"可被译为"Two by/times one equals two"。

除法（division）：divided by 意为"除"；"Six divided by two is three"意为"六除以二得三"。"2 ÷ 1 = 2"可被译为"Two divided by one equals two"。

正负号："He seems to have mistaken a plus for a minus"意为"他似乎把正号误作负号了"。minus two centigrade 意为"零下二度"。minus four 意为"负四"。

4.1.3 小数的表达

"小数"被译为 decimal；"小数点"被译为 decimal point；"1.5"被译为 one point five；"0.56"被译为 zero point five six 或省略 zero 而被译为 point five six；"21.23%"被译为 twenty-one point two three percent（注意：小数点后不念 twenty three）。

4.1.4 倍数的表达

"倍数"被译为 times 或 folds。"A 是 B 的两倍"可被译为"A is two times/folds of B"。"减半"可被译为 halve，如"在 2010 年之前将 XXX 病毒感染者数目减半"可被译为"to halve the people with XXX virus by 2010"。"翻一倍，翻一番"可用 double 作为核心词，如"在 2000 年之前实现 GDP 翻一番"可被译为"to double GDP by 2000"或"The GDP would be doubled by 2000"。"增长到原来的三倍"可用 triple 表示，如"我们的门诊量比 1999 年增长了两倍"可译为"Our outpatient visits triple over that of 1999"（即增加到 1999 年的三倍）。"增长到原来的四倍"可用 quadruple 表示。"我们的产量比 1999 年增长了三倍"（即增加到 1999 年的四倍）可被译为" Our production volume quadruples over that of 1999"。

4.1.5 分数（fraction）的表达

numerator 意为"分子"；denominator 意为"分母"。"二分之一"是 one half；"三分之一"是 one third；"四分之一"是 one fourth；"四分之三"是 three fourths。规律是分子用基数表达，分母用序数表达，如 one tenth（1/10）、four fifths（4/5）、one hundredth（1/100）、three two-hundredths（3/200）、one thousandth（1/1 000）、three thousandths（3/2 000）。"百分数"可被译为 percentage，如"10%"为 ten percent；"百分点"[1]为 percentage point。

4.1.6 方程式（equation）的表达

"一元二次方程"被译为 quadratic equation of one unknown；"一元三次方程"被译为 cubic equation of one unknown。"$x^2 + 3x + 2 = 12$ 是一个二次方程式"被译为"That x square plus 3 times x plus 2 equals 12 is a quadratic equation"。

表 4.2　常用方程式英汉表达

英文	中文
square	二次方，平方
cube	三次方，立方
the power of four / the fourth power	四次方
the power of n	n 次方
square root	二次方根，平方根
cube root	三次方根，立方根
the root of fourth power	四次方根
to extract a root	开方

4.1.7 指数／幂

exponential growth 意为"指数增殖、指数式生长、指数增长级、指数生长"；geometric growth 意为"几何级数增长"[2]；arithmetical growth 意为"算术级增长"，类似于等差数列，如 2、4、6、8、10 等。

1　百分点是指不同时期以百分数形式表示的指标的变动幅度。例如，"我国国内生产总值中，第一产业占的比重由 1992 年的 23.8% 下降到 1993 年的 21.2%"可被理解为：1993 年的国内生产总值中第一产业占的比重比 1992 年下降 2.6 个百分点（即 21.2 − 23.8 = −2.6，two point six percentage point），但不能说成是下降百分之 2.6（two point six percent）。

2　几何级数增长就是成倍数增长，类似于通常所说的"翻番"。如果 A = 2，A 的 n 次幂的增长就意味着可以得到 2、4、8、16、32、64、128 等；如果 A = 3，则可以得到 3、9、27、81 等。"几何级数增长"也可用 increase in a geometrical ratio 来表达。

- Population, when unchecked, increases in a geometrical ratio.
  如果不控制，人口将呈现几何级数增长。
- Subsistence increases only in an arithmetical ratio.
  生活资料只会以算术级增长。

4.1.8 约数

dozens of 意为"几十个"；hundreds of millions of 意为"几十万个"；well over thirty 意为"三十好几"。about、around、approximately 表示"大约"。拉丁文缩写 *ca* 意为"大约"，全写为 *circa*，发音是 /ˈsɜːkə/。

4.2 物理学、化学

4.2.1 测量单位的翻译

物理学、化学知识看似与医学口译并不相关，然而这两个学科的知识往往在生物医药领域的口译中频频出现。具体在重量、速度、质量等测量单位的口译上，相关知识对译员口译中的理解与表达较有帮助。比如，译员应掌握医学口译中常见的重量单位：千克、克、毫克、微克、纳克等，明了它们的概念内涵。特别是对日常生活中并不常见的微克、纳克，译员应该清楚纳克在谈及病毒相关科学实验中的剂量等语境中较为常用，微克则在谈及空气中 $PM_{2.5}$ 微粒的重量等语境中较为常用。译员还需知晓不同重量单位之间的换算关系：1 千克 = 1 000 克、1 克 = 1 000 毫克、1 毫克 = 1 000 微克、1 微克 = 1 000 纳克。在以上知识储备的基础上，译员还应掌握相应的英文表达：千克为 kilogram，克为 gram，毫克为 miligram，微克为 microgram，纳克为 nanogram。

4.2.2 物理学、化学知识的积累

医学口译译员可以通过日常增加自然科学学科英语语篇的阅读量，增进自身对相关知识的理解，积累相应表达。

请阅读下文，并学习其中的化学词汇（Anon, 2019）。

Chemical Formulae (化学式)

Any molecule (分子) can be represented by a formula (化学式) that lists all the atoms (原子) in that molecule. Each element (元素) is presented by its atomic symbols (化学元素符号) in the Periodic Table (元素周期表). For example, H for hydrogen (氢), Ca for calcium (钙). If more than one atom of a particular element is present, then it's indicated by a number in subscript (下标) after the atomic symbol. For example, H_2O means there are two atoms of hydrogen and one of oxygen.

If there is more than one of whole groups of atoms, then that's shown with a bracket（括号）around them. For example, calcium hydroxide（氢氧化钙）has one calcium (Ca) for every two hydroxides (OH)（氢氧化物）. So it is written as $Ca(OH)_2$.

If a charge（电荷）is present, it's indicated in superscript（上标）with a sign of +/- and a number if more than one charge is present. For example, calcium ions（离子）has have two positive charges（正电荷）so are written as Ca^{2+}.

Structural Formulae（结构式）

Sometimes a formula can be written in a way that gives an indication of the structure. For example, acetic acid（乙酸）contains two carbons（碳）, four hydrogens（氢）, and two oxygens（氧）, so it could be given as $C_2H_4O_2$—but is more usually written as CH_3COOH to emphasize the structure.

Chemical Equations（化学方程式）

A chemical equation shows a reaction taking place. On the left-hand side are the reactions（反应物）, the molecules that take part in the reaction. On the right-hand side are the products（产物）, the molecules that are created（产生的）in the reaction. Each side must contain the same number of each kind of atom. An arrow between them indicates the direction the reaction is expected to occur. For example, $Ca + Cl_2 \to CaCl_2$ (Calcium and chlorine produce calcium chloride).

If there are two or more of any molecule, that's indicated with the number in front of the molecule: $CH_4 + 2O_2 \to CO_2 + 2H_2O$ [One methane（甲烷）molecule + two oxygen molecules produce one carbon dioxide[1]（二氧化碳）molecule and two water molecules].

Phases（态）

An equation may sometimes specify which phase each molecule is in—whether it's solid, liquid, or gas, or if it's dissolved. This is written in brackets after the molecule—(s) for solid（固态）, (l) for liquid（液态）, (g) for gas（气态）and, (aq) for aqueous（溶解态）, meaning being dissolved in water.

For example, solid calcium carbonate（碳酸钙）reacts with carbonic acid（碳酸）in water to form calcium bicarbonate（碳酸氢钙）, which is much more soluble（可溶的）so it becomes dissolved in water. $CaCO_3 (s) + H_2CO_3 (aq) \to Ca(HCO_3)_2 (aq)$ (Solid calcium carbonate reacts with resolved carbonic acid and produces dissolved calcium bicarbonate).

Equilibriums（平衡）

All chemical reactions can actually proceed in either direction. Most of the time one direction

---

[1] CO_2 可念作 CO two，也可念作 carbon dioxide。其他化合物的念法也是如此。

is expected to take place more strongly, so the arrow is written in that direction. However, many common reactions happen in both directions simultaneously, creating an equilibrium where the reactions are taking place but there is no net change in concentration (浓度) from one side to the other. This is indicated with symbol (互换符号).

For example, carbonic acid in water is continually breaking down into (分解为) bicarbonate and hydrogen ions—but the ions are also continually joining back together. $H_2CO_3 \rightarrow HCO_3 + H$ (Carbonic acid → bicarbonate + hydrogen ions).

医学口译中，涉及营养学、生物化学、核医学等的会议常常提及微量元素、放射性元素、有机物名称等化学词汇。例如：

- 脂肪、糖类、蛋白质、维生素、水和无机盐是人体所需的六大类营养素。
  Fat, sugar, protein, vitamins, water and inorganic salts are the six types of nutrients needed by the human body.
- 人体所需的微量元素有碳、氢、氧、氮、钙、磷、镁、钠，还包括铁、锌、铜、锰、铬、硒、钼、钴、氟。
  The trace elements needed by human body include carbon, hydrogen, oxygen, nitrogen, calcium, phosphorus, magnesium and sodium, as well as iron, zinc, copper, manganese, chromium, selenium, molybdenum, cobalt and fluorine.

更多的物理、化学表达，参见本书附录。

4.3 统计学

由于医学会议常常涉及科研，所以有必要学习常用统计学表达。表 4.3 是常见统计学词汇（格里菲思、李芳，2011）。

表 4.3 常见统计学词汇中英文对照表达

英文	中文
dependent variable	因变量
covariate	协变量
independent variable	自变量
binary/dichotomous variable	二分变量
nominal variable	名义变量
continuous variable	连续变量
categorical variable	分类变量
descriptive analysis	描述性统计分析
mean	均值
mode	众数

第4章 数学、物理、化学、统计学名词及变化趋势相关表达译法

（续表）

英文	中文
median	中位数
standard deviation	标准差
t-test	t 检验
unpaired t-test	非配对 t 检验
paired t-test	配对 t 检验
chi-square test	卡方检验（chi 发音为 /kaɪ/）
factor score	因子得分
regression analysis	回归分析
reference group	参照组
univariate analysis	单因素分析
multivariate analysis	多因素分析
regression model	回归模型
odds ratio	比值比
hazard ratio	危险比
risk ratio	风险比
residual	残差
error term	误差项
linear regression	线性回归
generalized linear regression	广义线性回归
logistic regression	逻辑斯回归，罗吉斯回归，逻辑回归
binary logistic regression	二元逻辑回归
multinomial logistic regression	多分类逻辑回归
log transformation	对数转换
exploratory factor analysis	探索性因子分析
principal component analysis	主成分分析
factor load	因子载荷
eigenvalue	特征根
normal distribution	正态分布
skewed	呈偏态分布的
statistically significant	具有统计学显著意义
reliability	信度
validity	效度
threshold	阈值
confidence interval	置信区间
cohort	队列
panel data	面板数据

（续表）

英文	中文
longitudinal survey	纵向调查
cross-sectional survey	横截面调查
dimension	维度
indicator	指标
statistical model	统计学模型
parameter	参数
bias	偏倚
variance	方差
ANOVA (Analysis of Variance)	方差分析
MANOVA (Multivariate Analysis of Variance)	多因素方差分析

- α 值＜0.05 被认为具有统计学意义。
  When the α value is smaller than point o five, it is regarded as statistically significant.

同比和环比的概念和表达方式如下：同比发展速度主要是为了消除季节变动的影响，用以说明本期发展水平与去年同期发展水平对比而达到的相对发展速度。例如，"本期 2 月比去年 2 月""本期 6 月比去年 6 月"等。其计算公式为：同比发展速度＝本期发展水平÷去年同期发展水平×100%。在实际工作中，某年、某季、某月与上年同期对比计算的发展速度，就是同比发展速度。例如，"a year on year increase/decrease of... = increase/decrease... over/as compared with that of the same period of last year"意为"同比增长 / 降低……"。环比是指将现在的统计周期和上一个统计周期比较。例如，2005 年 7 月与 2005 年 6 月相比较可以被称为环比。"a month on month increase/decrease of..."意为"环比增长 / 降低……"。

4.4 描述变化趋势的常用表达

4.4.1 表示上升、提高、扩大

表示上升、提高、扩大最常用的动词是 increase、rise、raise，此外，还有 go up、go upward、upside expectation、soar、spiral、enlarge、expand、pick up 等相关表达。下文会进一步介绍这些词语和表达的具体用法。

1）go up = rise、increase。

- If a price, amount, or level goes up, it becomes higher or greater than it was.
  如果价格、数量或水平上升，它变得比以前更高或更大。

- Interest rates went up.
  利率升高。

- The cost has gone up to $1.95 a minute.
  费用提高到每分钟 1.95 美元。
- Prices have gone up 61 percent since deregulation.
  在放松管制以后，价格已经提高了 61%。

2）go upward：上行，走高。

- People now are not sure whether the mortgage rates go up or down.
  人们不确定抵押贷款利率究竟会上行还是下行。

3）upside expectation：上升预期。

- As a result, we should be conservative on the upside expectation of the likely rebound this week.
  因此，我们应该对本周可能出现反弹的上升预期持保守态度。

4）rocket：原意是"火箭"，引申为"急速上升"。

- His profits rocketed.
  他的利润猛增。

5）soar：飙升。

- Lower tariffs and the growth of population and industry caused trade to soar in the 19th century.
  较低的关税税率、人口的增长和工业的发展使 19 世纪的贸易突飞猛进。
- The prices of new cars have soared.
  新车价格暴涨。

6）spiral：螺旋上升 / 下降。

- If an amount or level spirals, it rises quickly and at an increasing rate.
  如果数量或水平呈螺旋状，则表示它上升得很快，而且速度越来越快。
- Production costs began to spiral.
  生产成本开始急剧上涨。
- a spiralling trend of violence
  暴力的态势越演越烈
- The divorce rate is spiralling upwards.
  离婚率不断攀升。
- Prices are still spiraling.
  价格仍然在急剧上涨。
- a vicious wage-price spiral
  工资与物价上升的恶性循环
- Experts watch the spiral development in industry with keen interest.
  专家们以很大的兴趣观察工业的螺旋式发展。

- Libraries have however remained locked in their growth spiral.
  然而，图书馆的发展仍停留在螺旋式上升阶段。

7）enlarge：扩大。

- When you enlarge something or when it enlarges, it becomes bigger.
  当你放大某物或者当它放大时，它变得更大。
- the plan to enlarge Ewood Park into a 30,000 all-seater stadium
  将埃伍德公园扩建为3万座体育馆的规划
- The glands in the neck may enlarge.
  脖子上的腺体可能增大。
- enlarge the foreign commerce
  扩大对外贸易
- The UN secretary-general yesterday recommended an enlarged peacekeeping force.
  联合国秘书长昨天建议扩大维和部队规模。

8）expand：扩大。

- If something expands or is expanded, it becomes larger.
  如果某物膨胀或被膨胀，它就会变得更大。
- Our foreign trade has expanded during recent years.
  近年来，我们的对外贸易有所扩大。
- We need capital to expand.
  我们需要资本以求扩展。

9）pick up：好转，改善；加速。

- If trade or the economy of a country picks up, it improves.
  如果一个国家的贸易或经济回升，它就会好转。
- Industrial production is beginning to pick up.
  工业生产开始好转。
- When a vehicle picks up speed, it begins to move more quickly.
  当车辆加速时，它开始更快地移动。
- Brian pulled away slowly, but picked up speed.
  布莱恩慢慢地启动了车子，但加快了速度。（= accelerate，加速）
- A pick-up in trade or in a country's economy is an improvement in it.
  贸易或一国经济的回升是一国经济的改善。
- a pick-up in the housing market
  楼市的好转/升温
- There are signs of a pick-up in high street spending.
  主要街道的消费出现了好转迹象。

4.4.2 表示减少、下降、降低、缩小

表示减少、下降、降低、缩小最常用的动词是 reduce 和 decrease，此外，还有 fall、go down、go downward、downside expectation、plummet、plunge 等相关表达。下文会进一步介绍这些词语和表达的具体用法。

1）fall：下降。

- We are expecting a fall in stock prices.
  我们预料股市价格将要下跌。
- Production costs fell by 30%.
  生产成本下降了 30%。

2）go down：下降。

- The price of eggs has gone down.
  蛋价下降了。
- Crime has gone down by 70 percent.
  犯罪率下降了 70%。
- Average life expectancy went down from about 70 to 67.
  平均预期寿命从 70 岁左右下降到了 67 岁。（= fall）

3）go downward：下行。

- So who supposedly made the economy go downward?
  那么是谁让经济下行呢？

4）downside expectation：下跌预期。

- The minimum downside expectation now is illustrated on the charts.
  最小下跌预期如表所示。

5）plummet：暴跌。

- Share prices plummet or plunge on the news of the devaluation.
  一有贬值的消息，股票价格就暴跌了。
- House prices have plummeted in this area.
  此地房价大跌。

6）plunge：猛跌；骤降；跳水。

- Since then prices have plunged.
  从那时起，价格猛跌。
- Prices started a downward plunge.
  价格开始猛跌。

4.5 句型练习

1）据估计，这一比例达到……
The ratio is estimated at...

2）XXX 占总数的百分之五。
XXX makes up for / accounts for 5% of the total.

3）总共有 100 人接受了调查，其中 32 人表示不知道。
Among the 100 respondents, 32 expressed ignorance.
100 people were surveyed and 32 of them said that they didn't know.
Out of the 100 people who were surveyed, 32 indicated that they didn't know.

4）这项技术开展以后，手术的成功率显著地提高了 20%。
After the application of this procedure, the success rate of operation was dramatically improved by 20%.

5）死亡率（mortality rate）从 1994 年的千分之十快速下降到 1995 年的千分之一。
The mortality rate plummeted from 10 per 1,000 cases in 1994 to 1 per 1,000 in 1995.

6）今年房价仍在缓慢而持续地上涨。
Housing price is going up slowly but consistently this year.
Housing price this year is undergoing a slow but consistent increase.

7）China is both the largest producer and consumer of tobacco in the world. The home to 20% of the world's population, China consumes 30% of the global tobacco products. There are nearly 300 million smokers in China, which is a quarter of the smokers in the world.
中国既是全球最大的烟草生产国，也是最大的消费国。中国人口占世界人口的 20%，消费全球 30% 的烟草产品。中国吸烟人数将近 3 亿，占全球吸烟者的 1/4。

8）The latest Chinese national epidemiological survey predicts that some 1 million Chinese will die as a result of smoking each year if current smoking trend continues. According to the survey, more than 350 million Chinese smoke, making the country's smoking population the largest in the world. Nicotine addiction is a growing problem, particularly in Asia, and international studies show that only around 3% of smokers who attempt to stop by using willpower alone can keep abstinence for more than one year.
最新的全国流行病学调查预测，如果中国目前的吸烟态势继续保持不变，每年将有约 100 万人死于与烟草相关的疾病。调查还显示，我国吸烟者总数超过 3.5 亿，居世界第一。尼古丁依赖是当今社会一个越来越严重的问题，在亚洲尤其是如此。国际研究表明，尝试凭借意志戒烟的吸烟者中，只有大约 3% 的人可以保持一年以上不复吸。

9）There has been a small but consistent decline, of about one per 1,000 births annually, in the proportion of boys being born in industrialized countries over the past 40 years.

第4章 数学、物理、化学、统计学名词及变化趋势相关表达译法

在过去的40年中,发达国家的男孩出生率一直以每年约千分之一的比率小幅下降。

10) Mathews and colleagues studied 740 first-time pregnant mothers in Britain and found 56 percent of those in the group with the highest energy intake at conception had sons, compared with 45 percent in the lowest group.

马修及其同事共对英国740名生了第一胎的妈妈进行研究。研究结果显示,在受孕期间饮食摄入热量最高的那组妈妈中,有56%的人生了男孩;而摄入热量最少的那组只有45%的人生了男孩。

11) Our company is the leading research-based biomedical pharmaceutical company in the world, investing some $10.1 billion in global research and development last year.

我们公司是全球领先的、以研发为基础的制药企业,去年,全球研发投入超过101亿美元。

12) We have been operating in China since the 1980s and is now one of the largest pharmaceutical investors in the country. To date, we have invested more than $400 million in China, with 3 pharmaceutical factories in Dalian, Suzhou and Chengdu, an R&D center in Shanghai, and our China corporate headquarters in Beijing. We currently employ some 5,700 employees, reaching patients in more than 100 major cities in China.

公司在20世纪80年代进入中国,累计投资额已超过4亿美元,是在华投资规模最大的跨国制药企业之一。在大连、苏州和成都拥有3个现代化制药厂,在上海有一个研发中心,中国分公司总部设在北京。目前,公司在中国共有约5 700名员工,业务范围涵盖中国100多个主要城市的患者。

13) 我国目前助产士人力资源匮乏,在发达国家,助产士与孕产妇的比例大约能达到1∶1 000,而我国的这一比例估计在1∶4 000。

Now China lacks human resources for midwifery. In the developed countries, the ratio of midwife to pregnant and lying-in women reaches about 1:1,000; however, in China, the ratio is estimated at 1: 4,000.

14) 国际助产联盟已有72个成员国,而且各会员国基本都实行独立的助产士注册制度和专门的助产学历学位教育体系。

The International Alliance for Midwifery has 72 member states, and each of them practices an independent system for midwife registration and a separate program with degree for midwifery.

15) 北京大学第三医院倪胜莲对4所医院的81名产房助产士进行问卷调查发现:被调查者中29.6%毕业于助产专业,其余毕业于护理专业;其中,67名在独立进行助产工作前接受过培训,但形式和时间不一,最长的24周,最短的仅1周。其中,通过临床带教和短期课堂培训的人员占85.0%,而通过专业培训班培训的人员只占10.5%。100%的被调查人员认为,对助产知识与技能进行专业培训可以减轻现实工作中所面临的压力;93.8%的被调查者认为,需要助产专业培训。

Ni Shenglian with Peking University Third Hospital surveyed 81 midwives working in the delivery room of four hospitals. And the finding is as follows: Among the respondents,

29.6% graduated from midwifery programs, while the remaining part graduated from nursing programs; 67 of them had received training in different forms and duration anywhere between 24 weeks and 1 week before they practiced midwifery independently. Those who have received clinical training and short-term in-class training account for 85.0%, while those received professional training sessions only make up for 10.5% of the total. 100% of the respondents think that professional training on midwifery knowledge and skills can help reduce the pressure they may encounter in work, and 93.8% think they need professional training for midwifery.

参考文献

格里菲思，李芳. 2011. 深入浅出统计学. 北京：电子工业出版社.

Anon. 2019. How to Read Chemical Equations. *Barista Hustle*. Retrieved July 22, 2022, from Barista Hustle website.

第 5 章
医学会议口译译前准备

医学会议往往涉及较多医学相关知识体系和大量术语,且来自世界各地的发言人可能会在英语、汉语发言中带有各种口音,译员务必要在译前进行充分准备。译前准备工作大致包括以下方面:了解会议目的和传译要求,查阅相关资料,整理资料并建立词汇表,了解发言人的口音特点,了解工作环境、工作方式并准备相关物料。

5.1 了解会议目的和传译要求

译员一定要问清翻译任务的目的、主题以及主持人、发言人、嘉宾、参会者等的背景情况和发言内容,了解参会者现场或在线交流的方式,并确定听众概貌,预测听众的知识背景和译文收听习惯。译员还可询问主办方有无译法特殊要求[1]。此外,译员一定要尽可能查证发言人和机构名称,务求正确。译员还可向主办方索取单语或双语资料,包括会议日程、相关机构及发言人介绍资料、发言人简历、机构简介、词汇表或术语表、产品宣传手册等。资料形式包括音像、视频、幻灯片、文字资料等。

5.2 查阅相关资料

译员需根据会议主题自行查阅相关资料,以补齐主办方提供材料的不足,建立会议相关主题知识体系。译员可广泛利用数据库、国内外视频网站等资源;还可绘制思维导图,梳理总结会议相关知识;也可查阅相关教科书、综述文章等,快速、系统地了解相关知识,构建会议主题相关知识体系。此外,译员还可参考临床顾问(up-to-date)数据库及《英国医学杂志中文版》。

临床顾问是临床疾病诊疗参考数据库,内容包括流行病学、病因、诊断与鉴别诊断、治疗方法、预后及患者教育等相关资料。该数据库原本只有英文版,后由 up-to-date 所属的 Wolters Kluwer 公司组织相关临床科室人员将其翻译为中文,并邀请相关专家审校,因此具有较高的权威性和参考价值。译员在搜索框输入关键词即可找到相应资料。但需要指出的是,并非所有英文资料都有中文版译本。此外,该数据库一般在医学院校购买使用,其余院校不一定

---

[1] 比如,在某跨国公司产品发布会翻译工作中,该公司要求把发言人讲话中的 new product 翻译为"创新产品"。

购买，使用者或许需要个人支付费用才可获取文献资料。

《英国医学杂志中文版》由中华医学会主办，每年出版12期，每期会针对一个专科内容进行文章的编译。所选文章来自BMJ出版集团旗下多本医学杂志，由来自全国知名医院、医学院的医疗卫生专业人士进行翻译，具有较高的权威性和参考价值。《英国医学杂志中文版》中的翻译文章，在每篇文章开头都有原文来源信息，可借此找到原文进行阅读。此外，在中华医学期刊全文数据库官网上，译员可检索该刊内容，找到想要参考的相关内容，再根据得到的文献开头部分的英文原文的参考信息，即可找到英文原文。译员可将中英文对照阅读，总结词汇和梳理知识点。

5.3 整理资料并建立词汇表

译员需要阅读、观看、梳理所有资料。若非英汉对照材料，译员可先阅读中文材料，然后再阅读英文材料；若是中英文对照材料，可中英对照阅读。从中文材料入手是因为母语材料更易理解和记忆。这是知识积累的过程。译员阅读和观看英文材料时也可了解相关词汇、短语的发音、使用方法、发言人口音等。

多模态译前准备在医学翻译中非常重要，因为医学会议可能涉及外科手术操作的内容，且往往是发言人边讲课边播放手术录像，或者是录像里已经录制好声音。图像是讲话的思路标记，两者相辅相成，因此译员也要考虑如何让自己的译文能够和图像同步发挥信息传递效果。医学会议广泛使用幻灯片，其中有大量图、表，译员也要考虑如何让自己的译文与图、表协同发挥作用。

此外，译员还需要准备好中英文对照词汇表。中英文对照词汇表是译员进行实地工作时必备的手边资料，需精心制备。词汇表中词汇顺序可按词汇在会议日程相关材料中出现的自然顺序（适用于上场前的准备阶段），也可以按照字母顺序（适用于上场时，便于快速检索），还可以归类编制，分为若干部分。以临床研究为例，译员可将其分为疾病、解剖、药物、器械、治疗方式等部分。词汇表可以包括专有名词，如机构名称、医学术语等；也可包括陌生的短语和词汇。

最初做好的词汇表到正式上场翻译之前可能需要缩减。译员在上场进行口译以前，应该将一些关键词汇牢记在心中；实在记忆困难的，应在方便译中查阅的纸质或电子词汇表中突出显示，以便随时查阅。有时，由于保密等缘故，直到最后一刻译员才知道翻译工作的具体内容，但只要还有时间和条件，译员一定要利用互联网、电子词典、讲稿等材料准备词汇表，以提高翻译的准确性，为现场翻译工作降低难度。

在词汇表制作中，译员有时会碰到中文或英文术语或词汇在主办方提供的资料中暂无对应译法的情况。此时，译员应该广泛查证和咨询专家，确定译法。查证的方法包括：（1）利用权威英英和汉英词典、英语搭配词典和英语同义词、近义词词典和百科全书等；（2）上网验证定义和检索命中数，并判断出处的权威性；（3）利用权威语料库，如英国国家语料库、美国国家语料库等。此外，我国出版的医学教材后面很多都有中英名词对照索引，也可作为词汇表制作参考资料。

第7章将详细介绍如何利用术语库工具建立术语库，协助医学口译工作。

5.4 了解发言人的口音特点

译员应尽可能了解发言人口音及特点。发言人口音可通过视频网站查阅发言人既往讲话进行了解，若找不到，可根据发言人个人社会人口学信息，了解其个人语言史。以某美籍华裔学者为例，译员从其简历中了解到他成年之前在浙江长大，成年后在北京接受教育，中年在美国工作，因此可大致推测他可能会有比较重的浙江方言口音。

在国际会议中，译员常会碰到发言人的英语发音带有母语口音的情况。下文按其与英语的关系从近到远分别分析印欧语系日耳曼语族的德语、罗曼语族的法语、意大利语、葡萄牙语、西班牙语，印欧语系印地语，阿尔泰语系日语、韩语，以及汉藏语系粤语为母语者的英文发音偏误。

德语为母语者，是欧洲人当中英语口音最轻的。英语和德语同属日耳曼语系，在发音、语法、用词上存在较多共通之处，因此德国发言人英语水平普遍较高，但也存在一些发音错误，如把 /w/ 发 /v/ 音，即把 work 念成 /vɜːk/；把 tomorrow 中的 /r/ 发小舌音或大舌音，听起来好似 /təˈmɔːʊʊ/。至于 th，不论本该发 /θ/，还是 /ð/，他们一律将其发 /d/，于是 think 成为 /dɪnk/，that 成为 /dæt/。

法语为母语者，由于受到法语 h 不发音的影响，容易把 Shanghai 念作 Shanggai，huge 念作 /juːdʒ/；会把 tomorrow 中的 /r/ 发小舌音，听起来好似 /dəmɔːˈəʊ/。他们把很多英法同源词汇按法语发音规则发音，如 organization 念 /ɔːgaːnɪzaːˈsɪɔn/，environment 念 /aːnvaɪrənˈmɒn/。此外，重音一律在后，如 hamburger，重读 ger 部分[1]。

意大利语为母语者，存在清辅音浊化现象，如把 today 念为 /dʊˈdeɪ/；还存在词尾辅音后添加元音现象，如将 moment 念为 /məʊməndə/ 或 /məʊmendəʊ/，甚至 /məʊmenda/。把 dr、tr 开头单词中的 dr 和 tr 分别处理为两个辅音且分开发音并在元音后分别添加辅音，念为 /dere/、/tere/，于是 drink，变为 /derɪnk/，train 变为 /teraɪn/。

西班牙语、葡萄牙语为母语者，除了存在意大利语的清辅音浊化、词尾辅音后添加元音现象，还存在弹舌音。他们也会把以 dr、tr 开头单词中的 dr 和 tr 分别处理为两个辅音且分开发音。

此外，由于医学术语来源于拉丁文的较多，在不同欧洲语言中的拼写相似，也会给母语为非英语者带来负面迁移，影响其重音和元音、辅音发音的准确性，如"解剖学"一词，英文为 Anatomy，德文为 Anatomie，法文为 Anatomie，葡萄牙文为 anatomia，西班牙文为 Anatomía，意大利文为 Anatomia。再如"妇科学"一词，英文为 Gynecology，德文为 Gynäkologie，法文为 Gynécologie，葡萄牙文为 ginecologia，西班牙文为 Ginecología，意大利文为 Ginecologia。而除德语以外，上述各语种均属于罗曼语，具有形容词后置于名词的特点，故"获得性免疫缺陷"的英文为 aquired immunodeficiency[2]，法文则为 immunodéficience

---

[1] 由于 hamburger 中 h 不发音，所以变成 /aːmbeˈgɜː/。同理，Henry 变为 /aːnrɪ/，其中 /r/ 发小舌音，en 被念为 /aːn/。甚至一些法国人会将何时该发 /h/，何时不该发 /h/ 记反，如将 iron 念为 /ˈhaɪrən/。

[2] 这个术语的德文为 erworbene Immundefizienz，词序与英文相同，其中 Immundefizienz 的发音比罗曼语诸语种更接近英语。

acquise，西班牙文为 inmunodeficiencia adquirida，葡萄牙文为 imunodeficiência aquosa，意大利文为 immunodeficienza acquifera。法、西、葡、意文术语与英文术语单词拼写相近，发音相似，但词序相反，会给这四种语言的学习者带来极大干扰。这在一定程度上解释了为何以罗曼语为母语者的英文发音乃至语法不如以日耳曼语（如德语）为母语者的英文发音和语法标准。

印度人或印度后裔，尤其是班加罗尔、泰米尔纳德等南方地区人士，将所有清辅音都发成相应的浊辅音，如将 /t/ 发 /d/；至于 th，不论本该发 /θ/，还是 /ð/，他们一律将其发 /d/，于是 think 成为 /dɪnk/，that 成为 /dæt/；他们没有长元音、短元音的区别，都发一个长度；每个单词没有重读音节、非重读音节之分，一律发重音；语速较快，且每个音节速度一样，句中无意群停顿、抑扬顿挫；他们将 /r/ 发成大舌弹音；词尾辅音一律省略不发，也不停顿；例如，"It's a great honor to be here and thanks for inviting me here to speak." 很可能被念为 /ɪt's a: gleɪ ɔːnə duːbi: hɪa: ən dæŋk pəʊ¹ ɪndaɪtɪn mi: hɪa: du: sbiːk/。不仅仅是口音，南部印度人的句法、词法等也常常出现偏误。印度北部人，如德里人，通常口音不太重，句法、词法相对比较规范。

澳大利亚人在英式英语基础上把 /eɪ/ 音发成 /aɪ/ 音，如把 "It's a good day today" 念成 "It's a good /dɪe/ to /dɪe/"。

新西兰人则在 /en/ 音前添加 /ɪ/ 音，如把 pen 念成 /pɪen/，把 eventual 念成 /eviental/。

日语为母语者，把 /rɪ/ 发成 /lɪ/，把 computer 念作 /gangbjuːda:/²（/k/ 浊化为 /g/，/p/ 浊化为 /b/，/t/ 浊化为 /d/，er 变为 /a:/），把 television 念作 /telɪbɪ/³，其中 /v/ 念作 /b/，sion 部分省略不念。日本明治维新后从西方音译了大量词汇⁴。但由于日语语音系统比英语语音系统简单，存在很多对应缺位现象，故导致日语会用一个相近音素（如 /b/）替代发音位置相似的音素（如 /v/）的发音，如 mother 一词中的 th 部分用 /d/ 替代。此外，由于片假名引入词已经融入日语日常使用中，日本人讲英文时，也难免不用片假名发音来念英文，从而导致偏误。再如，children 中的 dren 部分，按标准英语发音方式，dr 这两个字母合成一个辅音发音，日本人往往会将其拆开，念成 /delen/⁵，且这个单词中的 l 后面会被错误地添加短音 /ʊ/；于是这个单词会念为："齐鲁德伦"（/chɪlʊdelen/）。

韩国（朝鲜）语为母语者中的一些人吞音比较严重，把结尾 /l/ 音发成 /er/，把 ou 发成短音 /o/ 等。

母语为粤语者，语调受到粤语影响，且结尾清辅音发音往往过轻，如把 hurt 念作 /hɜː/。双辅音、多辅音发音存在障碍，如把 problem 念为 /pɒbləm/。

平时，要多听各国人士讲英语，并总结特点。此外，在上场翻译前，如果时间允许，译员

---

1 /f/ 念为 /p/。
2 日语为コンピュータ。
3 日语为テレビ台。
4 同时，用片假名表示发音。
5 /r/ 也被念作 /l/。

可以与发言人聊一聊较容易理解的日常生活话题，在此过程中了解发言人的口音特点。如有可能，可请发言人念如下这段文字[1]，译员可以从中归纳发言人发音的主要特点。

  Please call Stella. Ask her to bring these things with her from the store: Six spoons of fresh snow peas, five thick slabs of blue cheese, and maybe a snack for her brother Bob. We also need a small plastic snake and a big toy frog for the kids. She can scoop these things into three red bags, and we will go meet her Wednesday at the train station.

国际英语口音档案库和联合国多媒体中心也是收听和了解带有各种口音的英语的重要资源。此外，译者还应主动总结中国各大方言区持不同方言母语者讲英语的口音特征。

5.5 了解工作环境、工作方式并准备相关物料

  现场工作环境方面，译员应与主办方了解发言人在哪里发言，自己是坐着翻译，还是站着翻译；是有固定麦克风，还是需要译员手持麦克风，这会涉及是否方便记录交传笔记。若有搭档译员，要与搭档译员调好合作方式，约定各自负责翻译的话题或时间段。译员也可在上述第四步（即 5.4 小节）之前，就划分好各自负责的发言人、话题、时间段。译员还应准备好用于记交传笔记的材料，包括交传记录本和笔等，以及饮用水、方便食用的点心等物资。一些主办方甚至会邀请译者提前去现场彩排，并与发言人见面，以便熟悉工作环境和发言人口音、讲话方式和节奏，并厘清部分专业词汇译法，澄清知识偏误。

---

[1] 引自"The speech accent archive"（口语口音档案库）。此段文字能够体现英语发音的主要特点，是该档案库测量不同口音者发音偏误的标准语段。

第6章

语料库在医学会议口译中的应用

语料库（corpus，复数为corpora），顾名思义，是存放语言材料的仓库。在《语料库的应用》中，梁茂成、李文中、许家金（2010：3）认为："语料库是一个按照一定的采样标准采集而来的、能够代表一种语言或者某语言的一种变体或文类的电子文本集。"王克非（2012：9）认为，语料库是指"运用计算机技术，按照一定的语言学原则，根据特定的语言研究目的而大规模收集并贮存在计算机中的真实语料"。口译语料库在语料收集、数字化以及文字转写方面与笔译语料库有显著差异；此外，人们对于特定领域（如医学英语）的口译语料库研究也较少。

在理论上，任何平行语料库均可以转换为记忆库，方便之后使用软件辅助翻译时实现自动参考。此外，得到的平行文本还可供医学口译人员学习医学方面专业术语，获取专业知识，模仿更加地道的英语表达方式。

下文将介绍语料库的建立方法，并提供一个医学口译平行语料库建立案例。

6.1 语料库设计

开始建立语料库之前，我们需设计好要建设的语料库方案：首先，是该语料库的基本用途和应用范围；其次，是该语料库建设的基本流程。

医学口译语料库的基本用途是帮助医学口译人员在译前节省查词时间，增加译员专业知识储备量，译中迅速给出提示，提高翻译质量，译后还能训练译员地道的英语思维，提升译员能力。

大多数语料库的创建流程包括语料收集、语料清洗、语料对齐等环节。医学口译语料库收集到的语料可能是文本格式，也可能是音视频格式。口译语料库创建的具体流程如图6.1所示：

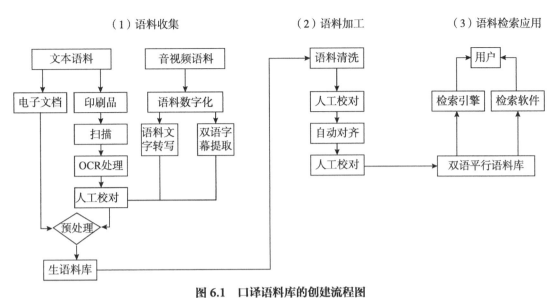

图 6.1 口译语料库的创建流程图

6.2 语料收集

6.2.1 文本语料

文本语料的收集方法有网络爬虫技术、字符识别技术、格式转换技术等；来源包括网络、文件、书籍等。字符识别（OCR，optical character recognition）技术是指对文件进行扫描转换为可编辑文字的技术。常见的 OCR 识别软件有 ABBYY FineReader、OmniPage Professional、Readiris 12 Corporate、LEADTOOLS、Dynamsoft OCR SDK、Tesseract、ExperVisionTypeReader、黑洞 OCR 等。

6.2.2 音视频语料

音视频语料的收集方法包括网络爬虫技术、口译现场录制、从权威网站（如联合国官方网站、世界卫生组织官网、TED 官网）下载等。对于音视频语料，我们下载之后需要进行文字转写和标注，有些网站上下载的音视频是有字幕的，这时候可将双语字幕提取出来，整理成文字语料。

6.3 语料数字化

通过录音和录像设备所获取的音频或视频材料，一般需要经过软件处理后，才可以成为计算机可读取或分析的音视频材料。这样的软件有 Cool Edit Pro、Adobe Audition、Gold Wave、SoundSoap Solo、AudioLava、iZotope RX 等。它们的工作原理是先获取一段纯噪声的频率特性,然后在掺杂噪声的音乐波形中,将符合该频率特性的噪声从声音中去除。

语音转写是指将语音转换为文字的过程。常见的语音转写工具有科大讯飞[1]、搜狗语音、百度语音、苹果语音、谷歌语音、微软语音、迅捷语音云服务[2]、Speechnotes[3]等。

科大讯飞:具有中英文音视频机器快转和人工精转两种模式,此外还支持维吾尔语音视频转写。对于发音标准、清晰、无背景噪声的语音音频,其准确率最高可达 95% 以上。转写文件类型支持 mp3、mp4、wav、pcm、m4a、amr、wma、3gp 格式。它支持多元化环境和多种设备,并且每一句文本处都有语音键,方便人工听辨,复核转写质量。

图 6.2 科大讯飞语音识别界面

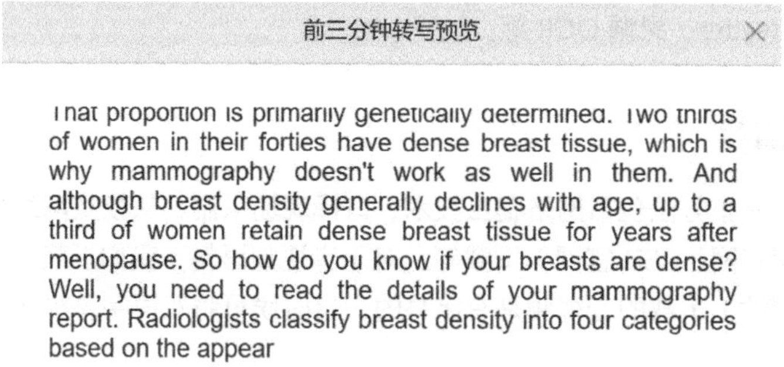

图 6.3 科大讯飞转写预览

---

1 参见讯飞听见官方网站。
2 参见讯飞听见"录音转文字助手"网站。
3 参见 Speechnotes 官方网站。

第 6 章 语料库在医学会议口译中的应用

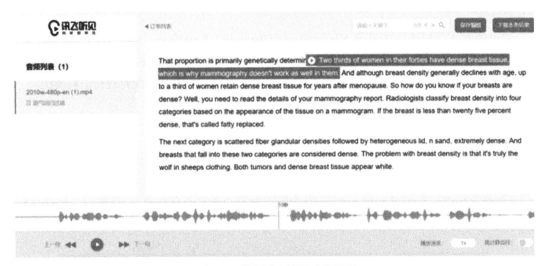

图 6.4　科大讯飞转写成功界面

百度语音：直接点击话筒即可即时转为文字。

图 6.5　百度语音识别界面

迅捷语音云服务：支持中英文语音转写，支持 mp3、m4a、wma、aac、flac、ac3、m4r、ape、ogg、wav 格式，识别率达 90%。

Speechnotes：对着麦克风说话即可即时辨识并转为纯文字；只要在辨识前先行切换到对应语言即可转换语言。

6.4　语料清洗

6.4.1　常用的文本语料清洗工具

语料清洗是将语料中无关的或错误的文字、标记、符号、公式、图标清除，为后续的对齐操作做准备。

常见的文本语料清洗工具有 Notepad++、UltraEdit、EmEditor、EditPlus、WinHex Hex Editor 等，这些工具均支持使用正则表达式对文本进行清洗。而在简单的人工清洗时，可使用 Microsoft Word 中的"清除所有格式"及"查找与替换"，然后利用通配符进行语料清洗。

6.4.2 语料清洗的基本操作

1）缺失内容补全。我们要对转写文本进行内容检查，对缺失的内容进行补充；若缺失过高，则需重新进行文字转写。

2）清除格式。我们可利用 Microsoft Word 中的"清除所有格式"，将底纹、特殊字体、颜色标记等版式清除，形成无格式的纯文本。

图 6.6　Microsoft Word 的清除格式功能

3）符号清洗。我们可利用 Microsoft Word 中的"查找与替换"功能，将错误的符号或段落进行清洗。以将软回车批量替换成硬回车为例，可单击"更多-特殊格式"，在"查找"中选中手动换行符，在"替换"中选中"段落标记"，单击"全部替换"即可将软回车批量替换成硬回车。

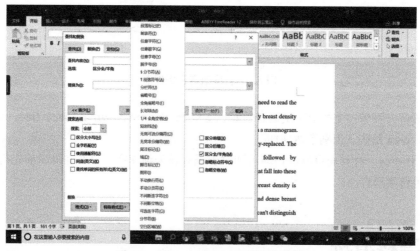

图 6.7　Microsoft Word 的替换功能

此处也可以使用 EmEditor 的"批处理替换"功能；打开 EmEditor，点击搜索 > 替换，会出现如图 6.8 中的批处理替换界面。在"查找和替换"处输入内容，添加至批处理，点击"批处理替换全部"即可。

第 6 章 语料库在医学会议口译中的应用

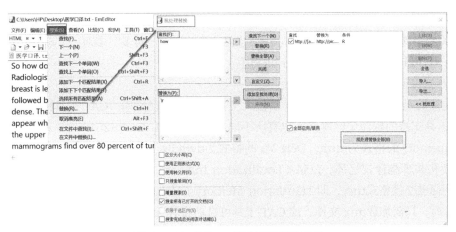

图 6.8　EmEditor 的批处理替换功能

4）内容清洗。我们要对文本中明显识别错误的内容进行修正，确保文本内容正确。

5）逻辑清洗。我们要对明显不对应的句对进行清洗。

6）非需求清洗。我们可根据自身需求，将完全重复、原文与译文完全相同、一句原文对应多种译文等不需要的句对进行清洗删除。

6.5　语料对齐

6.5.1　常见的语料对齐工具

语料对齐是指在两种语言或多种语言文本的不同语言单位之间建立对应关系，即确定源语文本的哪个语言单位和目标文本的哪个语言单位互为翻译关系（王斌，1999）。目前，我们在进行语料对齐时一般使用辅助工具来完成，而非简单的人工对齐。表 6.1 列出了常见的语料对齐工具，以供参考。

表 6.1　常见的语料对齐工具

CAT 工具自带	独立的工具
SDL Trados	Paraconc
MemoQ	ABBYY Aligner
Transmate	Tmxmall[1] 对齐工具
Déjàvu	xSegmenter
Wordfast	Bitext2tmx CAT bitextaligner
雪人 CAT	Bilingual SentenceAligner (Microsoft)
雅信 CAT	LF Aligner
	CopusSort
	CTexT AlignmentInterface

1　参见 Tmxmall 官方网站。

在了解语料对齐的相关工具后,我们还需要熟悉语料对齐规范,其基本规范如下:

1)原文与译文一般是一一对应的关系,当然也有少数"一对多""多对一""多对多"的情况。

2)一般以句号、分号、问号为分句标记。

3)尽量保证句子逻辑上的完整性。

要注意的是,搜索语料库需要借助搜索工具或转化为记忆库。CAT 工具种类繁多,不同的 CAT 工具支持的翻译记忆库格式也有所不同。例如,SDL Trados2019 的语料库文件格式为 sdltm,memoQ 的格式为 mtm,Déjà Vu 的格式为 dvmdb。为了方便使用不同 CAT 工具的译者能交换和共享翻译记忆库,LISA(Localization Industry Standards Association)推出了翻译记忆的标准交换格式 tmx,即 Translation Memory Exchange。译者使用不同的 CAT 工具加载记忆库时,只需加载 tmx 文件,该 CAT 工具可自动将其升级成适配于自身格式的文件。CAT 工具也都支持将记忆库直接导出为 tmx 格式;大多搜索工具支持的是 txt 格式(可用 Tmxmall 将 tmx 格式转换为 txt 格式)。

6.5.2 语料对齐工具实操

下面将以"世卫组织总干事世界防治疟疾日讲话"为例,分别演示 CAT 工具自带的对齐功能(以 SDL Trados Studio 2019 为例)和独立的对齐工具(以 ParaConc、ABBYY Aligner、Tmxmall 对齐工具为例)的对齐操作。

1. SDL Trados Studio 2019 对齐

1)添加翻译记忆库 TM。

图 6.9　SDL Trados Studio 2019 添加记忆库

图 6.10　SDL Trados Studio 2019 记忆库语言选择界面

第 6 章 语料库在医学会议口译中的应用

图 6.11 SDL Trados Studio 2019 记忆库创建成功

2）添加对齐文档。

点击对齐文档，选择对齐文档类型；添加上一步新建好的翻译记忆库，并添加原文和译文文件；点击"完成"后会出现自动对齐的界面。

图 6.12 SDL Trados Studio 2019 选择添加文件

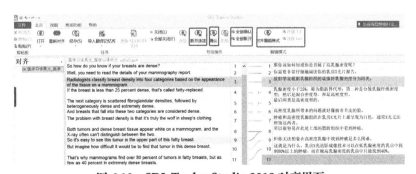

图 6.13 SDL Trados Studio 2019 对齐界面

在这个自动对齐后的界面中，虚线表示未确定对齐，如果确定某句对齐正确，可点击"确认"，之后就会变成实线。如果全部对齐正确，可点击"全部确认"。其中，线条的颜色越偏向红色，表示对齐的错误度越高。在图 6.13 中，我们可看到第 1—3 句检查无误，均已"确认"成为实线。

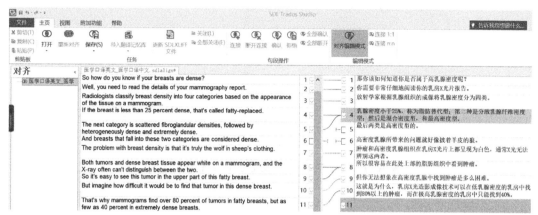

图 6.14　SDL Trados Studio 2019 对齐编辑模式

对于对齐不正确的，我们可先断开连接，再点击"对齐编辑模式"，选中原文和译文要对齐的句子，点击"连接 1∶1"或"连接 n∶n"。在图 6.15 中，原文第 4 句和第 5 句应该与译文的第 4 句对齐，这时，选择"连接 n∶n"，即可对齐。对齐成功后，可将对齐文件导出为 sdlalign 格式或者 sdlxliff 格式。

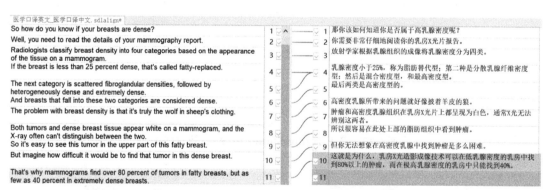

图 6.15　SDL Trados Studio 2019 对齐成功界面

2. ParaConc 对齐

1）进入 ParaConc 后，点击"File"，选择"Load Corpus File"，添加中英文对照的文本（这里只能添加 txt 文件），点击"OK"。

2）点击"File"，选中文本并点击"View Corpus Alignment"进行对齐。

3）对于对齐后的文本，我们可以进行进一步的操作，如"Split Sentences"（切分句子）、"Merge with Next Sentence"（同下一句合并）、"Merge with Previous Sentence"（同前一句合并）、"Split Segment"（切分对齐段）、"Merge with Next Segment"（同下一对齐段合并）、"Merge with Previous Segment"（同上一对齐段合并）、"Insert Empty Segment"（插入空对齐段）等。

第 6 章 语料库在医学会议口译中的应用

图 6.16 ParaConc 添加文件界面

图 6.17 ParaConc 对齐界面

图 6.18 ParaConc 操作界面

4）对齐后，点击"File"，选择"Export Corpus Files"，导出对齐文本。

3. ABBYY Aligner 对齐

1）先分别将源语文件和目标语文件导入 ABBYY Aligner 中。

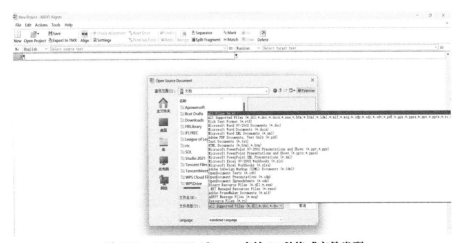

图 6.19 ABBYY Aligner 支持 24 种格式文件类型

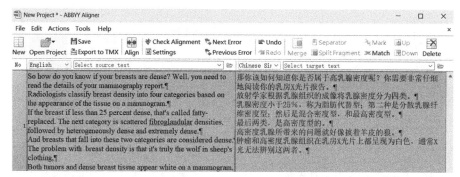

图 6.20　双语导入 ABBYY Aligner

2）点击对齐，自动实现句级对齐。

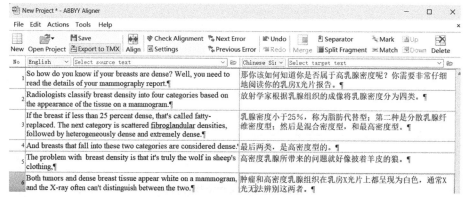

图 6.21　ABBYY Aligner 自动对齐界面

3）修改未自动对齐或对齐不正确的地方。同时选择多个句段（按住"Shift"键），再点击"Merge"按钮，可将所选句段合并；点击"Split Fragment"按钮，则可将句段从光标所在之处切分。

4）将对齐后的双语再次进行质量检查，并导出到 TMX，获得平行文本。平行文本可供医学口译人员学习医学方面的专业术语，获取专业知识，模仿更加地道的英语表达方式。我们也可将文件导出为双语 RTF。

So how do you know if your breasts are dense|Well, you need to read the details of your mammography report.	那你该如何知道你是否属于高乳腺密度呢？你需要非常仔细地阅读你的乳房 X 光片报告。
Radiologists classify breast density into four. categories based on the appearance of the: tissue on amammogram.	放射学家根据乳腺组织的成像将乳腺密度分为四类。
If the breast is less than 25 percent dense, that's called fatty-replaced. The next category: is scattered fibroglandular densities, followed-by-heterogeneously dense and extremely dense.	乳腺密度小于 25%，称为脂肪替代型；第二种是分散乳腺纤维密度型；然后是混合密度型，和最高密度型。
And breasts that fall into these two categories are considered dense.	最后两类，是高密度型的。
The problem with breast density is that it's truly the wolf in sheep's clothing.	高密度乳腺所带来的问题就好像披着羊皮的狼。
Both tumors and dense breast tissue appear white: on a mammogram, and the X-ray often can't: distinguish between the two.	肿瘤和高密度乳腺组织在乳房 X 光片上都呈现为白色，通常 X 光无法辨别这两者。

图 6.22　双语 RTF 文件

4. Tmxmall 对齐操作步骤

Tmxmall 在线对齐是由 Tmxmall 于 2015 年自主研发并发布的一款基于网页架构的专业语料对齐平台，主要用于制作翻译记忆库和双语平行文本。

1）进入 Tmxmall 官网并登录，点击"在线对齐服务"，选择"双文档"对齐模式，导入源语和目标语。

图 6.23　Tmxmall 双语对齐界面

2）点击"对齐"按钮进行对齐，然后再根据需要进行"合并""拆分""上移""下移""插入""删除""回退"以及"重做"等操作。句对对齐完成后，可以进行"一键去重""筛选功能""查找与替换""术语提取"等高级操作。

3）对齐完成后，点击"导出"，可导出多种格式，包括 tmx、xlsx、docx、txt 格式，可根据需要进行选择。

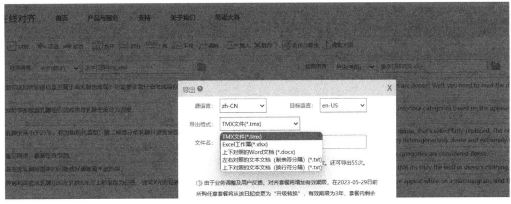

图 6.24　Tmxmall 导出对齐文本界面

6.6　语料格式转换

1）大多 CAT 工具均可导入 tmx 格式，它们也支持将记忆库直接导出为 tmx 格式。例如，在使用 SDL Trados Studio 2019 创建翻译项目时，在加载本地记忆库操作中，将 tmx 文件导入，它会提示如图 6.25 所示界面，单击"快速升级"，可自动将记忆库文件升级成 sdltm 文件。

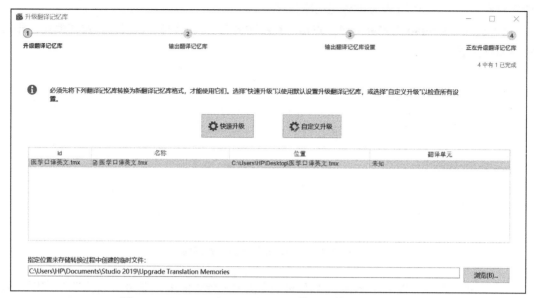

图 6.25　SDL Trados Studio 2019将tmx 转为sdltm 文件

2）使用Heartsome TMX Edior在"工具"选项中的"TMX 转换为"与"转换为TMX"功能，还可实现 docx、xlsx、txt、tbx、hstm 与 tmx 文件的双向转换；还可使用诸如"txt 文本批量转换编码工具""TMX-ParaConV"等工具进行相应的格式转换。

6.7　语料应用

对于口译工作者来说，语料的主要作用就是检索。检索大致分为三种：双语文本搜索、平行语料搜索和综合搜索。语料应用可以通过在之前建好的语料库中进行检索而实现，但在这个过程中，译员可能找不到确切的语料库，这时，可进行双语文本搜索。译员还可导入译前准备好的语料进行平行语料搜索，在现场口译时，还可使用在线语料平台进行搜索。

6.7.1　双语文本搜索

如果译员找不到具体的语料文件，可以利用 FileLocator 进行检索，该软件可以进行双语文本检索。操作步骤为：打开 FileLocator，选择查询位置，可以是特定的文件，也可以是多个文件，输入要查询的文本的关键词，点击"开始"，即可开始搜索。

第6章 语料库在医学会议口译中的应用

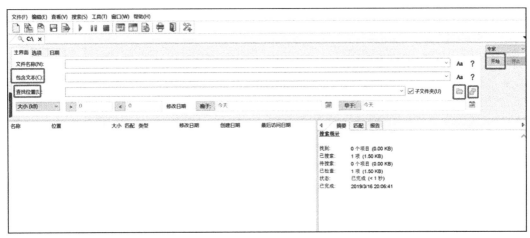

图 6.26　FileLocator 搜索界面

例如,搜索医学口译双语文件夹中 txt 文件里的"Radiologist",可显示出对应的双语内容(如图 6.27 所示)。该功能可帮助口译人员在高强度压力的口译现场迅速找到正确的术语对应译法及可能出现的相关用语。

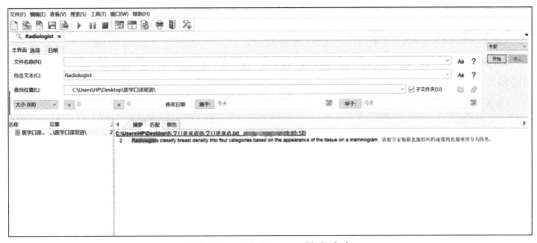

图 6.27　FileLocator 搜索成功

6.7.2 平行语料搜索

一般来说,可以创建语料库的软件或平台都可以进行平行语料搜索,此处使用 SDL Trados Studio 2019 来演示平行语料搜索,具体步骤如下:

1)打开该软件,新建翻译记忆库。

2)在新建的翻译记忆库里导入之前的语料。

3)在"TM"筛选处可对原文或译文进行搜索,点击"执行搜索",并且可以更改筛选条件,可对筛选条件进行添加、保存、删除、导入和导出。译员可对常用的筛选条件进行保存,在搜索文本时可直接导入筛选条件,节省时间。

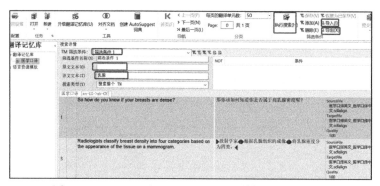

图 6.28　SDL Trados Studio 2019 语料搜索筛选条件

6.7.3 综合搜索

许多语料库、平台、软件都可用于综合语料搜索，如美国当代英语语料库（Corpus of Contemporary American English，COCA）[1]、柯林斯语料库（Collins-Cobuild）、英国国家语料库（British National Corpus，BNC）、Tmxmall 语料快搜等。下面以具体案例来演示美国当代英语语料库和 Tmxmall 语料快搜的操作步骤。

案例：明天有一个关于神经病学中海马的现场口译。

译员可采用以下综合搜索方式，做好译前准备：

1）美国当代英语语料库：是美国目前最新的当代英语语料库，也是世界上最大的英语平衡语料库。

（1）首先打开官网，注册并登录后，会看到如图 6.29 所示的界面，该界面表中第一列展示出 COCA 的 16 个子库。

图 6.29　COCA 语料库界面

1　参见美国当代英语语料库官方网站。

第6章 语料库在医学会议口译中的应用

（2）点击第一个语料库，即智能网络语料库，进入搜索界面。该语料库有一个特别功能——创建自己的虚拟语料库。虚拟语料库有助于译员在极短的时间内，从自行创建的虚拟语料库中查找到关键词。创建方式如图6.30所示，点击"Create corpus"即可。在图6.30中，检索方式有List、Word、Browse、Collocates、KWIC五种类型，其中KWIC为Key Word in Context的缩写，即文中关键词检索；Collocates指语义搭配。

图6.30　COCA搜索界面

下面分别对List和Word这两种检索方式进行介绍。

① 在List下检索：如图6.30所示，输入本次口译主题"hippocampus"（海马），点击"Find matching strings"后，在"FREQUENCY"界面会出现"hippocampus"，点击"hippocampus"即出现如图6.31所示界面。第二列显示与"hippocampus"相关的网站，点击第一个网址，进入如图6.32所示界面。用户可以对该语料进行分类选择（第三列至第五列的A、B、C表示分类选项），并保存到自己创建的虚拟语料库中，以备迅速检索。

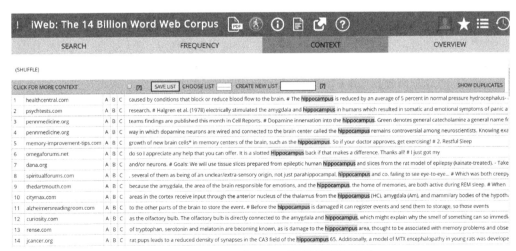

图6.31　COCA中List下的搜索结果界面

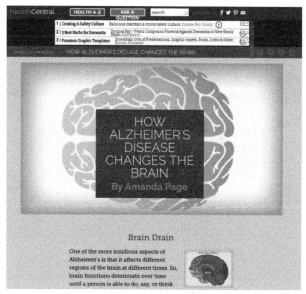

图 6.32　COCA 跳转到有关海马的新网站界面

对于医学口译人员来说，该功能可帮助他们快速补充了解医学方面的专业知识，同时也可为平时练习找到更多素材。

② 在 Word 下检索：输入"hippocampus"后，单击"See detailed info for word"，页面跳转到图 6.33 所示界面，该界面显示了该单词的词典页面、相关话题、搭配、词群、网站和检索语料并以高亮形式显示，每个类型都能点击"more"以查看更多。

2）Tmxmall：是由来自百度、华为等多家一流企业的管理及技术骨干共同创建，公司自主研发了语料检索与交换平台。

（1）打开官网，注册并登录，然后选择产品与服务中的语料快搜（如图 6.34 所示）。

（2）仍以前文所述神经学案例为例，输入"海马"，点击"语料快搜"（如图 6.35 所示）。在检索结果中有很多关于"海马"的语料，用户可根据语境进行筛选，选取自己需要的语块译法。同时，用户还可以在检索界面右边看到术语的注释信息。"海马"一词在两个领域使用：一是医药–卫生领域；二是轻工业–手工业领域。根据本案例情况，我们选取"海马"在医学–卫生领域的译法即可。

第 6 章 语料库在医学会议口译中的应用

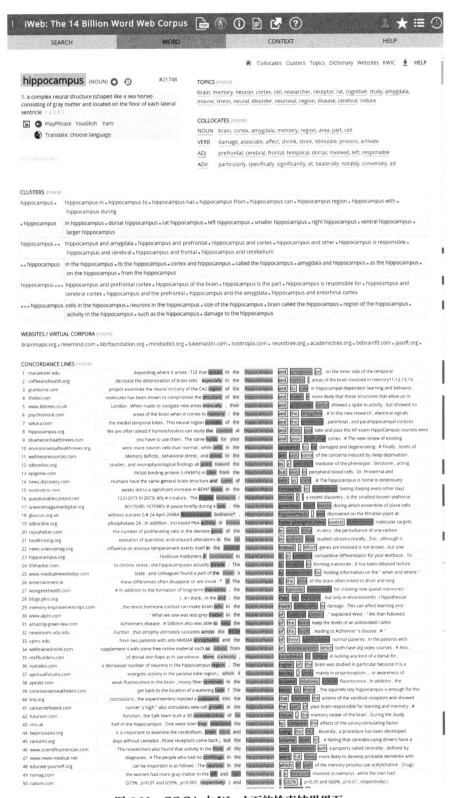

图 6.33　COCA 中 Word 下的检索结果界面

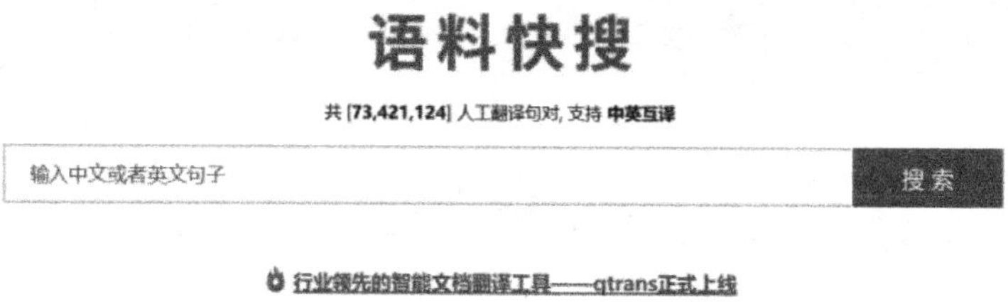

图 6.34 Tmxmall 语料检索界面

图 6.35 Tmxmall 中"海马"检索结果界面

参考文献

梁茂成，李文中，许家金. 2010. 语料库应用教程. 北京：外语教学与研究出版社.

王斌. 1999. 汉英双语语料库自动对齐研究. 北京：中国科学院研究生院（计算技术研究所）博士学位论文.

王克非. 2012. 语料库翻译学探索. 上海：上海交通大学出版社.

第7章
术语库在医学会议口译中的应用

7.1 术语与术语库

根据中华人民共和国国家标准 GB/T 15237.1—2000《术语工作词汇》的定义,"术语是在特定专业领域中一般概念的词语指称"。口译术语管理(王华树,张静,2017)是指为了满足特定的口译活动需求而对术语资源进行管理的实践活动,包括术语的收集、描述、处理、存储、编辑、呈现、搜索、维护和分享等,是口译人员职业翻译行为的主要表现。建立术语库的目的就是提高术语管理的效率和准确性。对于医学口译人员来说,在进行口译任务前的首要任务就是将准备材料中的术语快速、准确地查找出来,并制作成双语对照条目。有了术语库的帮助,口译人员就能在高强度、高压力下提高翻译准备效率,并保证译入语中术语翻译的准确性和前后一致性。

口译术语库建立的一般流程包括以下步骤:术语收集、术语提取、术语转换、术语搜索、术语维护。

7.2 术语收集

在译前,译员可以利用客户方提供的资料或自行收集材料,对口译任务中的医学知识进行理解和梳理,并提取高频词、新术语和行业特定用语(行话)。术语的来源和收集方法有以下四种:

1)客户方提供:有些客户会提供机构内部的权威资源以保证译入语中术语的准确性和一致性。

2)译员收集:在拿到口译准备资料后,译员通常会先将其中的术语整理出来,然后再查询权威词典;如有可能,还会与审校和术语专家进行商讨、校对,以确定术语的翻译,并建立术语表,以保证后续翻译的一致性。译员可通过访问大型术语库,如 UNTERM[1]、EuroTermBank[2] 等,搜索查询权威术语;也可以在 Google、Bing 中搜索相似的术语站点,或

---

1 参见联合国术语库官方网站。
2 参见 EuroTermBank 官方网站。

利用灵格斯、有道、金山词霸、句酷等电子词典来收集术语。但是，通过这种方法收集的术语存在权威性问题，译员要学会甄别术语的准确性。

7.3 术语提取

术语提取（term extraction）又称词汇提取（glossary extraction）、术语识别（term recognition）等，指利用技术工具将相关术语从特定的语料中提取出来的过程，是信息提取和知识获取领域中的重要任务类型。术语提取大致可分为人工手动提取和工具自动提取两种。口译人员在任务较少时可采取手动提取；口译任务较繁重时，可考虑利用工具自动提取术语，并进行人工审核和编辑。

7.3.1 常见的术语提取工具

常见的术语提取工具有三类：第一类是 CAT 工具自带的功能，如 SDL Trados、memoQ、Déjà Vu、Wordfast 等；第二类是独立术语提取工具，如 SDL MultiTerm、语帆术语宝、AntConc 等；第三类是专业口译员术语提取工具，如 InterpretBank[1]、Interplex UE、Intragloss、LookUp、Flashterm、Glossary Assistant、Interpreters' Help、Interpreter's Wizard。

7.3.2 语帆术语宝

语帆术语宝是一款在线术语管理软件，可进行单语术语提取和双语术语提取。其优点在于：文件上传速度和术语提取速度非常快；输入单语文本可提取双语术语库；可在线编辑修改术语表；可下载与 SDL Trados2015 匹配的插件，在 SDL Trados2015 中使用。

用户需打开官网，注册并登录（推荐使用 Chrome 浏览器）。术语提取具体操作步骤如下：

图 7.1　语帆术语宝管理首页

1　参见 InterpretBank 官方网站。

第 7 章 术语库在医学会议口译中的应用

1)单语术语提取。

(1)点击左侧导航栏的"提取术语",进行提取设置。选择好原文、译文语种后,可以到"标签管理"处添加标签设置。用户可以直接采用"输入文本"方式复制、粘贴,也可以直接"上传文件"进行提取,但是需要注意的是,它目前仅支持上传txt格式文件。

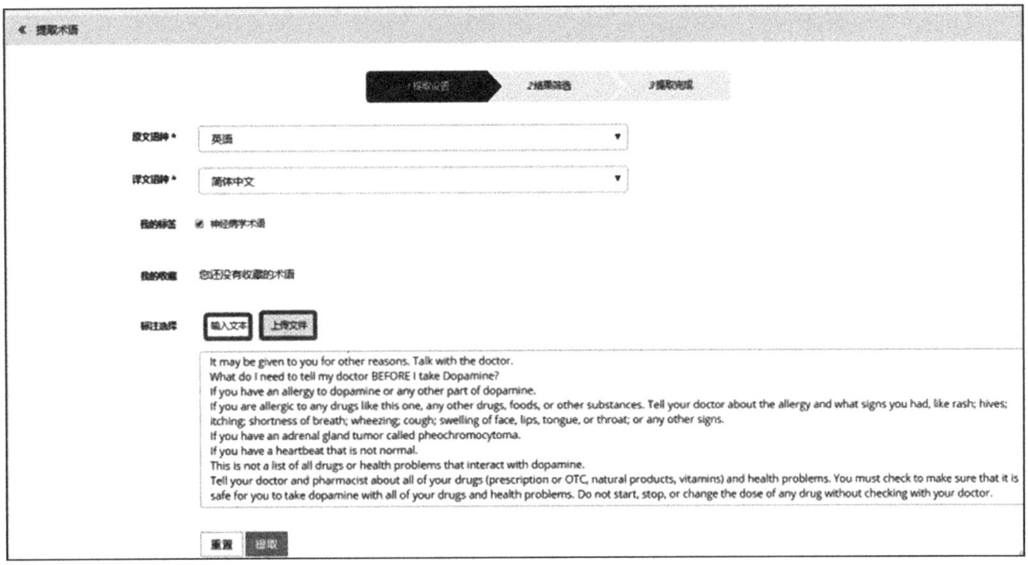

图 7.2　语帆术语宝语言选择及文件选择界面

图 7.3　语帆术语宝单语术语提取设置界面

设置完成后,点击"提取",即可显示筛选结果。用户可以根据词频进行调整,查看筛选结果,也可以看到每个术语的来源。对于给出多个译文的术语,用户可勾选复选框,选择合适的译文；也可以手动编辑调整译文，同时也可将不需要的术语删除。对于没有给出译文的术语，用户可以使用快捷键 F2 快速调取机器翻译译文。单击"术语原文"处，用户还可查看术语的上下文。

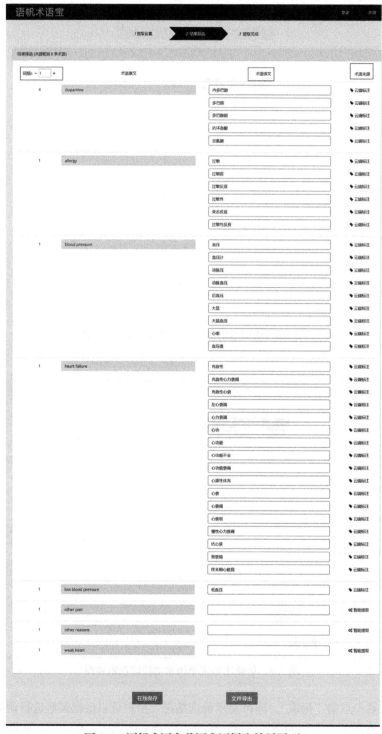

图 7.4　语帆术语宝单语术语提取结果界面

（2）筛选、修改完毕后，勾选要保存或导出的术语，点击"在线保存"，即可将其保存在自己的账号中；点击"文件导出"，即可生成术语文件，文件导出支持xls和tbx两种格式。

2）双语术语提取。

（1）点击左侧导航栏的"双语提取"，进行提取设置。语帆术语宝可提取tmx格式文件，若不是tmx文件，用户需前往Tmxmall进行对齐，导出tmx格式文件。目前，它支持的语种包括中日、日中、中英、英中四个语言对，文件大小不超过1M。

图7.5　语帆术语宝双语术语提取设置界面

（2）设置完成后，点击"提取"，即可显示筛选结果。与单语术语提取一样，用户可以对提取结果显示的术语进行查看、修改、删除等。此外，用户还可以按原文/译文的词长筛选术语，点击术语原文旁边的漏斗状按钮即可进行词长设置；

图7.6　语帆术语宝双语术语提取结果界面

（3）筛选、修改完毕后，点击"在线保存"或"文件导出"。

7.3.3 专业口译员术语提取工具

1）InterpretBank：是为专业口译员设计的 Windows 和 MacOS 桌面工具，主要用途是帮助口译员准备口译任务、管理术语，并在现场口译工作过程中访问术语。它具有六大主要功能：术语管理、术语创建、自动翻译、术语提取、术语查询、记忆库。

这里主要介绍术语提取功能，包括手动术语提取功能和自动术语提取功能。两种模式下都只需要将文档导入，点击提取按钮和添加按钮，即可完成术语提取。

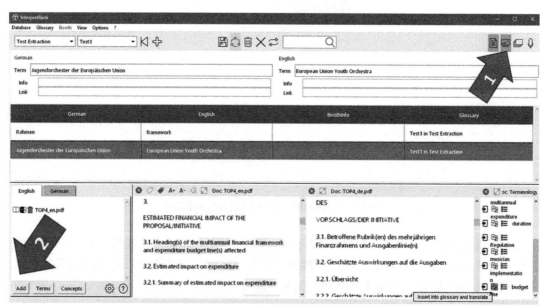

图 7.7　InterpretBank 术语提取界面

2）Interpreters' Help：会议口译员的专业工具，主要功能是译前术语管理、与同事或社区共享词汇表、从文本中快速提取术语以构建术语表、查询词典、查看词汇表等。在译中，译员可即时检索术语，同时它还有离线工具 BoothMate，方便译员离线查询事先准备好的术语。

7.4　术语格式转换

翻译时，不同的软件生成的术语库文件类型也不同，大致分为三种类型：xlsx、sdltb、tbx。xlsx 格式是 Microsoft Word 数据表格式；sdltb 格式是 MultiTerm 的术语格式；tbx 格式是国际术语交换格式。这三种格式的文件可通过 MultiTerm、Intragloss、Glossary Converter 工具进行转换。

7.4.1 xlsx → sdltb

1）打开 Glossary Converter，点击"settings"，进入"output format when converting termbase"（选择要转换的格式）页面，选择"MultiTerm Termbase"，勾选"Use the selected output format for any format"，点击"OK"。

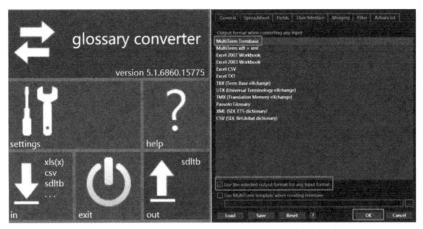

图 7.8　Glossary Converter 界面及选择转换格式

2）点击"in"，选择 xlsx 文件（注意：要将 xlsx 文件的首行设置为语言行，而不是术语），设置好语言，直接点击"OK"，即可导出 sdltb 文件，转换后的文件与源文件在同一目录下。

3）生成的 sdltb 文件，可直接用 MultiTerm2019 打开。

图 7.9　MultiTerm2019 导入 sdltb 文件界面

7.4.2 sdltb → xlsx

用 MultiTerm2019 打开 sdltb 文件，分别点击"术语库管理"→"导出"→"HTML export definition"→"处理"，导出 html 文件，然后用 Execl 打开 html 文件，再将文件另存为 xlsx 文件。

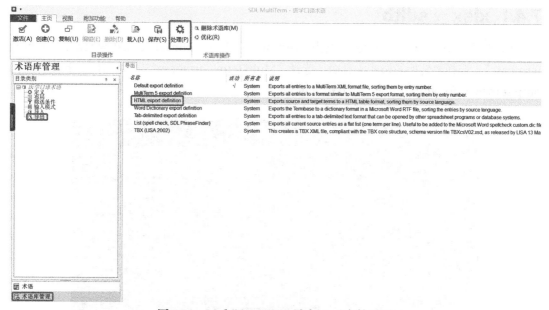

图 7.10 MultiTerm2019 导出 html 文件界面

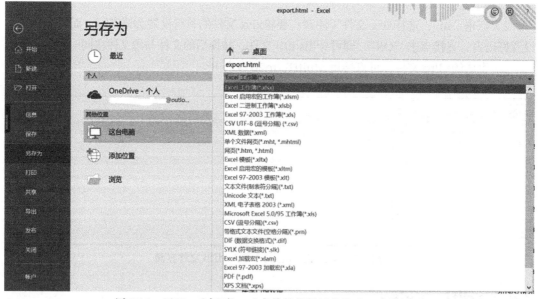

图 7.11 用 Excel 打开 html 文件并将其另存为 xlsx 文件界面

7.4.3 xlsx→tbx

1）与将 xlsx 转换为 sdltb 类似，打开 Glossary Converter，点击"settings"，选择要转换的格式，即 TBX（Term Base eXchange），勾选"Use the selected output format for any format"，点击"OK"。

2)点击"in",选择xlsx文件(注意:要将xlsx文件的首行设置为语言行,而不是术语),设置好语言,直接点击"OK",即可导出tbx文件,转换后的文件与源文件在同一目录下。

图7.12　Glossary Converter 中 xlsx → tbx 选择转换格式界面

7.4.4　tbx → xlsx

1)打开 Glossary Converter,点击"settings",选择 Excel 2007 Workbook,勾选"Use the selected output format for any format",点击"OK"。

2)点击"in",选择tbx文件,直接点击"OK",即可导出xlsx文件,转换后的文件与源文件在同一目录下。

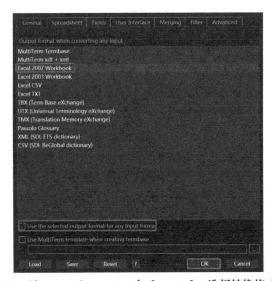

图7.13　Glossary Converter 中 tbx → xlsx 选择转换格式界面

7.4.5 sdltb → tbx

用 MultiTerm2019 打开 sdltb 文件，分别点击"术语库管理"→"导出"→"TBX(LISA2002)"→"处理"，即可导出 tbx 文件。

图 7.14　MultiTerm2019 导出 tbx 文件界面

7.4.6 tbx → sdltb

MultiTerm2019 只能打开 sdltb 格式的术语库，所以用户要用 MultiTerm2019，就需要将 tbx 格式转换为 sdltb 格式；也可以使用 Glossary Converter 和 SDL MultiTerm Convert 进行转换。具体步骤如下：

1）打开 SDL MultiTerm Convert2019，将 tbx 转换为 xdt 和 mtf.xml 文件。

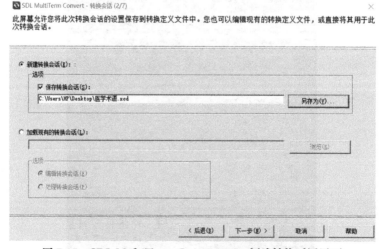

图 7.15　SDL MultiTerm Convert2019 新建转换对话界面

第 7 章 术语库在医学会议口译中的应用

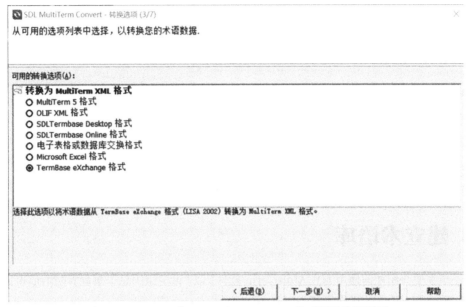

图 7.16　SDL MultiTerm Convert2019 格式转换选择界面

2）打开 SDL MultiTerm Convert2019，点击"新建术语库"，再点击"载入现有术语库定义文件"，导入 xdt 文件，生成一个新的 sdltb 文件。

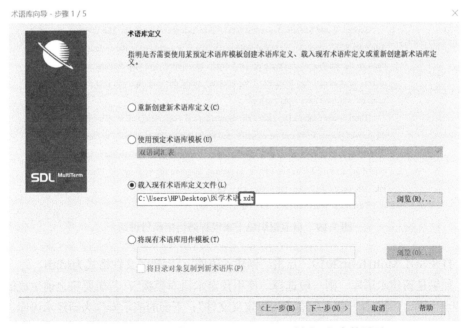

图 7.17　SDL MultiTerm Convert2019 导入 xdt 文件界面

3）点击"术语库管理"，导入 mtf.xml 文件，再点击"完成"。

图 7.18　SDL MultiTerm Convert2019 导入 mtf.xml 文件界面

7.5　建立术语库

本小节主要介绍如何使用 SDL MultiTerm 软件，以"世卫组织总干事世界防治疟疾日讲话"为语料，创建新术语库的操作步骤。

> The theme of World Malaria Day this year is "Ready to Beat Malaria". World Malaria Day is important for at least 3 reasons.
>
> First, it's an opportunity to celebrate our successes. Since 2000, millions of malaria deaths have been averted—especially among children. More and more countries have eliminated the disease.
>
> Second, World Malaria Day reminds us of the challenges that remain. The latest data from WHO show that the global malaria response is at a crossroads: the declining trend in the number of malaria cases and deaths has stalled, and vital funding for malaria programmes has flatlined. If we continue along this path, we will lose the gains for which we have fought so hard.
>
> Third, World Malaria Day unites all partners around a common goal: accelerating the pace of progress. We call on countries and the global health community to close the critical gaps in the malaria response. Together, we must ensure that no one is left behind in accessing life-saving services to prevent, diagnose and treat malaria. Please join us to get the malaria response back on track.
>
> I am ready to beat malaria—are you? I thank you.

图 7.19　世卫组织总干事世界防治疟疾日讲话

1）打开 SDL MultiTerm2019，点击"创建术语库"，创建的文件格式为 sdltb。

2）如果是新建术语库，则一般选择"使用预定术语库模板"；若想要将之前生成的 xdt 文件转化为术语库，则选择"载入现有术语库定义文件"；下面的演示操作为新建术语库。

第 7 章 术语库在医学会议口译中的应用

图 7.20 SDL MultiTerm2019 新建术语库界面

3）定义好名称，选择语言，将不需要的语言删除，选择需要的语言，点击"添加"，接下来可以对字段性标签等进行设置，设置完成后即创建了一个空的术语库。

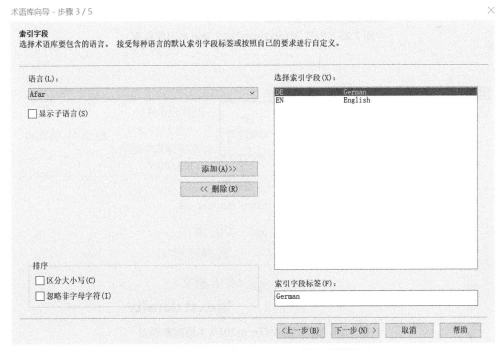

图 7.21 SDL MultiTerm2019 语言选择界面

4)点击"新加"或按快捷键 F3,可以添加术语;点击"保存"或按快捷键 F12 可将新术语保存到术语库中,然后 SDL MultiTerm2019 自动退出编辑模式,进入查看模式。

图 7.22　SDL MultiTerm2019 新加术语界面

5)口译人员在现场口译前可打开之前准备好的术语库(sdltb),进行查看和搜索。

图 7.23　SDL MultiTerm2019 导入术语库界面

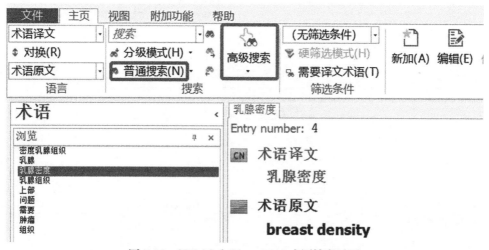

图 7.24　SDL MultiTerm2019 术语搜索界面

7.6 术语库应用

7.6.1 术语库搜索

有了术语库之后，译员可以在术语库中进行检索。MultiTerm 支持三种不同的检索模式：简单检索、进阶的简单检索和高级检索。

1）简单检索。

口译员在口译任务进行前将要检索的术语库或自己准备好的术语库打开，可以在搜索栏中找到一个搜索框，在搜索框中输入需要检索的术语，搜索结果会在左侧的"结果列表"中显示（如图 7.25 所示）。

图 7.25　SDL MultiTerm2019 简单检索界面

2）进阶的简单检索。

图 7.26　SDL MultiTerm2019 进阶的简单检索界面

译员在"显示"区可选择显示方式和文字大小。选择"Flags layout"时，各索引前会显示小国旗；选择"Full layout"时，它会显示该条目的创建者、创建时间、修改者及修改时间；选择"Language only"时，它只显示语言名称及术语内容；选择"Source/Target"时，它只显示源语言及目标语言的术语内容；"MultiTerm Classic"是最简洁的显示方式。

3）高级检索。

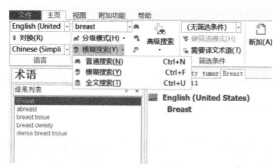

图 7.27　SDL MultiTerm2019 高级检索界面

（1）其普通搜索与简单检索一样。
（2）模糊搜索：其功能是搜索与此搜索格式类似的词。例如，我们搜索 breast 一词，结果会显示包含 breast 的术语以及 Breast、abreast 等（如图 7.28 所示）。

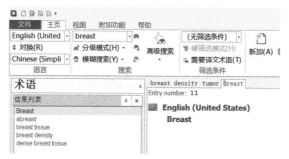

图 7.28　SDL MultiTerm2019 模糊搜索 breast 界面

（3）全文搜索：只能检索到包含了检索词的词。

7.6.2　综合搜索

译员可通过专门的便携式设备，充分利用译前创建的术语库和专门的术语管理系统，对口译过程中遇到的术语进行快速搜索。诸如 InterpretBank、Intragloss[1]、Interplex UN、LookUp、Flashterm、Glossary Assistant、Interpreters' Help、Interpreter's Wizard 等，或者智能电子笔（SmartPen），均可在翻译过程中自动识别提前准备好的口译文件中的术语。

1）Intragloss：一个为口译员设计的术语工具。它有五大主要功能：读取文件和查找术语、对比文档、使用已有术语、即时创建词汇表、使用网站功能。Intragloss 的这些功能能够帮助口译员节省多达 50% 的准备时间。下文主要介绍如何使用在线功能创建术语表。

Intragloss 有一个内置的 Web 浏览器，可以将一个或多个网页导入任务中。这是一个特别

1　参见 Intragloss 官方网站。

有用的功能，因为除了会议组织者提供的文件之外，口译员还经常使用其他在线资源（文件）做准备。

（1）使用 Intragloss 打开口译任务相关网页，可在网页中随意选取术语进行条目添加。

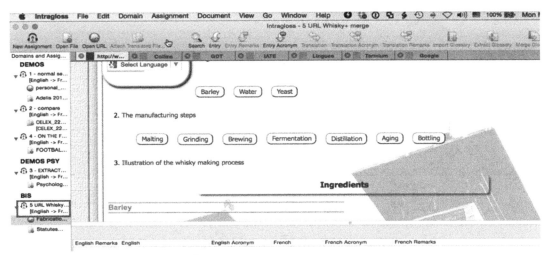

图 7.29[1]　用 Intragloss 打开口译相关网站界面

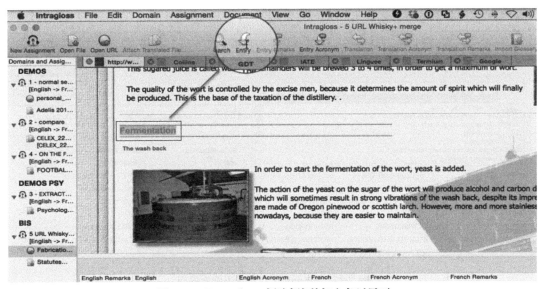

图 7.30　Intragloss 术语查询并加入条目界面

（2）可以看到添加的术语条目都在下方显示了出来；还可以选取网页中的术语，点击"Search"，就会跳转到各权威词典及谷歌中进行释义。

1　图 7.29 至图 7.31 均来自 Intragloss 官方网站。

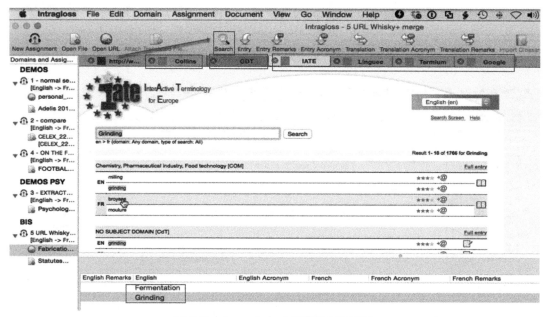

图 7.31　Intragloss 术语在线搜索界面

2）Interplex UN：这是一个术语检索软件，具有众多的术语库可供查询，检索操作简单，如图 7.32 所示，选择术语领域和语言，输入检索文本即可。

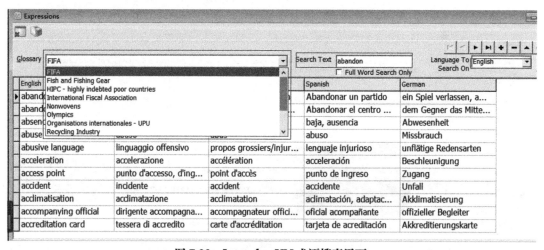

图 7.32　Interplex UN 术语搜索界面

7.7 术语综合技术应用

7.7.1 术语资源平台

1)联合国术语库(UNTERM)[1]:这是由联合国主要工作站点和各地区委员会共同维护的一个多语术语库。公开部分针对全球的普通用户,无须注册即可查询术语。

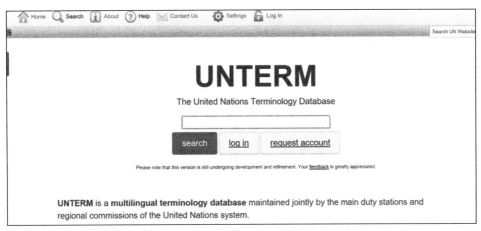

图 7.33　UNTERM 检索界面

该术语库查询方便快捷,输入查询单词即会出现相关词汇搭配,可快速唤起口译人员的记忆。

图 7.34　UNTERM 检索界面

2)术语维基(Term Wiki)[2]:该平台是一个社交型术语库,能够创建术语、查询术语、浏览术语、维护术语、分享术语等。

1　参见联合国术语库官方网站。
2　参见术语维基官方网站。

图 7.35 Term Wiki 检索界面

口译人员在使用术语库时可以选择专业领域，还可以建立口译社区，进行团队编辑、维护和分享。

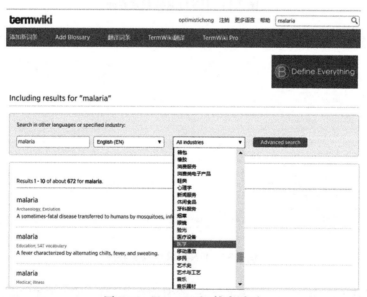

图 7.36 Term Wiki 检索界面

3）TAUS Data[1]：这是翻译自动化协会建立的多语术语库，口译人员可选择领域、内容类型等，其搜索显示结果包括双语平行文本，供口译人员参考。

---

1 参见 TAUS Data 官方网站。

第 7 章 术语库在医学会议口译中的应用

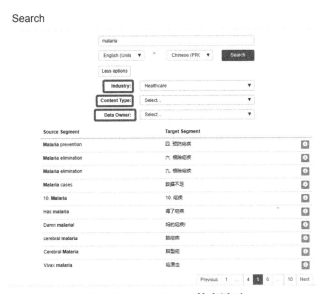

图 7.37　TAUS Data 检索界面

4）MyMemory[1]：这是目前世界上规模最大的多语术语库，收录了欧盟、联合国等多家多语网站的翻译记忆。口译人员不仅可以使用该术语库查询术语，还可以上传记忆库或者编辑已有词条。口译人员在口译准备阶段可以将查询到的专业术语或者记忆库上传到该库中，以便在口译过程中快速查询。

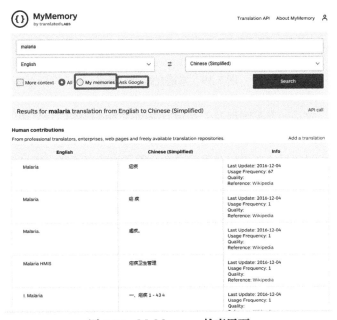

图 7.38　MyMemory 检索界面

1　参见 MyMemory 官方网站。

5)术语在线[1]:这是由全国科学技术名词审定委员会建立的一个术语知识服务平台。该平台的术语专业性较强,不仅可以帮助口译人员选择相关的专业领域,还可以显示相关技术名词推荐。

图 7.39 术语在线检索界面

6)WebCorp[2]:这是一家英国网站,利用万维网作为语料库信息来源,能够提供丰富的语言学信息。

对于医学口译人员来说,在译前准备阶段常常需要快速查找某一细分领域的术语等。他们可以利用 WebCorp,输入网址,搜索术语,该网站专业术语较多,非常具有参考意义。

案例:明天有一场关于神经病学中海马的口译任务。

现在,译员该如何准备呢?具体步骤如下:

(1)首先查找关于海马的相关网站,复制其网址。

---

1 参见术语在线官方网站。

2 参见 WebCorp 官方网站。

第 7 章 术语库在医学会议口译中的应用

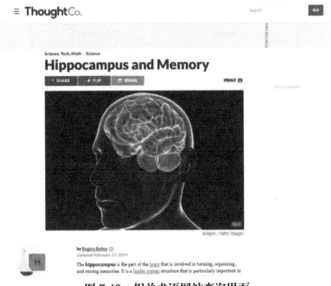

图 7.40　相关术语网站查询界面

（2）打开 WebCorp，点击"WebCorp Live"和"Wordlist Tool"，进入如图 7.41 所示界面。

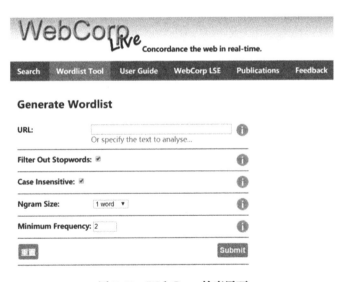

图 7.41　WebCorp 检索界面

（3）在 URL 一栏中输入网址，然后设置是否过滤掉禁用词、是否区分大小写、单词个数和最小词频，设置完毕后，点击"Submit"，会生成一个词语表，点击单词会显示该单词出现在原文中的句子，并且会显示出"词汇表"（Wordlist）中总共生成的单词[1]数量和每个单词出现的"次数"（Frequency）。如表 7.1 所示：

1　可进行设置，如将 N-gram 设置为 2，即可显示共同出现两个词的频率。

表 7.1　WebCorp 检索结果

Word	Frequency
hippocampus	24
brain	21
memory	11
science	9
memories	9
function	7
new	6
gyrus	6
cerebral	6
hippocampal	5
anatomy	5
lobes	5
biology	5
formation	5

7.7.2　术语综合搜索

1）维基百科（Wikipedia）[1]：维基百科是一个多语网络百科全书。口译员在翻译时，若碰到没有见过的术语，可查询该百科全书了解其意义。

图 7.42　维基百科检索界面

1　参见维基百科官方网站。

第 7 章 术语库在医学会议口译中的应用

维基百科中还有分类索引,介绍各个领域的百科知识,如在中华文化中可以找到中医,在自然与自然科学中可以找到生物学、医学和药学等(如图 7.43 所示)。

图 7.43 维基百科分类检索界面

例如,我们点击医学领域,它可以显示出具体的医学分类以及医学术语等(如图 7.44 所示)。

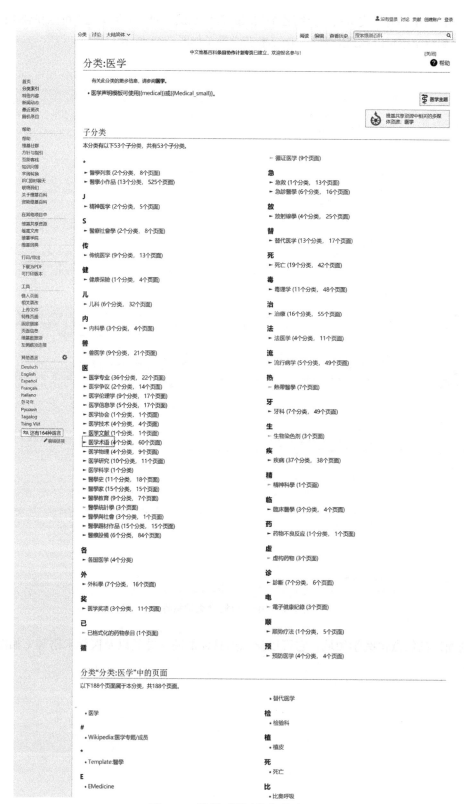

图 7.44 维基百科医学索引界面

第 7 章 术语库在医学会议口译中的应用

案例：现有一个关于阿尔茨海默病的演讲需要口译。

该案例需要译员提前对阿尔茨海默病相关知识及术语翻译进行掌握。操作过程如下：

（1）译员首先要对阿尔茨海默病的定义及相关词汇定义进行了解。打开维基百科，输入"阿尔茨海默病"，搜索结果如图 7.45 所示，阿尔茨海默病术语的英文在括号中显示为"Alzheimer's disease"，绿色高亮的术语点击后会显示英文，蓝色高亮的术语可以直接点击链接进行查看。同时，右侧还有阿尔茨海默病的基本知识，附有图片帮助理解，点击图片会显示中英文对照信息。

图 7.45　维基百科阿尔茨海默病检索结果界面

（2）若选择语言为英语，可以检索上文中的"Alzheimer's Disease"，检索结果如图 7.46 所示。它与上文中的中文内容完全相同，只是语言种类不同。译员可以对照中英文两个版本的词条进行术语学习和归纳。

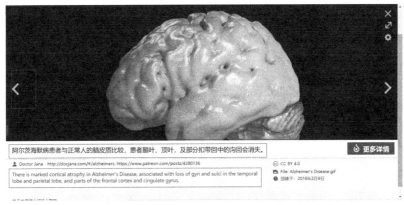

图 7.46　维基百科 Alzheimer's Disease 检索结果界面

2）利用 Google 检索确认译文：维基百科中的术语虽有参考意义，但是不一定完全正确，所以还要进一步确认。以前文案例中的"Alzheimer's Disease"及查询到的译文"阿尔茨海默病"为例，在谷歌中进行搜索，输入"阿尔茨海默病""Alzheimer's Disease"，搜索结果如图 7.47

115

所示；Google 学术以及中国医药生物技术网上对"Alzheimer's Disease"的译法均为"阿尔茨海默病"，这两个信息来源比较权威，故采纳这种译法。

图 7.47　Google 检索"阿尔茨海默病""Alzheimer's Disease"界面

参考文献

王华树，张静. 2017. 信息化时代口译术语管理及其技术应用研究. 外文研究，5（4）：72–77.

下 篇
案例实践

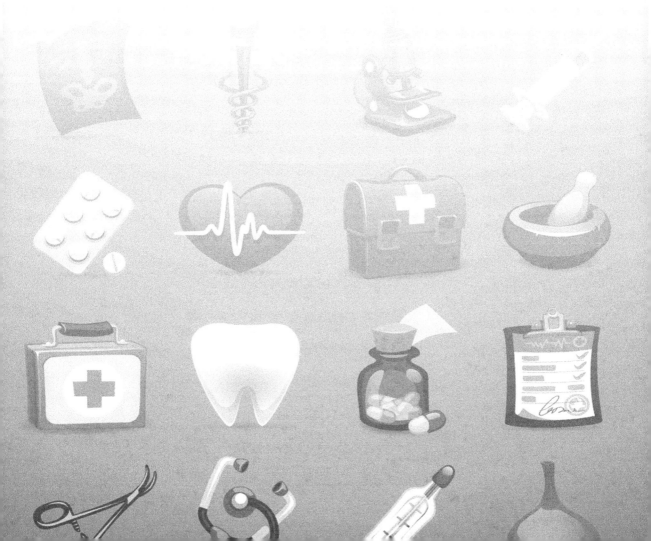

第 下
科学出版

第8章

人物和机构简介及仪式性讲话

8.1 人物和机构介绍

人物和机构介绍是医学会议中常有的环节，目的是方便与会各方的交流。在医学会议中，主持人可能会使用幻灯、发言稿等手段，辅助自己向听众介绍参加会议的主要人员及与会议相关的机构，因此译者也应做好相应的准备。此外，不少会议会提前做好中英文对照的人物和机构简介，译者应主动索要，用于译前准备。如果会议主办方邀请译者完成人物和机构介绍笔译任务，译者也可尽力协助，并与主办方协商相应的报酬。在对这些资料进行翻译的过程中积累的信息和译法，对完成会议口译工作会有帮助。

本节着重讲解几则人物简介及机构简介的翻译；涉及的人物身份包括临床专家、公共卫生专家、卫生经济学家等；机构类型包括医院、医学院、制药公司等。这些人物和机构类型都是会议口译中常见的。会议口译常常涉及医药公司和医疗卫生管理部门及其人员介绍，因此本节在词汇与表达拓展部分总结了相关译法。

8.1.1 背景知识

临床路径（clinical pathway）：是指以循证医学证据和指南为依据，针对某一疾病建立的一套标准化治疗模式与治疗程序，其目的在于促进治疗和疾病管理的标准化。

临床算法（clinical algorithm）：也被称作临床流程图，是用于表示临床决策顺序、教授临床决策和指导诊疗的特殊文本格式（Margolis，1983）。

8.1.2 人物介绍（一）

1. 相关词汇

associate director：副主任
Center for Disease Prevention and Control (CDC)：疾病控制中心
research fellow：研究员
Center of Public Health Information：公共卫生信息中心
initiative：项目；活动
in partnership with...：与……合作

2. 原文、参考译文及说明

Ms. A is currently an Associate Director with the Center of Chronic Diseases and Research Fellow of the Public Health Information Center of the China CDC. She has been involved in WHO projects in China and various initiatives in partnership with international organizations, including the US CDC.

A女士现任中国疾病预防控制中心慢性病中心副主任，是公共卫生信息中心的研究员；曾参与世界卫生组织在华项目并与美国疾病预防控制中心等国际机构进行过多项合作。

说明：人物简介中可能会使用一些该领域或行业常用的缩写，如此处的CDC，可查证后再翻译。

8.1.3 人物介绍（二）

1. 相关词汇

president (of a hospital)：（医院）院长
vice director：副所长
Institute of Public Health：公共卫生研究所
epidemiologist：流行病学家
National Committee for Hospital Tobacco Control：全国医院控烟委员会
campaign：运动；活动
health care professional：医疗卫生工作者
smoking-free hospital：无烟医院
under sb.'s leadership：在某人的领导下
push forward：推进
model smoking-free hospital：示范无烟医院
dedicate sb.'s effort into：致力于
smoking cessation：戒烟
adviser：顾问
municipal government：市政府
policy making：政策制定

2. 原文及参考译文 [1]

Professor B is currently the President of XXX Hospital and Vice Director of the Institute of Public Health. As one of the top epidemiologists, he founded the National Committee

---

[1] 本书"下篇"中选用了一些口语性较强的素材，为了让学习者能够体验真实的场景，编者尽量保留了素材的原汁原味，对于一些语法不够规范的句子未做较大改动。

for Hospital Tobacco Control, and promoted nationwide campaigns for tobacco control in health care professionals and the creation of smoking-free hospitals. Under his leadership, tobacco control campaigns have been pushing forward in more and more Chinese hospitals, and his hospital is a model smoking-free hospital. He has dedicated his effort to tobacco control for many years. His work covers a wide range, including public education, training, smoking cessation, information exchange, and research. He is also a main adviser of the central and municipal governments for tobacco control policy making.

B 教授现任 XXX 医院院长、公共卫生研究所副所长，是国内顶尖的流行病学家，创建了全国医院控烟委员会，积极推动全国卫生工作者控烟工作和创建无烟医院工作。在他的领导下，控烟工作已经进入越来越多的中国医院，他的医院也是无烟示范医院。他多年来一直投身于控烟相关工作，包括公共教育、培训、戒烟、信息交流和研究。他还是中央政府和市政府控烟政策制定顾问。

8.1.4 人物介绍（三）

1. 相关词汇

Department of Economics and Management, School of Management, XXX University：XXX 大学管理学院经济与管理系

Center for Health Economics Research：卫生经济研究中心

serve on... Committee：就任于……委员会

Advisory Committee of the Chinese Ministry of Health for Emergent Public Health Events：中国卫生部突发公共卫生事件专家咨询委员会

Asian Consortium for the International Society for Health Economics Research：国际卫生经济研究学会亚太联合会

Chinese Economists Society：中国（留美）经济学会

2. 原文、参考译文及说明

Professor C is the founder and Chair of the Department of Economics and Management, XXX University School of Management, and Director of the Center for Health Economics Research. Professor C now serves on the Advisory Committee of the Chinese Ministry of Health for Emergent Public Health Events, and he is the Vice-Chair of the Asian Consortium for the International Society for Health Economics Research. He was elected President of the Chinese Economists Society in 2000 and 2002.

C 教授是 XXX 大学管理学院经济与管理系主任，也是该系的创始人，是卫生经济研究中心主任，现任中国卫生部突发公共卫生事件专家咨询委员会委员、国际卫生经济研究学会亚太联合会副主席，曾担任中国（留美）经济学会 2000 和 2002 届主席。

说明：请注意，某些机构的中英文名称并非严格对应，如此处的 Chinese Economists

Society 被译为"中国(留美)经济学会",而非"中国经济学家学会"。再如,北京大学医学部被译为 Peking University Health Science Center,这是因为该机构名称中的医学是包括公共卫生等在内的大医学,而非临床医学。而国外的 medical school 一般仅指从事临床医学教育的医学院,与临床医学教育相关的公共卫生学院独立于医学院存在。中外在这一点上有较大差异。另一个类似的例子是北京大学医学人文学院,它译为 Peking University School of Health Humanities,如果用 medical humanities,国际上会误以为该机构仅仅开展临床医学人文的教研工作。由此可见,机构名称翻译需要名副其实,译名应与原文名称的实际所指一致。

8.1.5 人物介绍(四)

1. 相关词汇

Division of Health Education, National Training Center for General Practice / Family Medicine:国家全科医学和家庭医学培训中心健康教育部

Department of Social Medicine and Health Management:社会医学与卫生事业管理系

School of Health Administration and Education:卫生管理与教育学院

University of Medical Sciences:医科大学

legislation:立法

2. 原文及参考译文

Professor D is a professor at the Department of Social Medicine and Health Management, School of Health Administration and Education, XXX University of Medical Sciences. He has made a profound contribution to the making of public health policies in China, including the legislation of tobacco control in XXX city and the Public Health Development Plan of XXX city (2000–2015).

D 教授是 XXX 医科大学卫生管理与教育学院社会医学与卫生事业管理系教授。他为中国公共卫生政策制定做出了重大的贡献,包括 XXX 市控烟的立法和 XXX 市公共卫生发展规划(2000—2015)。

8.1.6 人物介绍(五)

1. 相关词汇

residency:住院医师培训

society:学会;协会

association:协会;社团

2. 原文、参考译文及说明

1）XXX, MD Ph.D., is the Director of XXX Unit, Department of XXX at XXX Hospital. He specializes in both adult XXX and XXX. Dr. XXX treats patients suffering from XXX to other XXX syndromes. Dr. XXX completed his doctoral program of Neuroscience at the University of XXX, and he completed his <u>residency</u> in the Department of Neurology at XXX University before taking on a clinical fellowship at the XXX Center and a research fellowship at the XXX Medical College at XXX University. Dr. XXX returned to the University of XXX as an Assistant Professor in the Department of XXX. He joined the Department of XXX at XXX Hospital in XXX Month, XXX Year.

XXX是医学博士、哲学博士，也是XXX医院XXX科XXX单元主任。他的研究方向是成人XXX和XXX疾病。XXX博士从事从XXX疾病到XXX综合征的一系列疾病的诊疗。XXX在XXX大学攻读神经科学博士，在XXX中心从事临床研究，在XXX大学XXX医学院从事研究工作。他还在XXX大学完成了神经病学系的住院医师培训。XXX博士回到XXX大学，担任XXX系助理教授。他于XXX年XXX月加入XXX医院XXX科室。

说明：（1）residency意为"住院医师培训"，而resident意为"住院医师"。（2）请注意本段中"研究方向""从事临床研究""从事研究工作"这几个表达的翻译法。

2）Dr. XXX is a member of <u>XXX Society</u> and XXX Academy of XXX. He is a fellow of XXX Association. He received a(n) XXX award. Previously, he was a recipient of a Fellowship Training Grant from the National XXX Institute from XXX year to XXX year. He was awarded XXX Research Prize by the XXX Association in XXX year and XXX Award in XXX year.

XXX博士是XXX协会、XXX学会成员，也是XXX协会会员。他获得了XXX奖。此前，他曾于XXX年—XXX年获得国家XXX学会的研究者培训奖学金。他在XXX年荣获XXX协会颁发的XXX研究奖，并在XXX年获得XXX奖。

说明：表达学会、协会时，除了使用society、association外，还可使用college、academy，如American College of Cardiology、American Academy of Neurology。注意：尽量避免使用"被XXX协会授予XXX奖励"等不太符合中文表达习惯的译法。

3）Dr. XXX is devoted to research, clinical practice / patient care and education to improve the current knowledge and management of XXX. He researches the molecular mechanisms of XXX in both laboratory and clinical settings. He sees patients in the XXX Clinic at XXX and <u>performs procedures</u> including XXX.

XXX博士致力于研究、临床实践/患者照护和教育，以提高XXX疾病的现有知识和管理水平。他在实验室和临床中研究XXX病的分子机制。他在XXX医院的XXX诊所出诊，并开展包括XXX在内的操作和治疗。

说明：perform procedures被翻译为"开展操作和治疗"。procedure既可指操作，又可指治疗，此处由于原文并无上下文可供译者判断其具体所指，故将两层含义都翻译出来。

8.1.7 机构介绍[1]

1. 相关词汇

北京大学人民医院：Peking University People's Hospital
北京中央医院：Peking Central Hospital
伍连德：Wu Lien-teh
医疗诊治：patient care

2. 原文、参考译文及说明

1）北京大学人民医院创建于 1918 年，是中国人自行筹资建设和管理的第一家综合性西医医院，最初命名为"北京中央医院"，中国现代医学先驱伍连德博士任首任院长。

Founded in 1918, Peking University People's Hospital was the first general hospital of Western medicine that was financed and operated by the Chinese nationals. Its initial name was "Peking Central Hospital". Dr. Wu Lien-teh, a pioneer of modern medicine in China, served as its first president.

2）北京大学人民医院 94 年发展历程，是中国医学进步的见证。医院成功进行了亚洲第一例、世界第四例异体同基因骨髓移植，诞生了中国第一支乙肝疫苗和中国第一台体外震波碎石设备，为中国医疗卫生事业的发展做出了重要的贡献。

In its 94-year history, the hospital has witnessed the progress of medicine in China. The hospital successfully performed Asia's first and also the world's fourth allogeneic bone marrow transplantation. It also gave birth to China's first hepatitis B vaccine and China's first extracorporeal shock-wave lithotripsy device. The hospital has made a substantial contribution to the development of health care in China.

说明：进行移植手术中的"进行"常用 perform 来表达。此外，需记住"异体同基因骨髓移植""体外震波碎石设备"的译法，可从中学习词根、词缀，如 allo- 意为"异体的"，geneic 意为"同种的"，hepat- 意为"肝脏"，itis 意为"炎症"，extra- 意为"以外的"，corpor- 意为"身体的，体的"。

3）经过 94 年的艰苦创业，北京大学人民医院发展成为集医疗、教学、科研为一体的现代化综合性大学医院，成为我国重要的医疗诊治、医学教育、医学研究中心。开放床位 1 693 张，设有 39 个临床科室、17 个医技科室；拥有血液内科、心血管内科、骨科、妇产科、眼科、泌尿外科、儿科、皮肤科、风湿免疫科、肾内科、病理科 11 个国家级重点学科；血液病研究所、肝病研究所、关节病研究所、应用碎石技术研究所 4 个北京大学级研究所。拥有教育部"视觉损伤与修复重点实验室（北京大学）"和"丙型肝炎和肝病免疫治疗""造血干细胞移植治疗血液病" 2 个北京市重点实验室。现有中华医学会各学科分会前任、现任和候任主任

---

[1] 这是关于北京大学人民医院的简介，选编自该医院官网。

委员12名。医院已经跨入国内医院队列的第一方阵。

With the great efforts of generations of medical workers throughout the 94 years, the hospital has been developed into a general teaching hospital for patient care, teaching, and research. It has 1,693 beds, 39 clinical departments, and 17 technological departments. It has 11 national-level key disciplines: hematology, cardiovascular diseases, orthopedics, obstetrics and gynecology, ophthalmology, urology, pediatrics, dermatology, immuno-rheumatology, nephrology, and pathology. It also has four university-level research institutes for hemopathy, hepatopathy, arthropathy, and lithotripsy. It has a Ministry of Education (MOE) key laboratory of vision impairment and repair (Peking University) and two municipal key laboratories—one for hepatitis C and immunotherapy for hepatopathy and the other for treating hemopathy by hemopoietic stem cell transplantation. Twelve of its physicians served, are serving, or will serve as the directors of the subcommittees of the Chinese Medical Association. It has become a top hospital in China.

说明：（1）"It has 11 national-level key disciplines"这一部分，按国外医院宣传习惯，一般强调临床科室，用clinical program表示，即"Eleven of its clinical programs are leading/ranked top in the country"。（2）注意积累词缀意义，如hemato-（血液）、cardio-（心脏）、vascular-（血管）、ortho-（正）、pedo-（足）、ophthalmo-（眼睛的）、opto-（光的）、uro-（尿液的）、iatry-（医学）（派生出iatrics, 学科）、dermo-（真皮的）、nephro-（肾脏）、patho-（病）、arthro-（关节）。（3）obstetrics and gynecology（/ˌgaɪnəˈkɒlədʒɪ/）在口语交流中可被简称为OBGYN，OB指obstetrics，GYN指gynecology。（4）中华医学会各专业分委会英文名使用Chinese Society of XXX（具体专业和专科名称）来表示。

4）医院承担着繁重的医疗任务，2011年全年门、急诊量2 193 593人次，出院病人总数52 190人次。在造血干细胞移植、肝移植、肾移植、白血病、关节置换、胃肠道肿瘤、恶性骨肿瘤保肢化疗、妇科恶性肿瘤、脊柱功能重建、骨与关节损伤、胸部微创手术、视网膜玻璃体手术、血液透析、心律失常、心血管疾病、自身免疫性疾病、肝脏疾病、内分泌系统疾病、糖尿病眼病、突发性耳聋等领域的诊断治疗均处全国领先水平。

The hospital has provided care to numerous patients. In 2011, it provided outpatient and emergency care to 2,193,593 patients and inpatient care to 52,190 patients. It takes the lead in China in many fields, including hemopoietic stem cells transplantation, liver transplantation, kidney transplantation, leukemia, joint replacement, gastrointestinal tumor, limb salvage chemotherapy for malignant bone tumor, gynecological malignancy, spinal function reconstruction, bone and joint injury, minimally invasive thoracic surgery, vitreoretinal surgery, hemodialysis, arrhythmia, cardiovascular diseases, autoimmune diseases, hepatopathy, endocrinopathy, diabetic ophthalmopathy, and sudden hearing loss, etc.

说明：（1）"承担着繁重的医疗任务"采取意译。（2）"出院病人"按字面翻译是patients discharged from the hospital。参考译文按西方医院统计口径对其进行了调整。译文字面意思是为一定数量的住院病人提供了诊疗。住院病人数和出院病人数这两个统计口径数字存在差异,需跟相关机构询问确切数字。(3)注意积累词根、词缀意义,如 leuko-(白色)、emo = hemo-(血液,译员联想法语中元音前的 h 不发音)、ia-(病症)、gastro-(胃)、intestine-(肠道)、vitro-(玻璃)、retino-(视网膜)、dia-(通过)、-lysis(溶解;分解)、ar-(不),-rhythm(节奏)、auto-(自身)、endo-(内)、crino-(分泌)。

5)近年来,医院开展"北京大学人民医院医疗质量持续改进工程",构建并不断完善医疗质量管控、检查、评价、反馈的长效机制;学习型临床路径应用管理系统的探索,突破临床路径实施瓶颈,极大地推动了医院诊疗规范和医疗质量的提高;组织临床专家修订的《知情同意书汇编》,得到卫生部的高度认可并向全国推荐使用;电子病历系统的上线实现了医疗质量的全过程实时管理,受到卫生部肯定并向全国推广;实时的医院感染控制检测随访系统为全方位监测医院感染并实现随访提供保障;医院全面实施移动护理管理信息系统,优质护理 100% 全覆盖,制定规章与流程(P&P),规范临床操作,提升护理安全和服务质量。

In recent years, the hospital has devoted itself to continuous improvement in the quality of medical services. It established and has constantly been enhancing a long-term mechanism, including managing, inspecting, evaluating, and feeding back, to improve the quality of services. With a self-learning clinical pathway/algorithm application management system, it overcame the bottleneck in implementing clinical pathways and drastically improved the level of standardization of diagnosis and treatment and the quality of services. It organized clinical experts to amend the Compilation of Informed Consents, which was highly recognized by the Ministry of Health (MOH) and recommended to health facilities throughout the country. It achieved whole-process real-time quality management with an electronic medical records system, which was also recognized by the MOH and rolled out across the country. The real-time control, detection, and follow-up system enabled all-round monitoring and following-up of nosocomial infection. The hospital applied a full-scale mobile nursing management information system and achieved 100% coverage of quality nursing. It has made protocols and procedures (P&P) to standardize clinical practice for safer nursing and higher quality of services.

8.1.8 制药公司介绍

1. 相关词汇

  biomedical pharmaceutical company:生物医药公司
  be committed to doing something:致力于
  manufacture:制造
  prescription medicine:处方药物[1]

---

1 "非处方药"为"over the counter or OTC medicine/drug"。

treat and cure：治疗和治愈[1]
across a broad range of areas：涵盖广泛领域
therapeutic：治疗的
cardiovascular disease：心血管疾病[2]
central nervous disease：中枢神经疾病
arthritis：关节炎
anti-infection：抗感染
male urology：男性泌尿
oncology：肿瘤科
investor：投资者
to date：到目前为止
R&D center：研发中心（全称是 research and development center）

2. 原文、参考译文及说明

Our company is a leading research-based biomedical pharmaceutical company in the world, with a sales volume of $XXX billion and investing some $XXX billion in global research and development last year. We <u>are committed to</u> discovering, developing, manufacturing, and promoting all kinds of leading prescription medicines for human and animal health care. We have a world-leading portfolio of medicines that prevent, treat and cure diseases across a broad range of therapeutic areas, such as cardiovascular diseases, central nervous diseases, arthritis, anti-infection, male urology, and oncology.

我们公司是全球领先的、以研发为基础的制药企业，去年销售额逾 XXX 亿美元，全球研发投入约 XXX 亿美元。公司致力于为人类及动物的健康发现、开发、生产和推广各种领先的处方药，以其无与伦比的产品组合在心血管、中枢神经、关节炎、抗感染、男性泌尿和抗肿瘤等治疗领域保持世界领先地位。

说明：（1）治疗领域是医药公司常见的宣传内容，译员可在日常学习过程中，积累不同治疗领域的中英文说法。（2）与 be committed to 类似的表达还有 specialize in doing something，后者更强调在某方面做得很专业。（3）词缀积累：onco- 意为"癌的"。

8.1.9 总结与点评

在人物与机构简介的翻译中，译员一定要注意文化差异导致的叙事内容和视角差异，从跨文化角度积极进行调和，具体做法包括同化法，即参考译入语叙事习惯翻译。译员可多阅读母语者撰写的个人简介和机构简介，以了解母语者的叙事内容和视角，让译文更容易被接受。

---

[1] 治疗和治愈有区别。treat 不一定能治愈患者。
[2] cardio- 意为"心的"；vascular- 意为"血管的"。

8.1.10 词汇与表达拓展

1. 公司部门及类型的翻译

advertising：广告
American-invested company：美国独资企业
branch：分公司；分部；分行
central-government owned enterprise / enterprise owned by the central government：央企
consulting：咨询
customer service：客户服务
daughter company：子公司
department：部门
enterprise：企业
finance：财务
firm/company/corporation/incorporation：公司
foreign-invested company：外商独资企业
government affair and relation：政府事务和关系
group：集团
home office / headquarters：总部
human resource：人力资源
information technology department：IT部，信息技术部
joint venture：合资公司
law and compliance：法务和合规
limited liability company (LLC)：有限责任公司
limited company (Ltd.)：有限公司
market access：市场准入
marketing：营销
medical affair：医疗事务
mother/parent company：母公司
multinational：跨国公司
partnership corporate：合伙企业
private enterprise：民营企业
project：项目
public relation：公共关系
sale：销售
share holding company：控股公司
share-controlling company：控股（母）公司
small and medium-sized enterprise (SME)：中小企业

small and micro enterprise：小微企业
sole proprietorship corporate：个人独资企业
state-owned enterprise (SOE)：国有企业
sub-company：分公司
subsidiary/affiliate：附属公司
technology development：技术发展
wholly-funded company：独资公司

2. 常见行政头衔（titles）的翻译

主席：chairman（男性）/ chairwoman（女性）/ chairperson/chair（不知道或不强调性别）
总统：president/chancellor（后者表示德国总统）
总理：premier
首相：prime minister（日本／英国首相，角色相当于其他国家的总理）
部长：minister
省长：governor
州长：governor
司长：director general
厅长：director general
市长：mayor
县长：county head
镇长：township head
乡长；村长：village head

3. 副职的翻译

1）常用词。
vice/deputy/under/associate
2）常见搭配。
vice president：副总裁；副总统
vice-chairman：副主席
vice-chancellor：副校长[1]
vice/deputy director：副主任
associate professor：副教授
associate (research) fellow：副研究员

---

[1] In a British university, the vice-chancellor [（行政和学术）副校长] is the person in charge of academic and administrative matters. In an American university, the vice-chancellor is the person next in rank below the chancellor, who acts as the chancellor's deputy（副手）or substitute.

4. 行政级别和机构的翻译[1]

1）行政级别。

national/state：国家的

federal：（美国）联邦的

provincial/municipal：省级的 / 直辖市级的 = state：（美国）州级的

city：市

county：县

town/township：乡；镇

village：村

2) 机构。

State Council：国务院

ministry：部（中国）

Ministry of Health (MoH)：卫生部

Ministry of Education (MoE)：教育部

Ministry of Commerce (Mofcom)：商务部

Ministry of Finance (MoF)：财政部

Foreign Ministry / Ministry of Foreign Affairs (FM)：外交部

Department of Labor (USDOL)：劳工部（美国）

Provincial Ministry of Education：省教育部（加拿大）

Provincial Ministry of Environment Protection：省环境保护部（加拿大）

National Development and Reform Commission (NDRC)：国家发展与改革委员会（国家发改委）

State Ethnic Affairs Commission (SEAC)：国家民族事务委员会（国家民委）

office：办

State Council Information Office：国务院新闻办公室（国新办）

State Council AIDS Working Committee Office (SCAWCO)：国务院艾滋病工作委员会办公室（国艾办）

administration：总署；总局

General Administration of Customs：海关总署

State Administration for Market Regulation：国家市场监督管理总局

department：司；厅（省级）

department/administration：局

the Department of International Cooperation of the Chinese Academy of Agriculture Sciences：中国农业科学院国际合作局

---

[1] 本部分主要以中国的行政级别和机构为例介绍这类名词的翻译方法，中间也会提到美国等其他国家的情况。

China Meteorological Administration：中国气象局
National Medical Products Administration：国家药品监督管理局
bureau/board：局（县级和市级）
County Board of Education：县教育局

5. 临床医学专业（specialty）和专科医师（specialist）的翻译

内科：internal medicine; physician / medical doctor / internist
心内科：cardiology; cardiologist
呼吸科：respiratory medicine; pulmologist
泌尿科：urology; urologist
神经内科：neurology; neurologist
消化科：digestive medicine/gastroenterology; gastroenterologist
生殖医学科：reproductive medicine; reproductive specialist
肿瘤科：oncology; oncologist
外科：surgery; surgeon
心胸外科：cardiac/thoracic surgery; cardiac/thoracic surgeon
泌尿外科：urological surgery; urological surgeon
神经外科：neurological surgery; neurological surgeon
整形外科，美容外科：plastic/cosmetic surgery; plastic surgeon
肛肠科：proctology; proctologist
骨科：orthopedics; orthopedist
妇科：gynecology; gynecologist
产科：obstetrics; obstetrician
男科：andrology; andrologist
儿科：pediatrics; pediatrician
五官科：otolaryngology; otolaryngologist
耳鼻喉科：ENT (ear, nose and throat); ENT doctor
眼科：ophthalmology; ophthalmologist
牙科：dentistry; dentist
口腔科：stomatology; stomatologist
皮肤科：dermatology; dermatologist
麻醉科：anesthesia; anesthetist/anesthesiologist
精神科：mental health/psychiatry; psychiatrist[1]
检验科：test lab; technician[2]

---

1 指精神科医生，注意其与心理医生（psychologist）的区别。
2 指技师。

中医科：traditional Chinese medicine (TCM); TCM practitioner[1]
药剂科：pharmacy; pharmacist[2]
社会工作：social work; social worker

6. 医学相关学院、学科和专业的翻译

school/college/faculty：学院
discipline：学科
major/program：专业
basic medicine：基础医学
clinical medicine：临床医学
pharmaceutical science：药学
public health：公共卫生
social medicine：社会医学
primary care：初级保健
preventive medicine：预防医学[3]
medical humanity：医学人文[4]
nursing：护理
physiology：生理学
pathology：病理学
bio-chemistry：生物化学
toxicology：毒理学
anatomy：解剖学
genetics：遗传学
pathophysiology：病理生理学

8.2 仪式性讲话

会议的仪式性讲话包括开幕词、闭幕词、祝酒词、欢送词等，本节选用开幕词、祝酒词、欢送词各一个，介绍此类讲话的口译要点。其中，开幕词选编自 2018 年举办的中国医师协会外科医师分会年会开幕式上王杉会长的发言，祝酒词和欢送词选编自其他口译素材。

---

1 指中医师。
2 指药师。
3 注意其与 defensive medicine（指医生为了免于患者控告而小心行医）的区别。
4 medical humanity 在国外指狭义的临床医学人文。我国的医学人文除包括临床医学人文外，还包括预防医学等领域的人文。

一般情况下，如果译者（尤其是同传译者）是第一次接触相关翻译内容，我们建议尽可能将这些重要稿件提前翻译为目标语言。一方面，便于译者提前熟悉和掌握有关会议内容；另一方面，也可避免译者对大型会议产生的临场紧张感所导致的失误。

8.2.1 开幕词、祝酒词、欢送词

1. 相关词汇

  同道：colleague
  中国医师协会：Chinese Medical Doctor Association
  （中国医师协会）外科医师分会：Chinese College[1] of Surgeons
  北京医师协会：Beijing Medical Doctor Association
  （北京医师协会）外科专科医师分会：Beijing College of Surgeons
  北京大学人民医院：Peking University People's Hospital
  年会：annual meeting
  北京国际会议中心：Beijing International Convention Center

2. 开幕词原文、参考译文及说明

  1）尊敬的各位外科同道及朋友，大家好！
  Dear Colleagues and Friends, good morning.
  2）由中国医师协会、中国医师协会外科医师分会主办（CCS），北京医师协会、北京医师协会外科专科医师分会联合主办，北京大学人民医院承办的第十一届中国医师协会外科医师年会将于 2018 年 5 月 17 日至 20 日在北京国际会议中心召开。

The 11th Annual Meeting of the Chinese College of Surgeons (CCS) hosted by the Peking University People's Hospital and jointly hosted by the Chinese Medical Doctor Association, Chinese College of Surgeons, Beijing Medical Doctor Association, and the Beijing College of Surgeons will be held from May 17 to 20, 2018 at the Beijing International Convention Center.

  3）中国医师协会外科医师分会于 2007 年 11 月 17 日成立，11 年来，分会秉承"规范行业行为、维权自律并重"的宗旨，充分发挥"服务、协调、自律、维权、监督、管理"的职能，弘扬以德为本、救死扶伤的人道主义，努力规范外科医师的执业行为、提高外科医疗水平和服务质量、维护外科医师的合法权益，为提升人民健康水平、全面建成小康社会和实现中华民族伟大复兴服务。

The Chinese College of Surgeons (CCS), established on November 17, 2007, has adhered to the mission of "regulating professional conduct, protecting rights, and promoting

---

1 College 在这里表示"学会"。类似表达有 American College of Cardiology（美国心内科学会）。

self-discipline" in the past 11 years. It has given full play to the functions of "service, coordination, self-discipline, rights protection, supervision and management", promoting the humanitarianism by taking morality as the foundation, saving lives and helping the wounded, striving to standardize the conduct of surgeons, improve the surgical capability and service quality, safeguard the legitimate rights and interests of surgeons, and serve to improve the population health, build a moderately prosperous society in an all-round way and realize the great rejuvenation of the Chinese nation.

说明：本段原文具有较浓厚的内宣视角，在对外传播的视角下，译者还可采取一定程度的编译策略，如概括性翻译等。

4）本着面向全国普通外科医师、发挥行业带头作用、搭建高水准医师交流与继续教育平台、促进外科学科发展与进步的目的，中国医师协会外科医师分会自2007年成立，连续成功举办了十届中国外科医师年会。本届年会我们将继续秉承历届年会的优秀传统，理论与实践相结合，力求加强医务工作者的综合能力。

In line with the purpose of serving general surgeons nationwide, playing a leading role in the profession, building a high-level exchange and continuing education platform, and promoting the development and progress of surgical disciplines, CCS has organized its annual meetings as international academic events in the past 10 years. In this year's meeting, we continue to adhere to the tradition of combining theory with practice to improve the overall competence of the surgeons.

说明：（1）本段中的"自2007年成立"属于重复信息，省去不译。（2）依据上文，本段提及的"医务工作者"实际上是指参会的外科医师，故译者将其翻译为the surgeons。

5）会议期间，我们将举办高质量的讲座，并设立手术视频影院，展示中国最好的外科医生进行的出色手术。我们倡导学术争鸣，聚焦国外先进技术，充分利用互动、国际化的现代信息技术平台，旨在将CCS年会打造成精品会议。

During the meeting, we will deliver high-quality lectures and set up surgery video cinemas to demonstrate the excellent surgeries conducted by the best surgeons in China. We advocate academic contention, focus on advanced techniques from abroad, as well as make full use of the modern information technology platform, featured with interaction and internationalization, aiming at making the CCS Annual Meetings boutique conferences.

6）截至2017年底，中国医师协会外科医师分会业已成立24个分支机构，在年会期间各分支机构都将设立分会场，并围绕各自专业领域中临床进展与多学科协作、手术和诊疗技术的演示与培训、执业规范和行业标准的研究与制定等主题，邀请国际和国内知名专家学者进行学术报告和现场演示，全方位展现普通外科学领域的最新成就和发展趋势。

By the end of December 2017, the CCS had established 24 sub-branches, which will hold parallel sessions during this annual meeting, themed with the clinical development and interdisciplinary cooperation, diagnostic methods demonstration and training of surgery, and study and establishment of practical rules and professional code of conducts. International and domestic experts will be invited to give presentations and live demonstrations, displaying the latest achievements and development trends of general surgery in an all-round way.

7）感谢各位同道参加此次盛会，很荣幸和您再次相聚北京，让我们在外科医学事业发展道路上携手并进，共创辉煌！

Thank you for joining us in this grand event. It's a great honor to meet you again in Beijing. Let's work together to create a brilliant future for surgery!

3. 祝酒词原文及参考译文

Now I wish to propose a toast, to the health of Prime Minister John Howard, to the friendship between China and Australia and between our peoples, and the lofty cause of world peace and development[1]! Cheers!

现在，我提议：为霍华德总理阁下的健康，为中澳两国和两国人民的友谊，为世界和平和发展的崇高事业，干杯！

4. 欢送词原文及参考译文（改编自戚文琴，2007）

1）Respected Dean, friends and colleagues, ladies and gentlemen,

尊敬的系主任、朋友们、同事们、女士们、先生们：

2）I'm very grateful to the Dean of the Department, Ms. Gao, and all my other friends here for giving me such a great send-off party. With your presence, you give me a warm feeling of being part of a big family. Thanks! Thanks very much for coming. A year ago, I came to this renowned university as an exchange scholar, and I do feel greatly honored to have had this opportunity. During my stay here, I received great help and support from Ms. Gao. I'd like to take this opportunity to extend my heartfelt thanks to her. My thanks also go to Wang Jun, who did so much excellent interpretation work for me. Thank you.

我非常感谢高主任和各位朋友为我举办欢送会。你们的到来给了我温暖的大家庭的感觉，感谢你们的到来。一年前，作为交换学者来到这所知名的学府，能有这样的机会，我非常荣幸。在这一年里，高主任给了我极大的帮助和支持。我想借此机会向她表达我衷心的谢意。也要感谢王军，感谢她为我做了很多很好的口译工作。谢谢！

8.2.2 总结与点评

仪式性讲话存在一定的固定模式，有很多套语，甚至连讲话的常见主题也具有一定的规律性。译员应多了解、总结各类礼仪讲话的规律，做到胸有成竹。翻译时，译员需关注会议的规格及用词，并选用恰当的语气和表达，传达讲话者的情绪，起到营造仪式气氛的目的。市面上

1　propose a toast to something or somebody：提议为某事或某人祝酒。

有一些会议用语教材、国际会议用语翻译教材,可参考使用。

8.2.3 词汇与表达拓展

1. 表示欢迎(雷天放、陈菁,2008)

1)On behalf of..., I am delighted to welcome all of you to...
我谨代表……,欢迎大家来到……

2)I'm honored to have this opportunity to welcome all of you to...
我十分荣幸地欢迎大家来到……

3)It is a great pleasure for me to welcome you all to... / It gives me great pleasure to welcome all of you to...
我非常高兴地欢迎各位出席……

4)It is my pleasant duty to extend a cordial welcome to you on behalf of...
我谨代表……,对各位的到来表示热烈的欢迎。

5)It is a real honor and privilege for us to welcome you to...
我们非常荣幸地欢迎大家出席……

6)It is with a profound feeling of pleasure and privilege that, on behalf of..., I extend a hearty welcome to you all, especially to the distinguished guests from...
我代表……,非常荣幸地欢迎大家的到来,尤其是来自……的贵宾们。

7)As the chairperson of this symposium, I have the pleasure and honor of welcoming all of you to this international meeting.
作为本届研讨会的主席,我十分高兴和荣幸地欢迎各位出席这次国际会议。

8)May I welcome all of you to...
欢迎各位参加……

9)On behalf of..., I bid a warm welcome to you all gathered here to participate...
我代表……,对前来参加……的各位朋友表示热烈的欢迎。

10)May I begin by welcoming you to...
首先,我对各位朋友前来参加……表示欢迎。

2. 表示荣幸

1)It's my privilege / great honor to be invited today for this meeting.
我非常荣幸能参加这次大会。

2)I'm honored to be here to attend...
我非常荣幸能够参加……

3)It gives me great honor to welcome you to... Workshop to discuss...
我非常荣幸欢迎各位参加……研讨会,就……问题开展讨论。

3. 表示感谢

1) I would like to take this opportunity to express/extend my sincere thanks to..., for honoring us by taking his busy time to preside over this important workshop, and I am very grateful to..., for taking time off from your busy schedule to come to this meeting.

我想借此机会对……表示诚挚的谢意，感谢他从百忙之中抽出时间主持这个重要的研讨会，我也非常感谢……从百忙之中抽出时间参加研讨会。

2) I wish to extend my sincere thank to... for preparing this excellent document and to the UNFPA for providing the funds to enable... to write the document and enable us to organize this workshop today.

我想对……表示诚挚的谢意，感谢他精心准备文件；也要感谢联合国人口基金会提供资金，正是这资金帮助了……完成文件的准备，帮助了我们今天研讨会的顺利召开。

3) I'm grateful for the company's support to me and China's athletic environment for all these years.

感谢公司多年来对我和中国田径运动的支持。

4) Thank you to the people of China, all the wonderful volunteers, and BOCOG!

感谢中国人民，感谢所有出色的志愿者，感谢北京奥组委！

5) Thank you very much for your gracious invitation for us to the party in such a magnificent hall.

非常感谢您的盛情邀请，让我们到如此华丽的大厅参加晚会。

6) I am deeply grateful to you for your wonderful arrangement and incomparable hospitality.

我对贵方的精心安排和盛情款待表示深深的感谢。

7) Permit me first to extend my heartfelt thanks to all of you for your presence.

首先，请允许我对各位的莅临表示衷心的感谢。

8) I would like to show my gratitude to Mr. Chairman for his presence.

感谢主席先生的光临。

9) I want to pay tribute not only to those who prepared the magnificent dinner but also to those who provided the splendid music.

我不仅要感谢为我们准备丰盛晚宴的人们，而且要感谢为我们演奏美妙音乐的人们。

4. 表示祝愿

1) I wish you a most fruitful day of interesting and stimulating discussions and sharing of knowledge.

祝大家今天的讨论生动活泼、成果丰硕，愿大家能够互相积极地分享知识。

2) I wish the conference a great / every success and every one of you a pleasant/enjoyable stay in Beijing.

祝愿大会圆满成功，祝各位在京期间生活愉快。

5. 表示提议或征求意见

1）I'd like to hear your comments. / Any comment is welcome.
欢迎大家发表看法和意见。

2）Now the floor is open for questions.
现在欢迎大家提问。

3）I'd like to make a motion (that)... / Shall I propose (that)...
我想提议……

6. 表示会议

研讨会：workshop/seminar/symposium

会场：venue

分会场：track

远程会议：teleconference

卫星会（指在主会场以外的城市通过远程会议的方式同时召开的会议）：satellite meeting

筹备会：preparatory meeting

表彰会：awarding meeting

新闻发布会：press conference

洽谈会：match-making conference

推介会：introductory meeting

访谈：interview

专访：one-on-one interview

小组采访：group interview

面对面的会谈：face-to-face meeting

背靠背的会议；一个紧接一个的会议：back-to-back meetings

开幕式：opening ceremony

闭幕式：closing ceremony

开幕词：opening remarks

闭幕词：closing remarks

演讲：speech

讲座：lecture

发言人，讲者：speaker

主席：chair/chairperson（不表示性别）/ Chairman（男）/ Chairwoman（女，该词使用较少）

秘书处：secretariat

秘书长：secretary general

司仪：master of ceremony (MC)

主持人：host/moderator

共同主持人：co-host/co-moderator
讲台：podium
（在主席台上的）小组讨论：panel discussion
小组讨论发言人：panelist
主席台：stage
问答环节：Q&A session
议程：agenda
日程：program
时间表：timetable/schedule
集会：convene
重新开始会议：reconvene
提案：proposal
议案：bill
动议：motion

参考文献

雷天放，陈菁. 2008. 口译教程. 上海：上海外语教育出版社.
戚文琴. 2007. 实用英语口译入门教程. 北京：旅游教育出版社.
詹成. 2015. 会议口译常用语手册. 北京：外语教学与研究出版社.
Margolis, C. Z. 1983. Uses of clinical algorithms. *JAMA*, *249*(5): 627–632.

第9章

公共卫生

9.1 流感大流行预警级别提升通告

世界卫生组织（World Health Organization，WHO）是全球公共卫生治理的主要国际机构，在流行病防控上扮演着举足轻重的作用。本节材料选编自世界卫生组织前总干事陈冯富珍宣布流感大流行预警级别升至五级的讲话。在人类高度全球化的背景下，疾病防控是全球事务。该讲话中有大量常见的疾病防控相关表达和术语，我们在日后的相关翻译中可能会用到。

9.1.1 背景知识

1）**有关"流行"的词汇辨析**：endemic、epidemic 和 pandemic 都有流行的意思，且都可作名词和形容词。endemic 指地方性流行（病），epidemic 指流行（病），pandemic 特指跨洲流行（病）。

2）**流感预警级别**：按照发生大规模暴发流行的可能性，划分为五级，包括Ⅰ级（较少发生、绿色）、Ⅱ级（可能发生、蓝色）、Ⅲ级（较易发生、黄色）、Ⅳ级（易发生、橙色）、Ⅴ级（极易发生、红色）。

3）**流感命名方式**：H 指的是血球凝集素（hemagglutinin[1]），N 指的是神经氨（neuraminidase[2]），这两种物质都是病毒上的抗原（antigen）。H 和 N 后面的数字代表具有血球凝集素第 X 型、神经氨酸酶第 X 型的病毒。流感病毒有 16 个 H 亚型（subtypes）（H1—H16）和 9 个 N 亚型（N1—N9）。感染人的禽流感病毒亚型主要为 H5N1、H9N2、H7N7，其中感染 H5N1 的患者病情重，病死率[3]（fatality rate）高。

4）**世界卫生组织**：Dedicated to the well-being of all people and guided by science, the World Health Organization leads and champions global efforts to give everyone, everywhere an equal chance to live a healthy life. Founded in 1948, WHO is the United Nations agency that connects nations, partners and people to promote health, keep the world safe and serve

---

1　hema- 意为"血"，glut 意为"凝固"，-in 意为"素"。
2　neur- 意为"神经"，amino 意为"氨基"，-ase 意为"酶"。
3　死亡率可用 mortality 来表达。病死率（fatality rate）指一定时期内（通常为一年），患某病的死亡者占该病全部患者中的比例。

the vulnerable (脆弱人群)—so everyone, everywhere can attain the highest level of health. WHO leads global efforts to expand universal health coverage (全民健康覆盖). WHO directs and coordinates the world's response to health emergencies (卫生紧急事件), and promote healthier lives—from pregnancy care (孕产妇保健) through old age care (老年照护). Our Triple Billion targets outline an ambitious plan for the world to achieve good health for all using science-based policies and programs[1].

5）**联合援助计划 (UNITAID)**：It is an international drug purchase facility, established to provide long-term, sustainable and predictable funding to increase access (可及) and reduce prices of quality drugs and diagnostics (诊断用品) for the treatment of HIV/AIDS, malaria (疟疾) and tuberculosis (结核) in developing countries.

6）**全球疫苗免疫联盟 (GAVI, Global Alliance for Vaccines and Immunization)**：By the late 1990s, the progress of international immunization programs was stalling. Nearly 30 million children in developing countries were not fully immunized against deadly diseases, and many others went without any immunization at all. At the heart of the challenge was an acute market failure; powerful new vaccines were becoming available, but lower-income countries simply could not afford most vaccines. In response, the Bill & Melinda Gates Foundation and a group of founding partners brought to life an elegant solution to encourage manufacturers to lower vaccine prices for the poorest countries in return for long-term, high-volume and predictable demand from those countries. In 2000, that breakthrough idea became the Global Alliance for Vaccines and Immunization.

9.1.2 流感大流行相关讲话

1. 相关词汇

　　alert level：预警级别
　　Director-General：总干事
　　assessment：评估
　　available：可用的；现有的
　　consultation：咨询
　　avian influenza：禽流感
　　pandemic：大流行病，洲间流行病
　　phase：级
　　undertake preparedness measures：采取预案措施
　　evolution：进化

1　选编自世界卫生组织官网。

make the results of their investigations publicly available：将调查结果公诸于众
by definition：从定义来看
notorious：臭名昭著的
mutation：变异
unpredictable：不可预测的
health authority：卫生管理部门
epidemiological：流行病学的
clinical：临床的
virological：病毒学的
activate：激活
preparedness plan：预案
remain on high alert for：对……保持高度警惕
influenza-like illness：流感样疾病
severe pneumonia：严重的肺炎
heightened surveillance：加强监测
detection：发现
case：病例
health facility：医疗机构
ministry of health：卫生部
pharmaceutical industry：医药行业
business community：商界
at an accelerated pace：以更快的速度
reach out to：接触
donor country：捐赠国
World Bank：世界银行
mobilize resources：调动资源
antiviral drug：抗病毒药物
ramp up production：加大产量
vaccine manufacturer：疫苗制造商
the full clinical spectrum：全临床疾病谱
data：数据
affluent country：富裕国家
mortality：死亡率
a window of opportunity：机遇；机会窗口
ramp up preparedness and response：更充分地准备，更快速地响应
solidarity：团结
humanity：人类
be under threat：受到威胁

2. 原文、参考译文及说明

1) Ladies and gentlemen, based on assessment of all available information, and following several <u>expert consultations</u>, I have decided to raise the current level of influenza pandemic alert from <u>Phase</u> 4 to Phase 5.

女士们、先生们，基于现有信息的评估和<u>专家会商</u>的结果，我决定将流感预警级别从目前的 4 <u>级</u>提高至 5 级。

说明：画线词汇需重点掌握。下同。

2) Influenza pandemics must be taken seriously because of their capacity to spread rapidly to every country in the world. On the positive side, the world is better prepared for an influenza pandemic than at any time in history. <u>Preparedness measures</u> undertaken because of the threat from H5N1 avian influenza were an investment, and we are now benefiting from this investment. For the first time in history, we can track the evolution of a pandemic in real-time.

流感大流行必须得到严肃重视，因为这种疾病有能力在世界各国快速传播。积极的一面是，我们目前的流感大流行应对准备比历史上任何一个时刻都更为充分。为应对 H5N1 禽流感而制定的<u>预案</u>措施是一项投入，而我们现在正受益于这项投入。纵观历史，我们目前是开了对大流行病的演进进行实时跟踪的先河。

3) I thank countries who are making the results of their investigations publicly available. This helps us understand the disease. I am impressed by the work being done by <u>affected countries</u> as they deal with the current outbreaks. I also want to thank the governments of the US and Canada for their support to WHO, and to Mexico.

我要感谢将调查结果公之于世的各国，此举有助于我们更好地了解禽流感。<u>遭受禽流感侵袭的国家</u>在处理目前的爆发中所做的工作也给我留下了深刻的印象。此外，我还想感谢美国和加拿大政府对世界卫生组织的支持和对墨西哥的支持。

4) Let me remind you. New diseases are, <u>by definition</u>, poorly understood. Influenza viruses are notorious for their rapid mutation and unpredictable behavior. WHO and health authorities in affected countries will not have all the answers immediately, but we will get them. WHO will be tracking the pandemic at the <u>epidemiological</u>, clinical, and virological levels. The results of these ongoing assessments will be issued as public health advice, and made publicly available.

请允许我提醒大家：新出现的疾病本身就有很多东西是我们所未知的。而流感病毒是出了名的变异快速、行为难于预测的病毒。世卫和出现疫情的各国卫生部门目前尚不能回答所有的问题，但一定会找到所有问题的答案。世卫将从流行病学、临床和病毒学的角度追踪禽流感的大流行，并发布评估结果，提出公众健康建议。

说明：（1）此处的 by definition，也可翻译为"顾名思义"。全句则可译为："新出现的疾病，顾名思义，就是那些本身还有很多东西是我们所未知的疾病。"（2）注意：epidemic (/ˌepɪˈdemɪk/)、epidemiology (/ˌepɪdiːmɪˈɒlədʒɪ/)、epidemiologist (/ˌepɪdiːmɪˈɒlədʒɪst/)、 epidemiological（/ˌepɪdiːmɪəˈlɒdʒɪkəl/）的发音在重音部分存在差异。此外，这几个词的英式发音和美式发音也有差异。类似的还有 economy 和 economist、economic(s) 和 economical 等。

5）All countries should immediately activate their pandemic preparedness plans. Countries should remain on high alert for unusual outbreaks of influenza-like illness and severe pneumonia. At this stage, effective and essential measures include heightened surveillance, early detection and treatment of cases, and infection control in all health facilities.

各国都应该立即激活大流行病预案，并对流感样疾病和严重肺炎的异常爆发保持高度警惕。在目前阶段，有效的关键措施包括加强监督、早期发现和预防病例、控制所有医疗卫生机构内的感染。

说明：（1）医疗卫生机构内的感染也称"院内感染"，医院日常工作中，简称"院感"。（2）pneumo- 意为"肺部的；空气的"，-ia 意为"病症"。

6）This change to a higher phase of alert is a signal to governments, to ministries of health and other ministries, to the pharmaceutical industry and the business community that certain actions should now be undertaken with increased urgency, and at an accelerated pace.

此次提高预警级别等于是向政府、卫生部和其他部委、医药行业和商界发出信号，提醒他们一定要快速采取一定形式的、更加紧急的措施。

7）I have reached out to donor countries, to UNITAID, to the GAVI Alliance, the World Bank and others to mobilize resources. I have reached out to companies manufacturing antiviral drugs to assess capacity and all options for ramping up production. I have also reached out to influenza vaccine manufacturers that can contribute to the production of a pandemic vaccine.

我与捐赠国、联合援助计划、全球疫苗免疫联盟、世界银行及其他方面的人士进行了接触，希望能够充分调动资源。我还与生产抗病毒药物的公司进行了接触，对他们提高产量的能力及所有提高产量的方式进行了评估。此外，我还接触了能对大流行疫苗生产作出贡献的流感疫苗制造商。

说明：vaccine 为名词，对应的动词"接种疫苗"是 vaccinate，抽象名词是 vaccination，近义词有 inoculate、inoculation。常见搭配有：get vaccinated/inoculated with a certain vaccine、to inoculate a certain vaccine against... disease 等。

8）The biggest question, right now, is this: How severe will the pandemic be, especially now at the start? It is possible that the full clinical spectrum of this disease goes from mild illness to severe disease. We need to continue to monitor the evolution of the situation to get the specific information and data we need to answer this question.

目前最大的问题是：这场大流行会有多严重，尤其是在目前的开始阶段？该疾病在临床上可能会从轻症发展到重症。我们需要继续监督形势的发展，掌握具体信息和数据，以便回答这个问题。

说明：full clinical spectrum of this disease 本意为"该疾病的全临床谱系"，此处所给参

考译文已对其进行灵活处理。

9）From past experience, we also know that influenza may cause mild disease in affluent countries, but more severe disease, with higher mortality, in developing countries. No matter what the situation is, the international community should treat this as a window of opportunity to ramp up preparedness and response.

过去的经验告诉我们：流感在富裕国家可能引起轻微病例，但在发展中国家可能引起更加严重的、死亡率更高的病例。不管形势如何，国际社会必须抓住当前的重要机遇期，把预案做得更好，把反应速度进一步提高。

10）Above all, this is an opportunity for global solidarity as we look for responses and solutions that benefit all countries, all of humanity. After all, it really is all of humanity that is under threat during a pandemic. As I have said, we do not have all the answers right now, but we will get them. Thank you.

最重要的是，目前是考验全球团结性的时机，我们期待造福各国、造福全人类的行动和解决方案。毕竟在大流行病时期，整个人类都受到威胁。我前面说过，我们目前没有所有问题的答案，但迟早会找到答案。谢谢大家。

9.1.3 总结与点评

上文在理解、记忆、表达方面并不存在太多障碍。做好传译工作的关键，是要熟悉术语的翻译方法。译者可依据下文"词汇与表达拓展"中列出的内容，进行术语与相关知识的积累。

此外，全球卫生治理相关讲话中，许多发言人并非英语母语者，可能会存在特殊口音。例如，以世界第二大语言西班牙语为母语的发言人，在使用英语作为通用语进行口头交际时，其特殊口音被称为西语英语变体；即使在英语本族语中，澳大利亚英语也带有显著区别于美国英语的鲜明特点（王炎强等，2022）。译者应积极了解发言人的口音特点，并提前索要讲话稿，检索、调研讲话稿涉及的知识内容。充分的译前准备是做好传译工作的前提。但在翻译中，译者要注意讲者是否更改了发言稿，并做出相应调整。故译前准备除讲话稿涉及的知识内容外，译者还应进行一定的拓展性调研，以便发言人脱稿讲话时，也能够应对自如。

上文选自书面讲话。此类讲话信息密集，做口译笔记时一定要抓住要点，多用符号，少写文字，以符号作为回忆的提示，以便回忆发言人的讲话内容，做好译文产出。

9.1.4 词汇与表达拓展

1. 联合国机构、国际组织及头衔

  International Court of Justice：国际法院
  Security Council：安全理事会
  Economic and Social Council：经济社会理事会
  General Assembly：联合国大会

Secretariat：秘书处

United Nations Commission on Narcotic Drugs (UNCND)：联合国麻醉药品委员会

United Nations Human Rights Council (UNHRC)：联合国人权理事会

United Nations Conference on Trade and Development (UNCTD)：联合国贸易发展会议

United Nations Drug Control Program (UNDCP)：联合国禁毒署

United Nations Office on Drugs and Crime (UNODC)：联合国毒品和犯罪问题办公室

United Nations Development Program (UNDP)：联合国开发计划署

United Nations Environment Program (UNEP)：联合国环境规划署

United Nations Joint Program on HIV/AIDS (UNAIDS)：联合国艾滋病规划署

United Nations Development Fund for Women (UNIFEM)：联合国妇女基金

United Nations Children's Fund (UNICEF)：联合国儿童基金会

United Nations Population Fund (UNFPA)：联合国人口基金会

United Nations Education, Science and Culture Organization (UNESCO)：联合国教科文组织

United Nations Industrial Development Organization (UNIDO)：联合国工业发展组织

World Health Organization (WHO)：世界卫生组织

International Labor Organization (ILO)：国际劳工组织

Food and Agriculture Organization (FAO)：世界粮农组织

World Trade Organization (WTO)：世界贸易组织

World Meteorological Organization (WMO)：世界气象组织

International Monetary Fund (IMF)：国际货币基金组织

World Bank：世界银行

International Atomic Energy Agency (IAEA)：国际原子能组织

Secretary-General：秘书长

Under-Secretary-General (USG)：副秘书长

Deputy-Secretary-General (DSG)：常务副秘书长[1]

Director General：总干事

Deputy Director General：副总干事

2. 我国规划免疫疫苗清单

重组乙型肝炎疫苗：recombinant hepatitis[2] B vaccine

---

[1] Under-Secretary-General 指副秘书长，从联合国诞生之日起就有了。而 Deputy-Secretary-General 的地位排在秘书长之下，却在所有 USG（副秘书长）之上，其职权是协助秘书长负责总体工作，而其他 USG 都各负责一摊工作或一个部门；在秘书长外出或不在总部时，DSG 代理秘书长职务，因此它被译为"常务副秘书长"。

[2] hepato- 意为"肝"；-itis 意为"炎症"。

皮内注射用卡介苗：BCG[1] for intradermal[2] injection
脊髓灰质炎灭活疫苗：inactivated poliomyelitis vaccine
脊髓灰质炎减毒活疫苗：live attenuated poliomyelitis vaccine
吸附无细胞百白破联合疫苗：acellular DPT[3] toxoids[4] adsorbed combined vaccine
吸附白喉破伤风联合疫苗：diphtheria and tetanus toxoids adsorbed combined vaccine
麻（疹）风（疹）腮（腺炎）联合减毒疫苗：measles, mumps, and rubella combined attenuated vaccine
A 群脑膜炎[5]球菌多糖疫苗：Group A meningococcal[6] polysaccharide[7] vaccine
A 群 C 群脑膜炎球菌多糖疫苗：Group A and Group C meningococcal polysaccharide vaccine
冻干甲型肝炎减毒活疫苗：lyophilized live attenuated hepatitis A vaccine

9.2 艾滋病防控

本节以艾滋病防控为例，介绍疾病防控常用语的译法。材料选编自 2007 年中国艾滋病现状简介及联合国前秘书长科菲·安南在第十五届国际艾滋病大会上的发言。

9.2.1 中国艾滋病现状简介

1. 相关词汇

HIV case：艾滋病毒感染病例
AIDS case：艾滋病病例
infection rate：感染率
new infection：新发感染
cumulative number：累计数量
HIV positive case：艾滋病病毒阳性病例
heterosexual transmission：异性传播

1　(BCG) Bacillus Calmette-Guerin：用于预防结核。
2　intra- 意为"内"；-dermal 意为"真皮的"。
3　指百日咳、白喉、破伤风，对应的英文分别是 diphtheria、pertussis、tetanus。
4　指 bacterial poison (toxin) that is no longer active but retains the property of combining with or stimulating the formation of antibodies。
5　对应英文为 meningitis。
6　meningo-：脑膜；-coccal 球状的（联想记忆：coconut 意为"椰子"）。
7　poly-：多；-saccharide：糖。

homosexual transmission：同性传播

　　injecting drug use：注射吸毒

　　commercial plasma donation：有偿血浆捐献（卖血）

　　blood transfusion：输血

　　contaminated blood and blood product：受污染的血液和血液制品

　　mother to child transmission：母婴传播

2. 原文、参考译文及说明

　　1）By the end of 2007, there were an estimated 700,000 HIV cases in China. The HIV infection rate among China's population is 0.05%. The estimated AIDS cases were 85,000; new HIV infections in 2007 were 50,000.

　　据估计，截至2007年底，中国有70万例艾滋病病毒感染，中国人口中的感染率为0.05%。艾滋病病例为85 000例；2007年，新发感染5万例。

　　说明："截至"与"截止"用法不同。"截止"表示到某个时间停止，强调"停止"，其后不能加时间词语作宾语，一般用于时间词语之后。"截至"则表示停止于某个时间，强调"时间"，"截至"后面需带时间词语作宾语。

　　2）By the end of October 2007, the cumulative number of reported HIV positive cases was 223,501, including 62,838 AIDS cases and 22,205 recorded deaths.

　　截至2007年10月底，累计报告艾滋病病毒阳性病例223 501例，其中包括62 838例艾滋病病例和22 205例有记录的死亡病例。

　　3）Among the 700,000 estimated HIV cases, 40.6% were through heterosexual transmission, 11.0% through homosexual transmission, 38.1% through injecting drug use, 9.3% through commercial plasma donation and transfusion of infected blood and blood products and 1.0% through mother to child transmission.

　　在估计的70万艾滋病病毒感染病例中，异性传播占40.6%，同性传播占11.0%，注射吸毒传播占38.1%，通过卖血（浆）和通过污染的血液和血液制品输血感染占9.3%，母婴传播占1.0%。

9.2.2 科菲·安南在第十五届国际艾滋病大会上的发言[1]

1. 相关词汇

　　leading light[2]：领导人物

1　这是按照事先写好的发言稿做的发言。发言中，讲者使用了多种修辞手法。翻译时，译者首先要达意；在此基础上，还应追求文采，以体现讲者的修辞运用。

2　If you say that someone is a leading light in an organization, campaign, or community, you mean that he/she is one of the most important, active, enthusiastic, and successful people in it.

fight against：抗击……的行动
dedication：投入
resolve：决心
struggle[1]：抗争，斗争
curb the spread of：遏制……的传播
recipe：（喻）方案；办法
visionary political leadership：有远见的政治领导力
allocation of critical resources：对关键性资源的分配
civil society：公民社会
massive campaign：大型运动
public awareness：公众意识
condom use promotion：安全套使用推广
virus：病毒
at an alarming rate：以惊人的速度
spin out of control：失控
health minister：卫生部长
General Assembly Special Session on HIV/AIDS：联合国大会艾滋病特别会议
a session devoted to a disease：专门讨论某一种疾病的会议
pledge：承诺
deliver the resources：提供资源
time-bound target：有时间规定的目标
the Declaration of Commitment：《承诺宣言》
front：方面
Member State：成员国
Global Fund to Fight AIDS, Tuberculosis and Malaria：全球抗击艾滋病、肺结核和疟疾基金[2]
the vast majority of：广大……
combat：抗击
full partner：全面伙伴
objective：目标
be on track[3]：在正轨上
epidemic[4]：流行病
emerge：出现

---

1 文中指代抗击艾滋病。
2 简称"全球基金"。
3 If someone or something is on track, he/she/it is acting or progressing in a way that is likely to result in success. （例句：It may take some time to get the British economy back on track.）
4 在文中指代艾滋病。

bear the brunt of[1]：首当其冲
sub-Saharan Africa：撒哈拉以南的非洲
care：关怀
live up to its name：名副其实
outline：列举
scale up：扩大规模
setting：条件；情况
impose from：由……强加
community center：社区中心
health worker：卫生工作者
have access to：能获得……
anti-retroviral therapy：抗逆转录病毒治疗
vicious circle：恶性循环
step up efforts：加大力度
call in reinforcements：请求增援
draw on：运用
enlist：纳入
empower：赋予权力，赋权
untapped：没有开发的
stigma：污名化；羞辱
pressing：紧迫的
priority：优先任务；要务
be vulnerable to：容易感染……
sexual partner：性伴侣
injecting drug user：注射吸毒者
unconscionable[2]：不合理的；昧着良心的；道德上不可接受的；肆无忌惮的
conspire[3]：共谋，合谋；密谋
abuse：虐待
violence：暴力

---

1 To bear the brunt or take the brunt of something unpleasant means to suffer the main part or force of it.（例句：Young people are bearing the brunt of unemployment. / A child's head tends to take the brunt of any fall.）

2 If you describe something as unconscionable, you mean that the person responsible for it ought to be ashamed of it, especially because its effects are so great or severe.（例句：It's unconscionable for the government to do anything for a man who admits to smuggling 135 tons of cocaine into the United States.）

3 相当于combine。If events conspire to produce a particular result, they seem to work together to cause this result.（例句：History and geography have conspired to bring Greece to a moment of decision... / But fateful forces beyond the band's control were to conspire against them.）

coercion[1]：强迫
concurrent：同时的
entrap sb. in：让某人陷入……陷阱
piecemeal：单个的
option：选择
necessity：必须
land ownership：土地所有权
right to inheritance：继承权
sb. be denied：某人被剥夺了……
microbicide：抗微生物制剂
become available：有
speak up about：大声谈论
stick head in the sand：将头埋进沙子
a veil of apathy：无情的面纱
translate into：转化为
mobilize：调动
state apparatus：国家机器
Ministry of Finance：财政部
Ministry of Defense：国防部
hold positions of power：掌权
affirm the rights of women：捍卫妇女权利
nurture the dreams and aspirations of girls：编织女童的梦想与希望
without judgment：不加评论
assume responsibility：承担责任
abstain from：不去做某事
cultural stereotype：文化定势思维
come into manhood：成为男人
sexual initiation：初次性行为
reach out to：外展至；涉及
devise approach：设计方法

2. 原文、参考译文及说明

1）I am delighted to be here today, among so many leading lights in the fight against HIV/AIDS. It is the dedication and resolve of people like you that is our best hope in the

---

[1] Coercion is the act or process of persuading someone forcefully to do something that he/she does not want to do.（例句：It was vital that the elections should be free of coercion or intimidation.）

struggle.

非常高兴来到这里，和各位抗击艾滋病的杰出领导人欢聚一堂，正是大家的决心和贡献才使我们燃起了希望。

2）It is fitting that we are meeting in Thailand, which has had such remarkable success in curbing the spread of HIV/AIDS. Prime Minister, your recipe for success was a powerful combination: visionary political leadership at an early stage of the epidemic; allocation of critical resources; strong civil society involvement; along with massive campaigns for public awareness and condom use promotion. Thank you, Thailand, for showing us that progress is possible. Continued leadership is now crucial in ensuring that you sustain that success, despite very real challenges.

我们在泰国相聚是非常合适的，这个国家非常成功地遏制了艾滋病的蔓延。总理先生，您提供的解决方式很好：既有在疾病早期富有远见的政治领导力，又有关键性资源的分配、民间社会的积极参与，以及促进提高公众意识和推广安全套使用的大型宣传运动。感谢泰国，向我们证明成功是可能的。现在，尽管还有各种非常实际的挑战，你们仍需要持续的领导力来确保持续性的成功。

3）It is also appropriate that this conference is being held in Asia, where the virus is spreading at an alarming rate. One in four infections last year happened on this continent. There is no time to lose if we are to prevent the epidemic in Asia from spinning out of control.

我们在亚洲举办这次会议也非常恰当，因为艾滋病正在以飞快的速度在亚洲传播，去年1/4的病例都出现在亚洲。我们不能浪费任何时间，不能让艾滋病在亚洲的蔓延失去控制。

4）At this conference, many countries around the world are being represented by their health ministers. But let us be clear: the fight against HIV/AIDS requires leadership from all parts of government—and it needs to go right to the top. AIDS is far more than a health crisis. It is a threat to development itself.

世界上许多国家都派出了卫生部长作为此次会议的代表。让我们明确一点：抗击艾滋病需要政府各个层面的领导力，包括最高层领导。艾滋病不仅是一个卫生方面的危机，也会对发展本身带来威胁。

5）That is why, three years ago, the governments of the world made a promise. At the General Assembly Special Session on HIV/AIDS—the first General Assembly session devoted to a disease—they pledged to deliver the resources and action needed to defeat the epidemic. They adopted a number of specific, time-bound targets, in a document we know as the Declaration of Commitment.

因此，三年前，世界各国领导人做出承诺。在联合国大会艾滋病特别会议上——也是第一个针对某一种疾病的联合国大会上——他们承诺投入抗击艾滋病所需的资源，并采取相关行动；他们还在名为《承诺宣言》的文件中确立了一系列具体的、有时间限制的目标。

6）Three years on, there has been progress on many fronts. Significant new resources have been pledged, both by individual Member States and through the Global Fund to

Fight AIDS, Tuberculosis and Malaria. The vast majority of Member States have adopted comprehensive, national strategies to combat HIV/AIDS. Increasingly, governments are working with civil society as a full partner in the struggle.

三年来，我们在许多方面都取得了进步。各成员国和全球抗击肺结核、艾滋病、疟疾基金认捐了大量新资源。广大成员国采取了综合的国家策略抗击艾滋病；越来越多的政府和作为全面合作伙伴的民间社会一起共同抗击艾滋病。

7）And yet, we are not doing nearly well enough. We failed to reach several of the objectives the Declaration set for last year. Even more important, we are not on track to begin reducing the scale and impact of the epidemic by 2005, as we had promised.

但是我们做得还不够好，我们没有实现《宣言》中为去年设定的许多目标。更重要的是，我们还没有着手落实我们所承诺的在 2005 年前缩小疾病规模，降低疾病影响的目标。

8）Meanwhile, over the past few years, we have seen a terrifying pattern emerge: All over the world, women are increasingly bearing the brunt of the epidemic. Women now account for nearly half of all adult infections. In sub-Saharan Africa, that figure is around 58 percent. Among people younger than 24, girls and young women make up nearly two thirds of those living with HIV.

与此同时，在过去几年当中，我们看到一种可怕的趋势：在全世界范围内，妇女越来越成为艾滋病的主要受害者。现在，成年女性感染者占到了成人感染者的一半；在撒哈拉以南非洲地区，这个数字约为 58%。在 24 岁以下人口当中，女童和年轻妇女占到了感染者的 2/3。

9）And yet, one third of all countries still have no policies to ensure that women have access to prevention and care. Knowing what we do today is associated with the path of the epidemic, how can we allow that to be the case? It is clear that if the Declaration of Commitment is to live up to its name, we will have to do much, much better on several fronts. Today, allow me to outline three specific areas we must focus on.

可是 1/3 的国家还没有建立相关的政策，使妇女能够得到预防和关怀。我们都知道，目前采取的行动和艾滋病的发展轨迹相关，我们怎么能够允许这种情况再继续下去？有一点是明确的，那就是如果《承诺宣言》名副其实的话，我们就必须在许多方面大力改进我们的工作。今天，请允许我指出三个我们必须关注的领域。

10）First, we need to scale up infrastructure to support both treatment and prevention. Successful programs in Africa, in Latin America, and here in Asia, have demonstrated that prevention and treatment can work <u>in any setting</u>, but only if:

interventions are scaled up to reach whole societies;

they are developed inside the country, rather than imposed from outside;

there is strong engagement by people living with and affected by HIV; and

there are enough trained people to implement successful programs—from community centers for awareness-raising, counseling and testing, to clinics for treatment and care.

首先，我们需要加大我们的基础设施规模，支持治疗和预防。在非洲、拉丁美洲和亚洲成功的项目都表明，预防和治疗<u>在任何环境下</u>都能够发挥作用，但前提是：

- 干预规模扩大到全社会；
- 项目在本国开发，而不是由外部势力所强加；
- 患有艾滋病或者受艾滋病影响的人群积极参与，以及
- 有足够的受过训练的人员来执行这些项目，包括在社区中心负责提高人们意识和咨询与检测的人员、在诊所负责治疗和关怀的人员等。

11）That means doing everything possible to ensure that health workers living with HIV have access to anti-retroviral therapy. In many of the most affected countries, AIDS drives a cruel and vicious circle by striking at those who are most badly needed to fight the epidemic. It means stepping up efforts to train new people, and calling in reinforcements among health workers not yet involved in the struggle. And it means drawing on unconventional capacity where formal skills may be lacking. Enlisting and empowering untapped talent among community workers, volunteers, and people living with HIV/AIDS will both help to scale up the efforts and contribute to breaking the stigma and silence.

这就意味着要确保患有艾滋病的医护人员能够获得抗逆转录病毒药物治疗。在艾滋病感染最严重的国家，艾滋病侵袭了我们在抗击艾滋病过程中最需要的人，形成了一种残酷的恶性循环。这就意味着我们需要加大力度来培训新的人员，呼吁尚未参与抗击艾滋病工作的医护人员增援。这就意味着在专业技术人员缺乏的地区，我们需要调动一些非传统力量。调动社区工作人员、志愿者和艾滋病感染者，给他们赋权，有助于扩大工作规模，并有助于消除羞辱和打破缄默。

说明：此段中的 where formal skills may be lacking 指"在专业技术人员缺乏的地区"。

12）No less pressing is our second priority: empowering women and girls to protect themselves against the virus. Why are women more vulnerable to infection? Why is that so, even when they are not the ones with the most sexual partners outside marriage, nor more likely than men to be injecting drug users? Usually, because society's inequalities put them at risk—unjust, unconscionable risk.

我们的第二项要务也同样紧迫：那就是给妇女和女童赋权，让她们能够保护自己免患艾滋病。为什么妇女更容易患艾滋病？她们不是有最多婚外性伙伴的人，也不像男性那样容易成为注射吸毒者，可为什么她们更容易感染艾滋病？往往是社会的不公平让她们面临风险——这些风险不公平，也不应该让她们来承受。

说明：unconscionable 意为 morally unacceptable。

13）A range of factors conspire to make this so: poverty, abuse and violence, lack of information, coercion by older men, and men having several concurrent sexual relationships that entrap young women in a giant network of infection. These factors cannot be addressed piecemeal. What is needed is real, positive change that will give more power and confidence to women and girls. Change that will transform relations between women and men at all levels of society.

一系列因素造成了这样的结果，包括贫穷、虐待和暴力、缺乏信息、被年长的男性胁迫、

男性同时保持多个性关系,导致妇女身陷感染艾滋病的巨大网络中。这些因素不能零敲碎打地加以解决。(我们)需要的是真正的、积极的变革,赋予妇女和女童更多的权力和信心。这种变革将改变社会各阶层男女之间的关系。

说明:(1) conspire 本意是"密谋;共谋;图谋",本处取基本意义"造成"。(2) Piecemeal means piece by piece, or one by one.

14) In other words, what is needed is the education of girls. Only when societies recognize that educating girls is not an option, but a necessity, will girls and young women be able to build the knowledge, the self-confidence and the independence they need to protect themselves from HIV/AIDS. Once they leave school, we must work to ensure they have job opportunities, as well as enjoy the rights to land ownership and inheritance that too many are denied today. And we must ensure they have full access to the practical options that can protect them from HIV—including microbicides, as they become available.

换言之,我们需要让女童受到教育。只有当社会认识到女童教育不仅是一种选择,而是一种必需的时候,女童和年轻的妇女才能够获得知识、自信和独立,保护自己免受艾滋病的威胁。我们应当确保她们一离开学校,就能有工作机会,能够享有继承土地所有权和财产的权利;今天,许多妇女没有土地继承权和财产继承权。我们还必须保证她们能够获得切实可行的方法,包括将会面世的抗微生物制剂,以保护自己免受艾滋病感染。

15) That brings me to the third priority: stronger leadership at every level — including at the top. Leadership means showing the way by example:

by breaking the deadly wall of silence that continues to surround the epidemic;

by achieving the cultural shift needed to fight it effectively;

by working to scale up the response—including providing treatment to all those who need it.

这就引出了我要讲的第三个要务:在各个层次加强领导力,包括最高层的领导力。领导力意味着通过范例展示方法,例如:

- 打破这可怕的围绕着艾滋病的缄默之墙;
- 改变有效抗击艾滋病所需要改变的相关文化观念;
- 扩大应对艾滋病行动的规模,包括向所有有需求的人提供治疗。

16) We need leaders everywhere to demonstrate that speaking up about AIDS is a point of pride, not a source of shame. There must be no more sticking heads in the sand, no more embarrassment, no more hiding behind a veil of apathy. Your leadership must then translate into adequate resources from national budgets. It must mobilize the entire state apparatus, from Ministries of Finance down to local governments, from Ministries of Education to Ministries of Defense. And it must generate partnerships with every sector of society—business, civil society, and people living with HIV/AIDS.

我们需要领导人在各种场合展示大胆谈论艾滋病不是一种羞辱之源,而是值得自豪的事情。不应当再将头埋到沙子里,不应当感到尴尬,也不应当隐藏到冷漠的面纱之后。你们的领导力必须体现在从国家预算中调拨充分的资源用于防治艾滋病上。应该调动从财政部到地方政府、从教育部到国防部的整个国家机器；也必须与社会各界建立伙伴关系，包括商界、公民社会、艾滋病感染者等。

17）But leadership comes not only from those who hold positions of power. Leadership comes from partners who make sure they always use a condom. Leadership comes from fathers, husbands, sons and uncles who support and affirm the rights of women.

领导力不单单来自掌权者，也来自愿意坚持使用安全套的性伙伴，来自支持并捍卫妇女权利的父亲、丈夫、儿子、叔伯、舅舅等。

18）Leadership comes from teachers who nurture the dreams and aspirations of girls. Leadership comes from doctors, nurses and counselors who listen and provide care without judgment. Leadership comes from the media who bring HIV/AIDS out of the shadows, and encourage people to make responsible choices. Leadership comes from men working to ensure that other men assume their responsibility—in abstaining from sexual behavior that puts others at risk.

领导力也来自编织女童梦想与希望的教师，来自不带评判地倾听和提供服务的医生、护士、咨询师，来自媒体——媒体让艾滋病成为可见的话题并鼓励人们做出负责任的选择，也来自男性的同伴教育者——同伴教育者要担负起责任，告诫同伴不要因性活动而给他人带来风险。

说明：同伴教育（peer education）是艾滋病预防中的常用健康教育策略。此处的 men working to ensure that other men assume their responsibility—in abstaining from sexual behavior that puts others at risk 即指同伴教育。

19）Leadership means freeing boys and men from some of the cultural stereotypes and expectations that they may be trapped in—such as the belief that men who don't show their wives "who's boss at home" are not real men; or that coming into manhood means having your sexual initiation with a sex worker when you are 13 years old.

领导力意味着将男童和男性解放出来，让他们免受文化定势思维和文化对他们的预期的影响。比如，有的文化相信男人如果不向妻子展示"在家里谁说了算"就不是真正的男子汉，有的文化相信要成为男人就要在13岁的时候和性工作者进行首次性行为。

20）Leadership means finding ways to reach out to all groups, and devising approaches for prevention and treatment that are suited to their needs—whether young people, sex workers, injecting drug users, or men who have sex with men. Leadership means daring to do things differently, because you understand that AIDS is a different kind of disease. It stands alone in human experience, and it requires us to stand united against it. I am grateful to every one of you for joining me in that mission. Thank you very much.

领导力意味着找出能够外展到所有群体的方式，并设计适合他们需求的预防和治疗方式，不管他们是年轻人、性工作者、注射吸毒者，还是男同性恋者。领导力意味着将艾滋病仅仅看作另一种疾病，大胆尝试新鲜事物。艾滋病在人类的经历中是一个独立的问题，却需要我们站在一起来共同抗击。我希望大家能和我共同加入这场斗争。谢谢。

9.2.3 总结与点评

医学会议中经常介绍疾病概况或流行病学情况,本节所选的艾滋病流行状况一段即为此类内容。此段的中英文表达方式可被"移植"到未来的会议翻译中。

科菲·安南的讲话属于有稿发言,现场讲话时,语速较快,译者可请求讲者事前提供讲稿,以便在译前做好准备。即使讲者给的并非最终版本,也有助于译者学习相关表达,并了解相关讲话要点和知识。此外,译者需注意该讲话中有较多的联合国固定表达译法,如 girl 翻译为女童,而非女孩;women 翻译为妇女,而非女人、女性。

9.2.4 词汇与表达拓展

1. 艾滋病

"Four Free and One Care" policy:"四免一关怀"政策
addiction:成瘾
anti-microbe:抗微生物制剂
bisexual:双性的
buy sex:买性,嫖娼
casual sex:随意的性行为
Center for Disease Prevention and Control (CDC):疾病预防与控制中心(疾控中心)
cissy:有娘娘腔的、柔弱胆小的、脂粉气质的男子
commercial sex:商业性行为
condom:安全套
female sex workers:女性性工作者
gay:男同性恋
heterosexual:异性的
homosexual:同性的
illegal blood collection:非法采血
injecting drug users (IDU):注射吸毒者
lesbian:女同性恋
male circumcision:男性包皮环切术
men who have sex with men (MSM):男同性恋者
multiple sex partners:多个性伙伴
needle exchange:针具交换
prevention of mother-to-child transmission (PMTCT):母婴传播阻断
prostitution:卖淫

safe sex：安全性行为
sex orientation：性取向
sex workers：性工作者
sexual intercourse：性交
single sex partner：单一性伙伴
solicitation：拉客
transmission route：传播途径[1]
unprotected sex：无保护性行为
voluntary counseling and testing (VCT)：自愿咨询与监测

2. 毒品和麻醉品

analgesic：止痛药
ecstasy：（指 methylene-dioxy-methyl-amphetamine，MDMA）摇头丸；亚甲二氧甲基安非他明
Dolantin：杜冷丁
heroin：海洛因
ice：（指 methylamphetamine）冰毒；甲基安非他明；去氧麻黄碱
k-amphetamine：K 粉；甲基安非他明；去氧麻黄碱
marijuana：大麻
opiate：鸦片类制剂
opium：鸦片
sedative：镇静剂
tranquilizer：镇静剂

3. 流行病及其他医学术语

abstinence, be loyal, condom (ABC principle)：禁欲、忠诚、安全套（ABC 原则）
acquired immune deficiency syndrome (AIDS)：获得性免疫缺陷综合征
anti-retroviral (ART) drug：抗逆转录病毒药物
antibody：抗体
bodily fluid：体液
bridge population：桥梁人群
cock-tail therapy：鸡尾酒疗法
communicable disease：传染病
contagious disease：（接触性）传染病

---

[1] 艾滋病传播途径有三条：性传播（sexual transmission）、母婴传播（mother-to-child transmission）、血液传播（blood transmission）。

第9章 公共卫生

discrimination：歧视
epidemic：流行病（的）
epidemiologist：流行病学家
epidemiology：流行病学
human immunodeficiency virus (HIV)：人类免疫缺陷病毒
incidence rate：发病率；疾病发生率
incubation period：孵化期；潜伏期
mosquito bite：蚊虫叮咬
mucosa：黏膜
negative：阳性的
onset of a disease：发病
pathogen：病原体
people living with HIV/AIDS (PLWHA)：艾滋病病毒携带者
phlebotomist：抽血员
phlegm：痰
positive：阴性的
prevalence rate：患病率；流行率；现患率
saliva：唾液
semen：精液
strain：毒株
surveillance：监测
T-cell critical volume：体细胞载量
vaccine：疫苗
vaginal secretion：阴道分泌物
virus load：病毒载量
window period：窗口期

4. 国际发展和援外机构

Australian Government Overseas Aid Program (AusAid)：澳大利亚国际发展署（澳发署）
Canadian International Development Agency (CIDA)：加拿大国际发展署
China International Development Cooperation Agency (CIDA)：国家国际发展合作署
Norwegian People's Aid (NPA)：挪威援助发展署
UK Department for International Development (DFID)：英国国际发展部
United States Agency for International Development (USAID)：美国国际发展署

5. 基金会

Bill and Melinda Gates Foundation：比尔和梅琳达·盖茨基金会

Ford Foundation：福特基金会
Global Fund Against AIDS, Tuberculosis and Malaria：全球抗击艾滋病、肺结核和疟疾基金会
Li Ka Shing Foundation：李嘉诚基金会
Sasakawa Foundation：世川基金会

6. 非政府组织

Chinese Association of Family Planning：中国计划生育协会[1]
Family Health International：家庭健康国际
Marie Stopes International：玛丽斯特普国际

9.3 烟草控制

中国是全球最大的烟草生产国，也是最大的消费国。中国人口占世界人口约20%，消费全球约30%的烟草产品。《中国吸烟危害健康报告2020》显示，我国吸烟人数超3亿，15岁及以上人群吸烟率约为26.6%。其中男性吸烟率高达50.5%。吸烟给中国的公共卫生带来了负面影响，我国已于2003年加入《烟草控制框架公约》，但履约情况不容乐观，在戒烟服务提供、服务开展和获得方面也仍然面临很多挑战。本节选编自烟草依赖治疗相关新闻报道及一位卫生官员在戒烟培训研讨会上的开幕词。

9.3.1 背景知识

《烟草控制框架公约》(the Framework Convention on Tobacco Control，FCTC): It is the world's first modern-day global public health treaty. It is also the first treaty negotiated under the auspices of the World Health Organization. The treaty entered into force in February 2005. To control tobacco use, countries can: protect people from exposure to tobacco smoke; ban tobacco advertising, promotion and sponsorship; ban tobacco sales to minors; require health warnings on tobacco packaging; promote tobacco cessation (戒烟); increase tobacco taxation; create national coordinating mechanisms for tobacco control (WHO, 2022). 2003年，中国加入了FCTC，同时制定了一系列全国性及地区性的烟草控制条例。

尼古丁依赖 (nicotine dependence): Nicotine dependence occurs when you need nicotine and can't stop using it. Nicotine is the chemical in tobacco that makes it hard to quit (戒烟). Nicotine produces pleasing effects in your brain, but these effects are temporary. So, you

---

[1] 这是与政府有关系的非政府组织，其英文为governmental non-governmental organization (GONGO)，GONGO的说法来自国外学者和实践者。

reach for another cigarette. The more you smoke, the more nicotine you need to feel good. When you try to stop, you experience unpleasant mental and physical changes. These are symptoms of nicotine withdrawal（尼古丁戒断症状）. Regardless of how long you've smoked, stopping can improve your health. It isn't easy but you can break your dependence on nicotine. Many effective treatments are available[1].

电子烟（e-cigarette）: E-cigarettes are sometimes called "e-cigs" "vapes" "e-hookahs" "vape pens" and "electronic nicotine delivery systems (ENDS)". Some e-cigarettes look like regular cigarettes, cigars, or pipes. Some look like USB flash drives, pens, and other everyday items (Centers for Disease Control and Prevention, 2022).《中国吸烟危害健康报告2020》称电子烟烟液中含有有害物质（hazardous substance），其中尼古丁会让使用者产生依赖性，还会增加心血管疾病和肺部疾病的发病风险，可能对胎儿和青少年大脑发育造成长期不良后果，导致学习障碍和焦虑症（anxiety）。电子烟气溶胶（aerosol）中的金属含量可能比可燃烟草卷烟中的多，同时二手气溶胶是一种新的空气污染源。和传统卷烟（cigarette）相比，电子烟产品常会添加不同香味，这些调味剂加热后可产生有害物质。而加味也是青少年尝试电子烟的重要原因之一。报告指出，青少年使用电子烟后成为卷烟使用者的风险，是从不使用电子烟者的2.21倍。由于大多数电子烟使用者同时使用卷烟或其他烟草制品（tobacco product），会出现两种或多种产品导致的健康危害叠加。

9.3.2 中国烟草控制

1. 相关词汇

smoking cessation：戒烟
public health：公共卫生
delivery of service：服务的开展
access of service：服务的获得
epidemiological survey：流行病学调查
smoking population：烟民群体
nicotine addiction：尼古丁成瘾
willpower：意志力
abstinence：戒断
therapy：治疗
licensed physician：注册医师
tobacco dependence therapy：烟草依赖治疗
first-line medicine：一线药物

---

1 引自妙佑医疗国际（Mayo Clinic）官方网站。

neuro-psychiatric disease：神经 – 精神疾病
drug dependence：药物依赖
addictive：成瘾的
heroin：海洛因
cocaine：可卡因
marijuana：大麻
withdrawal symptoms：戒断症状
dysphoric mood：烦躁
fatigue：疲倦
insomnia：失眠
anxiety：焦虑
restlessness：坐立不安
will：意志力
keep abstinent：保持戒断
restart smoking：复吸
fight against tobacco dependence：抗击烟草依赖
be attributable to：可以归因于
behavioral treatment：行为治疗
relieve：缓解
healthcare professional：医疗专业人士

2. 原文及参考译文一

1）最新的中国全国流行病学调查发现，如果目前的吸烟趋势继续下去，每年将有约 100 万中国人死于吸烟。该调查发现，我国吸烟者总数超过 3.5 亿，居世界第一，每年有一百万人死于烟草相关的疾病。烟草依赖是当今社会日益增长的问题，在亚洲地区尤为显著。全球研究数据表明，吸烟多年的烟民选择凭借个人意志戒烟，只有 3% 的人能保持一年以上戒烟成功率[1]。

The latest nationwide epidemiological survey in China found that about 1 million Chinese would die as a result of smoking each year if the current smoking trend continues. According to the survey, about 350 million Chinese smoke, making the country's smoking population the largest in the world. Nicotine addiction is a growing problem, particularly in Asia, and international studies show that only around 3% of smokers who attempt to stop by using willpower alone can maintain abstinence for more than one year.

2）但控烟及烟草依赖方面的专家在今天早些时候于北京举行的新闻发布会上指出，上述局面将有望得到改观。接受正规医生的指导和治疗，可以使戒烟的成功率至少翻一番。更可喜的是，近年来烟草依赖的治疗又取得了新突破。

1　选编自中国控制吸烟协会官网。

But according to experts on nicotine addiction and smoking cessation at a press conference held earlier today in Beijing, these are challenges that can be overcome. Receiving therapy under the direction of a licensed physician can at least double the success of smoking cessation. What is more inspiring is that new breakthroughs have been made in tobacco dependence therapy in recent years.

3）尽管几乎每个烟民都了解吸烟有害健康，但戒烟对大多数人而言始终是个巨大的挑战。这是因为烟草依赖其实是一种神经–精神疾病，其本质是尼古丁依赖。同海洛因成瘾一样，尼古丁依赖也属于药物依赖。事实上，尼古丁的成瘾性不亚于海洛因、可卡因，比大麻更强。

Although almost every smoker knows smoking damages their health, quitting remains a huge challenge for most individuals. This is because tobacco dependence is actually a neuropsychiatric disease, nicotine addiction. Similar to heroin addiction, nicotine dependence is a kind of drug dependence. In fact, nicotine is no less addictive than heroin or cocaine, and more addictive than marijuana.

4）正因为吸烟者形成了对尼古丁的依赖，所以一旦戒烟，往往会出现严重的戒断反应，表现为头痛、烦躁、疲倦、失眠、焦虑甚至坐立不安，这些表现与毒品的戒断症状多少有些相似。吸烟多年的烟民只凭个人意志戒烟，1年内保持成功戒烟的比例只有3%，绝大多数戒烟者都会走回复吸的老路。

When smokers dependent on nicotine try to quit smoking, serious withdrawal symptoms such as headache, dysphoric mood, fatigue, insomnia, anxiety, and even restlessness, which are more or less similar to heroin withdrawal symptoms, would occur. Among long-time smokers relying on their own will only without medication or counseling, only 3% can keep abstinent for one year, and most of them would restart smoking sooner or later.

5）和治疗其他疾病一样，要想治好烟草依赖这种疾病，最好还是去医院寻求专业的帮助。通过联合心理、行为以及药物治疗，可以很好地缓解戒断症状，大大地降低复吸率。研究表明，戒烟成功的病例中，大约有70%要归功于医生的帮助。所有药物治疗都是有利有弊的。因此，想戒烟者最好找到医生，一同选择适合他们的正确戒烟方法。

Like other diseases, the best way to fight against tobacco dependence is to seek professional help in hospital. The combined psychiatric, behavioral and medication treatments can well relieve withdrawal symptoms and hence greatly reduce the number of people who restart smoking. As studies have shown, about 70% of the successful quit cases are attributable to the help of physicians. All medications have both benefits and risks. For that reason, smokers who want to quit should speak with their doctors or healthcare professionals to determine the right treatment for them.

3. 原文、参考译文及说明二

1）Good morning, everyone. Thank you all for your participation and for your continuing dedication to tobacco control.

大家早上好,谢谢大家参加培训,感谢大家继续致力于烟草控制。

2) I am sure that you are all aware of the decision to make all health facilities in China smoke-free by the end of 2011. My counterparts from the Ministry of Health and China CDC, my WHO colleagues and I have been visiting provinces all over the country to monitor the implementation of the decision.

我相信大家都听说过 2011 年年底实现中国所有医疗卫生机构无烟化的决定。国家卫生部和中国疾病预防与控制中心以及世界卫生组织的同事们和我一同在全国各地走访和督导了此决定的执行情况。

3) In every province we have visited, we hear that it is hard to convince the visitors to the hospital, the patients and their families, not to smoke in the hospital. We hear that there is a need for cessation training for health workers who are in direct contact with patients.

在我们所到的每一个省,我们都听到,说服医院的访客、病人和探访他们的亲属不要在医院里吸烟非常困难。我们听说很有必要对直接接触病人的医护人员提供戒烟培训。

4) There must be an integrated approach to tobacco control that includes cessation. We must create smoke-free workplaces, public places and public transport, ban tobacco advertising, promotion and sponsorship, fully inform smokers and others of the harms of tobacco, especially with graphic health warnings on cigarette packs, and we must raise the price of tobacco products, so they are less affordable.

必须有一项综合的措施来控制烟草,包括戒烟。我们必须创建无烟工作场所、公共场所和公共交通工具,禁止烟草广告、促销和赞助,并告知吸烟者和他人关于烟草的危害,特别是在烟盒包装上使用逼真的健康警示。我们必须提高烟草产品的价格,使人们不能轻易地买到烟草产品。

说明:(1) graphic 意为 very clear and powerful,可被译为 "形象的,生动的,逼真的"。(2) affordable 在此处为意译。

5) You are at the cutting edge of this change. As cessation specialists, you can offer not only the best advice to your patients, but also to your colleagues. You can offer guidance and training to the health workers in your area of influence.

您正站在这种变化的最前沿。作为戒烟专家,您不仅可以为您的病人,也可以为您的同事提供最好的建议;可以在您所能影响的领域,为医护人员提供指导和培训。

6) Renowned Oxford epidemiologist Sir Richard Peto has projected that one out of every three young Chinese men alive today will die early from tobacco. China cannot afford to lose one third of its male talents. We need to work together to prevent this tragedy from becoming a reality.

著名的牛津大学流行病学家理查德·皮托爵士预测,今天活着的年轻中国男性中,每三人就有一人会因烟草相关原因过早死亡。中国损失不起三分之一的男性人才。我们需要共同努力,防止悲剧的发生。

7) Thank you again for your participation today and I wish you a productive and

successful training.

再次感谢你们今天的参与，预祝大家培训收获满满、圆满成功！

说明：结尾的祝词根据文化习惯进行了意译。

9.3.3 总结与点评

公共卫生指一个国家和地区，通过有组织的活动来预防疾病、延长生命、促进心理和身体健康，并能发挥更大潜能的科学、技术和政府职能。此外，它还指一个国家或地区中，与人类健康有关的生产和生活环境的卫生状况。公共卫生会议口译可能涉及与上述定义相关的方方面面，本节选取了一个常见的疾病防控主题——烟草控制，作为教学和练习材料，希望通过高频词汇与表达以及相关知识的总结与介绍，为学习者日后从事相关翻译打下基础。

9.3.4 词汇与表达拓展

1. 戒烟辅助药物

盐酸安非他酮：bupropion hydrochloride

尼古丁替代疗法：nicotine replacement therapy

尼古丁贴片：nicotine patch

尼古丁口胶：nicotine gum

尼古丁鼻喷剂：nicotine nasal spray

尼古丁吸入剂：nicotine inhaler

盐酸伐尼克兰：varenicline hydrochloride

2. 生理学相关名词

antagonist：拮抗剂

protagonist：激动剂

receptor：受体

参考文献

王炎强，等. 2022. 新概念大学英语口译教程. 上海：复旦大学出版社.

Centers for Disease Control and Prevention. 2022. Electronic cigarettes. *CDC*. Retrieved July 22, 2022, from CDC website.

WHO. 2022. Tobacco and the WHO Framework Convention on Tobacco Control. *WHO*. Retrieved July 22, 2022, from WHO website.

第10章

内科

10.1 肺癌靶向治疗

肺癌是目前发病率和病死率最高的恶性肿瘤,在世界范围内,每年因肺癌死亡的人数超过100万。根据临床和组织病理学特征,肺癌可以大致分为非小细胞肺癌（NSCLC, non-small-cell lung cancer）和小细胞肺癌（SCLC, small-cell lung cancer）两种类型,其中非小细胞肺癌约占全部肺癌的85%。

近年来,随着肿瘤分子生物学的不断进展,分子靶向药物（molecular target drug）正逐渐成为晚期（late-stage）非小细胞肺癌治疗中不可替代的重要手段。许多大型临床试验（clinical trials）表明,以EGFR-TKI为代表的分子靶向药物治疗可延长患者的生命,并因其毒性低（low toxicity）、使用方便越来越为患者所接受。根据EGFR突变状态选择患者接受EGFR-TKI治疗正逐渐成为大家的共识。

本节内容选自宋庆龄基金会主办的"肺YOUNG呼吸·中国肺癌精准医学好声音"系列讲座,讲者是北京协和医院呼吸内科王汉萍博士、医师。

10.1.1 背景知识

EGFR-TKI: "表皮生长因子受体酪氨酸激酶抑制剂"。EGFR（epidermal growth factor receptor）意为"表皮生长因子受体", TKI（tyrosine kinase inhibitor）意为"酪氨酸激酶抑制剂"。非小细胞肺癌患者,特别是肺腺癌（adenocarcinoma of lung）大约有30%—40%存在EGFR突变,有EGFR突变的患者服用EGFR-TKI类药物可获得很好的治疗效果。一代TKI有易瑞沙、特罗凯等;二代有阿法替尼;三代主要是奥希替尼（Osimertinib）。若是服用一、二代TKI治疗,晚期肺腺癌患者平均中位生存时间（average median survival）约为25个月。而可以服用三代TKI治疗的患者,其中位生存时间为30多个月。

PFS（progression free survival）: "无进展生存",又称"无瘤生存"。

AZD9291 (Osimertinib) Versus Platinum-based Doublet-chemotherapy in Locally Advanced or Metastatic Non-Small Cell Lung Cancer: "AZD9291（奥希替尼）与铂类双重化疗治疗局部晚期或转移性非小细胞肺癌的比较"。AZD9291是奥希替尼的代称,在药物研发阶段,为了保密等原因,不少候选药物都以代称形式指称。

T790M病人: 它在下文指非小细胞癌患者中的T790M基因突变者。

奥西替尼：药物类别为 EGFR 酪氨酸激酶抑制药；药物机制：奥西替尼能可逆地结合 EGFR 的突变形式（19 外显子缺失、L858R、T790M），通过与 EGFR 激酶区 ATP 结合域的半胱氨酸-797 残基不可逆共价结合，抑制其下游信号通路，从而发挥抑制肿瘤增殖的作用（李萍、王丽、贾乐川，2017）。

10.1.2 肺癌靶向治疗简介

1. 相关词汇

精准治疗：precise treatment

驱动基因：driver gene

敏感突变：sensitizing mutation

一线治疗：first line treatment

耐药机制：mechanism of drug resistance

EGFR 的扩增：amplification of EGFR

旁路的激活：activation of bypass pathways

EGFR 下游通路的激活：activation of EGFR downstream pathways

耐药突变：drug resistant mutation

多学科的合作：multidisciplinary cooperation

2. 原文、参考译文及说明[1]

1）作为一名肺癌的医生，我觉得自己是非常幸运的，因为我们现在正在把肺癌治疗做得越来越好，而且以后可能会更好。这得益于精准治疗在肺癌治疗领域方面的一个快速发展。现在，已经有很多驱动基因可以指导我们的治疗，那么其中表现最好的当然就是 EGFR-TKI。

As a doctor of lung cancer, I feel very fortunate because we are doing better and better in lung cancer treatment, and it may be better in the future. This is due to the rapid development of precision treatment in the field of lung cancer treatment. There are already a lot of driver genes that can guide the treatment, and of course, the best performer of all is EGFR-TKI.

2）这 10 年是 EGFR-TKI 从一代到三代发展的 10 年，这已经成为我们临床大夫治疗的一个利器。对于一些敏感突变的病人，一代和二代的 TKI 已经成为一线首选的治疗。它们带来的 PFS 持续 9 到 11 个月，但是我们并不满意这样的疗效，为什么？因为它们都会耐药，TKI 的耐药机制将是我们进一步进行精准治疗的一个关键。目前为止，我们发现 TKI 的耐药机制包括三种：第一个是在 EGFR 靶点上的变化，包括 T790M 的突变和 EGFR 的扩增。第二个是可能出现一些旁路的激活，例如 EGFR 下游通路的激活。另外，还有病理类型的转变，例如转化成小细胞。

---

[1] 该文由录音转写而成。

The decade has witnessed the development of EGFR-TKI from the first generation to the third generation, and it has become a useful tool for our clinicians. For some patients with sensitive mutations, the first and second generations of TKI have become the best choices. They bring the PFS from 9 to 11 months, but still, we are not satisfied with this effect. Why? Because they are all resistant. TKI's resistance mechanism will be the main challenge to the further development of precision treatment. So far, we have found three TKI resistance mechanisms. The first is due to changes in the EGFR targets, including T790M mutations and EGFR amplification. The second is due to the possible activation of some bypasses, such as the activation of the downstream pathway of EGFR. There are also transformations of pathological types, such as transformation into small-cell lung cancer.

说明："旁路的激活"可被译为 activation of bypass pathways（Huang & Fu，2015）。

3）在这些耐药机制中，最突出的就是T790M突变，占总耐药机制的50%—60%。俗话说："彼之砒霜，己之蜜糖。"虽然T790M是一个耐药突变，（但）幸好我们现在已经有了三代的TKI——奥希替尼。通过一系列AURA试验已经奠定了它在T790M病人身上首选的治疗地位。所以说，找出T790M突变对于病人来讲非常重要，因为如果使用奥希替尼，意味着又将赢得一个一年左右生活质量比较好的缓解期。

Among these resistance mechanisms, the most prevalent is the T790M mutation, which accounts for 50% of the total resistance cases. As the saying goes, "One man's trash is another man's treasure." Although T790M is a drug-resistant mutation, fortunately, we now have the third generation of TKI—Osimertinib, which has already established its position as a preferred choice for T790M patients through a series of AURA experiments. Therefore, finding the T790M mutation is very important for patients because if it is present, you can put the patient on Osimertinib, which means that your patient will win a one-year-or-so remission with higher life quality.

说明：（1）"突出"不能被直译为 prominent，《柯林斯高级英语学习词典（第五版）》将其解释为：Something that is prominent is very noticeable or is an important part of something else. 后文又说到其实是其比例较高，达50%，所以将其翻译为 prevalent 更妥。该词典将 prevalent 解释为：A condition, practice, or belief that is prevalent is common.（2）"耐药机制"在此处实际上指出现了耐药的病例。（3）"缓解期"被译为 remission。该词典将其解释为：If someone who has had a serious disease such as cancer is in remission or if the disease is in remission, the disease has been controlled so that they are not as ill as they were. 例句：Brain scans have confirmed that the disease is in remission. 可以将其与 relapse（复发）进行比较。（4）很多靶向抗癌药物都有 -nib 这个后缀，它的意思是小分子抑制剂，如 -tinib 意为 tyrosine kinase inhibitors，-anib 意为 angiogenesis（血管生成）inhibitors，rafenib 意为 rapidly accelerated fibrosarcoma（纤维瘤，RAF) kinase（激酶）inhibitors。（5）延伸与补充：凡是以 -mab 结尾的词均为单克隆抗体类（mono-clonal antibody）药物。

4）我们临床大夫应该在这种三代耐药之后进行一个再次活检，也许哪一天我们就发现了你的驱动基因。TKI 耐药之后组织再活检的意义是非常重大的。对于病人来讲，通过组织活检获得一个精准的耐药机制信息可以指导用药，他们能够得到更好的、一个更精准的治疗，可以带来更多生的希望。

We, as clinical doctors, should perform a re-biopsy in the case of resistance after the use of third-generation drugs. Perhaps a patient's driver gene would be found. Tissue biopsy after the occurrence of resistance after using TKI is very significant. For patients, the precise information obtained from tissue biopsy on drug resistance mechanisms can guide medication, thus bringing more hope to the living.

说明：（1）"三代耐药"意为"对第三代药物耐药"。（2）"也许哪一天我们就发现了你的驱动基因"中"你的"指的是一个病人的。（3）"活检"被译为 biopsy；"组织再活检"被译为 re-biopsy of tissues。

5）对于医生来讲，二次活检的过程可以提高我们的临床技能，更精准地治疗病人之后可以提高你的医疗能力，同时通过多学科的合作也能提高（本）科室和其他科室的各种能力；另外，也许能够建立医院自己的数据库，临床科研的素材也会更加充分，这整个过程最终能够推动科室和医院的整体发展，乃至推动精准医学的发展。

For doctors, the process of the second biopsy can improve our clinical skills. The precise treatment of patients can improve your expertise, and multidisciplinary cooperation can also improve your own department and other departments' ability. Perhaps the hospital's database can be established, and there would be more sufficient clinical research material/data. This whole process will eventually promote the overall development of the departments and the hospital and even promote the development of precision medicine.

10.1.3 总结与点评

本节内容节选自学术演讲，内容逻辑结构比较清晰。首先，是引入部分，说明 EGFR-TKI 作为精准医疗手段治疗肺癌的效果显著；其次，说明 EGFR-TKI 具有抗药性的缺陷。第二部分说明 EGFR-TKI 有三种抗药机制，其中 T790M 突变是最主要的一种耐药机制。最后，研究者提出，由于 EGFR-TKI 的耐药性，医生需要进行二次活检，而二次活检对于医生、病人、科室乃至医院都是有益的。

若进行交传，本节内容记忆会有一些困难，因为中间部分信息量大且密集，因此在记笔记的时候，译者一定要按逻辑结构来记并且要善于用逻辑符号；如果在笔记中使用大量汉字会加重记忆负担。虽然演讲人语速不快，但讲话逻辑不是特别清晰，这也造成了记忆困难。

在译文表达方面，如果将内容提炼出来，本节内容可以用简单的英文句式表达。但如果演讲人在讲话中使用重复的、逻辑关系不是很明确的长句，译者在听的时候需要多加注意；如果译文表达不脱离原文的外壳，表达出来的也必定是没有逻辑的长句，这会大大增加表达的难度。因此，译者在听的时候要注意把重点意思提取出来，再用合适的英文句式来表达。

10.2 多发性骨髓瘤

多发性骨髓瘤（multiple myeloma，MM）是一种以浆细胞终末分化、浆细胞浸润骨髓以及血清和/或尿液中存在单克隆球蛋白（或免疫球蛋白片段）为特征的浆细胞病。在2015年，全球约有48.8万人患有多发性骨髓瘤，其中101 100人因此死亡（Hallek, Bergsagel & Anderson, 1998）。

2014年，国际骨髓瘤工作组（International Myeloma Working Group，IMWG）更新了骨髓瘤的诊断标准，增加了三种可用于诊断无CRAB特征[1]患者疾病的特异性生物标志物：克隆性骨髓浆细胞大于或等于60%；在相关FLC水平为100mg/L或更高的情况下，高血清游离轻链（serum free light hain，FLC）比率大于或等于100；或在MRI结果中发现一个以上的局灶性病变。此外，它还对定义进行了修订，以便使用CT和PET-CT诊断骨髓瘤骨病。这些变化使早期诊断并开始有效的治疗以防止风险最高的患者发生末端器官损伤成为可能。

10.2.1 背景知识

浆细胞终末分化（terminal differentiation of plasma cell）：浆细胞谱系中的最后状态，细胞变得静止或只产生同样类型的后代。

浆细胞浸润骨髓（infiltration of plasma cells into bone marrow）：骨髓内浸入了浆细胞，某些病变组织向周围扩展的现象。

单克隆免疫球蛋白（monoclonal globulin）：单克隆浆细胞分泌的结构均一的免疫球蛋白或多肽链亚单位（轻链），又称M蛋白。

浆细胞病（plasma cell dyscrasias）：又称异常蛋白血症，单克隆免疫球蛋白生产细胞过度增殖，产生过多的单克隆免疫球蛋白所致的疾病，多伴有肾脏损害。

恶性浆细胞（malignant plasma cell）：正常浆细胞由于受到致癌因子的作用，不能正常完成细胞分化，因而变成了不受机体控制的、连续进行分裂的恶性浆细胞。

游离轻链（free light chain）：免疫球蛋白中分子量较小的游离肽链，含214个氨基酸，根据其结构和恒定区抗原性的差异分为κ轻链（kappa light chain）和λ轻链（lambda light chain）两种型别。

回顾（性）分析（retrospective study）：事件发生后，通过回顾访查方法，从事件的结果反推分析和探索其发生原因及规律的一类研究。

前瞻性研究（prospective study）：在临床研究方案中预设诊断或疗效标准，对非主观选定、自然顺序患者进行试验和随访，在原定计划的时间内结束研究，对结果进行客观评估的试验方法。实际评估结果独立于预期目标，能有效避免偏倚。

---

[1] 一种既包括标准的实验室预后标志物又包括高危细胞遗传学异常的新的分期系统也已经开发出来。

10.2.2 多发性骨髓瘤治疗进展简介

1. 相关词汇

多发性骨髓瘤：multiple myeloma
血液系统恶性肿瘤：hematological malignancies
国际骨髓瘤工作组：International Myeloma Working Group
微小残留病变：micro residual disease (MRD)

2. 原文、参考译文及说明

1）多发性骨髓瘤是一种血液系统恶性肿瘤。根据欧美的统计数据，它是血液系统中第二常见的恶性肿瘤，仅次于淋巴瘤。虽然我国还没有相关统计数据，但近年来多发性骨髓瘤在全球的发病率增高。幸运的是，近年来，在多发性骨髓瘤研究方面，科学界所取得的成果也非常显著。

Multiple myeloma (MM) is a hematological malignancy. According to the statistics from Europe and America, it is the second most common malignant tumor of the blood system, second only to lymphoma. Although we do not have statistical data on the MM prevalence in China, the incidence rate of MM in recent years has increased if we look at the global data. Fortunately, the achievements in the research of MM in recent years are also significant.

说明：（1）在医学口译中，一些术语由于发音比较复杂，译者往往在首次提及时使用全称，之后就用简称指代。本段译文中的 MM 指代 multiple myeloma。（2）malignant tumor、malignancy、cancer 都可以指代恶性肿瘤；tumor 指肿瘤，既可以是良性（benign）肿瘤，也可以是恶性肿瘤。（3）英语中表示成果显著的核心名词为 achievement。与 achievement 搭配的形容词和短语有 considerable、extraordinary、fine、great、important、impressive、major、no mean、notable、outstanding、real、remarkable、significant、tremendous 等。例句：This was no mean achievement for the government.

2）从这张幻灯片中，我们可以看到最近几十年骨髓瘤患者的生存情况变化。从 1971 年到 1995 年，骨髓瘤患者的生存情况是比较差的，中位生存时间不超过三年。

From this slide, we can see the change of the survival of MM patients in the recent decades. The survival was poor between 1971 and 1995, with a median survival time of no more than three years.

说明：（1）"生存情况"中的"情况"属于范畴词，可不译。（2）"比较差"中"比较"的使用是为了避免绝对化，可不译。

3）但随着近年来在临床诊疗和<u>科学研究</u>等方面所取得的进展，骨髓瘤患者的中位生存时间已经增加到了 88 个月。

However, with the advances in clinical care and <u>research</u> in recent years, the median survival time has increased to 88 months.

说明："科学研究"既可被译为 scientific research，也可被译为 research。此处，译者按照口译译文的简练原则,将其译为 research。

4)从 1995 年至今,从不到三年猛增到了 88 个月,这可以算得上是在多发性骨髓瘤治疗方面所取得的一个显著成就。

The median survival time has increased drastically from less than three years in 1995 to 88 months now. It can be said that it is one of the most outstanding achievements in the field of MM treatment.

5)为什么能够取得如此显著的成就呢?我想,这要得益于骨髓瘤的各方面的研究成果,包括诊断标准的改善、疗效评判标准的改善,以及预后预测因素的变化。此外,还需要特别提到的是诸多新药和新的治疗策略的相继问世。这些让我们感到骨髓瘤治疗的未来还是非常光明的。

Why could such remarkable achievement be made? I think the credits go to the research outcomes of various aspects of myeloma, including better diagnosis criteria, outcome criteria, as well as changes in the prognostic factors of myeloma. Besides, it is worth noting that many drugs and new treatment modalities had emerged. Altogether, they bring us more hope for curing MM.

说明:(1)criteria 是 criterion 的复数形式,其另一种复数形式是 criterions,无 criterias 这一用法。(2)对于原文最后一句,译者采用了改变叙事主体的方法,将原文的"我们"视角下的感受改为用 they 指代前文所述的种种研究成果。

6)我们首先来看一下诊断标准变化。最新的诊断标准是在 2014 年由国际骨髓瘤工作组所发布的。它和以往的诊断标准共识不一样的地方就在这三条,幻灯片里用红色字体显示出来了。这三条分别是:骨髓中恶性浆细胞超过 10%,游离轻链的比值超过 100,用 MRI 检测到 1 毫米以上、5 毫米以下的骨髓损害。这三条标准,如果病人符合其中任意一条及以上,<u>即使病人没有症状也要进行治疗</u>。这是与以往的诊断标准共识的主要差异。

Let's first look at the changes for diagnostic criteria for MM. The latest diagnosis criteria were released by the International Myeloma Working Group in 2014. It is different from the previous consensus on the diagnostic criteria in the three items marked in red in the slide. They are: There are more than 10% of malignant plasma cells in the marrow; The ratio of free light chains exceeds 100; One marrow damage larger than one millimeter and smaller than five millimeters is detected by MRI. If the patient meets one or more of the three criteria, <u>even if there are no symptoms</u>, he/she should receive treatment. This is the main difference compared with the previous consensus on diagnostic criteria.

说明:注意比较原文和译文中的画线部分。译文省略了 patient,用 there be 结构来体现有无,目的是避免 patient 在同一句话中的重复使用。

7)以往多发性骨髓瘤诊断后,要到患者有症状的时候才开始治疗。但现在只要有上述情况之一,即使没有症状,也要进行治疗。

In the past, the treatment only started as one is diagnosed with MM and has developed symptoms. Now, with any one of these conditions, the patient needs to receive treatment even if he/she has no symptoms.

说明：与 symptom 搭配的动词及短语有 display、exhibit、experience、have、present with、report、show、suffer from 等。

8）为什么会产生这种变化呢？因为科学家们通过回顾性研究发现，只要患者有上述的三个情况之一，两年内，患者中出现<u>疾病进展</u>的比例就可以达到 70% 到 90%。如果说等疾病已经带来了多器官损害才进行治疗的话，<u>治疗效果</u>往往不佳。一些器官损害往往是不可逆的。

Why? It is because that through retrospective analysis, it was found that in the patients that have one of the above conditions, 70 to 90 percent would <u>develop cancer</u> (or MM) within two years. If a patient already has multiple organ damages before undergoing treatment, the <u>treatment outcomes</u> are often sub-optimal. Some of the organ damages are often irreversible.

说明：（1）"疾病进展"指患多发性骨髓瘤，所以被译为 develop cancer。cancer 在此指多发性骨髓瘤。（2）"治疗效果"可被直译为 treatment effect，但业内常用 treatment outcomes，即用治疗结果或结局来指代的用法更为普遍。

9）这个诊断标准的改变给临床实践带来什么样的变化呢？它带来的变化主要是对于 10% 的病人来讲，原来是不需要这么早治疗的，现在需要对他们提前进行治疗，这样可以避免他们出现贫血、骨损害、肾功能损害等<u>并发症</u>。

What have the changes in the diagnostic criteria brought to the clinical practice? The changes are as follows. Most importantly, 10% of patients who, in the past, did not need such early treatment need it now. Such early treatment can avoid some <u>complications</u>, like anemia, bone damage, kidney damage, and so on.

10）患者的寿命，从无进展生存来看也得到了延长。至于 <u>OS</u> 是否有延长，现在还没有文献报道。但可以肯定的是，至少对 <u>PFS</u> 是有积极影响的。

In terms of progression-free survival, patients' life has been extended, but whether there is an extension to OS (overall survival), there is no literature that reported it. But, we are sure that at least it has a positive impact on PFS.

说明：（1）OS 指 overall survival，即"总体生存期"。（2）PFS 指 progression-free survival，即"无进展生存期"。

11）我们再来看下一个进步，那就是有关多发性骨髓瘤疗效标准的变化。这些变化出现在 2014 年发布的国际骨髓瘤工作组共识中。疗效标准的变化在于，和以往相比，除了依据传统的完全缓解之外，还增加了依据 MRD，也就是微小残留病变的检测结果。MRD 检测可通过流式细胞术、新一代测序技术以及影像学（CT）来进行。

Now, let's look at the next advance. It is the change in the outcome criteria for the disease, which appeared in the International Myeloma Working Group consensus (on diagnostic criteria) released in 2014. The difference from the past in terms of the outcome criteria is that, in addition to the conventionally used "complete remission", the test results for MRD, or micro residual disease, was also added. MRD detection could be done through flow cytometry, next-generation gene sequencing, and radiological investigations like CT.

12）用 MRD 来描述疗效对判断病人的生存预后有什么影响呢？我们从这条生存曲线可以看出，假如患者通过治疗，MRD 结果转阴，并持续转阴，那么患者在第 120 个月的时候还是处在生存状态。

What is the impact of using MRD to describe a patient's outcome? We can see from the survival curve that if the patient becomes MRD negative after treatment and continues to be MRD negative, he/she is still alive at the 120th month.

13）那就是说，如果经过治疗能够使微小残留病变都转阴，而且一直持续转阴性，可以预计病人的生存期会达到十年或者十年以上。这样的恶性肿瘤病人现在能存活十年以上，而以前这样的恶性肿瘤病人生存时间不超过三年。这是一个非常巨大的进步。

That is to say, if after the treatment, the micro residual disease results become negative in a sustained way, it can be expected that the patient can survive for ten years or more. For such a malignant tumor, now the patient can live for more than ten years. It represents an enormous improvement as the survival time was no more than three years in the past.

10.2.3 总结与点评

本节练习以多发性骨髓瘤的诊断和疗效标准变化的讲话口译为例，介绍了肿瘤诊疗和研究常用的词汇和句型的译法。肿瘤相关的学术会议较多，本节介绍的相关知识有助于学习者开展会议口译工作。在准备此类学术性较强的会议口译过程中，除了研读讲者的幻灯片，学习者还可通过会议相关主题词查找相关学术论文进行研读，以便了解主题相关背景知识、常用词汇和句型等。

10.3 心脏康复

心脏康复指使心脏病患者功能与结构改善、体力与精神优化、社会参与程度提高并预防心血管事件发生的康复评估、运动训练、饮食与行为模式转变、遵医依从性（compliance）等多种具有目的性的协同干预措施（马普亚，2015）。运动训练方式包括有氧运动（aerobics / aerobic exercises）、无氧运动（anaerobic exercises）、抗阻训练（resistance training）、耐力训练（endurance training）等。本节讲话主题是高风险患者的心脏康复，选自瑞士巴米韦德（Barmelweid）诊所的让－保尔·施密德（Jean-Paul Schmid）博士讲话。讲话介绍了高风险患者的辨识和管理等内容。

10.3.1 背景知识

纽约心脏协会分级Ⅲ级（New York Heart Association Class Ⅲ）：指根据纽约心脏协会开发的心血管功能和失能（cardiovascular function and disability）分级系统中两种最严重

（severe）的心功能不全（cardiac dysfunction）等级之一。Ⅲ级定义如下：心脏病患者活动受限明显，但休息时自感舒适；较轻微的体力活动也会导致症状。

博格评分（Borg scale）：一种评价呼吸困难程度的方法，通过 0—10 分描述呼吸困难强度的量表。测量时，要求受试者对呼吸不适的总体感觉给分，0 分代表完全没有呼吸困难感觉，而 10 分代表能想象到的最严重的呼吸困难感觉。

P 波（P waves）：P 波代表心房去极化（atrial depolarization）。在正常心电图中，P 波先于 QRS 波群（QRS complex）。它看起来像是从基线向上的一个小凸起，波幅（amplitude）通常为 0.05 至 0.25mV [0.5 至 2.5 个小格子（small boxes）]，正常持续时间为 0.06—0.12 秒（1.5 到 2.75 个小格子），形状通常是平滑的、圆形的（rounded）。

心肌梗死（myocardial infarction，MI）：指血液流动受阻（blockage of blood flow），导致心肌组织死亡。梗死发生在给心脏本身供血的动脉，即冠状动脉（coronary artery）。根据心肌组织受损的程度不同，心梗患者有可能存活并接受心脏康复治疗（cardiac rehabilitation），以增强剩余心肌的功能；也可因大量心肌组织受损而死亡。心肌梗死在日常英文中表述为 heart attack，字面意思是"心脏病发作"。

二尖瓣脱垂、狭窄、反流（mitral prolapse, stenosis, regurgitation）：心脏有四个腔室（chambers），每一侧的心房（atria）与心室（ventricle）由单向瓣膜（one-way valve）分隔，以使血液单向流过。左房室尤其重要，因为从肺部返回的新鲜含氧血液（oxygenated blood）会从心脏左侧循环到（circulated out of the heart）身体的其他部位。分隔心房与心室的瓣膜被称为房室瓣（atrioventricular valve），左侧的房室瓣也被称为二尖瓣（mitral valve）[1]。如果这个瓣膜的瓣叶（flap）因疾病而撕裂（tear away），这个过程被称为脱垂（prolapse），脱垂方向为血流方向，即心室侧。这将导致血液渗漏（leakage）和倒流（back flow），即反流（regurgitation）。有时，瓣膜异常狭窄（stenosis），造成部分阻塞。

心律失常（arrhythmia/dysrhythmia[2]）：指异常的心率和心律。心率是指心脏每分钟跳动的次数；心律是指心脏跳动的节律，意思是心脏跳动的规则性。心律失常包括室性心动过速（ventricular tachycardia）、心房颤动（atrial fibrillation）等。

心房扑动（atrial flutter）：是一种由心脏电系统问题引起的心律失常。发生心房扑动时，心房跳动节奏过快，导致心脏以快速但通常有规律的节奏跳动（Anon，2022a）。

心脏再同步治疗（cardiac resynchronization therapy，CRT）：是使用起搏器植入方式来帮助心脏恢复正常节律的治疗（Anon，2022d）。术中在右心房和左、右心室分别放置三根起搏导线（lead），在皮下（subcutaneously）埋入一个起搏器（pacemaker）。后者通过同时发送脉冲（pulse）来激活左心室和右心室，使左心室和右心室同时（synchronically）收缩，同步工作，纠正双心室收缩不协调，增加心输出量（cardiac output），从而改善心力衰竭（heart failure）症状。它需要将起搏导线放置在三腔中，所以又被称为三腔起搏器（three-chamber pacemaker）。

---

1 因其形状像倒置的主教帽（mitre = bishop's hat）而得此英文名。
2 这两个英文术语之间有细微的区别，但常交替使用。

二氧化碳通气当量斜率[1]（VE/VCO$_2$ slope）：指在运动试验（exercise testing）中获得的二氧化碳通气当量斜率（minute ventilation-carbon dioxide production slope）。反映通气效率（ventilatory efficiency）对心力衰竭具有预测价值。VE-VCO$_2$关系通常是线性的，因此无论用于计算的运动试验时间间隔多长，按照理论假设，都会产生类似的斜率值（Arena, Humphrey & Peberdy, 2003）。

乳酸阈（lactate threshold）：又称乳酸阈值，是划分有氧运动和无氧运动的临界点（threshold），在这个临界强度（intensity）以下的运动是有氧运动，而在这个临界强度以上的运动属于无氧运动。

陈－施呼吸（Cheyne-Stokes respiration）：是一种特殊形式的周期性呼吸（periodic breathing）[流量或潮气量的振幅增减（waxing and waning amplitude of flow or tidal volume）]，具有中枢性呼吸暂停（central apneas）或中枢性低通气（central hypopneas）之间呼吸呈渐增、渐减（crescendo-decrescendo）的规律（Rudrappa, Modi & Bollu, 2022）。

活性（ergoreflex）：指静息状态时通气（ventilation at rest）与运动后即刻通气（ventilation just after exercise）之间的呼吸生理学（respiratory physiology）差异。

变时性功能不全（chronotropic incompetence）：广义上被定义为心脏无法增加与活动或需求增加相称（commensurate with）的心率，常见于心血管疾病患者，产生运动不耐受（exercise intolerance），影响生活质量，是主要心血管不良事件（adverse cardiovascular events）和总体死亡率的独立预测因子（independent predictor）（Kitzman, 2013）。

10.3.2 高风险患者的心脏康复

1. 相关词汇

  brain natriuretic peptide (BNP)：脑钠肽
  extended coronary artery disease：扩展性冠状动脉疾病
  hypertension：高血压
  ejection fraction：射血分数
  echocardiography：超声心动图检查
  electrocardiogram (ECG/EKG)[2]：心电图
  restrictive filling pattern during diastole：舒张期限制性充盈模式
  left ventricular diameter：左心室内径
  mitral regurgitation：二尖瓣反流
  tricuspid regurgitation：三尖瓣反流

---

[1] 实际汉语医学交流中，因为简洁，"VE/VCO$_2$斜率"的使用非常普遍。
[2] electro- 意为"电"；cardio- 意为"心脏"；-gram 意为"图像"。ECG 为这三部分构词成分的首字母。临床上因为手写体的 C 容易被看成 e，导致 ECG 与 EEG（electroencephalogram，脑电图）混淆，故也使用 EKG 来表示 ECG，其中的 K 是因为 cardio- 中字母 c 的发音为 /k/。

right ventricular dilated：右心室扩张
post-acute myocardial infarction (MI) patient：急性心肌梗死后的患者
arrhythmia：心律失常
chronic heart failure：慢性心力衰竭
conditional cardiac surgery：择期心脏手术
post cardiotomy syndrome：心脏切开术后综合征
pericardial effusion：心包积液
valvular heart disease：瓣膜性心脏病
atrioventricular (AV) conduction problem：房室传导问题
chronic obstructive pulmonary disease (COPD)：慢性阻塞性肺病
oxygen saturation during exercise：运动时的氧饱和度
pulmonary auscultation：肺听诊
diuretic：利尿剂
fluid homeostasis：体液稳态
exercise intensity：运动强度
hypotension：低血压
fluid elimination：液体排出
laboratory value：实验室值
cardiopulmonary exercise testing：心肺运动试验
exercise prescription：运动处方
periodic breathing：周期性呼吸
implantable cardioverter-defibrillators (ICD) implantation：植入式心律转复除颤器植入
oscillatory ventilation：振荡通气
ventilatory efficiency：通气效率
Cheyne-Stokes respiration：陈－施呼吸，Cheyne-Stokes 呼吸
advanced heart rate：快速的心率
chronotropic incompetence：变时性功能不全
oxygen pulse：氧脉搏
ventricular function：心室功能
lactate threshold：乳酸阈
remodeling：重塑
negative remodeling：负性重构
systolic dysfunction：收缩功能障碍
cardiac decompensation of the exercise：运动性心脏失代偿
catabolic state：分解代谢状态
skeletal muscle atrophy：骨骼肌萎缩
respiratory muscle atrophy：呼吸肌萎缩

increased ergoreflex activity：运动反射活性增加
sympathetic activation：交感神经激活
treatment modality：治疗方式
left ventrical (LV) function：左心室功能
atrial fibrillation：心房颤动 [1]
ventricular arrhythmia：室性心律失常

2. 原文、参考译文及说明 [2]

1）Thank you very much. Dear chairperson, dear colleagues, thank you for the very kind invitation. It's also the second time I'm here to have the opportunity to talk to you about the specific topic of cardiac rehabilitation, which, this time, is cardiac rehabilitation in high-risk patients. High risk, probably, if you talk about high risk, it is about heart failure, but sometimes other problems can occur, which is not only related to left ventricular function. Now, if we talk about training rehabilitation, we also mostly talk about exercise. Let's just stress the point that rehabilitation, if you talk about rehabilitation, should always be multidisciplinary, so it is not only about exercise. Exercise is the core of the rehab but it should be multidisciplinary, and we know from the other slide we have seen today, the recommendation of rehabilitation and exercise in heart failure patients is Class-I Level-A evidence, so it's very good multi-center trial evidence about exercise.

非常感谢您。亲爱的大会主席、亲爱的同事们，感谢你们的盛情邀请。这是我第二次来到这里并有幸与你们专门交流有关心脏康复中的一个特定话题，这一次我要谈的是高危患者的心脏康复。当你们说到高风险的时候，想到的一般是心力衰竭，但有时也会出现左心室功能以外的其他问题。如今，谈到康复训练，我们也主要关注运动。我要强调一点，那就是康复，它应该是多学科的，不只包括运动。运动是康复的核心，但它应该是多学科的，对吧？我们今天已经从另一张幻灯片里看到了，对心力衰竭患者的康复和锻炼的建议是Ⅰ类推荐A级的证据。

说明：rehab 即 rehabilitation。

2）Now when we say "multidisciplinary", what should we talk about? If we say multidisciplinary, we have a specific standard within the program, which is the organization of the assessment of the patients in the hospital, and then sending the patients to the rehab clinic. So, it has to be well-organized, and it has to have a system within there. And this allows the best outcome for the patients with all the components of cardiac rehabilitation we normally know.

那么，当我们说多学科的时候，我们指的是什么呢？它指的就是，我们在心脏康复项目上有一个具体的标准，就是关于如何组织医院内的患者进行评估，然后把患者转到康复门诊去的

1　可简称房颤。
2　该文由录音转写而成。

标准。因此，它必须精心组织，并形成系统。这样才能让患者得到心脏康复应有的各种治疗，并获得最好的结果。

说明：（1）multidisciplinary 指 interdisciplinary treatment，即"多学科治疗"。（2）此处的 the program 指 heart rehabilitation program，需要注意 program 一词在临床、医院管理中的使用方式及含义。例如，"The clinical programs in the hospital have all been ranked high in a certain ranking."的字面含义为"该医院的多个临床项目在某排名中位居榜首。"临床项目，其实质内容在中国的语境下是存在的，但中文常用的表达方式有所不同，此处更恰当的翻译应为"该医院在疾病诊疗方面处于世界领先地位"。

3）Now what is important if you talk about high-risk patients? It is to determine what is the risk in a patient, and you have to get a <u>picture</u> of your patient. You have to know what the risk is, and there are some criteria with which you can judge the risk. For example, if you see a patient who has a functional classification of New York Heart Association Class Ⅲ, he has an elevated BNP; he has an extended coronary artery disease and hypertension, and his ejection fraction is 25%. The echo shows you a restrictive filling pattern during diastolic. The left ventricular diameter is increased. He has severe mitral regurgitation as well as tricuspid regurgitation, and the right ventricular is dilated. He has an elevated pulmonary pressure, and he has a low exercise capacity, and a high VE/VCO$_2$ slope. This is a high-risk patient. And if you see these values, then you know you have to be very cautious training this patient. If you have a patient who has not all these very important risk factors, it is a little bit of another story. So, making a whole picture and an initial assessment is very important.

现在，如果你们谈到高危患者，最重要的是什么呢？那就是确定患者的风险是什么，而这时你需要了解你的患者的整体情况。你需要知道他／她的风险，有一些标准可以来帮助我们判断风险。例如，如果你看到一个患者的纽约心脏病协会心功能分级是Ⅲ级，他的 BNP 升高，有长期的冠心病和高血压，射血分数是 25%，超声显示舒张期的充盈受限，左室内径增大，有严重的二尖瓣反流和三尖瓣反流，且右心室扩大，肺动脉压升高，运动耐量降低，且 VE/VCO$_2$ 斜率升高，这就意味着这是一个高风险的患者，如果你看到这些数值，那么你就会知道你训练这个患者时需要非常谨慎。如果你有一个患者没有任何上述非常重要的危险因素，那么情况则不同。所以，在起始阶段进行评估、了解总体情况是非常重要的。

说明：（1）此处的 picture 指代情况。（2）在实际医学交流中，医生往往采用最经济、最省力的方式来传递信息，因此临床对话和相关学术讲座中常常出现讲者中英文夹杂使用及使用英文缩略语、汉语缩略语等情况，如 BNP、VE/VCO$_2$。此外，这部分内容包含较多术语，但均出现在幻灯片中，译员应在译前对幻灯片进行充分查阅，制作对应的术语表。

4）When we talk about high-risk patients, there are different types of patients. We can have the post-acute myocardial infarction patient. This is a patient who has some kind of risk of arrhythmia. He has probably, if it's high-risk, reduced ejection fraction, which is the main problem in this patient. You can have a patient with chronic heart failure, and then you know that probably his problem is not an acute event. This is another picture of this patient:

He probably has decreased exercise capacity and decreased left ventricular function, but it's a little bit different from the post-acute myocardial infarction patient. Then you have patients with the status of <u>conditional cardiac surgery</u>. In these patients, you can have complications of surgery. You can have postcardiotomy syndrome; you can have pericardial effusion; you can have anemia, bleeding, so and so on. So, this is now the risk profile; so, this is now the picture again. And then you have patients with valvular heart disease. Here also... These are patients with post-surgical complications, but you also know that these patients can have AV conduction problems, so this is another risk. And this underlines the importance of having a picture of your patient, and you know: Is it the post-acute MI patients? Is it chronic heart failure? Has he had surgery? Which are the complications? This is very important.

我们谈到高危患者时，要清楚他们是分不同类型的。我们会遇到急性心肌梗死后的患者。这是一个有某种心律失常风险的患者。如果是高风险，他可能有射血分数的降低，这是这个患者的主要问题。你会遇到慢性心力衰竭的患者，你会知道他的问题可能不是急性事件。这位患者的另一方面情况是：他的运动耐量可能降低，左心室功能降低，但这与急性心肌梗死后的患者略有不同。然后，你还会遇到择期心脏手术的患者。这些患者可能会出现手术的并发症，可能出现心脏切开术后综合征、心包积液、贫血、出血等。这是对风险进行一个勾画，再次呈现患者的情况。你还会遇到心脏瓣膜病的患者，还有……这些是有术后并发症的患者，相信大家都知道这些患者可能有房室传导问题，这是这类患者的另一个风险。这些例子强调了了解患者整体情况的重要性。你得知道这是不是一个急性心肌梗死后的患者、是不是慢性心力衰竭患者、是否接受过手术、有哪些并发症，这一点非常重要。

说明：（1）此处，讲者用 conditional cardiac surgery 指代 elective cardiac surgery，意为"择期心脏手术"。（2）这一段术语较多，译员应做好译前准备，方法同前一段。

5）When you know these, then you have, on the one side, the risk associated with the <u>baseline disease</u>, and then, other risk associated with comorbidities. So, <u>has this patient renal failure</u>? Has this patient COPD? What is his oxygen saturation during exercise? So, this completes your picture and gives you an image of your high-risk patient.

当你知道了这些，那么你就会知道与基础疾病相关的风险，还有与患有并发症相关的其他风险。患者有没有肾功能衰竭？有没有慢性阻塞性肺病？他运动时的氧饱和度是多少？这些都能为你补充高危患者的信息，让你更全面地了解患者。

说明：（1）此处，讲者用 baseline disease 表示基础性疾病，此术语更常见的表达是 the underlying disease。（2）注意：此处，讲者的表达方式从语法上看较为随意，更严谨的表达方式为：... has the patient got/suffered from...

6）Now, what is special in high-risk patients? What differentiates the high-risk patient from the ordinary one? Of course, first of all, it is the reduced exercise capacity. So, these patients are unable to train very well, with training to be taken at low intensity. And this is not the risk in itself, but it shows you that the high risk, in general, is low exercise capacity, and accordingly, the exercise prescription has to be adapted. Certainly, these patients require more intensive medical supervision. If you have the example of the first patient, it's sure you have to see this patient every time he goes to exercise; you have to be sure that he is compensated, that his pulmonary auscultation is good, he's not in a pre-lung edema status to be sure that he has no arrhythmia. And you have to evaluate his progress very often. I mean a patient who has few symptoms and who progresses and does better during exercise. He's doing well, even though he has high risk. If a patient is not progressing after three, four, or five weeks, although he is well trained, you have to ask yourself what is the problem behind it. There's something that is going wrong. And the frequent problems of these patients are hypotension. You can imagine these patients with low ejection fraction on diuretics therapy, hypotensive, and not very well. So, sometimes you have to interrupt cardiac rehabilitation, and optimize medication for optimized diuretics to improve hypotensive symptoms. Dyspnea, if you have lung disease in particular, it's very difficult for these patients to do exercise, but you just try to make what is possible. You stay at low intensity, and always follow the symptoms of your patient. If he is able to do it, it's right; when he gets more dyspnea, you have to go down with the exercise intensity and keep the fluid homeostasis. As I have said, it is very important, and particularly you have to pay attention to also the problem of hypotension linked with fluid elimination.

那么，对于高危患者来说，有什么特殊的呢？高危患者与普通患者有何不同？首先，是运动耐量的降低，所以这些患者不能很好地进行训练，必须在很低的强度下训练。这本身并不是风险，高危患者普遍运动耐量下降，运动处方就必须相应调整。当然，这些患者也需要更严格的医疗监督。如果你遇到类似第一个例子那样的患者，你一定要在他每次运动的时候监督他，你必须确保他代偿得很好，肺部听诊是正常的，不处于肺水肿前期状态，并确保他没有心律失常。而且，必须经常评估他的进展。我的意思是，如果一个患者几乎没有症状，进步很快，在运动中表现得更好，说明即使他仍然有很高的风险，他情况还是不错的。如果患者在三至五个星期后仍然没有进步，即使他训练得很好，你还是要问问自己背后的问题是什么。背后一定有问题。你经常会遇到的问题是低血压。你可以想象那些射血分数低的患者在利尿剂治疗过程中会出现低血压，且状态不太好。因此，有时你不得不中断心脏康复，优化药物治疗，优化利尿剂治疗，来达到改善低血压症状的目的。呼吸困难的患者很难做运动训练，尤其是患有肺部疾病时，你只能去尝试，保持训练在低强度，而且密切关注患者的症状。若他能做到，就没问题；当他的呼吸困难稍有加重时，你就得降低运动强度和保持体液平衡。如前所述，这是非常重要的，也要特别注意与液体排出相关的低血压问题。

说明：（1）you have to be sure that he is compensated 指要确保他的心肺功能得到代偿。（2）hypo- 意为"低"；hyper- 意为"高"。"低血压"可用 hypotension 来表达；"高血压"可用 hypertension 来表达。（3）di- 意为"通过"；ur- 意为"尿"；etic 为形容词或名词词尾。其字面意思是"使尿液通过身体的物质"，该术语的标准译法为"利尿剂"。注意：在医学药学词汇中，形容词可活用为名词，如 antimalarial（抗疟疾药物）、anticoagulant（抗凝剂）等，既是形容词，又是名词。（4）symptom 的常见搭配动词是 relieve 或 ameliorate（缓解），此处可能是由于讲者为非英语母语者，用法存在偏误，译员应结合背景知识和上下文灵活处理。（5）dyspnea 本意为 shortness of breath（气短）。此处，讲者的语法使用并不十分规范，但该句大意为：呼吸困难的患者很难做运动训练，尤其是患有肺部疾病时。译员要依据背景知识和上下文进行理解。-pne/u、-pnea 的意思是 breath、air、lung，可构成术语 tachypnea、dyspnea、apnea（accelerated, difficult/painful, cessation of breathing：呼吸过快；呼吸困难；呼吸暂停）。（6）原文第六处下画线中的 you 实际指患者有肺病。（7）原文第七处下画线中的 you 指医师。（8）本段代词使用比较混乱，译员应结合上下文理解代词何时指代患者，何时指代医生。

7) Now when we talk about high-risk patients, of course, in these patients, you have to have the best assessment of what you have at your disposition. We talked about echo in these patients. In some post-acute MI patients, you do not necessarily need to do an echocardiography when they come to your cardiac rehabilitation institution. But for high-risk patients, I would really recommend it, to see whether there are post-surgical complications, what is the ejection fraction like, what's the severity of mitral valve regurgitation, etc. You have to complete your laboratory values and then cardiopulmonary exercise testing. It's really something that gives you a lot of information, not only about exercise prescription but also the severity of the disease, and I will show you that in a moment. But just to mention what is important, you have the exercise capacity <u>in itself</u>; then you have the ventilatory efficiency, which is reflected by the VE/VCO$_2$ slope. The higher it is, the more serious the disease is. And then the periodic breathing, which is also a sign of very severe disease. And finally, we always have to ask ourselves if we have patients with low ejection fractions, whether they improve, whether the ejection fraction improves, and, if it is not the case, whether they are candidates for an ICD implantation.

当我们谈到高危患者，当然，在这些患者中，你必须竭尽所能做最好的评估。我们谈到过高危患者的超声心动图。当一些急性心肌梗死后患者来到你的心脏康复机构时，你不一定需要做超声心动图，但对于高危患者，我建议评估是否有术后并发症、射血分数是多少、二尖瓣关闭不全的程度等。你需要补齐实验室的化验数值，然后是心肺运动试验。这样能给你提供很多信息，不仅是关于运动处方的信息，而且还有关于疾病严重程度的信息，稍后我会向你们展示这一点。那么，哪些指标是重要的？包括运动耐量本身的值，还有通气效率，这反映在 VE/VCO$_2$ 斜率上，斜率越高，疾病就越严重。然后是周期性呼吸，这也是一种非常严重的疾病征象。最后，我们总是要问自己，如果有射血分数低的患者，他们是否有改善，射血分数是否改善；如果没有改善，是否考虑 ICD 植入。

说明：in itself 指这个指标没有其他数值来表示，而是用其本身来表示。

8) So, <u>this</u> is just to give you an example of how <u>cardiopulmonary exercise testing</u> shows you the severity of the disease. In this patient, he has kind of an oscillatory ventilation. Normally this is [indistinct sound] in this ventilation, but it is kind of oscillated, you see, this is a kind of Cheyne-Stokes respiration, which occurs in the advanced heart rate.

If you see this, you know this is high risk. This patient also has chronotropic incompetence. Well, it is difficult to train this patient to make exercise prescriptions. You just follow the symptoms. Then you see that the oxygen pulse, which reflects the ventricular function during exercise, is reduced. You see that exercise capacity is very low: Below, maybe, let's say, 50% of the predicted value. You see this very elevated VE/VCO$_2$ slope. Normally, you should follow here this line, but this is very much increased, which shows you a mismatch between ventilation and circulation and shows you a patient who has probably kind of pre-edema status. He has a very early first lactate threshold, which means that the muscular function is very reduced, and he has a pulmonary comorbidity. You see that it is unable to increase his respiratory volume, or his tidal volume very much. He's doing everything he can just by increasing the respiratory rate. So, cardiopulmonary exercise testing completes your picture of a patient of high risk.

本页幻灯举例说明心肺运动试验如何体现疾病的严重程度。我们看，这位患者出现了振荡通气。通常情况下，通气的曲线都是大幅上升的，但本例呈振荡表现，这是一种陈－施呼吸，一般在心率快时出现。如果你看到这种现象，你就知道这是高危情况。这位患者也有变时性功能不全，很难给这位患者开运动处方，你只能根据他的症状调整。然后，你就会看到反映运动中心室功能的氧脉搏减少了。我们可以看到运动耐量是非常低的，大概低于预计值的50%。你可以看到这个非常高的 VE/VCO$_2$ 斜率。通常你会关注这条线，但此处的明显升高，就表明通气和循环之间不匹配，并表明了患者可能处于水肿前的状态。他有很早的乳酸阈值，这意味着肌肉功能降低明显，肺部有并发症，他的呼吸量、潮气量不能增加太多，他只能通过提高呼吸频率尽力代偿其他方面。因此，心肺运动试验能够完善对高危患者的了解。

说明：（1）结合视频中幻灯片翻页情况，可以看出 this 指的是本页幻灯片。（2）讲者幻灯片中的 CPX 指 cardiopulmonary testing，其中 C 指 cardio，P 指 pulmonary，X 指 testing。

9）Now, exercise in high-risk patients has, on the one hand, the point that we would like to have very much of benefit because these patients are the most severely diseased, so we would like to improve exercise. We would also like to improve remodeling. We know that exercise improves myocardial infarction, improve remodeling, and does not do any harm, so it's important to start early. We know the effects of exercise in the long term on slowing down atherosclerosis, and we also know that exercise improves the quality of life, morbidity, and mortality in the setting of cardiac rehabilitation. And on the other hand, what are the risks? The risk is negative remodeling, and I would say this risk is very low. Data show that the left ventricular function improves with exercise and the diameters come down and that arrhythmia during exercise is very rare. So, the exercise itself is not very high-risk, it is more about the underlying diseases, which are of risk, and cardiac decompensation of the exercise is almost impossible. So, the risks, even though the patients are at high risk of complications, are very low, and the key is the assessment of the patients and then the prescription of the low-intensity-adapted exercise capacity.

通过运动,一方面,我们想给高危患者带来最大的获益,因为这些患者病情最严重,所以我们想改善运动,我们也想改善重构。我们知道运动对于心肌梗死的患者来说能够改善重构,没有任何负面影响,因此应该尽早开始。我们知道长期来看运动能够减缓动脉粥样硬化,在心脏康复的场景下,运动能够提高生活质量,降低发病率和死亡率。另一方面,运动有何风险?风险是负性重塑,我认为这种风险很低。资料表明,随着运动的进行,左心室功能得到改善,内径变小,运动中心律失常非常罕见。因此,运动本身并没有很高的风险,更多的是基础疾病带来的风险,而心脏对于运动失代偿是几乎不可能的。因此,即使患者处于高风险,并发症的风险也很低,重点在于如何对患者进行评估和开具适应运动能力的低强度处方。

说明:(1)此处,remodeling 指 cardiac remodeling,即 a group of molecular, cellular, and interstitial changes that clinically manifest as changes in size, shape, and function of the heart resulting from the cardiac injury(Cohn, Ferrari & Sharpe, 2000)。(2)此段中,讲者多次使用 improve,若其后为负面性的名词,如文中的 morbidity and mortality,或具体病症,可将其当作 relieve 或 ameliorate 来理解。(3)athero- 意为"粥样";scler- 意为"硬";-osis 意为"症"。

10) This is a very long circle, a vicious circle of inactivity in heart failure patients. You have, at the start, the systolic dysfunction, whether this is cardiomyopathy or myocardial infarction, and you see what is happening coming down at the catabolic state, skeletal muscle atrophy and respiratory muscle atrophy, the increased ergoreflex activity, sympathetic activation, all these negative impacts of a reduced ejection fraction, and we know that exercise is good for all these aspects. It ameliorates the catabolic state, so it increases muscle mass if you do it well; it increases skeletal and respiratory muscle; it improves the ergoreflex; it decreases sympathetic activity; and it is a kind of vasodilation treatment; so it is very important to have this exercise treatment modality in these patients.

这是一个路线很长的圆圈,展示的是一个心力衰竭患者不活动所带来的恶性循环。无论是心肌病,还是心肌梗死,在开始时都是收缩功能障碍,往下走可以看到分解代谢更加明显,骨骼肌和呼吸肌萎缩,运动反射活动增加,交感神经激活,所有这些都是射血分数降低带来的负面影响。我们知道,运动对这些方面都有非常好的作用,它能缓和分解代谢状态,增加肌肉质量,增强骨骼肌和呼吸肌,改善运动反射,降低交感神经活性,而且还是一种血管扩张治疗,因此对这些患者进行这种运动治疗是非常重要的。

11) The question is, then, how can we improve systolic dysfunction? There are some data we have heard about: <u>High-intensity interval training</u> can improve ejection fraction. We have also heard that it is probably not for all patients but heart failure patients who are in a good functional state. They can do high-intensity exercise and probably improve their LV function. They are candidates for CRT. CRT is also very good for improving ejection fraction, especially if combined with a training program. Then we have resistance training and

respiratory muscle training, particularly to improve skeletal and respiratory muscle atrophy, and endurance training, which works more for ergoreflex and sympathetic activation.

那现在，问题就是我们怎样才能改善心脏收缩功能不全？我们所了解的一些数据表明，高强度间歇训练可以提高射血分数。我们还知道，HIIT 并不适用于所有患者，只适用于功能状态好的心衰患者。他们可以进行高强度的运动，且很可能改善左室功能。他们是 CRT 治疗的候选对象。CRT 也能够很好地改善射血分数，特别是在与训练计划相结合的情况下。而抗阻训练和呼吸肌训练尤其能够改善骨骼肌和呼吸肌的萎缩。此外，我们还有耐力训练，更多的是对运动反射和交感神经的激活起作用。

说明：high-intensity interval training 常缩写为 HIIT，意为"高强度间歇性训练"。

12）Now, this shows you the complete picture of rehabilitation. One question about safety in high-risk patients is the question of monitoring. Shall we monitor patients when they are doing exercise with the ECG? And when we look at the recommendation, it says that in high-risk patients, at the beginning, it might be very useful to have some kind of monitoring because it gives you some hints about how they improve during exercise and whether there is <u>arrhythmia</u>, and it is very useful. Of course, you know that monitoring during endurance training is very easy. We can have the ECG. However, when we do respiratory muscle training or resistance training, it's more difficult.

这体现了康复的完整情况。高危患者的安全问题之一是监测问题。当患者做运动时，我们是否应该用心电图监测他们？我们在训练监督指南里看到，建议高危患者在开始运动时，做一些监测可能是非常有用的，因为它会给你一些提示，看到患者在运动中改善的情况、是否有心律失常，这是非常有用的。当然，在耐力训练中，监测是很容易的，我们可以做心电图，但当我们做呼吸肌训练或抗阻训练时，难度就比较大了。

说明：a- 意为"非，不"；rhythm 意为"节奏"；-ia 意为"症"。注意：将这三部分词根、词缀构成词汇，连接前缀 a- 和词根 rhythm 时，要多写一次字母 r。

13）So, you don't have to monitor all the time your heart failure patients; however, during some time during exercise, it can be useful, especially when starting. An ECG is one thing, and what is sure is that you have to look at your patients' physical examination, blood pressure response, and their heart rhythm. These are very important points to look at when you have patients doing exercise.

因此，你不必一直监测心力衰竭的患者，但是在运动的某些时期，它可能是有用的，特别是在开始时。心电图是关注的内容之一，此外你一定还要关注患者运动时的体格检查结果、血压反应、心律，这些方面对于运动中的患者也非常重要。

14）This is an example of a patient who is starting exercise. He feels a little bit more tired than the last days—his Borg scale score during training is higher than usual. And you see this typical scattering of the heart rate, around 135–150, during exercise. And you know that, if you look at the monitored ECG, this patient has developed atrial fibrillation, which also has to be treated. You have to look at whether the patient is having atrial fibrillation.

这是一个刚开始训练的患者的例子。他看起来比过去几天更累,因为训练中的呼吸困难评分量表数值比平时要高。你看,这是典型的运动中的心率散点图,大约135—150次/分。如果你去看监测的心电图,就会发现这位患者已经发生了房颤,这也是必须要治疗的,你必须确定患者是否处于房颤状态。

15)This is now the patient with some shortness of breath newly. And if you look at his recording of that—you see the training here, and you see his heart rate just a little bit lower than 150. And as you expect on the ECG—you see here, frequent P waves in patients with atrial flutter. Or this patient who reports sudden weakness and slight oppression in the chest. You see that he has a very strange behavior of his heart rate. He has to lower his exercise intensity because he did not feel well. He had sudden weakness and oppression, and if you look at the ECG, you will see that he has mild ventricular arrhythmia all of a sudden, which you detect with monitoring and which you would not if you don't have this.

这是一个新近出现呼吸急促的患者。如果你看到他训练时的记录,你会看到他的心率略低于150次/分。正如你在心电图上看到的,心房扑动患者会有高频的P波。你再看一下这个患者,他自诉突然出现乏力和胸部的轻度压迫感。你会发现,他的心率表现得十分异常,他不得不降低他的运动强度,因为他感觉不适。他会突然出现乏力、压迫感,如果你看心电图,你会发现他突然出现了轻度的室性心律失常;你可以通过监测来发现,而如果你没有监测,就不会发现这次心律失常。

16)So, I think it is important to have this opportunity to monitor patients at starting of exercise until we know that they are doing well, and to tailor exercise, as we have heard, to get a picture of the complicated case of your patient—whether it is at very high risk or not. If you want to know more about how to do exercise, not only in high-risk patients but also in low-risk patients, how to improve their exercise capacity, how to perform resistance training, and how to perform respiratory muscle training, I would like to show you this picture of our course, of this year's international course, on cardiac rehabilitation and sports cardiology, to which you are also invited if you're able to join us. We do this course on the 20–23 of November this year. It will be taught by an international panel, and it's a course on 4 days. I will just show you what we are talking about.

因此,我认为重要的是有机会在患者一开始运动时进行监测,直到我们知道他们做得很好。然后正如刚才提到的那样,为他们定制个性化的运动,来真正了解患者的复杂情况,了解他是否高危。如果你想更多地了解如何在高风险患者以及低风险患者中实施运动康复、如何提高他们的运动能力、如何进行抗阻训练、如何进行呼吸肌训练,我想向你展示这张图片,这是我们今年的"心脏康复和运动心脏病学"国际课程介绍。我们邀请各位能够参加的同道参加。我们在今年 11 月 20—23 日开课。讲师团由一个国际性的小组组成，总共有 4 天的课程。我给大家看一下我们将要研讨的一些话题。

17）On Thursday, it is on heart failure, which is <u>the state of the art</u>, evidence of rehabilitation, stress testing, multidisciplinary approach, exercise training in high-risk patients, what we've talked about, and then the exercise in special exercise modalities. And on the other days, you will see that we have an overview of cardiac rehabilitation in general and its principles. Then there is a day on sports cardiology. And we try to cover everything, which ranges from the theory to exercise testing to exercise prescription in this four-day course. We know that some of your colleagues have already attended this course, and you may have the opportunity to attend it this year. And thank you for your attention.

星期四的内容包括心力衰竭的研究和临床实践前沿状况、康复的证据、负荷试验、多学科方法、我们刚才谈到的对高危患者的运动训练、特殊的运动康复治疗模式中的运动。另外的几天中，我们会讲心脏康复概述、原则。然后，有一天是关于运动心脏病学的。我们试图在四天的课程中涵盖从理论到运动测试，再到运动处方的所有内容。我知道你们的一些同事已经参加了这门课程，也欢迎你们参加。感谢大家！

说明：the state of the art 指 the best and most modern of its type。

10.3.3 总结与点评

1. 理解

讲者存在代词混用、误用情况，需根据上下文理解具体所指并传译。

2. 记忆

如果本讲话采用同声传译模式翻译，反而较为容易。如果翻译前索取到讲者幻灯片，依据幻灯片做好词汇和背景知识的准备，在现场翻译时，译者只需紧跟讲者顺句驱动即可做好翻译。如是交传，需要注意参考讲者幻灯片，并将口译笔记与幻灯片内容结合，作为回忆讲者所讲内容的提示。讲者来自一个多语种国家——瑞士，需提前了解具体口音情况，了解其受到该国官方语言中的哪一种（德语、法语、意大利语、列托－罗曼斯语）影响更大，以便结合既往总结的不同语种英语口音进行听辨。

3. 表达

讲者的有些句子重复内容较多，有很多都是讲者在思考措辞过程中带出的无意义表达，可酌情删减。母语为非英语讲者在讲话中普遍存在这种现象，译者应酌情处理。

10.3.4 词汇与表达拓展

循环和血液系统常用词汇与表达

1）-cardi/o- = heart

endocarditis (inflammation of the lining)：心内膜炎（指心脏内层的炎症）

myocarditis (inflammation of the muscle layer)：心肌炎（指肌肉层的炎症）

pericarditis (inflammation of the outer layer of the heart)：心包炎（指外层的炎症）

2）brady-/tachy- = slow/fast

bradycardia (rate < 60 beats/minute)：心动过缓（心率 < 60 次 / 分）

tachycardia (rate > 100 beats/minute)：心动过速（心率 > 100 次 / 分）

3）angi/o- = vessel

angiogram (X-ray of artery)：血管造影图（动脉 X 射线造影图[1]）

angiography：血管造影术

4）veno-/phlebo- = vein

phlebitis (inflammation of veins)：静脉炎（静脉炎症）

venogram (X-ray of veins)：静脉造影图（静脉 X 射线造影图）

5）-stasis/-stat = stop

hemostasis (stop bleeding)：止血

hemostat (a clamp-like instrument)：止血钳（钳形器械）

6）-cyte = cell

erythrocytes (red blood cells)：红细胞

leucocytes (white blood cells)：白细胞

7）hem/o- / -emia = blood

hematosalpinx (blood in the uterine tubes)：输卵管出血（输卵管内出现血液）

hypoxemia (low oxygen)：低氧血症（低氧）

参考文献

李萍，王丽，贾乐川. 2017. 第 3 代表皮生长因子受体抑制药——奥西替尼研究状况. 中国临床药理学杂志，33（14）：1371–1373.

马普亚. 2015. 心脏康复的过去、现在和未来. 中国胸心血管外科临床杂志，22（8）：709–718.

全国科学技术名词审定委员会. 2006. 遗传学名词：第 2 版. 北京：科学出版社.

1　X 射线造影图在日常口语中又称 "X 光片"。

全国科学技术名词审定委员会. 2007. 免疫学名词. 北京：科学出版社.
全国科学技术名词审定委员会. 2014. 组织学与胚胎学名词：第2版. 北京：科学出版社.
全国科学技术名词审定委员会. 2017. 老年医学名词. 北京：科学出版社.
全国科学技术名词审定委员会 . 2018a. 呼吸病学名词 . 北京：科学出版社 .
全国科学技术名词审定委员会. 2018b. 核医学名词. 北京：科学出版社.
全国科学技术名词审定委员会. 2018c. 呼吸病学名词 . 北京：科学出版社.
全国科学技术名词审定委员会. 2019. 感染病学名词. 北京：科学出版社.

Anon. 2008. *Cambridge Academic Content Dictionary.* Cambridge: Cambridge University Press.

Anon. 2022a. Atrial flutter. *MayoClinic.* Retrieved November 10, 2022, from MayoClinic website.

Anon. 2022b. New York heart association class Ⅲ/Ⅵ. *NCBI.* Retrieved August 17, 2022, from NCBI website.

Anon. 2022c. The free dictionary by Farlex. *Medical Dictionary.* Retrieved November 10, 2022, from Medical Dictionary website.

Anon. 2022d. What is cardiac resynchronization therapy? *Hopkins Medicine.* Retrieved August 17, 2022, from Hopkins Medicine website.

Arena, R., Humphrey, R. & Peberdy, M. A. 2003. Prognostic ability of VE/VCO$_2$ slope calculations using different exercise test time intervals in subjects with heart failure. *Eur J Cardiovasc Prev Rehabil*, *10*(6): 463–468.

Cohn, J. N., Ferrari, R. & Sharpe, N. 2000. Cardiac remodeling-concepts and clinical implications: A consensus paper from an international forum on cardiac remodeling. *J Am Coll Cardiol*, *35*(3): 569–582.

Des Moines University. 2022. Online medical terminology course. *DMU.* Retrieved August 17, 2022, from DMU website.

Hallek, M., Bergsagel, P. L. & Anderson, K. C. 1998. Multiple myeloma: Increasing evidence for a multistep transformation process. *Blood*, *9*(1): 3–21.

Huang, L. H. & Fu, L. W. 2015. Mechanisms of resistance to EGFR tyrosine kinase inhibitors. *Acta Pharmaceutica Sinica B*, *5*(5): 390–401.

Kitzman, D. W. 2013. Chronotropic incompetence: Causes, implications, and management. *Dialogues in Cardiovascular Medicine, 18*(3): 139–153.

Rajkumar, S. V. 2016. Updated diagnostic criteria and staging system for multiple myeloma. *Am Soc Clin Oncol Educ Book*, (35): 418–423.

Rajkumar, S. V. et al. 2014. International Myeloma Working Group updated criteria for the diagnosis of multiple myeloma. *The Lancet Oncology*, *15*(12): 538–548.

Rudrappa, M., Modi, P. & Bollu, P. C. 2022. Cheyne stokes respirations. *NCBI.* Retrieved August 17, 2022, from NCBI website.

第 11 章

外科

11.1 残胃癌治疗研究

中国医师协会外科医师分会是隶属于中国医师协会的外科医师行业学会，成立 12 年来已经成为拥有 24 个委员会、2 000 多名委员和专科委、2.23 万余名会员的行业组织。该分会每年 5 月在北京举行年度会议（CCS Annual Meeting），参会人数约 8 000 人，包括来自十余个欧、美、亚等国家的国际专家和同道。年会开幕式是最核心的全体活动，中外普外科领域的专家云集，半天的会议日程安排密集，介绍普外科专业发展、前沿学术及培训管理的最新进展，采用同传作为现场口译模式，对同传译员的专业素养及临床外科知识掌握的要求极高。

本节节选外科医师分会 2018 年年会王杉会长关于残胃癌的专题报告作为英译中口译案例，向读者展示外科学术会议口译工作的前期准备、开展过程及主要问题处理等要领。讲者发言的主要内容包括：残胃癌诊断困惑（diagnostic criteria dilemma on gastric stump cancer[1]）、胃癌复发的三种类型（three types of gastric cancer recurrence）、中国残胃癌诊断困境（current status of diagnostic dilemma for GSC in China）、全世界范围残胃癌研究进展（current development of GSC）、筛查服务情况（screening）、手术治疗（surgery）等。本节选择其中关于残胃癌诊断、治疗及专业发展现况的部分，分析有关专业内容的翻译及准备工作。

本节编者为该会议译员，为学会召开的会议提供过多次口译服务，比较熟悉该学会的会议程序、形式及发言人基本情况等。会议秘书处人员较为认真、负责，译员在会前两天获得了开幕式发言中英文稿件，并应邀对英文发言稿进行审校，这对于译员熟悉发言内容、提前热身发挥了积极作用。

对于外科专业内容口译任务，译员应做好充分准备，提前熟悉会议流程、形式、参会人及发言人情况，中英文日程及发言基本主题应该在会前至少 2—3 周获得，如果发言讲稿提前不可得，建议在有关机构网站、新媒体网站、学术期刊库检索有关主题信息与资料，以做好充分准备。

主旨发言是会议的灵魂，尤其是对于外科医师分会年会这样高规格、高要求的临床专业会议，学术内容的主旨发言往往是准备的重点和难点。此类会议发言稿和幻灯片获取耗时费力，且发言人往往不会提前太久提供发言幻灯片或讲稿，甚至出于保密等原因不提供幻灯片或发言

1　gastric stump cancer 简称为 GSC。

稿，这需要译员耐心与会议组织方及发言人进行沟通，使其明白提前提供发言材料的重要性。会前准备的具体技巧包括：（1）不断向会议组织方联系人催要发言资料，包括前期会议的资料，以做参考；（2）如有可能，可直接与发言人取得联系，代替组织方催要幻灯片；（3）请求发言人提供保密发言内容的摘要及专业内容指引；（4）根据主题内容进行学术研究文献检索，提前阅读有关文献，熟悉专题内容；（5）在互联网上寻找讲者既往在其他场合的类似主题发言。

这次会议，译员提前3天获得了有关内容，在取得幻灯片前，一边催要资料，一边检索有关专业文献，阅读了2—3篇学术期刊文章，并创建了基本词汇表。幻灯片取得后，译员结合具体发言内容，又做了细化、具体的准备，进一步完善了词汇表。

11.1.1 背景知识

同时癌：下文讲话中指同时性多原发癌。同时诊断或间隔时间小于等于6个月者称为同时性多原发癌，诊断间隔时间大于6个月者称为异时性多原发癌。

切缘阳性：指肿瘤切除术中，切除部位的边缘有残留的癌细胞存在。

11.1.2 残胃癌简介

1. 相关词汇

残胃上的癌：carcinoma in the remnant stomach / carcinoma in the gastric stump

残胃癌：gastric stump cancer (GSC)

残端：stump

恶性肿瘤：carcinoma

胃切除术/胃（癌）切除：gastrectomy

肝切除术：hepatectomy

根治术：curative resection

远端的：distal

局部复发：local recurrence

切除：resection/excision/removal

切缘阳性：positive margin

良性：benign

恶性：malignant

癌症筛查：cancer screening

原发病灶：primary lesion

病变：lesion

内镜下：endoscopic

指南：guidelines/guidance

残留癌：residual tumor/cancer

同时癌: synchronous cancer

异时癌: metachronous cancer

微转移癌: micrometastasis cancer

溃疡: ulcer

2. 原文、参考译文及说明

1）感谢介绍！行业学会要关注到我们临床实际问题。其实对于残胃癌，我们在座的，无论是年长的专家，还是年轻的专家，都有一个共同的概念，那就是良性病变切除术后 5 年在残胃上发生的癌，就叫作残胃癌。近两年，因为良性病变越来越少，恶性病变手术后发生的新发癌也出现了。刚才，季加孚教授也谈到了胃癌手术的疗效也在逐渐提高[1]，胃癌恶性病变 10 年以后在残胃上发生的癌，也不罕见。

Thank you for introduction! The professional society should pay attention to the practical issues in clinical settings. For gastric stump cancer (GSC), all the colleagues, junior or senior, share a common definition, namely carcinoma developed 5 years after incision of a benign lesion. In recent years, benign lesions are less common, while post-surgical malignant lesions increase. Just now, Prof. Ji Jiafu mentioned improved outcomes of surgeries for gastric cancer. Carcinoma in the gastric stump 10 years after the surgery is also common.

说明：（1）发言人切入发言主题前，一般会脱稿发表一些感受，译员要做好充分准备，提前预习幻灯片，甚至阅读发言人关于发言题目的著作简介等，以备不时之需。（2）原文是"近两年"，译员将其处理为 in recent years，此处的两年是一个约数。（3）所有画线词汇乃本段翻译的关键词，需译员重点掌握讲者原意并准确翻译。余同。

2）其实这种困惑来自我们一直追踪世界上胃癌治疗最先进的国家——日本。日本同道们出了一个叫作 Carcinoma of the Remnant Gastric Stump 的指南，我们翻译为《残胃癌》，残胃癌的概念就产生了困惑。英文中，有 GSC、GRC、RGC、carcinoma in the remnant stump 等概念，且常常互换使用。而中文里，绝大多数同行用的是残胃癌的概念。

Actually, such confusion of definition comes from Japan—the country leading the world in gastric cancer treatment. The Japanese colleagues published a guidance on carcinoma of the remnant gastric stump. We translated it into Chinese as gastric stump cancer or *Can Wei Ai*. In English, GSC, GRC, RGC, and carcinoma in the remnant stump are used interchangeably, while in Chinese we only have the term "gastric stump cancer".

说明：（1）本段作为发言的第一部分，提出了残胃癌的多种定义以及与残胃癌容易混淆的几个概念，如残留癌、复发癌、微转移癌等，这些基本的专业术语及定义均出现在讲者幻灯片中。译员在译前准备期间应充分熟悉幻灯片内容，尤其是医学专业词汇，应做到中英文均可熟识。此外，译员还可利用百度翻译等线上平台查阅词汇发音，缩短现场翻译时的听辨反应时间，以便快速、准确地翻译有关词汇。（2）两个关键术语"残胃癌"和"残胃上的癌"是发言的主线。

---

1 所谓疗效提高，指的是生存时间变长，所以才会有后文的 10 年一说。

译员应对术语名称及定义有一定的了解,以保障翻译的准确性。

3)日本一位放射科医生提出"残胃上的癌"的概念,因为他没法区分是复发还是新发的,因此他提出了残胃上的癌。在我们中日韩专家交流时,他表示,他提出这个定义的目的是想让临床研究的入组病例类型尽量完全。如果存在这些项目,你就需要注意。

A Japanese radiologist has proposed the definition of carcinoma in the remnant stump, for it is difficult to tell whether the carcinoma in the remnant stump is primary or secondary. When we held the summit of the general surgeons of China, Japan and Korea, he mentioned that he hoped to include all types of cases in clinical studies. You need to pay attention to see if there are the above-mentioned classifications.

说明:(1)此处原文提及的"专家"实际上是"普外科专家",因此译员进行了具体化措辞——general surgeons。(2)讲者说的"如果存在这些项目"应该是指上述的各种相关分类,译文进行了具体化体现。

4)日本的分类从第二版、第三版,都在提出用残胃上的癌。如果用这个名词命名,它涵盖了哪些病例?包括新发癌,与原发癌无关系,由于手术后产生的系列变化,但是还可能包括残留癌、异时癌、复发癌、微转移癌等,也是残胃的癌所涵盖的概念。

The Japanese guidelines Versions 2 and 3 mentioned the term "carcinoma in the remnant stump". What can be covered under the specific term? It includes newly-developed cancer, which has nothing to do with the primary lesion, but is caused by a series of postoperative changes. It may include cancer remaining in the remnant stomach, metachronously developed gastric cancer, recurrent cancer, and micrometastasis in the remnant stomach.

说明:(1)"包括新发癌,与原发癌无关系,由于手术后产生的系列变化"可被理解为"包括与原发癌无关系的、术后因各种变化产生的新发癌"。译员按此理解翻译。

5)那么从胃癌复发的类型上看,如果用残胃的癌的概念,它几乎涵盖所有的类型,那么我们在肝切除术后,肝的残肝上的癌就是残肝癌,就没有癌复发的概念了吗?一定不是,一定包括局部复发、区域复发、远端复发。

Does it suggest that there is no such concept of cancer recurrence if we use the almost all-inclusive concept of carcinoma in the remnant stump? The same concept can be used for carcinoma in the liver stump after hepatectomy. No! There is local recurrence, regional recurrence, and distance recurrence.

说明:此段出现了"肝切除术"这个专业词汇,幻灯片里没出现,需要译员随机应变。一旦出现不熟悉的医学词汇,翻译时,译员可采取"普通词汇替代专业词汇"的方式,即用外行说法传递内行专业信息。比如在此段,"肝切除术"除了可被翻译为术语 hepatectomy 外,还可以被翻译为日常表达 liver removal/resection。如果条件允许,译员也可请教搭档译员或查询在线词典。

6)此外,还存在同时癌和异时癌。在我们进行手术的时候,发现同时存在不同部位的癌,即同时癌的病例,达到了5%—8%。如果继续做连续切片,这个比例还更大,可高达13%—15%。早期胃癌手术后,有0.6%—3%的病例存在异时癌。这些比例,是否用一个简单的"残胃癌"就都涵盖了呢？

Besides, there are also synchronous and metachronous gastric cancers. Each cancer must be anatomically separate and distinct. Synchronous cancer accounts for 5%–8%. The ratio can reach 13%–15% with serial sections. After gastrectomy for EGC, metachronous cancers occur in 0.6%–3% of patients. Can carcinoma in the remnant stump cover all the above-mentioned types?

说明：此段中，译员根据背景信息，灵活增补了"Each cancer must be anatomically separate and distinct."，以便听众理解。

7) 为此，2年前我们成立了一个工作组，集合了全国27家研究中心病例，残胃癌病例3 018例，是目前所能看到国内外报道的最大例数；这27家中心都是中国权威机构，在残胃癌诊断方面，有4个中心依然用最原始标准，即良性病变术后5年发生的癌，有7个中心用了最新概念，即良性病变5年以上、恶性病变10年以上单一的标准来诊断残胃癌。到目前为止，仅有4个中心，是用的日本标准，就是残胃上的癌，来诊断残胃癌。其他这些机构，即便在同一个机构中也有不同标准。这就是中国实际，也确实给临床实践带来了困惑。

To answer this question, 2 years ago, we set up a working group and pooled 3,018 cases of gastric stump cancer from 27 medical centers (study sites), the biggest cohort in the world. Among the 27 centers, 4 centers used the most conventional diagnosis standard, namely carcinoma developed 5 years after gastrectomy of benign tumor, 7 centers use the latest definition of carcinoma developed 5 years after gastrectomy of benign tumor and 10 years after gastrectomy of malignant tumor, and only 4 centers use the Japanese standard—the carcinoma in the remnant stump—to diagnose gastric stump cancer. Other institutions use different standards; even standards of diagnosis in the same center may vary. This is the reality in China—full of confusions in clinical practices.

说明：此段如果需要进行同声传译，译员需要注意同声传译的即时性特点。这一特点要求译员和讲者基本保持同步，译员为保持语言连贯和翻译及时性，很少有时间对源语的结构进行较大调整，而是根据原文的顺序，把句子切成一个个意群，再把这些意群单位自然地连接起来，翻译出整体原意。这种方法就是"顺句驱动"，即常说的"顺译"技巧，顺译能够节省译员时间，缓解译员压力，也是同传培训的重要内容。

8) 我们来回顾一下残胃癌历史。首先要提到 Balfour。他很明确地讲了溃疡到胃癌恶变，并提出了我们传统的残胃癌定义，就是良性病变5年以上发生的癌是残胃癌。他在《新英格兰杂志》1988年发表的这个研究做了这个贡献。其实它得出的结论也是很明确的——绝大多数良性病变发生癌的，是在5年以上，良性病变5年以上胃手术后病变，这个一直没有改变。虽然日本的同道，从《规约》[1]一直在讲残胃的癌的概念——这是在（19）85年的研究，发现在10年之内，残胃发生新发癌的概率是极低的，因此在胃恶性病变10年以上，我们就视同为新发癌，就是残胃癌。这是（20）07年日本全国范围大规模调研，近万名患者中，有108人

1　指日本从1962年开始制定和出版的《胃癌临床和病理处理规约》。该《规约》后来经历多次修订。

确诊为残胃癌。这项研究也明确地讲，10年以上的癌，在残胃上的新发癌。通过日本这么多年的研究的演进过程，我们发现，他们把10年以上恶性病变界定为残胃的新发的癌。这是日本同道最新发表的论文，也是大样本的研究，虽然《规约》是说用残胃上的癌（carcinoma in the remnant stump）。

Let's review the history of gastric stump cancer. First it was Dr. Balfour who clearly defined the connection between ulcer and gastric cancer. He set up the conventional definition of gastric stump cancer; that is carcinoma developed 5 years after gastrectomy of benign tumors. The study published in the *New England Journal of Medicine (NEJM)* in 1988 concluded with clarity: The majority of carcinoma developing out of benign tumors occurred 5 years after surgical intervention of the lesion. This remains unchanged, although the Japanese colleagues have been discussing about carcinoma in the remnant stump since the issuance of *Guidelines*. This was a study done in 1985. Within 10 years, there was a very low incidence of primary carcinoma. Therefore, we regard cancers occurring 10 years after gastrectomy of the malignant lesion as a primary lesion, namely the remnant gastric carcinoma. This is the large-scale survey done in Japan in 2007. 108 out of nearly 10,000 patients were diagnosed with gastric stump cancer. It clearly conveyed the message that the carcinoma developed 10 years after the gastrectomy is defined as the primary lesion on the gastric stump. Through the years of intensive studies done by the Japanese, you can see the evolution of their concept. They gradually defined the primary lesion on the stump as the carcinoma in the remnant gastric stump. This paper is the latest publication of the kind—another large-sample study. The *Japanese Guidelines* states it as carcinoma on the gastric stump.

说明：（1）此段具有典型的口语语言风格，译员应避免使用过多的书面语言，以免翻译得过于生硬，建议可采用与发言人类似风格的口语语言。此段中，译员需要注意的是《新英格兰杂志》的翻译，这本杂志全称是《新英格兰医学杂志》（*New England Journal of Medicine*）。现场讲话中，讲者幻灯片里出现了杂志名称缩写 NEJM，若是翻译时间紧张，译员可将其直接翻译为 NEJM。（2）《规约》是日文汉字，等同于中文的《指南》，译员可视上下文将其直译为 guidelines 或意译为 guidance。

9）从日本国内来讲，我们也当面同日本同道讨论了概念，就是良性病变5年以上，恶性病变10年以上，作为残胃癌诊断标准。中国、日本和韩国都是胃癌高发的国家，到今天为止只有日本和韩国把癌症筛查作为国家策略，我国、欧美，以及同样胃癌高发的巴西，到目前为止都没有把癌症筛查作为国家策略。

We also had face-to-face discussion about the local diagnosis standard for gastric stump cancer with the Japanese colleagues. They also use the same standard, namely 5 years after the benign lesion removal and 10 years after the malignant lesion removal. China, Japan and Korea all see a high prevalence of gastric cancer. However, only Japan and Korea have developed a national strategy of gastric cancer screening. No national strategy of gastric cancer screening has been found in China, American and European countries, and other high-burden countries like Brazil.

说明：（1）这段话术语不多，需要注意的是流行病学词汇"高发"，它指的是"患病率高"，可以被翻译为 high prevalence 或 high burden。（2）讲者提到的"良性病变 5 年以上，恶性病变 10 年以上"信息不完整，译员在翻译时增补了相关信息，即 5 years after the benign lesion removal and 10 years after the malignant lesion removal。

10）那么我们可以看，这是日本不算胃镜下切除的早期胃癌的比例。胃癌手术病人中，早期胃癌手术比例，在日本已经达到了 51%，而我们国家，刚才季加孚教授也讲了，小于 20%，在 19% 左右。我国胃癌的进展期的病人在胃癌手术中的比例还是非常大的。虽然季加孚教授率领的这个联盟在推动胃癌的标准化的手术，但是与日本相比，我们还是有相当大的差距。它的 D 2 根治术接近 70%，而即使是 70% 的前提下，仍然有接近 12% 的残留。我们期待着季教授的研究结束，并等待研究数据发布出来。这说明什么？这说明日本胃癌手术中早期胃癌的比例已经相当大，而我们国家胃癌手术仍然以进展期胃癌为主。日本在胃癌根治术的标准化方面是非常高的，而我们国家距离标准化还有相当大的距离。这是胃癌术后镜下残留，我国实际上也有相当大的比例，21% 的有残留。这就提示我们，虽然我们国家比西方国家的局部复发率要稍微低一些，但我们和日韩还是有相当大的距离。

We can see the percentage of early cancer in Japan (endoscopic resection cases excluded) is 51%, while that in China is less than 20%, as mentioned by Prof. Ji Jiafu. It is 19%. Quite some patients are at the local advanced stage. Although Prof. Ji is leading the alliance and promoting standard procedure for gastric cancer, we still see big gaps between the Chinese and Japanese data. The share of D2 dissection is big, nearly 70%. Even with such a high proportion, there are still 12% of definite residual tumors. The Chinese data analysis result by Prof. Ji is pending. But we already see big gaps here. This shows that the share of early stage cancer in Japan is bigger than in China, and the majority of the Chinese patients are encountered at the local advanced stage. Japanese doctors performed curative resection in a much more standardized way, while we still have a long way to go to standardize the procedure. This is microscopic positive margin, which is 21%. This reminds us that we are inferior to Japan and Korea in terms of the local recurrence rate, though we are superior to the Western countries.

说明：本段术语较多，主要是关于肿瘤分期的词汇，包括"早期"和"进展期"，还有部分外科手术常用术语，如"根治术"和"镜下残留"，译员应在理解内容情况下准确翻译有关词汇。另外，"率""比例""占比"是医学口译常见的词汇，译员应注意掌握有关词汇的准确翻译，"率"反映事物发生的强度与频率，一般被翻译为 rate，单位可以是百分之一、千分之一、十万分之一等。"比例"和"占比"表示事物内部各组成部分的频数所占的比重和分布，一般是 percentage、proportion 或 share。

11）这是我们沈凌教授在 07 年发表在《新英格兰杂志》上的一篇文章，大家看，在 5 年内发生复发有近 60%，而日本是 30%。这就提示我们，我们国家无论从筛查到规范化手术到诊断治疗都需要进一步规范，因此使用残胃癌概念会对我们整个的诊治产生不是很积极的元素，所以我们建议也很明确，仍然建议大家在临床上使用残胃癌的定义。它是新发的癌的定义，是不包含残留和复发的癌的，否则的话，会导致我们整个业界已经达到治疗水平的及没有仔细的关注这个问题的同道之间，没有一个筛查手术行业规范。所以我们把良性病变5年以上发生的癌，恶性病变胃癌手术后10年以上在残胃上发生的癌临床诊断为残胃癌。在临床上我们要继续使用残留的癌，包括镜下、复发癌、多灶癌等。在有条件的机构——在这里有条件指的是无论是胃癌的筛查水平，还是胃癌手术的规范水平，以及病案记录的完整水平——我们不反对应用残胃上的癌的标准进行诊断。这样将来就不影响我们在全国层面的多中心的统计分析。如果要用残胃上的癌进行诊断，一定要参照日本同道的标准进行诊断，记录详细的间隔时间、原发灶的性质，以及各种的手术方式，达到残胃上的癌诊断标准。

This is Prof. Shen Ling's study, which was published in the *New England Journal of Medicine* in 2007. Let's look at the data. There is nearly 60% of recurrence after curative resection among the Chinese patients, while for the Japanese patients it is only 30%. This reminds us that we need to develop guidelines for screening, diagnosis and surgical procedures. But the use of gastric stump cancer may have a negative impact on the whole care pathway. Therefore, we have clear recommendations here. We suggest that gastric stump cancer will be kept as the definition of the primary cancer, excluding residual and recurrence tumors. Otherwise, confusion may be brought to those advanced medical centers or those colleagues who do not pay enough attention to the issue. This could constrain the development of guidelines, namely the standard of screening and surgical interventions. Therefore, we define gastric stump cancer as the tumor developing 5 years after the gastrectomy of benign lesion or the tumor developing 10 years after the gastrectomy of cancer. Meanwhile, we will need to use the concept of residual cancer, recurrent cancer, and multiple lesions in the remnant cancer. In advanced medical centers, namely those with high competence in cancer screening, surgical interventions and complete case reports, we do not object to their usage of carcinoma in the remnant stomach. In this way, the multiple-center analysis results will not be negatively influenced. When using the concept of carcinoma in the remnant stomach, we must refer to the Japanese standard of diagnosis, and keep a close record of the intervals, nature of the primary lesion, and all the procedures performed. There is a requirement for complete record keeping for the case of carcinoma in the remnant stomach.

说明：本段较长，专业术语多，译员应注意词汇的翻译。同时，译员要注意断句，讲者的句子较长时，需要将其切为短句，适当补词以保证完整性。

12）经过1年多全国专家共同努力探讨，多次讨论，就形成了大家在桌上可以看到的中国残胃癌定义的外科专家共识。这是非常完整的一个文件，内容包括共识的形成，以及对共识的详细解读，包括残胃癌和残胃上的癌应用的分组的、不同机构的分析。希望大家关注今后临床诊断残胃癌时，定义的应用。我们展望，今后一些新技术的建立，能够指导残胃癌诊断体系的建立。这些新技术能真正区分出哪些是残胃新生的癌，哪些是复发的癌，当然还包括残留癌。至于多灶癌是同时还是异时，应用新的技术鉴定之后，新的残胃癌的诊断体系就建立了。第二，希望作为胃癌高发大国，希望能建立筛查体系，为我们近8万普通外科医师建立规范，包括开展根治性手术的规范。谢谢大家！

After more than one year's effort and discussion made by all the experts nationwide, we produced "the Chinese Surgeons' Consensus Opinion for the Definition of Gastric Stump Cancer (2018 Version)". It is on your table now. It offers a complete description of the consensus formation and gives a detailed explanation of the definition. It also includes analysis of the use of definition of gastric stump cancer and the carcinoma in the remnant stomach in different centers. I hope all of you could pay attention to the clinical use of the concept of gastric stump cancer. In the future, we look forward to new technologies which could help to establish the diagnosis of gastric stump cancer. With these technologies, we can truly tell which is the newly developed lesion, and which is the recurrent one or residual one. As for multi-lesion cancer, we need to tell whether it is synchronously or metachronously developed gastric cancer. Only after diagnosis with the new technologies can we set up the diagnosis system for the disease. Secondly, being a high-burden populous country, China should build a cancer screening system, to provide nearly 80,000 general surgeons with the guidance for standard procedures including curative resection. Thank you!

说明： 译员在译前准备时应仔细阅读幻灯片，不漏过每个可能提及的词汇及知识点。此段是讲话的总结部分，讲者提到了"专家共识"。幻灯片最后部分的图片里有"共识"的英文翻译，译员可以参考。另外，前面提及的诸多词汇在这里有一个汇总，专业术语密度大，对于译员挑战较大，译员可将中英文对照幻灯片放在手边，随时参考词汇。

11.1.3 总结与点评

1. 理解

理解专业主题内容、理解发言人表达、理解术语实际含义是医学口译的基本要求，交传是如此，同传更是如此。

首先，熟练掌握专题内容是做好医学口译的前提条件，译员需要在会前就专题内容进行精心准备，提前索取幻灯片及其他参考资料。如果无法索要到幻灯片及其他参考资料，译员则需要阅读至少1—2篇相关主题的中英文文献，以熟悉知识内容及词汇。

其次，发言人表达好坏是不可控因素，往往对口译效果有较大影响。不管发言人临场发言状态如何，译员都应做到仔细聆听并尽力理解内容，便于准确翻译。

最后，专业词汇是医学口译的关键，准备资料时，应反复强化对于专业术语的外形、发音及含义的认知，便于快速、准确地进行专业词汇的翻译。

对于手术视频/现场演示手术的翻译，译员理解起来难度较大。如果能提前知道手术的术式（如胰十二指肠切除术），译员可参考手术教材，了解手术的适应证、禁忌证、过程（包括关键的解剖结构和手术器械）、要点等，这样才能在口译过程中理解发言人的语言。

对于手术视频的翻译，译员最好能够在脑海中回忆手术步骤，然后将记忆中的步骤一步一步地翻译出来。但是一般而言，译员很难在短时间内达到如此高深的境界。尽管如此，经过精心准备，译员仍然可以记住发言人讲述的关键词汇和结构，对照手术视频画面上的场景进行翻译。虽然大多数手术视频不像讲座幻灯片那样有文字说明，但是视频中可以看到实际的步骤和操作，译员可以结合发言人的语言来理解手术的过程，并且进行翻译。

为了在现场更迅速地理解发言人的语言，译员可以把提前准备好的关键词汇中英文对照的文件打印出来，带到会场，以备不时之需。这样能够辅助理解。

2. 记忆

医学译员的背景大致可以分为三类：第一类是以外语和翻译为专业的译员；第二类是以医学为专业的译员；第三类是有医学和口译两个专业背景的译员。但是由于现代医学高度分科化，医学词汇庞杂，不管是哪一种背景的译员，都很难记住各个专科的医学词汇。

对于医学词汇的记忆，译员除了依靠在训练和医学教育过程中学到的知识之外，最重要的还是依靠会议前的准备工作和会议翻译工作中对于词汇的了解和学习。为了加强记忆，总结和整理各个专业的医学词汇相当重要。比如，骨科是外科的一个分支，而骨科里面还有脊柱外科、关节外科、骨肿瘤、创伤骨科等多个亚专业。所以，在工作中，译员要想记住更多的专业词汇，就需要建立自己的专科知识库和词汇表（比如关节置换相关词汇、关节镜相关词汇等）。记住更多的专业词汇，在口译过程中，译员就会有更高的译出率，就能让听众更加深入地理解发言人所讲的内容，也能为译员获得更好的口碑。

医学口译往往涉及专业内容及词汇术语，若是没有提前准备，译员就难以取得较佳效果。译员在会前应尽量向会议主办方索取材料，为了提高翻译质量，会议主办方一般也会积极配合。拿到材料后，译员应仔细阅读，并提取核心词汇，将其做成专业术语表，进行强化记忆，包括对于词汇发音的记忆，便于做出及时反应和准确翻译。

对于医学同声传译，在发言人发言过程中，译员如遇到句子较长或开头句意不清楚的情况，可以对前半句话进行短期记忆存储（换言之，采用等待策略），等后半句出来后再进行句型结构调整和翻译。

3. 表达

医学口译对于译员表达的要求较高，除了准确、连贯、简洁等常规口译要求外，还应做到专业性。

首先，要求专业词汇翻译准确，不可错译、漏译，发音也应准确。

其次，医学专题发言的句式应符合医学科技英语特点，语气客观，以被动句为主，句子尽量简化，不用过多修饰描述性词语。但是，在开幕式、颁奖现场等特定发言场景，译员可根据发言内容及发言人情绪进行适当调整，要符合具体场景语言表达需要。

最后，译员的语音、语调及声音素质是影响表达的重要因素，译员应控制语速，避免过快或过慢（包括插入过多语气词或转承词），同时避免音调单一，应略微保持抑扬顿挫，声音不可过低或过高，避免影响听众情绪。

对于手术视频的翻译，表达方面最重要的是简洁、准确，翻译出最关键的术语。听众往往有相关背景知识，能根据译员说出的简短的关键术语来理解手术过程。

11.2 乳腺肿瘤的外科手术治疗

乳腺癌是发生在乳腺腺上皮组织的恶性肿瘤。本节选编自乳腺肿瘤外科手术治疗的科普节目，目的是让学习者逐渐熟悉日常相关医疗词汇表达及翻译。

11.2.1 背景知识

开放静脉通路（start intravenous line）：指使用金属或者管状的无菌材料，通过皮肤穿刺到静脉里，使静脉与外界相通，是静脉给药的常用方法。

11.2.2 乳腺肿瘤简介

1. 相关词汇

  breast cancer：乳腺癌
  breast tissue：乳腺组织
  lymph node：淋巴结
  intravenous line：静脉通道
  breathing tube：呼吸用的管子（讲话中指气管插管）
  lumpectomy：肿块切除术
  mammectomy：乳腺切除术
  modified radical mastectomy：乳腺癌改良根治术
  sentinel node biopsy：前哨淋巴结活检

2. 原文、参考译文及说明

1）Surgical removal of the tumor[1] is a common treatment for breast cancer. There are a number of surgical techniques, and your doctor will help you decide which is best for your situation. In addition to removing your breast tissue, it may be necessary to remove some or all of the lymph nodes under your arm.

手术切除肿瘤是乳腺癌的常规治疗手段。有许多种外科手术方式，医生会帮助你选择最适

---

1 注意区别癌（cancer / malignant tumor / malignancy）和肿瘤（tumor）。cancer / malignant tumor / malignancy 都是恶性的，tumor 可能是良性的，也可能是恶性的。

合你病情的手术方式。乳腺癌手术中，除了切除乳腺组织外，还可能需要切除腋下的部分或全部淋巴结。

2）Before the procedure, an intravenous line will be started and you may be given an oral sedative to help you relax. Breast surgery usually requires general anesthesia, a breathing tube will be inserted through your mouth and into your throat, and you will be given medications to put you to sleep for the duration of the procedure.

术前，建立静脉通路，医生可能用口服镇静剂来帮助你放松。乳腺手术通常需要全身麻醉，医生会将用于呼吸的管子通过口腔插入喉咙。手术过程中，由于药物作用，你会进入睡眠状态。

说明：（1）"全身麻醉"可简称为"全麻"。（2）此处，breathing tube（可直译为"呼吸管"）可被调整为"用于呼吸的管子"。（3）you will be given 可省略不译。

3）Depending on the types of produce, breast cancer surgery usually takes one to three hours. The main surgical procedures are lumpectomy and mastectomy. A lumpectomy preserves the appearance of the breast. The tumor along with a margin of surrounding tissue is removed. In this procedure, your surgeon will make an incision in the skin and separate the tumor and the margin of the healthy tissue from the breast with a scalpel. Then your surgeon will remove the mass with forceps, send it to the pathology lab for examination and close the wound with sutures.

根据手术类型不同，乳腺癌手术通常需要1—3个小时。主要的手术方式是乳房肿块切除术和乳房切除术。乳房肿块切除术保留乳房外观，将肿瘤及其周边部分一并切除。在此手术中，医生会在皮肤上做切口，用手术刀将肿瘤与乳腺健康组织边缘分离开。然后，使用手术钳取出肿瘤，送病理实验室检查，用缝合线缝合伤口。

说明：（1）lumpectomy 也可被译为"乳房肿瘤切除术"，但其使用不如"乳房肿块切除术"普遍。（2）lumpectomy 和 mammectomy（乳腺切除术）可分解为词根 lump（肿块）+ ectomy（切除术）和 mammo（乳房）+ ectomy。（3）注意：margin 指边缘，意思是不能只切肿瘤，要一并切除肿瘤周边的部分组织。

4）In a mastectomy, the entire breast is removed. This is usually indicated when the tumor is too large for a lumpectomy. In a simple lumpectomy, only your breast tissue is removed. Your surgeon will begin by making an incision around your nipple. He or she will then separate your breast tissue from the muscle underneath, and remove it for examination. Finally, your surgeon will insert drains to prevent fluid collection before closing the wound.

乳房切除术中，切除整个乳房，通常适用于肿瘤过大，不适合行乳腺肿块切除术的患者。单纯乳房切除术只切除乳腺组织。首先，在乳头周围做一切口，然后将乳腺组织与其下方的肌肉分离开，切除后送病理检查。最后，缝合伤口前，为预防积液，会插入引流管。

说明：（1）be indicated 在医学中指"其适应证是……"，此处，结合语料目标受众为大众这一特点，译员将其灵活处理为"适用于……的患者"。（2）simple 在此段不能被翻译成"简单"。（3）参考译文画线处中的"病理"二字是译员根据上下文添加的，目的是让译文更加清楚。

5）The most common type of mastectomy is a modified radical mastectomy in which the entire breast and some or all of the lymph nodes under your arm are removed. In this procedure, your surgeon will make an incision along the length of the breast, separate your breast tissue from the muscle underneath and remove it for examination.

最常见的乳房切除术是改良乳腺癌根治术。此手术将切除整个乳房以及腋下部分或全部淋巴结。手术过程中，医生将沿着乳房的长径做切口，将乳腺组织与其下方的肌肉分离，并切除乳腺组织做病理检查。

说明：make an incision along the length 可被翻译为"沿着长径做一个切口"。

6) To remove the lymph nodes under your arm, many surgeons use a technique called sentinel node biopsy. In this procedure, dye is injected into your breast to determine which lymph nodes drain fluid first. It is these lymph nodes that are most likely to contain cancer. Your surgeon will remove one to three of these lymph nodes for examination, insert drains and close the wound with sutures.

在切除腋下淋巴结时，往往会采用前哨淋巴结活检的方法。在此操作中，医生会将染料注入乳房，以确认哪些淋巴结先引流染料。这些淋巴结最可能含有癌细胞。医生会切除1—3个淋巴结进行病理检查，之后会插入引流管并缝合伤口。

7) In a radical mastectomy, the breast, underlying tissue, and muscle beneath the breast and all visible lymph nodes are all removed. Your surgeon will begin by making an incision along the length of the breast. Next, he or she will separate all of the breast tissue, muscles from the chest wall and visible lymph nodes, and remove them for examination. Finally, your surgeon will insert drains before closing the wound.

乳腺癌根治术中，乳腺、乳腺下的组织、肌肉，以及所有可见的淋巴结均被切除。医生将沿着乳房长径做切口，之后将所有的乳腺组织、肌肉与胸腔壁和可见的淋巴结分离开，切除送病理检查。最后，插入引流管并缝合伤口。

说明：此处，原文多次用主谓宾结构句子陈述操作过程。翻译时，按汉语习惯，译员通常会省略第二、第三个句子的主语，如 he or she、your surgeon。

8) After your breast surgery, your breathing tube will be removed and you will be taken to the recovery areas for monitoring. Lumpectomies are often done as outpatient procedures. In this case, you will be able to leave the hospital after several hours. If your surgery is done as an inpatient, your doctor will generally have you remain in the hospital for one to two days to monitor your recovery.

手术后，移除气管插管，病人将被转入术后恢复区进行监测。乳腺肿块切除术常常在门诊开展，数小时后即可出院。如果是住院手术，医生一般会让病人留院观察1—2天，以监测恢复情况。

说明：（1）比较有无"在这种情况下"（in this case）的译文效果，去除后，译文意思不变，且更加简洁。（2）注意"在门诊开展"（be done as outpatient procedures）的说法。

11.2.3 总结与点评

国外科普材料用语特点是：直接用称呼语 you 来将观众"拉入"介绍的科普内容场景，也会出现 your、your doctor、your tissue or organ 等表达。而中文科普材料往往是用第三方称谓，如病人、切除的组织等来做叙述的主体。翻译时，译员要注意转换。按照中文习惯，译员可删除这些人称代词。

要准确翻译术语，就要经常阅读目标语言的文献和文章，了解在该领域的术语乃至行话。在具体操作时，译员如果不确定，可将自己猜测的译法输入百度学术进行验证。验证时，除了关注检索命中数量，译员还需要观察文献来源、作者、时间、地区或国别等权威性判断信息。

11.2.4 词汇与表达拓展

1. 外科常用词汇

切口：incision
切除：dissection
缝合/缝线：suture
固定：fix
插管：intubation
撤管：extubation
移除：remove
纱布：gauze
敷料：dressing
手术刀：scalpel
手术钳：forceps
手术剪：scissors
游离：dissociation/free
吻合：anastomosis
端对端吻合：end-to-end anastomosis
侧对侧吻合：side-to-side anastomosis
侧对端吻合：side-to-end anastomosis
止血：hemostasis
电凝术：electrocoagulation

2. 解剖学和外科中的方位表达

trans-：经
transesophageal：经食道的
sub-：下

subcutaneous：皮下的

epi-：上

epigastric artery：腹上动脉

internal iliac artery：髂内动脉

external iliac artery：髂外动脉

lateral：侧的

lateral fixation：外侧固定

unilateral：单侧的

unilateral ovary：单侧卵巢

contralateral：对侧的

contralateral testis：对侧睾丸

11.3 脓肿切开引流

外科是临床医学的重要分支，一般以需要手术为主要疗法的疾病为对象。外科的主要亚专业包括普通外科（general surgery）、胸外科（thoracic surgery）、心外科（cardiac surgery）、骨科（orthopaedics）、泌尿外科（urological surgery）、整形外科（plastic surgery）、神经外科（neurosurgery）等。外科的专业术语除疾病相关术语之外，还包括手术相关的解剖学名词和手术器械。这些专科和各专科术语在医学会议中经常出现。

本节选编自《新英格兰医学杂志》网站介绍脓肿切开引流的教学视频。视频发布时间是 2007 年 11 月 8 日，主要内容是脓肿切开引流的适应证、禁忌证、所需器械、术前准备、手术操作、术后护理，以及并发症（indications, contraindications, required instruments, preoperative preparation, surgical procedures, postoperative care, and complications）等内容。选编目的是让学习者熟悉这类发言的口译。

在医学会议，特别是外科相关的会议中，手术视频是非常精彩而重要的环节。特别是讲者事先剪辑好的手术视频，环环相扣，进度极快，留给译员的反应时间相当短，给译员带来极大挑战。医学口译员需要进行外科手术录像翻译的训练。该杂志网站上有该视频的 PDF 文档，可下载参考，以便熟悉讲者的讲解脉络。

11.3.1 背景知识

脓肿（abcess）：是急性感染过程中，组织、器官或体腔内因病变组织坏死、液化而出现的局限性脓液积聚。四周有完整的脓壁。

知情同意（informed consent）：指患者对自己的病情和医生据此做出的诊断与治疗方案明了和认可。它要求医生必须向病人提供做出诊断和治疗方案的根据，即病情资料，并说明这种治疗方案的益处、不良反应、危险性及可能发生的其他意外情况，使病人能自主地做出决定——接受或不接受这种诊疗。

敷料（dressing）：用于覆盖伤口的材料，最常见的是纱布。

引流（drainage）：将伤口的液体引出体外的材料，常见的有引流管和引流条。

蜂窝织炎（cellulitis）：细菌引起的皮肤和皮下组织的广泛性、弥漫性炎症。

11.3.2 脓肿切开引流简介

1. 相关词汇

  incision：切开
  drainage：引流
  cutaneous abscess：皮肤脓肿
  loculated：分叶状
  localized：局限性的
  antibiotic：抗生素
  axilla：腋窝
  buttock：臀部
  extremity：四肢
  outpatient procedure：门诊手术
  urgent care：急诊治疗
  emergency department：急诊科/部
  physical examination：体格检查
  fluctuance：波动感
  needle aspiration：针穿刺
  anesthetize (v.)：麻醉
  anesthesia (n.)：麻醉
  sole：脚掌
  preoperative antibiotic：术前抗生素
  artificial heart valve：人工心脏瓣膜
  cosmetic：美容的；美观的
  sterile gauze：无菌纱布
  local anesthetic：局部麻醉药
  syringe：注射器
  lidocaine：利多卡因
  epinephrine：肾上腺素
  bupivacaine：布比卡因
  irrigation：冲洗
  bacterial culture：细菌培养

dress the wound：包扎伤口
antibacterial：抗菌的
face shield：面罩
chlorhexidine：氯己定
povidone iodine：聚维酮碘
intradermal tissues：皮内组织
abcess cavity：脓腔
puncture：穿刺
hemostat：止血钳
wound-packing material：伤口填充材料
quadrant：象限
local bacterial-culture susceptibility data：本地细菌敏感性培养结果数据
community-acquired methicillin-resistant Staphylococcus aureus (MRSA)：社区获得性耐甲氧西林金黄色葡萄球菌
pathogen：病原体
non-adherent：无黏性的
tetanus：破伤风
healing by secondary intention：二期愈合
acidic：酸性的
local anesthetic agent：局部麻醉剂

2. 原文、参考译文及说明

1）This is a video in clinical medicine from the *New England Journal of Medicine.*
这是来自《新英格兰医学杂志》的临床医学视频。

说明：《新英格兰医学杂志》是世界上影响最大的医学杂志之一。杂志每周出一期，官方网站上会有这期杂志的音频摘要（audio summary），概括了本期杂志的主要内容。认真听音频摘要，不但可以学习医学英语，而且可以了解医学的最新进展，对医学生和医学翻译学习者而言，是很好的学习材料。《新英格兰医学杂志》官网上有从量血压到伤口缝合的一系列临床医学视频，也都是很好的学习材料。近期，该杂志与国内合作提供其所发表的论文的中文译文，可供广大学习者进行双语阅读学习，也有助于译员积累医学知识和词汇。

2）Incision and drainage is the primary therapy for cutaneous abscess management. As antibiotic treatment alone is inadequate for treating many of these <u>loculated</u> collections of infectious material. Most localized skin abscesses without associated cellulitis can be <u>managed</u> with simple <u>incision and drainage</u> and do not require antibiotic treatment.

切开引流是皮肤脓肿的主要治疗方法。单独使用抗生素往往无法治疗这些<u>分叶状</u>积聚的感染性物质。大多数不伴蜂窝织炎的局限性皮肤脓肿可以通过简单的<u>切开引流</u>治疗，不需要抗生素治疗。

说明：（1）译员没有按字面意思将 management 翻译为"管理"，而是根据目标语言的表达习惯将其翻译为"治疗"。（2）incision and drainage 在原文是并列关系，但译员在译文中没有添加表示并列的"和"字，目的是让译文更加简洁。

3）Cutaneous abscesses have been described in all areas of the body but are commonly found in the axilla, buttocks, and extremities. This outpatient procedure is appropriate for many office settings, as well as for urgent care, and emergency department practicing environments.

全身各个部位都可能发生皮肤脓肿，最常见的部位是腋窝、臀部和四肢。这一门诊手术可以在许多地方开展，包括急诊。

说明：（1）注意：have been described 并非字对字翻译。（2）urgent care 和 emergency department 都表示急诊。翻译时，译员只说一遍即可。

4）Diagnosis of a skin abscess is the first step in a successful procedure. This can be accomplished in three ways. Physical examination of the affected area will often allow diagnosis of an underlying abscess based on swelling, pain, redness, and fluctuance. Spontaneously draining skin abscesses are also amenable to diagnosis by physical examination alone. Needle aspiration of a suspected skin abscess can assist clinicians in making the diagnosis of a localized abscess when results of physical examination are equivocal. Bedside ultrasound is a valuable adjunctive tool for identification of localized areas of fluid under the skin that may represent isolated areas of infection. An abscess that is diagnosed in one of these three ways may be appropriate for incision and drainage if it is larger than approximately 5 mm and found in an accessible location.

皮肤脓肿的诊断是成功手术的第一步，可以通过三种方式完成。当出现肿胀、疼痛、变红和波动感时，对受累部位的体格检查往往可以诊断脓肿。自发破溃的皮肤脓肿可以仅靠体格检查确诊。当体格检查不能确诊时，针穿刺可疑的皮肤脓肿有助于医生诊断局限性脓肿。床旁超声也是一种有价值的辅助手段，可明确代表局限性感染的皮下积液区。通过以上三种方式诊断的脓肿，如果直径大于 5 mm 且位于可处理区域，则适合切开引流。

说明：（1）procedure 有"步骤""程序"等意思，在此处表示"手术"。译员将 based on 灵活处理为"当……时"。（2）amenable 在此处的意思是 suitable for a particular type of treatment，如"Such conditions may be amenable to medical intervention."；译员将 be amenable to 翻译为"可以"。（3）与 localized 对应的概念是 wide-spread。（4）equivocal: If something is equivocal, it is difficult to understand, interpret, or explain, often because it has aspects that seem to contradict each other. (Formal) 例句：Research in this area is somewhat equivocal... / He was tortured by an awareness of the equivocal nature of his position. （5）译员根据汉语表达习惯将 tool 转换为近义词"手段"。（6）译文"可明确代表局限性感染的皮下积液区"中，"明确"作谓语动词，"代表……的皮下积液区"作宾语，核心词是"皮下积液区"。（7）注意：中文习惯笼统，英文精确性更高，如原文中的 one of these three，中文只是提及"三种"，未强调"三种方式之一"。（8）注意：accessible 可被翻译为"可处理"。

5) Extremely large or deep abscesses in areas difficult to anesthetize may <u>be more appropriate to treat</u> in a formal operating room setting. Abscesses of the palms, soles, or <u>nasolabial folds</u> can be associated with complications and may <u>require consultation with</u> an appropriate specialist. Incision and drainage <u>is not indicated for</u> cutaneous cellulitis <u>without an underlying abscess</u>. The need for preoperative antibiotics for conditions, such as abnormal or artificial heart valves, may require reconsideration of the timing for the procedure. <u>Input</u> from an appropriate specialist may be important for areas of the body with cosmetic concerns, because <u>the expected</u> scar formation after the abscesses drainage.

极大的或深部脓肿因其麻醉困难，更适合在正规的手术室环境进行治疗。手掌、脚掌或鼻唇沟处的脓肿可能出现并发症，应咨询合适的专家。不伴脓肿的皮肤蜂窝织炎不需要切开引流。术前需要进行抗生素治疗的情况（例如心脏瓣膜异常或人工心脏瓣膜），可能需要重新考虑手术时机。因为脓肿引流后会形成瘢痕，因此对于有美观需求的身体部位，合理的专家建议很重要。

说明：(1) 注意：appropriate 后用的是 treat 的主动语态，而非被动语态。(2) in a... setting 意为"在……环境"。该句也可不翻译，即译为"更适合在正规手术室治疗"。(3) A be not indicated for B 可被翻译为"B 不需要 A"。翻译时，施动者和受动者互换。(4) 注意：without an underlying 可被翻译为"不伴……的"。(5) input 在此处意译为"建议"。(6) 注意：expected 可被处理为"会"。

6) Appropriate universal <u>precautions</u> for potential exposure to bodily fluids should always <u>be used</u>. Materials needed for the incision and drainage of an abscess are similar to those needed for a <u>laceration repair</u>. <u>A pre-assembled laceration kit</u> may contain many of the necessary <u>items</u>.

对可能的体液接触应始终遵守常用的合理预防措施。脓肿切开引流需要的材料和外伤缝合所需要的材料相似。预配的外伤包里有许多必需的器械。

说明：precautions 与 use 搭配，此处用了被动语态。

7) For preparation and anesthesia, obtain a <u>skin-cleansing agent</u>, sterile gauze, local anesthetic, and a 5-to-10-ml syringe, with a 25 to 30-gauge needle. One percent lidocaine is an appropriate <u>anesthetic</u> for this procedure. Lidocaine with epinephrine offers advantages such as reduced bleeding and extended <u>duration of action</u>, but <u>is typically avoided</u> in areas with a single blood supply. Bupivacaine is another option that offers an increased duration of action for the anesthesia.

在准备和麻醉阶段，需要皮肤消毒液、无菌纱布、局麻药、5—10 ml 注射器、25—30 G 针头。这个手术可使用 1% 的利多卡因麻醉。利多卡因和肾上腺素连用具有减少出血并延长作用时间等优点，但是一般禁用于身体单一血供的区域。也可选择可延长麻醉作用时间的布比卡因。

说明：(1) 利多卡因是临床上最常用的局部麻醉药物，加入肾上腺素可以减少出血、延长作用时间。布比卡因是常用的长效麻醉药物。(2) anesthetic 在此处是名词。医学类文本中类似的表达有很多，如 antineoplastic（抗肿瘤药物）、antihypertensive（降压药）、

diuretic（利尿剂）均是用常见的形容词形式作名词。（3）在翻译"One percent lidocaine is an appropriate anesthetic for this procedure."时，译员进行了词性的灵活转换。贴合原文的译法（字面翻译）是："1% 的利多卡因是该手术合适的麻醉剂。"交流翻译法译文是："这个手术可使用 1% 的利多卡因麻醉。"交流翻译法译文更符合汉语表达习惯。（4）typical 释义如下："You use typical to describe someone or something that shows the most usual characteristics of a particular type of person or thing, and is therefore a good example of that type."其核心词是 usual，因此此处的 typically avoided 可被翻译为"一般是禁止的"。（5）areas with a single blood supply 可被译为"单一血供的区域"。

8）Items important for the incision and drainage itself include a scalpel blade with handle, a small curved hemostat, normal saline with a sterile bowl, and a large syringe with a splash guard or a needleless 18-gauge angiocatheter for irrigation of the wound. Swabs for bacterial culture, wound-packing material, scissors, gauze, and tape should all be available to complete the procedure and dress the wound.

切开引流必需的器械包括手术刀片和刀柄、小弯血管钳、无菌碗、生理盐水，以及用来冲洗伤口的带有防喷罩的大注射器或 18 号无针留置针。细菌培养拭子、伤口填充材料、剪刀、纱布和胶带都要准备好，用来完成手术并包扎伤口。

说明：（1）本段主要介绍手术相关器械和材料。画线词汇是本段翻译的关键词，译员需要重点掌握，准确翻译。（2）注意：important 可被灵活翻译为"必需的"。（3）scalpel blade 表示刀片，handel 表示刀柄。（4）词根 hemo 意为"血液"。（5）注意如下外科常用表达：irrigation of the wound（冲洗伤口）、bacterial culture（细菌培养）、wound-packing（伤口填充）、dress the wound（包扎伤口）。

9）Obtaining informed consent by discussing the risks and benefits of this procedure, including pain, bleeding, and scar formation. Wash your hands with antibacterial soap before beginning the procedure. Protect yourself from exposure to bodily fluids as many abscesses are under pressure. A face shield and gloves should be used.

告知患者手术风险（包括疼痛、出血和瘢痕形成）和益处并签署知情同意书。手术开始前使用抗菌肥皂洗手。因为许多脓肿都有压力，为了保护你自己避免体液接触，应使用面罩和手套。

说明：（1）"Obtaining informed consent by discussing the risks and benefits of this procedure, including pain, bleeding, and scar formation."没有被翻译为"通过讨论手术的风险（包括疼痛、出血和瘢痕形成）和益处而获得知情同意。"原因在于：在临床，实际上告知手术风险和益处发生在签署知情同意书之前。所以，原文的表达精确度有待商榷。

10）Place all equipment on a bedside table that is easy to reach. Position the patient so that the area for drainage is fully exposed. Apply a skin cleanser, such as chlorhexidine or povidone iodine, in a circular motion, starting at the peak of the abscess. Cover a wide area outside the wound to prevent contamination of other equipment.

将所有器械放在床旁桌上，以便于取用。摆好患者体位，使引流区域充分暴露。从脓肿的顶部开始以圆周运动的方式涂抹皮肤消毒剂（例如氯已定或者聚维酮碘）。消毒需覆盖伤口外大面积区域，以防污染其他器械。

说明：(1)此段是操作说明，因此有大量无主句出现。(2) position 作动词。

11) Anesthetize the top of the wound. This should be done by inserting a 25 or 30-gauge needle parallel to the skin and injecting it into the intradermal tissues. Once the entire open bore of the needle is under the skin, gentle pressure should be used to infiltrate with the anesthetic agent. You will note blanching of the tissue as the anesthetic spreads out. Continue with infiltration until you have covered an area over the top of the abscess large enough to anesthetize the area of incision. Some abscesses may require additional injections of anesthetic in a local field block pattern or modern procedural sedation for additional patient comfort.

使用 25 G 或 30 G 针头平行插入皮肤，并将麻药注射入皮内组织来麻醉伤口顶端。当整个针头进入皮肤下方时，使用温和的压力将麻药浸润皮肤。你可以看到随着麻药扩散，组织会变白。继续浸润直到覆盖脓肿顶端足够大的区域，足以麻醉皮肤切口。为了增加患者的舒适度，一些脓肿需要额外进行局部阻滞麻醉或术中镇静。

说明：(1)这段主要涉及麻醉方法，包括局部浸润麻醉（infiltration）、阻滞麻醉（field block）、镇静麻醉（sedation）。除了局部麻醉（local anesthesia）之外，还有全身麻醉（general anesthesia），本文也有提到。现代手术的发展离不开麻醉的进步。(2)注意原文中其他画线词语的对应译法。

12) Hold the scalpel between your thumb and forefinger. Make an incision directly over the center of the abscess that is oriented along the long axis of the fluid collection. Resistance may be felt as the incision is initiated and steady, firm pressure will allow a controlled entry into the subcutaneous tissues. Purulent drainage will begin when the abscess cavity has been entered successfully. Cosmetic results can be optimized if the incision is made parallel to existing skin-tension lines.

用大拇指和食指握住手术刀，直接在皮肤脓肿的中心切开；切口方向应沿着积液的长轴方向。开始切开时，你会感受到阻力，稳定的压力可以可控地进入皮下组织内。成功进入脓腔后，可以开始进行脓液引流。如果切口平行于现存皮肤张力线，伤口会最美观。

说明：注意以下两句的译法："Hold the scalpel between your thumb and forefinger. Make an incision directly over the center of the abscess that is oriented along the long axis of the fluid collection." 可将 "Hold the scalpel between your thumb and forefinger." 看作意义单位 A，将 "Make an incision directly over the center of the abscess" 看作意义单位 B，将 "that is oriented along the long axis of the fluid collection" 看作意义单位 C。原文是 A 为一句，B+C 为另一句；翻译时，将第二句进行了拆分，并将拆出的 B 与 A 重新合成了译文的第一句。

13) The incision should be extended to create an opening large enough to ensure adequate drainage and to prevent recurrent abscess formation; it may need to extend the length of the abscess borders. Care must be taken to control the scalpel during the stab

incision to prevent puncturing through the back wall of the abscess. The goal is to allow enough access for introduction of a hemostat to break up loculations and place internal packing. Using a swab to obtain a sample from the interior of the cavity for bacterial culture. Most patients will not require antibiotics after abscess drainage. Culture information is useful if the patient's condition later worsens and antibiotic treatment becomes necessary.

延长切口，使之足够长，保证充分引流，并且避免脓肿复发；可能需要延长至脓肿的边界。在切开的过程中，需要小心控制手术刀，避免刺穿脓肿后壁。目的是有足够的区域放进止血钳来打破分隔，并且放置填充物。使用拭子从脓腔内获得标本用来细菌培养。虽然大多数患者在脓肿引流后不需要抗生素治疗，但病人状态恶化需要抗生素治疗，培养结果就十分有用。

说明：（1）本段主要描述脓肿切开引流的相关细节。脓肿里面有的时候会存在分隔，如果不打断分隔，就无法充分引流脓液。所以，手术中的一个重要任务是把分隔打开，使脓肿能充分引流。（2）stab incision 中 stab 本意是"刺入"。（3）医学中常见方位词有 interior（内）、exterior（外）、internal（内）、external（外）、inferior（下）、superior（上）、anterior（前）、posterior（后）。

14）After allowing the wound to drain spontaneously, gently express any further contents. Additional injections of local anesthetic may be helpful during this portion of procedure if there is significant patient discomfort. Use a curved hemostat for further blunt dissection to break loculations and allow the abscess cavity to be completely opened up. Insert the hemostat into the wound until you feel the resistance of normal tissue; then open the hemostat to perform blunt dissection of the internal portion of the abscess cavity. Continue this procedure of breaking up loculations in a circular motion until the entire abscess cavity has been explored and any deep tracts that extend the surrounding tissues have been identified. Gent irrigation of the wound should be performed using sterile normal saline. An appropriate wound incision size will enhance irrigation and prevent excessive buildup of pressure within the abscess cavity. The irrigation should continue until the effluent is clear.

当伤口可以自然引流之后，轻柔按压，挤出内容物。在手术过程中如果患者有明显的不适，补充注射局麻药是有用的。使用弯钳进一步钝性分离，打断分隔，使得脓腔完全开放。把弯钳放入伤口，直至感受到正常组织的阻力，然后打开弯钳钝性分离脓腔的内部区域。通过圆周运动持续破坏分隔，直到探查整个脓腔并探查任何延伸到周围组织的瘘道。用无菌生理盐水轻柔冲洗伤口。适当的切口大小有利于冲洗并防止脓腔内压力过高。持续冲洗直到液体清亮。

说明：（1）perform 意为"行"。perform blunt dissection 意为"行钝性分离"。（2）tract 本意为"管道"，结合上下文，此处可被翻译为"瘘道"。瘘道还可表达为 fistula。（3）buildup 意为"形成"。此处的 excessive buildup of pressure 可被灵活处理为"压力过高"。（4）effluent 意为"流出液，流出物"，根据上下文，此处可被灵活处理为"液体"。

15）Using wound-packing material, such as 1/4- or 1/2-in packing strips, gently pack the abscess by starting in one quadrant and gradually working around the entire cavity. Place sufficient packing to keep the walls of the abscess separated and to allow further drainage of <u>infected debris</u>. Overpacking may cause <u>ischemia</u> of the surrounding tissues or interfere with desired wound drainage and should be avoided. An appropriate packing will <u>allow healing by secondary intention</u> and avoid premature closure of the wound, which can lead to re-accumulation of bacteria and recurrent abscesses.

使用伤口填充材料,例如 1/4—1/2 英寸的填充条,从一个象限开始轻柔地填充脓腔,直至填满整个腔隙。使用足够的填充物将脓腔壁隔开,可以进一步引流出感染物。过度填塞会导致周围组织的<u>缺血</u>或阻碍引流,因此要避免过度填塞。合理的伤口填塞可以<u>使伤口二期愈合</u>,并避免伤口过早愈合。伤口过早愈合会导致细菌再次聚集和脓肿复发。

说明:(1)脓肿引流之后,需要在脓腔里面放置填充物,有利于引流,并避免在脓肿全部引流出来之前发生伤口过早愈合的情况。如果没有相关的背景知识,译员在翻译本段时会比较困难。如果要翻译手术视频,译员需要提前自学手术过程,这样才能储备足够的背景知识,在听到讲者介绍的时候,能够在脑海中复现手术的场景,达到准确翻译。

16) For a simple abscess, the now openly draining wound allows the body's <u>host defenses</u> to clear the infection without the need to expose patients to side effects or risks of <u>antimicrobial therapy</u>. After most incision and drainage procedures are performed in healthy patients, antibiotics are not required. Patients with extensive cellulitis beyond the abscess area or with significant <u>comorbidities</u> may require supplemental antibiotic treatment. Providers are encouraged to use local bacterial-culture susceptibility data to guide any such empiric therapy.

对于单纯的脓肿,开放引流伤口就可以使机体的<u>自身免疫系统清除感染</u>,患者可以避免<u>抗菌治疗</u>的副作用和风险。大多数健康患者切开引流后不需要抗生素治疗。脓肿区域以外广泛蜂窝织炎或有明显共患病的患者可能需要辅助抗生素治疗。鼓励医生使用本地细菌敏感性培养结果数据来指导此类经验性治疗。

说明:(1) co- 意为"共同"; morbid 意为"病的";所以 comorbidity 意为"共患病"。比较: complication 意为"并发症"。(2) local bacterial-culture susceptibility data 指的是在某个区域内收集的细菌对药物敏感性的数据。(3) empiric therapy 意为"经验性治疗",指的是医师在给药时,按照既往经验,首先从对此类感染有效的药物开始给药,然后再按照病情进展情况调整用药。

17) Community-acquired methicillin-resistant Staphylococcus aureus (MRSA) has garnered heightened attention because of its increasing prevalence in skin infections. It is imperative to know and follow your regional management guidelines for this pathogen.

因为在皮肤感染中的发生率日益升高,社区获得性耐甲氧西林金黄色葡萄球菌(MRSA)获得了高度关注。必须要了解和遵守关于这类病原菌的当地管理指南。

说明:MRSA 的全称比较复杂,包括了抗生素名称和细菌名称。如果译者不熟悉,或者反应不过来,直接说 MRSA(/'ma:sa:/)也是可以的。医生一般能听懂 MRSA 这个英文缩写。

18) Cover the abscess wound with a sterile, non-adherent dressing. <u>Topical</u> antibiotics

have a limited benefit and are not required. As with any wound, be certain that patients' tetanus immunizations are up-to-date. All abscesses should have packing removed in a few days, and most patients with wounds that have packing in place should be <u>scheduled for a returning visit for follow-up</u> and packing remove 2 to 3 days after the procedure. Patients should <u>be given return instructions telling them to return earlier</u> if there are any signs of worsening. On subsequent visits for wound care, packing should be removed to allow assessment of the ongoing healing by secondary intention. Using fresh packing material may be necessary to continue the healing process, if significant wound drainage is still long going. A follow-up visit should then be rescheduled 2 to 3 days later. This is common for abscesses that require extensive drainage and in the absence of other <u>complications</u>, the need for repacking is not an <u>indication</u> for antibiotic treatment.

使用无菌、无黏性的敷料覆盖脓肿伤口。<u>外用</u>抗生素获益有限，因此不是必需的。因为有伤口，因此需要确定病人破伤风疫苗接种的最新情况。在几天后取出脓肿的所有填充物，大多数患者应<u>预约</u>术后 2—3 天的<u>随访</u>，取出伤口填充物。如果有任何恶化的迹象，<u>应告知患者及早就诊</u>。在随后的伤口照护随访中，应去除敷料以评估伤口的二期愈合情况。如果伤口引流仍需较长时间，需要更换新的填充物，有利于伤口愈合，并预约 2—3 天后的随访。脓肿经常需要持续引流；需要再次填充，但没有其他<u>并发症</u>，并不是使用抗菌治疗的<u>适应证</u>。

说明：（1）returning visit for follow-up 意为"随访"，也可单独使用 returning visit 或 follow-up visit 来表达这一含义。（2）indication 意为"适应证"，其反义词 contraindication 意为"禁忌证"。

19）The acidic environment of infected tissue leads to difficulties with adequate anesthesia provided by local anesthetic agents. Using appropriate amounts of anesthetic, allowing sufficient time after injection, or supplementing with <u>oral or parenteral agents</u> can increase the patient's comfort. Finally, additional complications to watch for include progression to surrounding cellulitis, development of fever, or other signs of clinical worsening. <u>This may prompt consideration for</u> repeat incision and drainage of an abscess or the need for antibiotic therapy. Most abscesses will respond well to simple incision and drainage and will not require treatment beyond packing changes and <u>local wound care practices</u>.

感染组织的酸性环境导致局麻药难以提供充分的麻醉。使用合适剂量的麻醉药、注射后留有充分的作用时间或补充口服或肠外药物可以增加患者的舒适度。此外，其他的并发症包括发展到周围的蜂窝织炎、发烧或者其他临床恶化的征象。<u>这意味着需要考虑再次切开引流或使用抗菌治疗</u>。对于大多数脓肿来说，单纯切开引流疗效良好，除了更换填充物和<u>局部伤口照护</u>之外，不需要其他治疗。

说明：（1）比较三个表示给药途径的词：topical（局部外用）、oral（口服）、parenteral（肠外，para- 意为"周围"，-entero 意为"小肠的"）。（2）注意：翻译 local wound care practices 时，译员省掉了 practices，因为照护已经将 practices 的意思包含在内了。

11.3.3 总结与点评

对于手术视频的翻译，表达方面最重要的是简洁、准确，翻译出最关键的术语。听众往往有相关背景知识，能根据译员说出的简短的关键术语来理解手术过程。

医学名词中往往有很多缩写，比如本章节中出现的 MRSA，在时间紧张的情况下，这样的专业术语就可以不翻译成中文，直接说英文缩写，既能省下宝贵的时间用来理解和表达讲者的其他重要内容，也不会影响听众的理解。但是，此类缩写往往有行业内固定的念法，可能与译者常规接触的习惯不同，如 MRSA 念 /'mɑːsɑː/，NOAC（new oral anti-coagulants，新型口服抗凝药）念 /'nəʊæk/。

11.3.4 词汇与表达拓展

1. diagnosis 的常见搭配（克劳瑟，2006）

accurate, correct, right, incorrect, wrong, definite, definitive, firm, positive, provisional, tentative, early

- Without the results of the blood test, the doctor could only make a tentative diagnosis.
- Early diagnosis is critical for successful treatment.

initial, final, clinical, medical

- psychiatric clinical diagnosis of schizophrenia, AIDS, and cancer

establish, give, make, reach

- The doctor cannot give a diagnosis without knowing the full medical history.

confirm

- Further tests have confirmed the diagnosis.

2. precaution 的常见搭配（同上）

sensible, wise, adequate, proper, reasonable, necessary, elaborate, basic, simple

- You'll be quite safe if you observe certain basic precautions.

every

- We take every precaution to ensure that you have a comfortable journey.

extra, special, fire, safety, security, follow, observe, take, as a precaution

- She had to stay in hospital overnight, just as a precaution.

precaution against

- a precaution against customers who try to leave without paying

precaution for

- Staff are expected to take reasonable precautions for their own safety.

precaution of

- I took the precaution of turning the water supply off first.

11.4 提上睑肌腱膜缩短术

外科手术视频翻译是医学会议口译中的常见任务。本节选编视频介绍了提上睑肌腱膜缩短术，可帮助学习者进一步学到与外科手术操作相关的表达。

11.4.1 背景知识

提上睑肌腱膜缩短术：是一种眼科手术，适应证包括中度上睑下垂、提上睑肌肌力在中度及以上的先天性及后天性上睑下垂等。

11.4.2 提上睑肌腱膜缩短术简介

1. 相关词汇

1）术式和症状/疾病
上睑提肌腱膜缩短术：levator advancement
重睑成形术：double eyelid operation
上睑下垂：ptosis

2）药物和器械
美兰：methylene blue
利多卡因：lidocaine
压板：protector
直剪：straight scissors
血管钳：hemostat
可吸收线：absorbable suture
丝线：silk

3）解剖学相关
重睑线：double eyelid line

上睑皮：upper eyelid
上穹窿：upper fornix
睑板：tarsal plate
提上睑肌：levator
结膜：conjunctiva
角膜：cornea
眼轮匝肌：orbicularis oculi muscle
眶隔：orbital septum
眶缘：orbital rim
内眦部：medial canthus
外眦部：lateral canthus
Müller 肌：Müller muscle
节制韧带：Whitnall ligament
内外脚：medial horn and lateral horn
滑车：cochlea
上斜肌：superior oblique muscle
兔眼：lagophthalmus

4）操作
浸润麻：infiltration anesthesia
分离：dissect
去除；剪除：remove
切开：incise
置入：insert
烧灼止血：hemostasis with electrocautery
夹住：clamp
形成三针褥式缝线：make three matrasses sutures
打活结：make temporary knots
结扎缝线：tie the knots

5）其他
弧度：contour

2. 原文、参考译文及说明

1）提上睑肌腱膜缩短术
Levator advancement.
2）适应证：中度上睑下垂、提上睑肌肌力在中度及以上的先天性及后天性上睑下垂者。
Indications: Congenital and acquired ptosis patients with moderate ptosis, whose strength of levator is no worse than moderate.

说明：积累常见表达：中度（moderate）、重度（severe）、轻度（mild）、先天性的（congenital）、后天性的（acquired）。

3）手术方法：沿重睑线以美蓝画线。

Procedure: Draw the incision line according to the double eyelid line with methylene blue.

说明：此处的"画线"指"画切口的线"，因此可将其补充翻译为 draw the incision line；可将"沿"翻译为 according to。

4）2% 利多卡因上穹窿部、结膜下及上睑皮下浸润麻醉。

Infiltration anesthesia with 2% lidocaine in upper fornix, conjunctiva, and upper eyelids.

5）切开皮肤。

Incise the skin.

6）剪除睑板上缘中 1/3 处睑板前轮匝肌。在睑板中外 1/3 或中内 1/3 处做一牵引线。置入睑板压板。

Remove the pretarsal obicularis oculi from the middle 1/3 tarsal plate. Make a traction suture in the lateral 1/3 or medial 1/3 of the tarsal plate. Insert the tarsal plate protector.

说明：（1）注意这句话的断句：剪除 / 睑板上缘 / 中 1/3 处 / 睑板前 / 轮匝肌。在睑板中 / 外 1/3/ 或内 1/3 处 / 做一牵引线。（2）可将"做一牵引线"翻译为 make a traction suture，即做一个牵引缝合。

7）分离提上睑肌：于睑板上缘近内眦部或外眦部用直剪剪断一小部分提上睑肌。然后将直剪深入提上睑肌下面，将提上睑肌完全分离，剪断其与睑板上缘的联系。

Dissection of the levator: Cut a small portion of levator along the upper margin of the tarsal plate, near medial canthus or lateral canthus. Then insert the straight scissors under the levator; dissect it completely. Cut the connections between the levator and the tarsal plate.

8）分离 Müller 肌：于睑板上缘 8—10 毫米处分离 Müller 肌，将其与提上睑肌之间的联系切断。

Dissection of Müller muscle: Dissect Müller muscle 8–10 mm above the upper margin of the tarsal plate. Cut the connections between Müller muscle and the levator.

9）打开眶隔，将眶脂肪上推，或经烧灼止血后去除。

Open the orbital septum. Push the orbital fat upward, or remove it after hemostasis with electrocautery.

说明：此处，烧灼是指电烧灼。

10）在眶隔下将提上睑肌完全分离并清除，此时提上睑肌上表面及下方均已得到分离。断内外角及节制韧带。用直剪顺提上睑肌两侧向上伸，剪开内外脚及节制韧带，此时可感觉提上睑肌向外松动，注意剪开内侧角时勿过于近眶缘，否则有伤及滑车和上斜肌的可能。

Completely dissect the levator below orbital septum. Now, the upper and lower surfaces of levator have been dissected. Cut the medial horn, lateral horn and Whitnall ligament. Use the straight scissors to cut the medial horn, lateral horn and Whitnall ligament. Now the levator becomes loose laterally. Be careful not to be too close to the orbital rim when cutting the medial horn to avoid injuring the cochlea or superior oblique muscle.

11）缝合提上睑肌，以血管钳夹住提上睑肌，用5-0可吸收线或5-0丝线于睑板上缘2毫米处缝合睑板板层三针，然后将此缝线缝于拟定缩短的提上睑肌腱膜处，形成三针褥式缝线。

Suture the levator. Clamp the levator with hemostat, and then make 3 sutures on the 2 mm upper margin of the tarsal plate. The suture could be 5-0 absorbable suture or 5-0 silk. Then take the suture through the advanced levator, making three mattress sutures.

说明：（1）表示几号的缝线、器材等时，可用gauze（"号"）表示，在上下文明晰时，也可省略不说。（2）外科常见缝合方法经常在外科口译中出现，请注意积累。

12）先打活结，嘱病人平视。如为全麻病人，先将眼球拉至正常位置，观察上睑的高度、弧度及兔眼大小，如矫正满意，则结扎缝线；如矫正不满意，需要行缝线调整。

First, make temporary knots, and then ask the patient to open the eyelids. If the patient is under general anesthesia, the eyeball should be pulled to the normal position, and the doctor should evaluate the height and contour of the upper eyelid, and lagophthalmus. If the result is satisfactory, then tie the knots. If not, adjust the suture.

13）在缝线下2毫米处剪除提上睑肌腱膜。以重睑成形术方式缝合皮肤，缝合皮肤时，注意睑缘位置、睫毛方向。

Cut the levator aponeurosis 2 mm below the suture. Suture the skin with the technique the same as double eyelid operation. During skin suture, you should pay attention to the position of the lid margin and the direction of the eyelash.

14）术后处理：加压包扎48到72小时，7天拆除皮肤缝线。术毕时，上睑缘位于角膜缘下1毫米为最佳。

Postoperative care: Compression dressing for 48–72 hours. Skin sutures will be removed in 7 days. When the upper eyelid margin is 1 mm below the cornea upper limbus after the operation, the optimal result is achieved.

11.4.3 总结与点评

医学口译，尤其是同声传译，难免会出现突发状况，如发言人提及不认识的专业词汇、句子没听清或翻译思考时间不足出现语误等情况，建议平时练好心态，临场就能处变不惊。

对于不认识或临时忘记的专业词汇，译员在临场应急时可用转换法，将其替换成普通词汇来表达。长期来看，译员可通过记忆医学词根、词缀等方式，熟悉构成，尽量做到专业术语的专业翻译。

在交替传译时，若是出现没听清的情况，译员可当场打断发言人求证，不建议在没有把握的情况下，硬翻有关内容，造成失误，引起听众不满。对于同声传译，若是出现未听清或未完全理解的句子，译员可暂时进行短期记忆存储，不做翻译，听见后面的句子后再结合上下文语境进行补译。如果译员对句子理解无把握，则建议放弃，而不建议硬翻，造成错误，因为错译误导听众的后果往往比漏译带来信息损失的危害性更大。

口译中若出现语误,一旦发现,译员可对听众进行补充说明。同声传译的语误问题,两三句话以内发生的失误,译员可找寻适当时机进行弥补修正,其他情况则不建议修正,因为打断听众连续性的后果更严重。

11.4.4 词汇与表达拓展

1. 外科常见术式

1) -pexy = surgically reattach, fix in a normal position:通过手术重新连接;固定到正常位置

hepatopexy:肝固定术

nephropexy (surgically attach the kidney in a normal anatomical position):肾脏固定术

splenopexy:脾固定术

2) -plasty = reconstruction:重建

rhinoplasty (surgical reconstruction of the nose):鼻成形术

3) -ectomy = cut out / remove:切除

appendectomy:阑尾切除术

tonsillectomy:扁桃体切除术

4) -otomy = cut into:切开

tracheotomy (cut into the windpipe, a temporary opening):气管切开术

5) -ostomy = make a "mouth":造口

colostomy (make a permanent opening in the colon):结肠造口术

2. 其他外科常见手术 / 操作

anastomosis:吻合术

drainage:引流术

extraction:摘除术

参考文献

克劳瑟.2006. 牛津英语搭配词典. 北京:外语教学与研究出版社.

Adminms. 2012. 新版日本《胃癌处理规约》. Medsci. Retrieved November 10, 2022, from Medsci website.

Michael, T. et al. 2007. Abscess incision and drainage. *New England Journal of Medicine*, (357): 20.

第 12 章

基础医学

12.1 艾滋病和流感的疫苗策略

艾滋病的流行对社会和经济产生了极大的负面影响。直到 21 世纪,人们还没有找到针对艾滋病的特效治疗方法,虽然高效抗逆转录病毒疗法(highly active antiretroviral therapy, HAART)已经在减轻患者痛苦、延长患者寿命等方面取得了一定的效果,但用于治疗艾滋病病毒感染的药物只能控制病毒复制,不能彻底清除病毒,而且抗艾滋病药物非常昂贵,还具有较严重的副作用,药物使用不当也会诱发耐药株的产生。因此,研制安全、有效的疫苗是控制艾滋病传播的重要手段之一。艾滋病易感者通过接种艾滋病疫苗,发生免疫反应,从而产生对疾病的特异抵抗力,提高免疫水平,达到预防和治疗艾滋病的目的。

本节讲话选自 2010 年 2 月流行病学家赛斯·伯克利(Seth Berkley)在 TED 上的演讲 "HIV and Flu—The Vaccine Strategy"。

12.1.1 背景知识

1918 年大流感:1918 年,在第一次世界大战的末尾,由甲型 H1N1 流感病毒引发的流感大流行,横扫美洲、欧洲、亚洲,甚至因纽特人聚集区,造成全球超过 5 亿人感染、5 千万至 1 亿人死亡,可谓是人类历史上最严重的流行病疫情。

Rock of Gibraltar: a small area of land in the south of Spain that is controlled by the UK. If someone says something is "like the Rock of Gibraltar", they mean it is very solid and strong and will not be destroyed.

Vaclav Smil's "massively fatal discontinuity" of life:"The Next 50 Years: Fatal Discontinuities"(Smil, 2005)一文作者瓦茨拉夫·斯米尔(Vaclav Smil)认为:Modern civilization is subject to gradual environmental, social, economic, and political transformations as well as to sudden changes that can fundamentally alter its prospects. He examines in this article a key set of such fatal discontinuities by quantifying the likelihood of three classes of sudden, and potentially catastrophic, events—natural disasters; viral pandemics; and transformational wars—and by comparing their likelihood with other involuntary risks (including terrorism) and voluntary actions and exposures.

12.1.2 艾滋病和流感疫苗策略简介

1. 相关词汇

vaccine：疫苗

neutralize：中和

mucosal barrier：黏膜屏障

immune cell：免疫细胞

replicate：复制

dendritic cell：树突细胞，树状细胞

macrophage：巨噬细胞

memory cell：记忆细胞

activated：激活的

plasma cell：浆细胞

squadron：中队

antibody：抗体

flu：流感

rendering of the flu virus：流感疫苗图

spike：刺突，病毒粒子表面的突起结构

mutate：变异

strain：毒株

prevail：流行

influenza A：甲流

recombine：重组

wild aquatic bird：野生水禽

mortality rate：死亡率

avian：禽类的

swine：猪的

transmit：传播

pathogen：病原

decoy：诱骗

evade：逃逸

genome：基因组

genetic variation：基因变异

cure：治愈手段

clinical trial：临床试验

neutralizing antibody：中和抗体

disable variations of the virus：使病毒变异体失去作用

vaccine candidate：疫苗候选物
retro-vaccinology：反向疫苗技术
universal HIV vaccine：适用于不同艾滋病病毒的疫苗
binding site：结合位点
three-dimensional structure：三维结构
rational vaccine design：合理/理性疫苗设计
protuberance：突起
severe disease：重症
mild case：轻症
vaccine delivery：疫苗递送
pandemic：跨洲际大流行（的）[1]
dose：剂
cumbersome：麻烦的
swine flu：猪流感
avian strain：禽流感毒株
poultry flock：禽群
pellet：球团；颗粒
contamination：污染
plant：工厂
spark the immune system：激活免疫系统
lop off：切除
bacterium：细菌
E. coli：大肠杆菌
swine-origin flu vaccine：猪源性流感病毒
be/get vaccinated：接种疫苗
vulnerable：脆弱的；易感的

2. 原文、参考译文及说明

1）A vaccine trains the body in advance on how to recognize and neutralize a specific invader. After HIV penetrates the body's mucosal barriers, it infects immune cells to replicate. The invader draws the attention of the immune system's front-line troops. Dendritic cells, or macrophages, capture the virus and display pieces of it. Memory cells generated by the

---

[1] 注意区分下面这三个词。endemic：(of a disease or condition) regularly found among particular people or in a certain area，地方病。epidemic：(of a disease or condition) affecting or tending to affect a disproportionately large number of individuals within a population, community, or region at the same time，流行病，又叫"时疫""瘟疫"等。pandemic：occurring over a wide geographic area (such as multiple countries or continents) and typically affecting a significant proportion of the population。

HIV vaccine are activated when they learn HIV is present from the front-line troops. These memory cells immediately deploy the exact weapons needed. Memory B cells turn into plasma cells, which produce wave after wave of the specific antibodies that latch onto HIV to prevent it from infecting cells, while squadrons of killer T cells seek out and destroy cells that are already HIV-infected. The virus is defeated. Without a vaccine, these responses would have taken more than a week. By that time, the battle against HIV would already have been lost.

疫苗预先训练我们的身体怎样识别和压制入侵者。一旦艾滋病病毒穿过身体黏膜障碍，它就开始破坏免疫细胞，不断进行自我复制。入侵者会吸引人体免疫系统"前线部队"的注意力。树突细胞或巨噬细胞会吞噬病毒，同时在自身表面展现它的一些片段。一旦前线部队发现艾滋病病毒，艾滋病疫苗产生的记忆细胞就会被激活。这些记忆细胞迅速分派特定的武器来应对。记忆细胞 B 变成（成熟）浆细胞，而浆细胞会产生一波又一波特异性抗体。这些抗体会"抓住"艾滋病病毒以阻止艾滋病病毒感染其他细胞。杀伤 T 细胞会寻找并破坏已经被艾滋病病毒感染的细胞。病毒就这样被打败了。如果没有疫苗，我们的身体可能会要一周多的时间才会对病毒作出反应。到那时，与艾滋病病毒的战斗必然是失败的了。

说明：本段文字来自讲者在现场播放的讲解疫苗工作原理的录像配音。本段后为赛斯·伯克利的讲话。

2) Really cool video, isn't it? The antibodies you just saw in this video, in action, are the ones that make most vaccines work. So, the real question then is: How do we ensure that your body makes the exact ones that we need to protect against flu and HIV? The principal challenge for both of these viruses is that they're always changing. So, let's take a look at the flu virus. In this rendering of the flu virus, these different colored spikes are what it uses to infect you. And also, what the antibodies use is a handle to essentially grab and neutralize the virus. When these mutate, they change their shape, and the antibodies don't know what they're looking at anymore. So that's why every year you can catch a slightly different strain of flu. It's also why in the spring, we have to make the best guess at which three strains are going to prevail the next year, put those into a single vaccine and rush those into production for the fall.

非常酷的视频，是吧？你们刚刚所看到视频里的抗体行为就是大部分疫苗起作用的过程。所以真正的问题是：我们怎样确保我们的身体能产生我们需要的特定抗体来抵抗流感和艾滋病病毒呢？面对大部分病毒，最大的挑战就是病毒总是在变换。我们一起来看一看流感病毒。在这个流感病毒示意图中，那些不同颜色的突起就是病毒用来感染你身体的工具，同样也是抗体用来抓住并且中和这些病毒的工具。一旦病毒开始变异，开始改变自己的形状，抗体这时候就难以识别这些病毒。所以，这就是你每年总是感染稍稍不同的流感病毒的原因。这也就是为什么每年春天我们都要预测一下明年哪三类病毒会流行，然后制作出一种疫苗，在秋季加紧投入生产。

3) Even worse, the most common influenza, influenza A, also infects animals that

live in close proximity to humans, and they can recombine in those particular animals. In addition, wild aquatic birds carry all known strains of influenza. So, you've got this situation: In 2003, we had an H5N1 virus that jumped from birds into humans in a few isolated cases with an apparent mortality rate of 70 percent. Now luckily, that particular virus, although very scary at the time, did not transmit from person to person very easily. This year's H1N1 threat was actually a human, avian, swine mixture that arose in Mexico. It was easily transmitted, but, luckily, was pretty mild. And so, in a sense, our luck is holding out, but you know, another wild bird could fly over at any time.

可更糟糕的是，最常见的流感病毒——流感病毒A会感染动物，而那些动物就生活在人类身边，病毒会在这些动物中再次重组。还有就是，野生水生鸟类会携带众所周知的多种流行性感冒病毒。你们已经经历过以下这些事情了：2003年，我们遭遇了一种叫作H5N1的病毒。在一些病例中，它从鸟类传染到了人类，死亡率高达70%。幸运的是，尽管这个病毒当时令人害怕，但是它不会轻易地在人与人之间传播。今年的H1N1病毒其实是人类、禽类、猪的混合病毒，这种病毒首先在墨西哥产生。这种病毒很容易传播，但幸运的是，它的毒性并没有那么强。所以，在某种意义上，我们仍是很幸运的。但是，说不定什么时候另一只鸟就飞来了呢。

4）Now let's take a look at HIV. As variable as the flu is, HIV makes flu look like the Rock of Gibraltar. The virus that causes AIDS is the trickiest pathogen scientists have ever confronted. It mutates furiously, it has decoys to evade the immune system, it attacks the very cells that are trying to fight it and it quickly hides in your genome. Here's a slide looking at the genetic variation of flu and comparing that to HIV, a much wilder target. In the video a moment ago, you saw fleets of new viruses launching from infected cells. Now realize that in a recently infected person, there are millions of these ships; each one is just slightly different. Finding a weapon that recognizes and sinks all of them makes the job that much harder.

现在，我们来看看艾滋病病毒。尽管流感多变，但艾滋病病毒更加多变。这让流感病毒相形见绌，就像直布罗陀海峡的岩石一般显眼。艾滋病病毒是最狡猾、最难缠的病毒，也是科学家面对的最难对付的病毒。艾滋病病毒急剧变异，甚至可以欺骗并躲过免疫系统。它会攻击那些攻击它的免疫细胞，之后会迅速地把自己隐藏在你的基因组里。这里的幻灯片向我们展示的是流感基因的变异情况，并将它与艾滋病病毒在基因变异方面进行对比。艾滋病病毒是一个更加狂野、不易击中的目标。之前，我们在视频中看到从感染细胞中产生出一批批新病毒。我们要意识到，在每一个新感染者的体内，病毒有成千上百万个，但是每一个都稍有不同。所以，要找到一种可以识别并且击败所有病毒的有效武器是一件更为艰难的事。

说明：（1）"As variable as the flu is, HIV makes flu look like the Rock of Gibraltar." 这句话中，讲者的逻辑似乎有误。其字面意思应该是像那块石头那样明显和重要。（2）genetic variation 意为"基因变异情况"。（3）a much wilder target 意为"一个更加狂野的目标"。

5）Now, in the 27 years since HIV was identified as the cause of AIDS, we've developed more drugs to treat HIV than all other viruses put together. These drugs aren't cures, but they represent a huge triumph of science because they take away the automatic death sentence from a diagnosis of HIV, at least for those who can access them. The vaccine effort though is really quite different. Large companies moved away from it because they thought the science was so difficult and vaccines were seen as a poor business. Many thought that it was just impossible to make an AIDS vaccine, but today, evidence tells us otherwise.

艾滋病病毒被确认为引起艾滋病的元凶已经有27年了。我们已经研制了越来越多的药物来治疗艾滋病，这些药物的种类比我们用于治疗所有其他病毒的加起来都要多。这些药物并不能治愈艾滋病，但是科学在对艾滋病病毒的战斗中已经取得了巨大的胜利，因为这些药物让确诊艾滋病不再等同于宣判死刑，至少对于那些有途径取得这些药物的人来说不再如此。但在疫苗研发方面，情况很不一样。一些大公司也不再做疫苗，因为他们认为科学如此艰辛，且做疫苗又不是什么赚钱的行业。很多人都认为研制出艾滋病病毒的疫苗简直是天方夜谭，但是现在，证据显示这是有可能的。

说明：vaccine effort 指疫苗研发工作。

6) In September, we had surprising but exciting findings from a clinical trial that took place in Thailand. For the first time, we saw an AIDS vaccine work in humans—albeit, quite modestly—and that particular vaccine was made almost a decade ago. Newer concepts and early testing now show even greater promise in the best of our animal models. But in the past few months, researchers have also isolated several new broadly neutralizing antibodies from the blood of an HIV infected individual. Now, what does this mean? We saw earlier that HIV is highly variable, that a broadly neutralizing antibody latches on and disables multiple variations of the virus. If you take these and you put them in the best of our monkey models, they provide full protection from infection. In addition, these researchers found a new site on HIV where the antibodies can grab onto, and what's so special about this spot is that it changes very little as the virus mutates. It's like, as many times as the virus changes its clothes, it's still wearing the same socks, and now our job is to make sure we get the body to really hate those socks.

今年九月，我们在泰国的临床实验中有一个令人惊奇和兴奋的发现。这是我们第一次发现艾滋病病毒疫苗在人体中能够发挥作用，尽管作用还比较弱，而且这种疫苗在十多年前就研制出来了。较新的理念和早期测试显示该疫苗在动物模型中有很好的效果和巨大的前景。但是在过去的几个月中，研究人员已经从感染艾滋病病毒个体的血液中分离出一种新的广谱中和抗体。那这意味着什么呢？早些时候，我们看到艾滋病病毒有多种变异体，而这种具有广泛中和能力的抗体能够与病毒结合，并破坏多种病毒变异体。如果把这样的疫苗注入猴子模型中，抗体可对其提供全面的保护，使其免受感染。另外，这些研究发现艾滋病毒上有抗体能结合的新位点，这个位点在病毒变异时基本不发生改变。这就好像，尽管病毒换了自己的衣服，但是它仍然穿着同样的短袜。现在，我们的工作就是让我们的身体能够明确地识别并厌恶这些短袜。

说明：（1）clinical trial 是"临床试验"，而非"临床实验"。（2）animal models 意为"动物模型"。（3）site 意为"位点"。（4）spot 意为"位点"。

7) So, what we've got is a situation. The Thai results tell us we can make an AIDS vaccine, and the antibody findings tell us how we might do that. This strategy, working backwards from an antibody to create a vaccine candidate, has never been done before in vaccine research. It's called retro-vaccinology, and its implications extend way beyond that of just HIV. So, think of it this way. We've got these new antibodies we've identified, and we know that they latch onto many, many variations of the virus. We know that they have to latch onto a specific part, so if we can figure out the precise structure of that part, and present that through a vaccine, what we hope is (that) we can prompt your immune system to make these matching antibodies. And that would create a universal HIV vaccine. Now, it sounds easier than it is because the structure actually looks more like this blue antibody diagram attached to its yellow binding site, and as you can imagine, these three-dimensional structures are much harder to work on. And if you guys have ideas to help us solve this, we'd love to hear about it.

我们现在的处境如下。泰国的实验结果告诉我们，我们能研制出艾滋病病毒疫苗。抗体的发现告诉我们，我们能做到。这样的策略——从抗体出发，然后再制造疫苗——之前的疫苗研究从未尝试过。我们称这一过程为反向疫苗技术，这一理论的应用已经超出艾滋病领域。我们可以这样想：我们已经取得了这些结构确认的新抗体，我们知道这些抗体能结合很多不同的病毒变异体。我们知道抗体需要与病毒的某一部分结合，那么如果把这个部分更为精确的结构搞清楚，并通过疫苗呈现这种结构，我们希望就能促使免疫系统产生相匹配的抗体。这样就能产生一种通用的艾滋病病毒疫苗。现在，这听起来比实际操作容易，因为它的结构看起来实际上像这幅图里结合在黄色位点上的蓝色抗体所示。正如你们可以想象的，这些三维结构是非常难以做出来的。如果你们知道如何帮助我们解决这个问题，我们愿闻其详。

8) But, you know, the research that has occurred from HIV now has really helped with innovation with other diseases. So, for instance, a biotechnology company has now found broadly neutralizing antibodies to influenza, as well as a new antibody target for the flu virus. They're currently making a cocktail—an antibody cocktail—that can be used to treat severe, overwhelming cases of flu. In the longer term, what they can do is use these tools of retro-vaccinology to make a preventive flu vaccine. Now, retro-vaccinology is just one technique within the <u>ambit</u> of so-called rational vaccine design.

但是，现在，我们对于艾滋病的研究为我们发明其他病毒的疫苗提供了巨大的帮助。例如，一个生物科技公司现在已经发现对付流感、具有广泛中和能力的抗体，外加一个流感病毒上可供抗体结合的新位点。他们正在研制一种鸡尾酒类型的混合抗体，这种抗体能治疗重症流感。长远来看，我们能做的就是使用反向疫苗技术来生产预防性流感疫苗。现在，反向疫苗技术是一种所谓的"理论疫苗设计"技术。

说明：ambit 意为"范围"，可略去不译。

9) Let me give you another example. We talked about the H and N spikes on the surface of the flu virus before. Notice these other, smaller protuberances. These are largely hidden

from the immune system. Now it turns out that these spots also don't change much when the virus mutates. If you can cripple these with specific antibodies, you could cripple all versions of the flu. So far, animal tests indicate that such a vaccine could prevent severe disease, although you might get a mild case. So if this works in humans, what we're talking about is a universal flu vaccine, one that doesn't need to change every year and would remove the threat of death. We really could think of flu, then, as just a bad cold.

再举个例子。我们之前说到过在流感病毒表面的 H 和 N 刺突。注意看这些更小的突起物。这些突起物很大概率都可以逃逸我们的免疫系统。现在人们发现，这些突起物在病毒变异之时并没有发生显著改变。如果体内的特异性抗体能识别这些小突起，那么你的身体就能抵抗所有类型的流感病毒。到现在为止，动物测试显示这样一种疫苗能预防流感重症，尽管动物还是会表现出流感的轻微症状。如果这种疫苗在人体中也能发挥作用，它将会是一种通用的流感疫苗。这样，我们就不用每年再去研制新疫苗，也可以永远消除来自流感的死亡威胁。到那时，我们就可以认为，流感就仅仅是一次重感冒。

10）Of course, the best vaccine imaginable is only valuable to the extent we get it to everyone who needs it. So, to do that, we have to combine smart vaccine design with smart production methods and, of course, smart delivery methods. So, I want you to think back to a few months ago. In June, the World Health Organization declared the first global flu pandemic in 41 years. The US government promised 150 million doses of vaccine by October 15 for the flu peak. Vaccines were promised to developing countries. Hundreds of millions of dollars were spent and flowed to accelerating vaccine manufacturing. So, what happened?

当然，当需要的人都可以得到时，疫苗才能发挥它的价值。所以，为了达到这样的目的，我们必须同时拥有精巧的疫苗设计和优良的生产方式，以及良好的疫苗运输方法。你们回想几个月前，6 月份，世界卫生组织宣布 41 年来第一个全球流感大流行。美国政府承诺将会在 10 月 15 日前生产出来 1 亿 5 千万剂疫苗，以应对流感高峰，同样也承诺会向发展中国家提供疫苗。为提高疫苗产量，要花费数亿美元。那这过程是怎样的呢？

11）Well, we first figured out how to make flu vaccines, how to produce them, in the early 1940s. It was a slow, cumbersome process that depended on chicken eggs, millions of <u>living chicken eggs</u>. Viruses only grow in living things, and so it turned out that, for flu, chicken eggs worked really well. For most strains, you could get one to two doses of vaccine per egg. Luckily for us, we live in an era of breathtaking biomedical advances. So today, we get our flu vaccines from... chicken eggs, [Laughter] hundreds of millions of chicken eggs. Almost nothing has changed. The system is reliable but the problem is (that) you never know how well a strain is going to grow. This year's swine flu strain grew very poorly in early production: basically 6 doses per egg. So, here's an alarming thought. What if that wild bird flies by again? You could see an avian strain that would infect the poultry flocks, and then we would have no eggs for our vaccines. So, Dan [Barber], if you want billions of <u>chicken pellets</u> for your fish farm, I know where to get them. So right now, the world can produce about 350 million doses of flu vaccine for the three strains, and we can up that to about 1.2 billion doses if we want to target a single variant like swine flu. But this assumes that our factories are humming because, in 2004, the US supply was cut in half by contamination at one single plant. And the process still takes more than half a year.

在20世纪40年代初期，我们研制出流感疫苗并实现了生产。其过程缓慢而复杂，整个过程都要依赖鸡蛋——上百万的新鲜鸡蛋。病毒只能在活物中生长，事实证明，用鸡蛋生产流感病毒效果很好。对于大部分种类的病毒株，每个鸡蛋可能会产出一到两剂疫苗。我们是幸运的，因为我们生活在生物医药飞速发展的时代。那么今天，我们用什么生产流感疫苗呢？还是鸡蛋——这数以亿计的鸡蛋。这几乎没有改变过。这种方法是可靠的，但问题是我们不知道一个病毒株生长得如何。今年的猪流感病毒株早期很难生产，基本上，每只蛋产6剂疫苗。这时，人们就产生了一种令人不安的想法：如果野生鸟类又飞来了，怎么办呢？我们都知道禽流感病毒能感染家禽，那时，我们就没有生产疫苗的鸡蛋了。丹，如果你的养鱼场需要上百亿个球团形鸡饲料，我知道从哪里可以搞到。现在，全球能生产3.5亿剂针对3种流感病毒的疫苗。如果我们只生产一类病毒的疫苗，例如猪流感，总产量就能到12亿剂，但前提是工厂还能正常生产。2004年，仅仅是由于一家工厂出现了污染，美国疫苗产量就减少了一半。而这一生产过程仍然需要半年多的时间。

说明：（1）living chicken eggs 被译为"新鲜鸡蛋"，其实是指活鸡胚。（2）chicken pellets 意为"鸡饲料"。

12）So, are we better prepared than we were in 1918? Well, with the new technologies emerging now, I hope we can say definitively, "Yes". Imagine we could produce enough flu vaccine for everyone in the entire world for less than half of what we're currently spending now in the United States. With a range of new technologies, we could. Here's an example: A company I'm engaged with has found a specific piece of the H spike of flu that sparks the immune system. If you lop this off and attach it to the tail of a different bacterium, which creates a vigorous immune response, they've created a very powerful flu fighter. This vaccine is so small (that) it can be grown in a common bacterium, E. coli. Now, as you know, bacteria reproduce quickly, it's like making yogurt, and so we could produce enough swine-origin flu vaccines for the entire world in a few factories, in a few weeks, with no eggs, for a fraction of the cost of current methods.

我们现在是否比1918年时准备得更充足？随着新科技兴起，我希望我们可以确定地说"是"。想象一下，如果我们能用现在美国花费的一半为全球生产足够的流感疫苗，那该多好。如果我们运用新技术，这是可以实现的。这里有一个例子：我工作的公司已经发现流感病毒H刺突蛋白的一个片段能激发免疫系统。如果你能切下这个片段，并且把它加在另一种不同细菌的尾巴上，这样就可以激起免疫系统的强烈反应，变成一种强有力的流感病毒"战士"。这种疫苗片段非常小，在普通的大肠杆菌中就能生长。我们都知道大肠杆菌繁殖非常快，就好像做酸奶一样，几个工厂就能在几周内生产够全世界用的猪流感病毒，但是并不需要使用鸡蛋，而且我们只要花费现有生产方式所需费用的一个零头就可以了。

13) Here's a comparison of several of these new vaccine technologies. And aside from the radically increased production and huge cost savings, for example, the E. coli method I just talked about, look at the time saved. This would be lives saved. The developing world, mostly left out of the current response, sees the potential of these alternate technologies, and they're leapfrogging the West. India, Mexico, and others are already making experimental flu vaccines. And they may be the first place we see these vaccines in use. Because these technologies are so efficient and relatively cheap, billions of people can have access to lifesaving vaccines if we can figure out how to <u>deliver</u> them.

这只是几种疫苗新科技的比较。除了从根本上显著提高产量和大幅度节约生产成本之外，我们刚才说到的利用大肠杆菌的方法还能节约时间，这就意味着能够拯救更多的生命。大部分比较落后的发展中国家，他们看到了这些替代技术的巨大潜力，并且正在大幅度追赶西方。印度、墨西哥以及其他发展中国家正在做实验性的流感疫苗。这些国家也可能是最先应用这些疫苗的地方。这些技术如此高效而且相对便宜，只要我们能够搞清楚如何运输疫苗，几十亿的普通大众就能获得这些救命的疫苗。

说明：结合上下文，deliver 应该是指将疫苗从生产工厂运输至所需地点，故译员将其翻译为"运输"，而非"递送"。"递送"是指疫苗的施用方式。

14) Now think of where this leads us. New infectious diseases appear or reappear every few years. Someday, perhaps soon, we'll have a virus that is going to threaten all of us. Will we be quick enough to react before millions die? Luckily, this year's flu was relatively mild. I say, "luckily" in part because virtually no one in the developing world was vaccinated. So, if we have the political and financial foresight to sustain our investments, we will master these and new tools of vaccinology, and with these tools we can produce enough vaccines for everyone at low cost and ensure healthy, productive lives. No longer must flu have to kill half a million people a year. No longer does AIDS need to kill two million a year. No longer do the poor and vulnerable need to be threatened by infectious diseases, or indeed, anybody. Instead of having Vaclav Smil's "massively fatal discontinuity" of life, we can ensure the continuity of life. What the world needs now are these new vaccines, and we can make it happen. Thank you very much.

现在，大家来想一下这些研究会给我们带来什么。新的感染性疾病每隔几年都会出现。某一天，也许很快又会出现一种威胁我们的新病毒。我们能及时做出反应，从而挽回数百万人的生命吗？幸运的是，今年的流感病毒相对温和。我刚才说"幸运"，是因为在过去发展中国家几乎没有一人接种过疫苗。如果我们有政治和金融远见来持续投资疫苗生产，我们将掌握疫苗技术的新工具。运用这些新工具，我们能生产出低廉的、普通大众都买得起的疫苗，从而保障大家都健康并能为社会创造更多价值。每年，流感不会再夺走 50 多万人的生命，艾滋病也不会再夺走 200 多万人的生命。穷人或易感人群，甚至可以说是所有人，都不会再受到感染性疾病的威胁了。不会再有瓦茨拉夫·斯米尔预言的大规模导致人类不能继续繁衍生息的致命疾病了，我们能保证生命的延续。现在，世界需要的就是这些新疫苗，我们有能力生产出来。谢谢大家！

12.1.3 总结与点评

对于这类主题明晰的演讲，译员应做好有针对性的译前准备。比如，本篇材料主题为艾滋病疫苗，讲者的身份是流行病学家，译员在译前可查看关于疫苗作用机制的科普文献、视频等，还可学习流感等流行病学的相关知识。这对于译员更好地理解讲者的意思很有帮助。

针对本篇所提及的疫苗作用机制、原理，译员可采用创意型的笔记方式来记录，如通过画图来表现艾滋病病毒表面的凸起部分以及不随病毒变异而改变的部分。

在本篇讲话中，讲者用了许多比喻，如 front-line troops、squadrons、powerful flu fighter 等。为了贴近讲者的讲话风格，译员在翻译时不能回避这些具有个人特色的语言，要运用自己的母语知识储备来快速调取相应的中文表达。

译员应在理解原文的基础上对多个分散的英文句子进行整合，将其输出为有逻辑的、方便听众理解的中文。例如，讲者在第七段描述疫苗作用机制时，使用了大量以 we 开头的主动句，若译员直接将其翻译成"我们……我们……"会显得非常机械、生硬，要适当进行调整。

对于此类带有演示文件（PPT 或其他幻灯片）的演讲，译员在翻译时不能只关注自己的口译笔记和聆听讲者发言，还应适当关注讲者的肢体动作和演示文件，以辅助理解和记忆。

12.2 慢性疲劳综合征

慢性疲劳综合征（chronic fatigue syndrome），也叫作疲劳综合征、肌痛性脑脊髓炎（myalgia encephalomyelitis, ME）或慢性疲劳免疫功能紊乱综合征，是一组以持续或反复发作的疲劳，伴有多种神经、精神症状，但无器质性及精神性疾病为特点的症候群。其临床症状复杂，表现不同，轻重不一，一般体检及实验室检查结果无重大异常，却是一种严重损害正常活动，使人逐渐衰弱的疾病。它常被误诊为神经衰弱、更年期综合征、内分泌失调、神经官能症等，导致患者延误治疗。

患有慢性疲劳综合征的患者至少具备以下症状中的四项：(1) 轻微发烧；(2) 淋巴结疼痛；(3) 时常头痛；(4) 肌肉无力；(5) 肌肉疼痛；(6) 时常咽痛；(7) 睡眠不佳；(8) 游走性关节疼痛；(9) 运动后长时间疲累；(10) 有以下神经性或心理问题：脑筋混沌、健忘、容易烦躁、易怒、忧郁、对强光敏感、无法集中精神；(11) 上述症状突然间出现。

慢性疲劳综合征的病因尚不明确，与长期过度劳累（包括脑力和体力）、饮食生活不规律、工作压力和心理压力过大等精神环境因素以及应激等造成的神经、内分泌、免疫、消化、循环、运动等系统的功能紊乱关系密切。过去，人们认为慢性疲劳综合征是一种分离转换障碍（又称癔症性精神症状）。

分离转换障碍是一类以解离和转换症状为主的精神疾病，由重大生活事件、内心冲突、情绪激动、暗示或自我暗示等精神因素作用于易病个体所致。

TED 研究员（fellow）詹妮弗·布雷亚（Jennifer Brea）是一名慢性疲劳综合征患者。在病情严重的时候，她甚至无法忍受床单的摩擦声。本节选编自她的 TED 演讲"What Happens

When You Have a Disease Doctors Can't Diagnose"。演讲中，她描述了自己的症状以及寻求治疗的过程。由于大多数人医生并不了解该疾病，她也一直无法得到准确的医学诊断。她调查发现，人们对于这类自身免疫病存在根深蒂固的错误观念和偏见。尽管近年来自身免疫病发病率越来越高，人们却仍没有重视这类疾病，也没有研究出有效治疗方案。她呼吁人们纠正错误观念和偏见，把更多的精力投入到自身免疫病的研究中去。

12.2.1 背景知识

Galen：Latin Galenus, (born in AD 129, Pergamum, Mysia, Anatolia—died in c. 216), Greek physician, writer, and philosopher. He became chief physician to the gladiators in AD 157. Later, in Rome, he became a friend of Marcus Aurelius and physician to Commodus. Galen saw anatomy（解剖学）as fundamental and, based on animal experiments, described cranial nerves（颅神经）and heart valves（心脏瓣膜）and showed that arteries（动脉）carry blood, not air. However, in extending his findings to human anatomy he was often in error. Following Hippocratic（希波克拉底）concepts, he believed in three connected body systems—brain and nerves for sensation and thought, heart and arteries for life energy, and liver and veins for nutrition and growth—and four humours（体液）—blood, yellow bile（黄胆汁）, black bile（黑胆汁）, and phlegm（痰液）—that needed to be in balance. Few had the skills to challenge his seductive physiological（生理学的）theory. He wrote about 300 works, of which about 150 survive. As they were translated, his influence spread to the Byzantine Empire（拜占庭帝国）, Arabia, and then Western Europe. A revival of interest in the 16th century led to new anatomical investigations（解剖学研究）, which caused the overthrow of his ideas when Andreas Vesalius found anatomical errors and William Harvey correctly explained blood circulation（血液循环）(Encyclopedia Britannica, 2022a).

Sigmund Freud：born on May 6, 1856, Freiberg, Moravia, Austrian Empire—died on September 23, 1939, London, England, Austrian neuropsychologist（神经生理学家）, founder of psychoanalysis（精神分析）, and one of the major intellectual figures of the 20th century. Trained in Vienna as a neurologist, Freud went to Paris in 1885 to study with Jean-Martin Charcot, whose work on hysteria（癔症，旧称歇斯底里症）led Freud to conclude that mental disorders（精神疾病）might be caused purely by psychological rather than organic factors（器质性因素）. Returning to Vienna (1886), Freud collaborated with the physician Josef Breuer (1842–1925) in further studies on hysteria, resulting in the development of some key psychoanalytic concepts and techniques, including free association（自由联想）, the unconscious（无意识/潜意识）, resistance（阻抗）(later defense mechanisms), and neurosis（神经症）. In 1899, he published *The Interpretation of Dreams*（《梦的解析》）, in which he analyzed the complex symbolic processes underlying dream formation: He proposed that dreams are the disguised expression of unconscious wishes. During World War Ⅰ, he wrote papers that clarified his understanding of the relations between the unconscious and conscious portions of the mind and the workings of the id（本我）, ego（自我）, and superego（超我）(Encyclopedia Britannica, 2022b).

Eliot Slater: August 28, 1904–May 15, 1983, was a British psychiatrist（精神病学家）who was a pioneer in the field of the genetics of mental disorders.

phase-3 clinical trial（三期临床试验）：临床研究有不同种类、分期，各自有不同的主要研究目的。表 12.1 是癌症疗法临床研究的种类、分期及主要研究目的介绍（American Cancer Society，2022）。

表 12.1 临床研究的种类、分期及主要研究目的

Types	Phases	Purposes
Pre-clinical (or laboratory) studies	Cell studies	These are often the first tests done on a new treatment. To see if it might work, researchers look for effects of the new treatment on cancer cells that are grown in a lab dish or a test tube. These studies may be done on human cancer cells or animal cancer cells.
	Animal studies	Treatments that look promising in cell studies are tested next on cancers in live animals. This gives researchers an idea of how safe the new treatment is in a living creature.
The investigational new drug (IND) application		Before a clinical trial can be started, the research must be approved. An investigational new drug or IND（研究性新药）application or request must be filed with the FDA when researchers want to study a drug in humans.[2]
Clinical trials	Phase 0	Exploring if and how a new drug may work (mechanism)
	Phase Ⅰ	Is the treatment safe? (safety)
	Phase Ⅱ	Does the treatment work? (efficacy，药效)
	Phase Ⅲ	Is it better than what's already available? (superiority，优越性)

Scleroderma（硬皮病）**:** an autoimmune connective tissue and rheumatic disease（风湿性疾病）that causes inflammation in the skin and other areas of the body. When an immune response tricks tissues into thinking they are injured, it causes inflammation, and the body makes too much collagen（胶原蛋白）, leading to scleroderma（局限性硬皮病）. Too much collagen in your skin and other tissues causes patches of tight, hard skin. Scleroderma involves many systems in your body. There are two major types of scleroderma: (1) Localized scleroderma only affects the skin and the structures directly under the skin. (2) Systemic scleroderma（系统性硬皮病）, also called systemic sclerosis, affects many systems in the body. This is the more serious type of scleroderma and can damage your blood vessels and internal organs, such as the heart, lungs, and kidneys. There is no cure for scleroderma. The goal of treatment

---

1 The IND application must contain certain information, such as results from studies so that the FDA can decide whether the treatment is safe for testing in people; how the drug is made, who makes it, what's in it, how stable it is, and more. Detailed outlines for the planned clinical studies, called study protocols（研究方案）, are reviewed to see if people might be exposed to needless risks. Details about the clinical trial team to see if they have the knowledge and skill to run clinical trials. The research sponsor must commit to getting informed consent from everyone on the clinical trial. They must also commit to having the study reviewed by an institutional review board (IRB)（机构审查委员会，负责伦理等方面的审查）and following all the rules required for studying investigational new drugs.

is to relieve symptoms and stop the progression of the disease. Early diagnosis and ongoing monitoring are important（National Institutes of Health, 2022）.

12.2.2 慢性疲劳综合征患者自述

1. 相关词汇

  dizzy：头晕的
  dizziness：头晕
  neurological symptom：神经学症状
  specialist：专科医师
  dermatologist：皮肤病医师
  endocrinologist：内分泌医师
  cardiologist：心内科医师
  psychiatrist：精神科医师
  psychiatric：精神科的
  neurologist：神经科医师
  conversion disorder：转换障碍
  sore throat：喉咙痛
  sinus infection：鼻窦感染
  gastrointestinal symptom：肠胃症状
  cardiac symptom：心脏症状
  emotional trauma：情感创伤
  statistics：统计学
  probability theory：概率论
  mathematical modeling：数学建模
  experimental design：实验设计
  counter-intuitive：违反直觉的
  spinal cord：脊髓
  excruciating pain：极度疼痛
  rare disease：罕见病
  exert oneself physically or mentally：费力或费心
  sore：肌肉酸痛的
  bedridden：卧床不起的
  multiple sclerosis：多发性硬化症
  physical function：生理功能
  congestive heart failure：充血性心力衰竭
  home-bound：在家待着无法出门

hysteria：癔症

sexual deprivation：性生活缺乏

uterus：子宫

paralysis：瘫痪

unconscious/conscious mind：无意识/有意识心理

physical symptom：身体症状

susceptible：易受影响的；易感的

Los Angeles County General Hospital：洛杉矶郡总医院

polio：脊髓灰质炎（俗称小儿麻痹症）

mass hysteria：群体性癔症

cohort：人群

undiagnosed condition：未诊断出的情况/疾病

epilepsy：癫痫

verbatim：逐字的

psychogenic illness：心因性疾病

enterovirus：肠病毒

Epstein-Barr virus：EB 病毒

Q fever：Q 热 [1]

scleroderma：硬皮病

autoimmune connective tissue disease：自身免疫性结缔组织病

esophagus：食管

ovarian cancer：卵巢癌

early menopause：绝经期提前

autoimmune disease：自身免疫病

hypochondriac：疑病症患者

be forcibly institutionalized：被强制收治入院（精神病医院）

EEG (electroencephalogram[2])：脑电图

hysterical paralysis：癔症性瘫痪

CAT scan：CT 扫描 [3]

MRI：核磁共振成像 [4]

lesion：损伤

stomach ulcer：胃溃疡

---

1 这是一种自然疫源性疾病，其病原体为 Q 热立克次氏体，多途径感染人，偶由蜱叮咬而传播。
2 electro- 意为"电"；encephalo- 意为"脑"；-gram 意为"图"。
3 即 a computed tomography or a computer-aided tomography scan，我国习惯用 CT 作为此种检查手段的简称。
4 即 magnetic resonance imaging，也被称作 NMR（nuclear magnetic resonance），我国习惯用核磁共振（英文习惯用 MRI）来表示。

stress：压力
H. pylorus：幽门螺旋杆菌
autoimmunity：自身免疫性
energy metabolism：能量代谢
standard deviation：标准差
remission：缓解

2. 原文、参考译文及说明

1）Hi. Thank you. So, five years ago, this was me. I was a PhD student at Harvard, and I loved to travel. I had just gotten engaged to marry the love of my life. I was 28, and like so many of us when we are in good health, I thought I was invincible. Then one day I had a fever of 104.7 degrees. I probably should have gone to the doctor, but I'd never really been sick in my life, and I knew that usually, if you have a virus, you stay home and you make some chicken soup, and in a few days, everything will be fine.

嗨！谢谢你们！这是五年前的我，那时我是哈佛大学的一名博士生，热爱旅行。当时，我刚与人生的挚爱订婚。28 岁，和大部分人一样身体健康，我觉得自己无所不能。有一天，我高烧 40.4 摄氏度，可能我应该去看医生，但当时我还从没真的生过大病，而且我知道，通常来说如果你被病毒感染，在家躺着休息，喝点自制的鸡汤，过几天就什么事都没有了。

说明：讲者说的 104.7 degrees 是华氏度（Fahrenheit degree），译员应将其换算成摄氏度。美国人习惯使用华氏度。换算方法：摄氏度 = 5/9（华氏度 –32）。口译时，若来不及换算，译员可直接按华氏度翻译，但翻译为摄氏度更能实现讲者预期的交流效果。

2）But this time it wasn't fine. After the fever broke, for three weeks I was so dizzy; I couldn't leave my house. I would walk straight into door frames. I had to hug the walls just to make it to the bathroom. That spring I got infection after infection, and every time I went to the doctor, he said there was absolutely nothing wrong. He had his laboratory tests, which always came back normal. All I had were my symptoms, which I could describe, but no one else can see. I know it sounds silly, but you have to find a way to explain things like this to yourself, and so I thought maybe I was just aging. Maybe this is what it's like to be on the other side of 25.

但是这一次它没有好，高烧之后，整整三个星期我头昏眼花到无法出门，我直走都能撞到门框上，我不得不扶着墙才能去洗手间。那个春天，我反复受到病毒感染。但是我每次去医院，医生都确定我的身体完全没什么问题。他的实验室检查结果永远都显示正常，所有的都正常，如果我不描述，其他人都无法察觉我的症状。我知道这听起来很蠢，但我不得不找到一个方式来解释发生在自己身上的一切，所以我想我大概只是年龄大了，或许这就是 25 岁的另外一面。

3）Then the neurological symptoms started. Sometimes I would find that I couldn't draw the right side of a circle. Other times I wouldn't be able to speak or move at all. I saw every kind of specialist: infectious disease doctors, dermatologists, endocrinologists, cardiologists. I even saw a psychiatrist. My psychiatrist said, "It's clear (that) you're really sick, but not with anything psychiatric. I hope they can find out what's wrong with you."

接下来，神经方面的症状开始出现，我发现有时候我无法画出圆的右半边，有时候发现我完全不能说话、不能动。我看了各种专科医师：感染病医师、皮肤科医师、内分泌医师、心内科医师。我甚至去看了精神病医生。我的精神病医生说："很明显，你现在生病了，但这和精神疾病没有任何关系，我希望其他医生可以找到你的病因。"

4）The next day, my neurologist diagnosed me with conversion disorder. He told me that everything—the fevers, the sore throats, the sinus infection, all of the gastrointestinal, neurological and cardiac symptoms—were being caused by some distant emotional trauma that I could not remember. The symptoms were real, he said, but they had no biological cause.

第二天，我的神经科医师诊断我得了转换障碍。他告诉我所有症状——发烧、嗓子疼、鼻窦感染，所有的胃肠、神经和心脏方面的症状，都是由某些早期发生的、我都不记得了的精神创伤引起的。他说这些症状是真实存在的，但没有任何生物学病因。

5）I was getting training to be a social scientist. I had studied statistics, probability theory, mathematical modeling, and experimental design. I felt like I couldn't just reject my neurologist's diagnosis. It didn't feel true, but I knew from my training that the truth is often counter-intuitive, so easily obscured by what we want to believe. So, I had to consider the possibility that he was right.

我正在接受社会科学课程的训练，已经学习了统计学、概率、数学建模和实验设计。我觉得我没有办法反驳我的神经科医师做出的诊断。我不愿相信这个诊断，但我的专业训练告诉我，真相往往与直觉相悖，而且很容易被我们偏好的主观想法所掩盖。所以，我不得不考虑他的诊断可能是对的。

6）That day, I ran a small experiment. I walked back the two miles from my neurologist's office to my house, my legs wrapped in this strange, almost electric kind of pain. I meditated on that pain, contemplating how my mind could have possibly generated all this. As soon as I walked through the door, I collapsed. My brain and my spinal cord were burning. My neck was so stiff (that) I couldn't touch my chin to my chest, and the slightest sound—the rustling of the sheets, my husband walking barefoot in the next room—could cause <u>excruciating pain</u>. I would spend most of the next two years in bed.

当天，我做了一个小实验，从距离两英里的神经科医师的办公室走回家。路上，我的腿被一种奇怪的、近乎电流穿过般的疼痛包裹。我认真思考，大脑怎么能产生这种疼痛。我走到家门口的时候，摔倒在地上。我的大脑和脊髓产生灼烧般的痛感，脖子很僵硬，甚至无法用下巴触碰胸部。最轻微的声音，比如纸张发出的沙沙声，甚至我丈夫赤着脚在隔壁房间走路的声音，都能引发巨大的痛苦。而接下来的两年，我大部分的时间都是在床上度过的。

说明：ex- 意为"穿过"；-crux = cross，意为"十字架"。excruciating pain 可被译为"巨大的疼痛"。

7) How could my doctor have gotten it so wrong? I thought I had a rare disease, something doctors had never seen. And then I went online and found thousands of people all over the world living with the same symptoms, similarly isolated, similarly disbelieved. Some could still work, but had to spend their evenings and weekends in bed, just so they could show up the next Monday. On the other end of the spectrum, some were so sick (that) they had to live in complete darkness, unable to tolerate the sound of a human voice or the touch of a loved one.

我的医生怎么会弄错呢？我认为我是得了一种罕见病，一种医生都没有见过的病。于是我上网搜索，发现无数人和我有相同的症状。他们和我一样孤独，一样地被人怀疑。他们中一些人仍然可以工作，但是不得不在晚上和周末都躺在床上休息，这样在下个星期一才可以继续去工作。在这个疾病谱系的另一端，有一些人病情太重，以致不得不彻底生活在黑暗中，而且无法忍受任何声音，甚至无法接受爱人的触碰。

8) I was diagnosed with myalgia encephalomyelitis. You've probably heard it called "chronic fatigue syndrome". The key symptom we all share is that whenever we exert ourselves—physically, mentally—we pay and we pay hard. If my husband goes for a run, he might be sore for a couple of days. If I try to walk half a block, I might be bedridden for a week. It is a perfect custom prison. I know ballet dancers who can't dance, accountants who can't add, and medical students who never became doctors. It doesn't matter what you once were; you can't do it anymore. It's been four years, and I've still never been as well as I was the minute before I walked home from my neurologist's office.

我被确诊为肌痛性脑脊髓炎。你可能也听说过它被称为"慢性疲劳综合征"。这个病的关键症状就是，每当我们费心、费力的时候，我们就会付出代价，而且付出的代价相当惨重。如果我丈夫出去跑步，他可能会全身酸痛几天。如果我想要走半个街区，我也许就会整整一周卧床不起。这是一个完美的定制监狱。我知道有再也不能跳舞的芭蕾演员，再也不能计算的会计师，永远无法成为医生的医学生。和你曾经做什么毫无关系，无论你以前做什么，患病之后再也不能继续了。患病四年了，我却仍然无法恢复到得病前的状况。

说明：(1) custom 指 specially designed for a particular person or purpose, custom prison 意为"量身打造的监狱"。(2) 最后一句的直译是：我一直没有恢复到我从我的神经科医师诊室处回到家之前的一分钟的状态。直译可读性（可听性）较差，翻译时，译员用"获得诊断"替代"从我的神经科医师诊室处回到家之前"。

9) It's estimated that about 15 to 30 million people around the world have this disease. In the US, where I'm from, it's about one million people. That makes it roughly twice as common as multiple sclerosis. Patients can live for decades with the physical function of someone with congestive heart failure. Twenty-five percent of us are home-bound or bedridden, and 75 to 85 percent of us can't even work part-time. Yet doctors do not treat us and science does not study us. How could a disease this common and this devastating have been forgotten by medicine?

据估计，全世界有 1 500 到 3 000 万人患有这种疾病。在我所在的美国，大约有 100 万人，普遍性是多发性硬化症的近两倍。患者患病的几十年中，会像充血性心肌衰竭病人一样，遭受各种生理功能问题。而我们当中 25% 的人无法跨出家门或干脆卧床不起，75% 到 85% 的人连兼职工作都没有办法完成。但是没有医生治疗这种疾病，也没有科学家研究这个疾病。一个如此常见且有杀伤力的疾病，怎么能被医学给遗忘了呢？

说明：为了行文逻辑，译员把"科学"（science）变为"科学家"。

10）When my doctor diagnosed me with conversion disorder, he was invoking a lineage of ideas about women's bodies that are over 2,500 years old. The Roman physician Galen thought that hysteria was caused by sexual deprivation in particularly passionate women. The Greeks thought the uterus would literally dry up and wander around the body in search of moisture, pressing on internal organs—yes—causing symptoms from extreme emotions to dizziness and paralysis. The cure was marriage and motherhood.

当医生诊断我患了转换障碍时，他引用了一系列有 2 500 年历史的关于女性身体的观点。古罗马医师盖伦认为，癔症是由性生活不足造成的，性欲旺盛的女性尤其容易患该病。希腊人认为，子宫会变干燥，会在身体中四处游走寻找水分，给体内的器官压力，从而引起从极端情绪到头晕、瘫痪的一系列症状，而治愈方法就是结婚、生子。

11）These ideas went largely unchanged for several millennia until the 1880s, when neurologists tried to modernize the theory of hysteria. Sigmund Freud developed a theory that the unconscious mind could produce physical symptoms when dealing with memories or emotions too painful for the conscious mind to handle. It converted these emotions into physical symptoms. This meant that men could now get hysteria, but of course women were still the most susceptible.

这种想法在几千年里都没有太大的变化，直到 19 世纪 80 年代，神经科医师们试图使癔症理论现代化。奥地利精神分析学家西格蒙德·弗洛伊德发展出一个学说，认为一些记忆或情感过于痛苦，意识心理无法处理，无意识心理在处理这些记忆或情感时，会产生一些生理症状，将这些情感转化成生理症状。这意味着男性也可能会患癔症，但女性仍然是最主要的患病人群。

说明：第二句是一个复杂句，翻译难度较大，注意分析句子结构。译员添加"奥地利精神分析学家"，以帮助译文听众理解。

12）When I began investigating the history of my own disease, I was amazed to find how deep these ideas still run. In 1934, 198 doctors, nurses and staff at the Los Angeles County General Hospital became seriously ill. They had muscle weakness, stiffness in the neck and back, fevers—all of the same symptoms I had when I first got diagnosed. Doctors thought it was a new form of polio. Since then, there have been more than 70 outbreaks documented around the world, of a strikingly similar post-infectious disease. All of these outbreaks have tended to disproportionately affect women, and in time, when doctors failed to find the one cause of the disease, they thought that these outbreaks were mass hysteria.

当我开始对我自己患的这个病的历史进行调查研究时，我非常吃惊地发现这些观点是多么根深蒂固。1934 年，洛杉矶郡总医院的 198 名医生、护士和工作人员得了严重的病。他们的肌肉无力、颈部及背部僵硬，并伴有发热。这些症状和我最初接受诊断时的所有症状一模一样。医生们认为这是一种新型的脊髓灰质炎。从那之后，全世界记载了 70 多次该病的暴发，而且症状都与之惊人地相似。每一次暴发，都是以女性患者为主。随着时间的推移，医生们由于无法找到病因，就认为这是一种群体性癔症。

13）Why has this idea had such staying power? I do think it has to do with sexism, but I also think that fundamentally, doctors want to help. They want to know the answer, and this category allows doctors to treat what would otherwise be untreatable, to explain illnesses that have no explanation. The problem is that this can cause real harm. In the 1950s, a psychiatrist named Eliot Slater studied a cohort of 85 patients who had been diagnosed with hysteria. Nine years later, 12 of them were dead and 30 had become disabled. Many had undiagnosed conditions like multiple sclerosis, epilepsy, brain tumors. In 1980, hysteria was officially renamed "conversion disorder". When my neurologist gave me that diagnosis in 2012, he was echoing Freud's words verbatim, and even today, women are 2 to 10 times more likely to receive that diagnosis.

为什么这个观点一直延续至今？我认为这与性别歧视有关，但是我也认为，医生们本质上是想提供帮助的。他们想知道答案，而癔症这个归类可以让医生有机会治疗这个本来无法治疗的疾病，去解释这个本来无法解释的疾病。问题在于，这种做法会造成真切的伤害。在 20 世纪 50 年代，一位叫艾略特·斯莱特的精神病学家研究了 85 名被诊断为患有癔症的患者。9 年之后，患者中的 12 人死亡，30 人残疾。许多人得多发性硬化、癫痫以及脑肿瘤等病，却没能被诊断出来。在 1980 年，癔症正式被重新命名为"转换障碍"。当我的神经科医师在 2012 年给我下这个诊断的时候，他照搬了弗洛伊德的理论。时至今日，女性患这个疾病的概率仍然是男性的 2 到 10 倍。

说明："弗洛伊德的理论"指弗洛伊德有关转化障碍的理论。

14）The problem with the theory of hysteria or psychogenic illness is that it can never be proven. It is, by definition, the absence of evidence, and in the case of ME, psychological explanations have held back biological research. All around the world, ME is one of the least funded diseases. In the US, we spend each year roughly 2,500 dollars per AIDS patient, 250 dollars per MS patient and just 5 dollars per year per ME patient. The ignorance surrounding my disease has been a choice, a choice made by the institutions that were supposed to protect us.

癔症或心因性疾病的"理论"问题在于无法证实。既然是心因性的，那顾名思义，就无法提供证据，进而由于缺乏证据，就阻止了生物学研究的继续；至于 ME，则是心理学的解释阻止了生物学研究的继续。全世界范围内，ME 是研究经费最少的疾病之一。在美国，我们每年为每名艾滋病患者投入大约 2 500 美元，为每名多发性硬化症患者投入 250 美元，而对于每名 ME 患者只有 5 美元。对我疾病的无视是有意而为之，是那些本该保护我们的研究机构有意而为之的。

说明：ME 即 myalgia encephalomyelitis，意为"肌痛性脑脊髓炎"。

15) We don't know why ME sometimes runs in families, why you can get it after almost any infection, from enteroviruses to Epstein-Barr virus to Q fever, or why it affects women at two to three times the rate of men. This issue is much bigger than just my disease. When I first got sick, old friends were reaching out to me. I soon found myself a part of a cohort of women in their late 20s whose bodies were falling apart. What was striking was just how much trouble we were having in being taken seriously.

我们不知道为什么 ME 会具有家族遗传性，为什么任何一个传染病——从肠道病毒到疱疹病毒到 Q 热——感染之后都可能会导致 ME，也不知道为什么女性得这个病的概率会是男性的两到三倍。这些问题比我得这个病本身更严重。我第一次生病的时候，老朋友们都来联系我。很快，我发现自己成为年近 30 身体就开始衰弱的女性人群中的一员。深受打击的是，在我们争取受到重视的过程中，遇到了很多困难。

说明：原文最后一句是倒装句，详见本节末尾的"总结与点评"。

16) I learned of one woman with scleroderma, an autoimmune connective tissue disease, who was told for years that it was all in her head—Between the time of onset and diagnosis, her esophagus was so thoroughly damaged (that) she will never be able to eat again; another woman with ovarian cancer, who for years was told that it was just early menopause; and a friend from college whose brain tumor was misdiagnosed for years as anxiety.

我听说有一位得了**硬皮病**的女性。硬皮病是一种自身免疫性结缔组织病。在几年的时间里，医生都告诉她，这个病纯粹是她个人想象出来的。从发病到确诊，她的食道由于疾病进展完全受损，再也无法进食。另外一位得了卵巢癌的女性，在很长时间里都被医生告知，她只是绝经期提前。另外我大学时的朋友，得了脑瘤却被错误地诊断为焦虑症，长达数年。

说明：（1）硬皮病是一种自身免疫性结缔组织病，病因尚不明确，临床上以局限性或弥漫性皮肤增厚和纤维化为特征，累及心、肺、肾、消化道等内脏器官。（2）原文第二处画线部分究竟是要表达由于诊疗操作造成损伤，还是疾病进展造成损伤，译员需结合有关硬皮病的背景知识来判断。

17) Here's why this worries me: Since the 1950s, rates of many autoimmune diseases have doubled to triple. Forty-five percent of patients who are eventually diagnosed with a recognized autoimmune disease are initially told they're hypochondriacs. Like the hysteria of old, this has everything to do with gender and with whose stories we believe. Seventy-five percent of autoimmune disease patients are women, and in some diseases, it's as high as 90 percent. Even though these diseases disproportionately affect women, they are not women's diseases. ME affects children and ME affects millions of men. And as one patient told me, we get it coming and going—if you're a woman, you're told you're exaggerating your symptoms, but if you're a guy, you're told to be strong, to buck up. And men may even have a more difficult time getting diagnosed.

让我感觉忧虑的原因如下：从 20 世纪 50 年代起，许多自身免疫病的患病率比以前高了一两倍,但45%最终被诊断为已知自身免疫病的患者,其最初的诊断是疑病症。就像古时的癔症,这与性别偏见和我们相信谁的话有关系。75%的自身免疫病患者都是女性,并且在某些疾病中女性患者比例甚至高达90%。尽管这些疾病的患者大多数是女性,但它们并非女性独有的疾病。成千上万的儿童和男性也患有ME。就像一位患者告诉我的那样,医生也没有什么好办法——如果你是女性,医生和其他人会说你夸大了症状,但如果你是男性,他们鼓励你要坚强,要振作起来。男性甚至会更难以被诊断出来。

说明: have someone coming and going 意思是 leave someone with no viable options or solutions,据此,get it coming and going[1] 可以被理解为医生没给患者任何合适的选择或解决方案,结合上下文,可被译为"医生也没有什么好办法"。

18) Here's the good part: Despite everything, I still have hope. So many diseases were once thought of as psychological until science uncovered their biological mechanisms. Patients with epilepsy could be forcibly institutionalized until the EEG was able to measure abnormal electrical activity in the brain. Multiple sclerosis could be misdiagnosed as hysterical paralysis until the CAT scan and the MRI discovered brain lesions. And recently, we used to think that stomach ulcers were just caused by stress, until we discovered that H. pylorus was the culprit. ME has never benefited from the kind of science that other diseases have had, but that's starting to change. In Germany, scientists are starting to find evidence of autoimmunity, and in Japan, of brain inflammation. In the US, scientists at Stanford are finding abnormalities in energy metabolism that are 16 standard deviations away from normal. And in Norway, researchers are running a phase-3 clinical trial on a cancer drug that in some patients causes complete remission.

但是,仍然有好的一面。尽管上述种种,我依然满怀希望。有太多的疾病在科学揭示出其生物学机制之前,都被认为是心理问题。癫痫患者被强制收容治疗,直到脑电图能够测出脑部的异常电活动。多发性硬化症被错误地诊断为癔症性瘫痪,直到CT扫描和核磁共振发现脑损伤。更近一点的例子是,我们曾经认为胃溃疡是压力所致,后来才发现幽门螺杆菌才是罪魁祸首。ME从来未得益于其他疾病所获得的科学帮助,但是这一切开始在转变。在德国,科学家开始发现自身免疫病的证据;在日本,科学家开始发现脑炎症的证据。在美国,斯坦福大学的科学家发现与正常值相差16个标准差的能量代谢异常;在挪威,研究者正在进行可以使一些患者得到缓解的一种抗癌药物的三期临床试验。

19) What also gives me hope is the resilience of patients. Online we came together, and we shared our stories. We <u>devoured</u> what research there was. We experimented on ourselves. We became our own scientists and our own doctors because we had to be. And slowly I added five percent here, five percent there, until eventually, on a good day, I was able to leave my home. I still had to make ridiculous choices: Will I sit in the garden for 15 minutes,

---

1 The Free Dictionary by Farlex 对 have (someone) coming and going 的定义为: to put someone in an inescapable position or situation; to leave someone with no viable options or solutions。

or will I wash my hair today? But it gave me hope that I could be treated. I had a sick body; that was all. And with the right kind of help, maybe one day I could get better.

患者的韧性也同样给了我希望。我们相聚在互联网上，分享各自的故事。我们如饥似渴地了解研究的进展。我们在自己身上做实验。我们不得不成为自己的科学家和医生。然后慢慢地，我在某方面有了 5% 的进展，在某方面又有 5% 的进展，直到最终，在我身体状况较好的一天，我能够走出家门。我依然需要做愚蠢的选择：比如，我今天是在花园里待 15 分钟，还是去洗头呢？ 但是，这给了我可以治愈的希望。我身患疾病，这就是全部，如果得到了正确的治疗，也许有一天我就可以康复。

说明：devour 意为"如饥似渴地去了解"。

20）I came together with patients around the world, and we started to fight. We have filled the void with something wonderful, but it is not enough. I still don't know if I will ever be able to run again, or walk at any distance, or do any of those kinetic things that I now only get to do in my dreams. But I am so grateful for how far I have come. Progress is slow, and it is up and it is down, but I am getting a little better each day.

我和全世界的患者联合起来，我们开始战斗，我们用一些美好的东西把这片空白填满，但这远远不够。我仍然不知道我是否还能再一次奔跑，或者行走一段距离，或者做任何只能在梦里做的运动。但是，我对现在所能走到这一步表示感恩，进展虽然很慢，而且情况时好时坏，但是我每天都在变得好一点点。

21）I remember what it was like when I was stuck in that bedroom, when it had been months since I had seen the sun. I thought that I would die there. But here I am today, with you, and that is a miracle.

我记得我被困在卧室里，好几个月没见到阳光。那时，我以为我也许是要死了，但是今天我在这里，和你们一起，这已经是个奇迹。

22）I don't know what would have happened had I not been one of the lucky ones, had I gotten sick before the Internet, had I not found my community. I probably would have already taken my own life, as so many others have done. How many lives could we have saved, decades ago, if we had asked the right questions? How many lives could we save today if we decide to make a real start?

我不知道如果我不是这其中的一个幸运儿，如果我在有互联网之前生病，如果我没有找到属于我的社群，将会发生什么。我或许就像很多人一样，已经自杀。如果在数十年前，我们提出了正确的问题，有多少生命可以得救？ 如果决定现在开始认真对待这个疾病，又有多少生命可以得救？

23）Even once the true cause of my disease is discovered, if we don't change our institutions and our culture, we will do this again to another disease. Living with this illness has taught me that science and medicine are profoundly human endeavors. Doctors, scientists and policymakers are not immune to the same biases that affect all of us.

即使人们发现了慢性疲劳综合征的真正原因，但如果我们的制度和文化没有改变的话，下一次我们还是会用同样的方式去对待另外一种疾病。与这个疾病共生教会我,科学和医学在很大程度上是人的工作,医生、科学家和决策者也是人,也难免受到偏见的影响。

说明：institutions 意为"制度"或"机构",这两种理解在此处似乎都合理。

24) We need to think in more nuanced ways about women's health. Our immune systems are just as much a battleground for equality as the rest of our bodies. We need to listen to patients'stories, and we need to be willing to say, "I don't know." "I don't know" is a beautiful thing. "I don't know" is where discovery starts. And if we can do that, if we can approach the great vastness of all that we do not know, and then, rather than fear uncertainty, maybe we can greet it with a sense of wonder. Thank you.

我们需要用一个更细致的方式来思考女性健康。我们的免疫系统就和我们身体的其他部分一样,都是争取平等的战场。我们需要去聆听患者的故事,我们需要乐意说："我不知道。"说"我不知道"是好的。"我不知道"就意味着探索的开始。如果我们可以做到这一点,如果我们可以去探索所有的、未知的广袤领域,也许我们就可以用惊叹,而不是恐惧,向那些未知的领域致敬。谢谢大家！

12.2.3 总结与点评

本篇讲话逻辑结构比较清楚,但在理解、记忆、表达方面,译员仍需注意以下要点。

1. 理解

整体来看,本篇讲话涉及的专业知识不是很深奥,也不难理解。翻译过程中,译员应注意讲者对慢性综合征病症的描述,并参考知识背景和术语解释,这样才能全面、准确地理解讲者本意。讲话中有一些长难句,译员需仔细琢磨方可理解准确。例如,"What was striking was just how much trouble we were having in being taken seriously." 一句存在倒装结构,正常语序是 we were having much trouble in being taken seriously。如果译员无法识别倒装句,可能就无法理解讲者的意思。

2. 记忆

本篇讲话存在较多的长句、复合句。这会增加交传中的记忆负担。做交传口译笔记的时候,译员应注意基于对演讲内容的理解和对知识背景的掌握来记录核心信息。一般来说,译员不可能记下所有信息,应使用口译笔记作为提示,辅助回忆。

3. 表达

本篇讲话涉及多种疾病名称等术语,翻译时,译员一定要确保术语译法准确、发音清晰。译员可使用译前准备的词汇表辅助译文的产出。此外,讲者使用的长句较多,译员可结合背景知识,根据汉语习惯,把一些长难句分拆成简单句,便于听众理解。

12.3 免疫疾病及免疫治疗

免疫性疾病（immune disease）是免疫调节失去平衡影响机体的免疫应答而引起的疾病。正常情况下，免疫系统只对侵入机体的外来物，如细菌、病毒、寄生虫以及移植物（implant）等产生反应，消灭（eliminate）或排斥（reject）这些异物。在某些因素影响下，机体的组织成分或免疫系统本身出现某些异常，致使免疫系统误将自身成分当成外来物来攻击。这时，免疫系统会产生针对一些机体自身成分的抗体及活性淋巴细胞，损害、破坏自身组织脏器，导致疾病。

免疫系统是一个复杂而高度发达的系统，但它的任务很简单：寻找并杀死入侵者。如果一个人天生免疫系统有严重缺陷，就会死于病毒、细菌、真菌或寄生虫（parasite）感染。在严重的系统性免疫缺陷中，缺乏一种酶（enzyme）意味着有毒废物在免疫系统细胞内堆积，从而破坏免疫系统。免疫细胞的缺乏也是迪格奥尔格综合征的基础，即由于胸腺发育不正常，T细胞的产生减少。

大多数其他的免疫紊乱要么是由于过度的免疫反应所致，要么属于"自身免疫性攻击"。哮喘、家族性地中海热和克罗恩病（炎症性肠病）都是免疫系统过度反应的结果，而自身免疫性多腺体综合征和糖尿病的某些类型是免疫系统攻击自身的细胞和分子所致。免疫系统的一个关键作用是区分入侵者和身体自身的细胞——当它不能做出这种区分时，就会对自身的细胞和分子产生反应，从而导致自身免疫性疾病。

本节材料选自董晨在未来论坛上的讲话。讲话人董晨时任清华大学医学院教授、院长，主要致力于免疫学的研究，重点关注免疫耐受和免疫应答的分子调控机制，以理解自身免疫和过敏疾病的发病机理，并探索新型肿瘤免疫治疗。

12.3.1 免疫疾病及免疫治疗简介

1. 相关词汇

免疫调节（immunomodulation）：指免疫系统中的免疫细胞和免疫分子之间，以及与其他系统，如神经内分泌系统之间的相互作用。免疫调节使得免疫系统以最恰当的形式应答，并使机体免疫反应维持在最适当的水平。

免疫应答（immune response）：指身体识别和保护自己免受细菌、病毒和外来有害物质侵害的过程。

抗体（antibody）：也叫免疫球蛋白，是免疫系统对外来物质（抗原）做出反应而产生的一种保护性蛋白。

淋巴细胞（lymphocyte）：是白细胞的一种，是体积最小的白细胞。它由淋巴器官产生，主要存在于淋巴管中循环的淋巴液中，是机体免疫应答功能的重要细胞成分，几乎是淋巴系统全部免疫功能的主要执行者，是对抗外界感染和监控体内细胞变异的一线"士兵"。淋巴细胞是一类具有免疫识别功能的细胞系。

体液免疫（humoral immunity）：以浆细胞（plasma cell）产生抗体来达到保护目的的免疫机制。

细胞免疫（cellular immunity）：狭义的细胞免疫仅指 T 细胞介导（T cell-mediated）的免疫应答（response），即 T 细胞受到抗原刺激后，分化（differentiate）、增殖（proliferate）、转化（transform）为致敏（sensatized）T 细胞，对抗原的直接杀伤作用及致敏 T 细胞所释放的细胞因子（cytokine）的协同（synergic）杀伤作用（killing effect）。T 细胞介导的免疫应答的特征是出现以单核细胞（monocyte）浸润（infiltration）为主的炎症（inflammatory）反应和/或特异性（specific）的细胞毒性（cytotoxicity）。广义的细胞免疫还应该包括原始的吞噬作用（primitive phagocytosis）以及 NK（natural killer）细胞介导的细胞毒作用（cytotoxicity）。

浆细胞（plasma cell）：又称抗体分泌细胞（antibody secreting cell），是免疫系统中释放大量抗体的细胞。成熟 B 细胞接受抗原刺激后，在抗原提呈细胞和 Th 细胞的辅助下成为活化 B 细胞，进而分化为浆细胞，合成和分泌各类免疫球蛋白，同时表达浆细胞抗原-1（plasma cell antigen-l，PCA-1）等浆细胞特异性标志，而 mIg、MHC Ⅱ 类分子、CD19、CD20、CD21 等标记消失。

迪格奥尔格综合征（DiGeorge syndrome）：又称 22q11.2 缺失（deletion）综合征，是一种罕见的先天性疾病，其症状因人而异，但通常包括反复感染、心脏缺陷和特征颜面外观（characteristic facial feature）。

胸腺（thymus）：是淋巴系统的主要器官，位于上胸部，它的主要功能是促进免疫系统 T 淋巴细胞[1]的发育。

T 细胞（T cell）：胸腺中成熟的淋巴细胞，能够通过细胞表面的受体识别由抗原提呈细胞提呈的抗原。

哮喘（asthma）：是一种慢性或长期的疾病，会间歇性地导致肺部发炎并使肺部的气道变窄。

家族性地中海热（familial Mediterranean fever）：是一种遗传性疾病，其特征是腹部、胸部或关节反复出现疼痛性炎症。

克罗恩病（Crohn disease）：是一种炎症性肠病（inflammatory bowel disease，IBD）。它会引起消化道炎症，导致腹痛、严重腹泻、疲劳、体重减轻和营养不良。

自身免疫性多腺体综合征（autoimmune polyglandular syndrome）：一种遗传性自身免疫性疾病，具有一系列不同寻常的临床特征，但最常见的特征是甲状旁腺功能低下和肾上腺功能不全。

靶向治疗（targeted therapy）：是一种使用药物来治疗癌症的方法。靶向治疗的工作原理是针对癌症的特定基因、蛋白质和有助于癌症生长和生存的组织环境进行干预。

---

1 简称 T 细胞。

2. 原文、参考译文及说明

1)我今天演讲的主题是免疫疾病与免疫治疗,而且更多的是从我自己作为免疫学家的角度,跟大家分享我过去走过的研究历程。我希望通过三个方面来给大家介绍。

What I'd like to talk about today is immunological disease and its immunotherapy. And I'd like to, from the perspective of immunologists, talk about what I have done in my research journey and I'll introduce it to you from three aspects.

2)首先,在进入这个具体的科研领域的介绍之前,我还得跟大家稍微介绍一下我们的免疫系统。免疫系统实际上是我们的"解放军"(在国外叫国防军),它起到对我们人体最有效的一个保护作用。大家可以想象,我们体内有各种细胞,<u>组成我们人体的最主要、最基本的单位也是细胞</u>。为了使人体能够不受外界的干扰,而且当人体内部有了一些问题以后能够及时地进行修复,我们肯定还是需要类似于解放军战士、类似于武警,甚至交警等等这样的一些角色。

But first of all, before I go to the specific scientific research field, I have to tell you a little bit about the immune system. The immune system is like "People's Liberation Army" (or any defense forces abroad), which plays the main role in protecting our body. We can imagine that we have various cells in our body. As we know, the most basic unit in our body is cells, and in order to prevent our body from external interference and repair our body in a timely manner when our body has some problem, we certainly need People's Liberation Army soldiers, armed police, traffic police, etc. to support us.

说明: 画线部分可被译为 the most basic unit in our body is cells。译员要抓住原文的主要意思,并将其转为目的语。这一句话的主要意思是我们人体最基本的单位是细胞,所以不需要逐字翻译"组成",也不必重复翻译"最主要""最基本"。

3)实际上免疫系统也就是起到这样的作用。当有外界<u>感染</u>侵入我们体内(时),免疫系统能够及时地产生反应、进行抵抗、把病菌清除掉。从另外一个角度讲,如果体内有一些异常情况,如组织损伤,免疫系统也必须能够应答。

In fact, the immune system just plays such a role. When there is external pathogens coming into our body, the immune system can response, resist and remove the germs timely. On the other hand, if you have some abnormal conditions, like tissue damage, the immune system has to respond, too.

说明:(1)"当有外界感染侵入我们体内"中的感染实际上指"病原体",译员将其译为 pathogens。(2)注意比较病菌(germ)和细菌(bacterium,复数为 bacteria)。病菌包括细菌、病毒、真菌(fungus,复数为 fungi)、支原体(mycoplasma)、衣原体(chlamydia)、放线菌(*Actinomyces*)、<u>立克次体(rickettsia)</u>、<u>螺旋体(spirochetes)</u>等。

4)但是既然谈到了解放军、谈到了部队,大家可以想象,这种任务不是单一的部队能够完成的。我们国家有空军、陆军、海军还有火箭军等等,而我们的免疫系统如果要发挥很好的功能,而且要应对千变万化的外界侵入的病菌,它就必须要有不同的组成成分。

But as we are talking about the People's Liberation Army and the armed forces, you can imagine that this task cannot be accomplished by a single force. We have the air force, army, navy, the rocket army and so on in China. And our immune system has different components, too, if it's going to function well and to be able to cope with the ever-changing invading germs.

5)通过进化,免疫系统发展出来一整套的细胞体系。在它的细胞体系里面,有红细胞、血小板等等,这些细胞都是免疫系统的组成部分,此外,还包括我们所说的巨噬细胞、中性粒细胞、<u>树枝状细胞</u>等等。但是在这个里面还有一个比较大的分支,那就是淋巴细胞。

The immune system has developed a cell system through evolution. And the cells, including the red blood cells, the platelets, macrophage, neutrophils, dendritic cells and so on, are the components of the immune system. But there is a broad category called lymphocyte.

说明:(1)讲者在列举细胞类别时,先想到了一些,之后又补充了一些。译员根据逻辑进行了语序调整。(2)树枝状细胞就是树突细胞(dendritic cells, DC)。(3)术语 platelets、macrophage、neutrophils 解析:plate 意为"板子";-let 意为"小";macro- 意为"巨";-phage 意为"吞噬"(联想记忆 esophagus,食道);neutro = neutral,意为"中性的";-phil 意为"爱好,嗜好"(联想记忆 philharmonic,用于乐队、音乐团体等名称中,意为"爱好音乐的;交响乐团;爱音乐的人;爱乐团体"。扩展:嗜酸性粒细胞,eosinophil;嗜碱性粒细胞,basophil)。

6)淋巴细胞最主要的有两类:一类是叫 B 细胞,这一类细胞有什么用处呢?它发挥的作用实际上类似于我们国家的火箭军。它对病菌的感染进行抑制,并且对病菌进行清除,这是体液免疫的一个主要功能或组成部分。另外还有一部分淋巴细胞叫 T 淋巴细胞。T 细胞参与我们所说的细胞免疫。我今天想讲的三部分的故事都跟 T 细胞有关。

There are two kinds of lymphocytes. One is called B cell. What function does this kind of cell have? Actually, it's like our rocket army, and it inhibits the infection of the germs, and clears the germs. That's one of the main functions or components of the humoral immunity. And then there is the second kind of lymphocytes which is called T lymphocytes, which get involved in what we call cellular immunity. The three aspects of story that I want to tell you today are all about T cells.

7)免疫系统的所有细胞,与<u>造血</u>系统的细胞一样,都是从造血系统产生的,而且造血系统会不断地更新这些细胞。

All of these immune system cells, just like the cells from the <u>hematopoietic</u> system, are produced by the hematopoietic system, and the hematopoietic system is constantly renewing these cells.

说明:hemato- 意为"<u>血液的</u>"。

8)T 细胞也分成两个主要的大类:第一类是杀伤性 T 细胞,就是 CD8 细胞。因为它表达的分子叫 CD8,所以被称为 CD8 细胞。这个细节对于绝大多数在场的人士来说,实际上不重要,大家只要记住 CD8 细胞就好,是有专门的杀伤能力的,而且它上面有特异的受体,能够识别<u>一些物质</u>。

T cells are also divided into two major groups. The first group is the killer T cell, which is also called CD8+ cells, because the molecule it expresses is called CD8, hence the name CD8+ cells. This detail doesn't matter to most of you, but please do remember that CD8+ cells have special ability to kill, and express <u>distinctive</u> receptors to recognize <u>some ligands</u>.

说明：（1）此处译文中的 distinctive 也可用 specific 来代替，但是在免疫学中，大家习惯用 distinctive 来表达受体本身是特别的、特殊的，是 CD8 所特有的；而用 specific 来指在受体和配体结合过程中，receptor 相对于 ligand 是特异性的。（2）此处，译员可根据背景知识将"一些物质"具体化为 some ligands（配体），以便听众理解。但如果听众是无生物医学背景的普通人，译员可将其翻译为 some materials。

9）比如说，被病毒感染的细胞所表达出来的病毒来源的一些分子，它就能够识别并杀死<u>这一类</u>被感染的细胞。这个 CD8 细胞也能够识别一些肿瘤细胞来源的抗原，并杀死这些肿瘤细胞。

For example, some cells that are infected by virus express molecules of viral origin. CD8+ T cells can recognize and kill these infected cells. Also, CD8+ T can recognize antigens that are originated from tumor cells and kill them.

说明："这一类"实际上是指前文所说的"被病毒感染的"，故译员将其翻译为 these。

10）另外一类 T 细胞叫 CD4 细胞。可能在场的很多人都知道这类细胞，为什么知道呢？因为它不仅在免疫系统中很重要，同时它还能被一种病毒所利用。<u>这个病毒就是 HIV，也就是艾滋病的病毒</u>。这个病毒通过识别 T 细胞分子，能够感染 CD4 T 细胞。

Another type of T cell is called <u>CD4+ cells</u>, and many of you here probably know this. Why do you know it? Because it's not only important in the immune system, but it's also utilized by a virus. <u>The virus is HIV and is able to infect CD4+ cells by recognizing T cell molecules</u>.

说明：（1）CD4+ cells，讲者可以念出"+"（positive），因为"+"表示"有"CD4 分子，也可以省略不念。（2）"这个病毒就是 HIV，也就是艾滋病的病毒"被译为"The virus is HIV and is able to infect CD4 by recognizing T cell molecules"。因为 HIV 对于源语言来说是一个外来语，且是一个首字母缩略词，所以讲者用中文进一步解释了这个词。但是，在目的语中，译员就不需要这个解释部分了，因为目的语的受众知道 HIV 的意思。

11）大家知道，这是感染了 HIV 的人，免疫系统会受损，这是因为感染 HIV 使得这一类 T 细胞在血液和免疫系统里面大量地下降，导致免疫系统不能发挥它应有的功能。所以这些 HIV 感染者一般都有很严重的免疫系统问题[1]。他们对于其他的病原体，比如细菌、真菌等的感染非常敏感。HIV 就是通过把这一类 T 细胞去除掉，使得我们的免疫系统丧失对外界的抵抗力。这就说明这一类 T 细胞非常重要，但这一类 T 细胞不是杀伤性 T 细胞，不能直接把其他的细胞杀死。

It's known that people who have been infected with HIV might have a compromised immune

---

1 患者感染后，如果及时采取治疗措施，可避免或延缓发生严重的免疫问题。

system, because HIV virus resulted in the massive drop of the number of this type of T cell in the blood and the immune system and the immune system can't do its job. Therefore, HIV-infected people usually have severe immune system problems, and are very sensitive to outside harmful bacterial infections, such as germs, fungi, and etc. The reason HIV can ruin the immune system is that it annihilates CD4+ T cells. We can tell that this type of T cell is very important, but it cannot directly kill other cells.

说明：感染 HIV 后，若能及时采取治疗措施，可避免或延缓发生严重的免疫问题，所以讲者所说的"一般都有很严重的免疫系统问题"可能不够准确，译员若具备相关知识，且处在交传模式，并被允许与讲者协商，那么可将其修正为 would have immune system problems。

12）它起到什么作用呢？我们在免疫学中，经常把这一类 T 细胞叫作免疫系统交响乐团指挥。它实际上发挥的是指挥其他的免疫细胞的作用，包括刚才讲的肥大细胞、中性粒细胞等等。这些细胞如何发挥它们的功能？就是靠 T 细胞。T 细胞能够使整个免疫系统有效地组织起来。T 细胞是免疫系统中比较重要的调节、整合、组织者。

Then, what role does it play? In the immune system, we often refer to this type of T cell as the conductor of symphony orchestra, and it actually directs how other immune cells, the mast cells, neutrophils and other cells function. All the immune responses are related to this kind of T cells who are the important regulators and organizers.

说明：（1）"这些细胞如何发挥它们的功能？就是靠 T 细胞。"属于重复信息，可省略不译。（2）"T 细胞能够使整个免疫系统有效地组织起来。"译员可根据背景知识将这句话翻译为"All the immune responses are related to this kind of T cells..."其中，responses 是译员根据知识储备补充的。若不具备背景知识，译员可按讲者的字面意思将其翻译为"T cells can orchestrate the whole immune system."（3）译员将"调节、整合、组织者"翻译为 regulators and organizers，省去了"整合"，原因在于"整合"和"组织"在免疫学上的结果相似，T 细胞联合树突状细胞和巨噬细胞（macrophages）来完成清除（clearance）或其他免疫应答，这个整合（integrate）的过程就是 organize immune response 的过程。如果三个词都翻译，译文会显得冗余，故译员省译了"整合"。

13）所以我今天讲的三个方面的工作跟这两类的 T 细胞，也就是 CD8+ T 细胞和 CD4+ T 细胞都有关系。在免疫系统里面，大家知道，需要维持一个比较好的平衡。如果免疫系统因为某些原因不能有效地发挥它的功能，比如被 HIV 感染后，人体就会对外界的感染非常敏感。有一些慢性感染，比如乙型肝炎等，是因为免疫系统不能有效地清除病毒感染所导致的。

What I'm going to talk about today has something to do with these two types of T cells, CD8+ T cells and CD4+ T cells. The immune system, you know, needs to maintain balance. And if the immune system doesn't function effectively, like when infected by HIV, patients will be very sensitive to infections. There are some cases of chronic infections, such as hepatitis B, where the immune system is unable to clear these infections effectively.

说明：译员译出了 you know（大家知道）。这个短语既可被视为讲者的无意义口语，又可被视为讲者试图与听众建立联系的方式。若是后者，译员应保留并翻译。若是前者，译员可省

第 12 章 基础医学

略不译。

14)还有另外一个情况,就是在有些情况下,一般来说免疫应答不是那么强。我们希望能够增强免疫应答,增强免疫系统的能力,这是现在对抗肿瘤的新兴的免疫治疗手段,这是一方面。我们希望能够依靠增强免疫应答来抵抗肿瘤内部起源的需要免疫系统发挥功能的情况。

The other circumstance is that sometimes the immune response is not that strong, and we want to be able to enhance it. And this is the new strategy of immunotherapy against tumors. We hope we can enhance the immune response so it can fight against the virus originated from tumors and function well.

15)另外,在很多情况下,免疫系统因为功能过强,或者调节不恰当,就引起各种各样的病变。现在是春天,在座的各位可能很多人都有过敏的问题。过敏就是因为免疫系统不能够有效地耐受外界,比如春天出现的新的植物的花粉,把这些外界物质当成是对人体非常有危害的一些物质,所以过度反应。等春天过了,花粉没有了,这些过敏的人士就没有这个问题了。

Besides, in many cases, the immune system reacts too strongly and regulates improperly. That will cause a variety of diseases. Now it's spring, and many of you may have allergies. Allergy is caused by the inability of the immune system to tolerate the stimulation from the outside world, for example, pollens. Instead, it takes these as hazards to the human body and overreacts. By the time spring goes by and the pollen is gone, those of you with allergies won't be bothered by it.

说明:(1)译员将"过敏就是因为免疫系统不能够有效地耐受外界,比如春天出现的新的植物的花粉"翻译为"Allergy is caused by the inability of the immune system to tolerate the stimulation from the outside world, for example, pollens"。译员添加了 the stimulation,让译文逻辑更加严密。(2)译员将"对人体非常有危害的一些物质"概括翻译为 hazards。(3)译员将原文中的"人士"译为 those of you,承接译文上文中的 many of you。

16)还有一些情况就不是季节性的,实际上后果更严重,等一下也会提到,那就是诸多的自身免疫疾病。就是因为免疫系统把关节、神经组织等等一些对自身功能都非常有用的组织和细胞当成了被外界感染过的细胞,所以它不断地浸润这些组织,然后来消灭、破坏这些自身的组织。这就是我们常说的自身免疫疾病或者炎症疾病。所以在这样的情况下,在过敏和自身免疫疾病情况下,免疫应答太强,没有受到很有效的控制,那么就会引起很多免疫疾病。

There are some cases that are not seasonal, but with more severe consequences. Those are autoimmune diseases, and we'll talk about them in a minute. Because the immune system is treating the useful and normal tissues and cells of joints, nerves and other body parts as infected tissues and cells, it keeps infiltrating into these tissues and cells, and destroys them. That is what we call autoimmune diseases or inflammatory diseases. So, in this case where there are allergy and autoimmunity and the immune response is out of control, a lot of immune diseases will be triggered.

说明:译员依据背景知识和上下文添加了 and normal。

17)这个图就说明我们希望免疫系统维持比较好的平衡,一方面,机体拥有较强的免疫力去清除慢性感染或肿瘤引起的反应；另一方面，我们希望机体免疫系统不会对花粉或自身组织产生超敏反应，以此使我们的机体免受免疫系统紊乱的影响。

This picture/diagram of the immune system can show us that we hope the immune system could maintain a good balance. On the one hand, the body has a strong immune system to clear reactions caused by chronic infections or tumors; on the other hand, we hope that the body's immune system will not be hypersensitive to pollen or its own tissues, so that our body is protected from immune system disorders.

说明：（1）diagram 意为"示意图"，picture 意为"图片"，译员可根据讲者幻灯片实际展示的内容选词。（2）译员用了 we could prevent our body from disturbances caused by the immune system，而非 we could prevent our body from disturbances from the immune system，是为了避免重复使用 from，并依据背景知识将 from 替换为 caused by。

18）所以第一方面我跟大家讲一讲肿瘤的免疫治疗。这一点大家都很关心，而且在社会上报道很多。它的原理是怎样的呢？2013 年，美国《科学》杂志把肿瘤的免疫治疗正式列为肿瘤的第四种治疗。

So, I want to talk to you first about immunotherapy for tumors, which is of great concern to you and has been widely reported. How does it work? In 2013, the American journal *Science* officially listed immunotherapy for cancer as the fourth treatment for cancer.

19）以前的肿瘤治疗主要是通过手术、放疗、化疗等手段。在化疗里面，因为对于肿瘤细胞的突变的了解越来越多，所以衍生出靶向治疗，也就是用特定的一些小分子、大分子来控制肿瘤细胞的一个手段。

Previous tumor treatments mainly utilize surgery, radiotherapy, and chemotherapy. For chemotherapy, as more and more mutations in tumor cells are known, targeted therapy is developed, a mean of controlling tumor cells with specific small and large molecules.

说明：（1）"等"字在中文中，不一定代表还有未列举完全的项目，而仅仅表示列举的终止，翻译时，译员需酌情判断。（2）"对于肿瘤细胞的突变的了解越来越多"实际上指的是对突变类型了解得越来越多，而非了解得更加深入，所以译员将其译为 as more and more mutations in tumor cells are known。

20）免疫治疗是一个什么样的办法呢？实际上，免疫治疗就类似于我们每年需要接种的流感病毒的疫苗，你一旦有了这种免疫力，免疫系统就不需要你来指挥，不需要你给药，它自动地就能够抵抗这些被外界病毒感染的细胞。如果免疫细胞能够识别我们的肿瘤细胞，自己就能够产生抵抗力，那么对于癌症的治疗，这是非常有利的，也是很多免疫学家很多年来一直期盼的一个结果。

Then what is immunotherapy? In fact, the mechanism of immunotherapy is similar to the flu vaccine that we need to get every year. Once you are armed with such immunity, the immune system doesn't need you to direct it again by administration of medicine. It automatically recognizes cells infected by viruses. If immune cells can recognize tumor cells and defend on their own, it could be very beneficial for cancer treatment, and many immunologists have been anticipating that for years.

说明：the mechanism 是译员依据上下文逻辑进行的补译。

21）在这个过程中，大家就发现免疫系统 CD8 T 细胞在肿瘤免疫里面起着非常重要的作用。它有两个特点，第一个是它有特异性，如果能够让这些 T 细胞识别肿瘤产生的特异的抗原、能够有效地清除肿瘤，那么这个特异性就非常好，而且它不会干扰到正常的组织。

During this process, it is found that CD8+ T cells play a very important role in tumor immunity. It has two characteristics. The first is that it has specificity. If these T cells can recognize specific antigens produced by tumors, and can effectively clear tumors, then they would have good specificity and would not disturb normal tissues.

说明："大家就发现"中的"大家"指的是科学家，并非本句的重点信息，故译员将其翻译为 it is found that。

22）另外一方面，这些 T 细胞能够产生记忆，如果给儿童接种疫苗，那么儿童就能够终身获得对这种病菌的保护。我们如果有一类 CD8 T 细胞对肿瘤有杀伤力，那么它一般来说最后都能够发展成为一个具有记忆性的免疫细胞，能够使得我们人体终身免遭肿瘤的侵害。

On the other hand, these T cells are able to generate memories. We know that if children are inoculated with a certain kind of vaccine against a germ, they can have lifelong protection against the germ that the vaccine protects people from. If we could have kind of CD8+ T cells that is lethal to a kind of tumor, they generally end up being immune cells with memory that protect us from the tumor for the rest of our lives.

说明：（1）译员在"如果给儿童接种疫苗"之前添加了 we know that，提示听众注意这是举例，是话题的切换。（2）译员在"接种疫苗"后，添加了 with a certain kind of vaccine against a germ，这是因为讲者接着就说了"获得对这种病菌的保护"。（3）"我们如果有一类 CD8 T 细胞对肿瘤有杀伤力"里的"肿瘤"，指的是某一种特定肿瘤，所以译员将其处理为 a kind of tumor。

23）很多化疗药物一开始效果很好，但是后续这些肿瘤都能够通过突变来规避这些药物的治疗，所以如果 CD8 T 细胞能够对肿瘤产生比较好的控制作用，那么这是我们免疫学家希望能够达到的目的。

Many chemotherapy drugs work well at the beginning, but later tumors are able to escape from the effect of these drugs through mutations. So, we'll be very happy to see that CD8+ T cells can better clear tumors.

24）怎么达到这个目的呢？最早大家就想研发肿瘤疫苗。就像我们通过接种疫苗对病毒和病菌产生抵抗力，如果研发出一种肿瘤疫苗，使得接种者产生针对肿瘤的免疫力，以后不得肿瘤，或者对肿瘤有抵抗力，这就是最好的一个结果。

How to realize that? In the early days, scientist wanted to develop the tumor vaccines. Just as we obtained immunity against viruses and bacteria, if we can develop a vaccine which will later generate the immunity in the inoculated, people will not get cancers anymore. And this will be the best results.

25)但是多年来,大家发现这个肿瘤抗原不是那么容易做,这是第一。第二,这一类的疫苗对于病毒引起的肿瘤是有预防作用,比如说对乙肝病毒引起的肝癌,比如说对 HPV 引起的宫颈癌等等,这些疫苗是有预防作用。但是一旦病人得了肿瘤,这些疫苗的干预性就比较差了。包括后来的细胞疫苗,都有<u>这些问题</u>。

However, after so many years, we found it is not easy to do that. This is the first <u>challenge</u>. Secondly, this type of vaccine has preventive effect on the tumor caused by viruses, such as liver cancer caused by hepatitis B virus, cervical cancer caused by HPV and so on. But once a patient already <u>bears a tumor</u>, these vaccines won't have very good efficacy. The later cellular vaccines have such a limitation too.

说明:(1)challenge 属于依据上下文补译。(2)注意专业表达: bears a tumor。(3)"这些问题"实际上是"这个问题",译员按"这个问题"来翻译。

26)后来就有一些新的进展,<u>这个主要是美国癌症研究中心的 Steve Rosenberg 博士</u>。他是一个外科医生,他经常做黑色素瘤手术。他发现黑色素瘤里面有大量的 CD8 T 细胞,所以他就想,如果把这个 T 细胞拿到体外来扩增,然后再输回病人,是不是能够起到比较好的<u>抵抗作用</u>。

And then there was some progress made mainly by Dr. Steve Rosenberg in American Cancer Research Center. He is a surgeon who often performed melanoma operations. He found there are a lot of CD8+ T cells infiltrating in melanoma, so he wondered if he can expand the T cells *in vitro*, and then bring them back to patients for better clearance of melanoma.

说明:(1)"这个主要是美国癌症研究中心的 Steve Rosenberg 博士"表意不完整,漏掉了"所做出的贡献"。译员将其整合补译为 some progress made mainly by Dr. Steve Rosenberg。(2)译员将原文中的"起到比较好的抵抗作用"意译为 for better clearance of melanoma。

27)他就这样做了,他发现确实有比较好的<u>抵抗作用</u>,因为在肿瘤里面的 CD8 T 细胞一般都是识别肿瘤的一些抗原,但是应用到其他的肿瘤里面,你肯定还是要找到一些办法能够使得 CD8 T 细胞能够识别肿瘤,那怎么办呢?

He did it and he found it did have better clearance, because inside the tumors, CD8+ T cells can generally recognize some of tumor antigens. If you want to apply it to treat other tumors, you have to find some other ways to enable CD8+ T cells to recognize tumors. How to make it happen?

说明:同上一段一样,本段中的"抵抗作用"也被翻译为 better clearance。

28)后来科学家就想了一个办法,就是如何让 CD8 T 细胞长一对眼睛——这个办法让我们在对白血病的治疗里面获得了比较大的成功,就是在 CD8 T 细胞上面加上人工的受体,让它能够结合到白血病的细胞上面,而且能够对白血病细胞起到杀伤的作用。

Then scientists came up with an idea on how to equip CD8+ T cells with a pair of "eyes". This was a great success in the treatment of leukemia. Artificial receptors were integrated into CD8+ T cells which could bind with leukemic cells and kill them in the end.

12.3.2 总结与点评

本节原文中，发言人主要介绍了免疫系统和免疫系统的两种反应机制，并介绍了治疗肿瘤的新方法——免疫治疗。在实际的口译工作中，译员会发现，发言人在思考时，会增加一些无意义的词，比如"这个""那么""一个""所以"等，译员需要自己辨别该词是否能发挥逻辑联系作用，否则应删译。本节中，译员已对发言人在讲话中使用的一些无意义的词进行了删减。

一般情况下，要理解发言人的意思，难度不大，但是发言人的表达习惯会给译员的理解增加难度，译员需要理解主要意思，厘清原文逻辑。本节出现的免疫专业术语较多，译员需要做好相关的译前准备。有些发言人讲话时，会在思考措辞的过程中说出的一些无意义的语气词，或出现短暂停顿等，译员可趁机去梳理发言人的讲话逻辑。

有些发言人喜欢重复某些讲话内容，便于观众或听众理解，而译员可能会根据翻译时间是否充裕、主办方是否对译文的简洁性提出要求、现场听众的反应等实际情况，适当简化源语言，输出简洁的目的语。

如果译员不慎漏译重要信息，可酌情在后面进行补充和解释，因为口语发言的特点（照着稿子宣读除外），往往是先讲出部分信息，然后再不断地补充和解释。

参考文献

王洪江. 2016. 基于反向遗传学技术的新型黄病毒减毒活疫苗的合理设计. 北京：中国人民解放军军事医学科学院博士学位论文.

赵爱华，白东亭. 2004. 构建更好的结核疫苗. 生物制品快讯，（12）：2.

American Cancer Society. 2022. Types and phases of clinical trials. *Cancer*. Retrieved November 10, 2022, from Cancer website.

Anon. 2022. Macmillan Dictionary. *Macmillan Dictionary*. Retrieved November 10, 2022, from Macmillan Dictionary website.

Donnelly, R. F. 2017. Vaccine delivery systems. *Human Vaccines & Immunotherapeutics*, *13*(1): 17–18.

Encyclopedia Britannica. 2022a. Galen. *Britannica*. Retrieved November 10, 2022, from Britannica website.

Encyclopedia Britannica. 2022b. Sigmund Freud. *Britannica*. Retrieved November 10, 2022, from Britannica website.

National Institutes of Health. 2022. Scleroderma. *Niams*. Retrieved November 10, 2022, from Niams website.

Smil, V. 2005. The next 50 years: Fatal discontinuities. *Population & Development Review*, *31*(2): 201–236

附录 I

常见物理学和化学单位及公式英汉对照表

1. The International System of Units (SI): Base Units (国际单位制基本单位)

Base Quantity 物理量	Unit Name 单位名称	Unit Symbol 单位符号
Amount of substance 物质的量	Mole 摩 [尔]	mol
Electric current 电流	Ampere 安 [培]	A
Length 长度	Meter 米	m
Luminous intensity 发光强度	Candela 坎 [德拉]	cd
Mass 质量	Kilogram 千克 / 公斤	kg
Time 时间	Second 秒	s
Temperature 温度	Kelvin 开 [尔文]	K

2. SI Derived Units (国际单位制衍生单位)

Derived Quantity 物理量	Name (Symbol) 单位名称 (符号)
Area 面积	Square meter (m^2) 平方米（m^2）
Volume 体积	Cubic meter (m^3) 立方米（m^3）
Speed/Velocity 速度 / 速率	Meter per second (m/s) 米每秒（m/s）
Acceleration 加速度	Meter per second squared (m/s^2) 米每平方秒（m/s^2）

（续表）

Derived Quantity 物理量	Name (Symbol) 单位名称（符号）
Frequency 频率	Hertz (Hz) 赫兹（Hz）
Force 力/重力	Newton (N) 牛[顿]（N）
Pressure/Stress 压强/压力	Pascal (Pa) 帕[斯卡]（Pa）
Energy/Work/Quantity of heat 能量/功/热量	Joule (J) 焦[耳]（J）
Power 功率	Watt (P) 瓦[特]（W）
Electric charge 电荷量	Coulomb (Q) 库[仑]（C）
Electric potential difference 电压/电动势	Volt (V) 伏[特]（V）
Electric resistance 电阻	Ohm (Ω) 欧[姆]（Ω）

3. **Prefixes Used to Designate Multiples of a Base Unit**（国际单位制前缀：表示该单位的倍数/分数）

Prefix 前缀	Symbol 符号	Meaning 含义	Multiple of Base Units 倍数/分数	Scientific Notation 幂次
tera- 太拉	T 太[拉]	trillion 万亿	1,000,000,000,000	10^{12}
giga- 吉咖	G 吉[咖]	billion 十亿	1,000,000,000	10^{9}
mega- 兆	M 兆	million 百万	1,000,000	10^{6}
kilo- 千	k 千	thousand 千	1,000	10^{3}
centi- 厘	c 厘	one hundredth 百分之一	1/100 or 0.01	10^{-2}
milli- 毫	m 毫	one thousandth 千分之一	1/1,000 or 0.001	10^{-3}
micro- 微	u 微	one millionth 百万分之一	1/1,000,000 or 0.000001	10^{-6}
Nano- 纳诺	n 纳[诺]	one billionth 十亿分之一	1/1,000,000,000 or 0.000000001	10^{-9}
pico- 皮可	p 皮[可]	one trillionth 万亿分之一	1/1,000,000,000,000 or 0.000000000001	10^{-12}

In general, when converting from base units (m, l, g, etc) or derived units (m^2, m^3, m/s, Hz, N, J, V, etc) to a multiple greater (kilo, mega, giga, or tera) than the base or derived unit, then <u>divide</u> by the factor. For example, 10 m = 10/1,000 km = 1/100 km = 0.01 km. When converting from base units or derived units to a multiple smaller (centi, milli, micro, nano) than the base or derived unit, then <u>multiply</u> by the factor. For example, 10 m = 10 × 100 cm = 1,000 cm.

一般来说，基本单位（米、升、克等）或衍生单位（平方米、立方米、米每秒、赫兹、牛、焦、伏等）向高倍（公斤、兆、千兆或太）转换时，<u>除以</u>该系数，例如 10 m = 10/1 000 km = 1/100 km = 0.01 km；向低倍（厘、毫、微、纳）转换时，<u>乘以</u>该系数，例如 10 m = 10 × 100 cm = 1 000 cm。

4. Subatomic Particles（次原子粒子）

Particle Name 粒子名称	Charge 电荷	Mass 质量	Location 位置
Proton 质子	+1	1	nucleus 原子核
Neutron 中子	0	1	nucleus 原子核
Electron 电子	−1	0	outside the nucleus 原子核外部

5. Common Cations（常见的阳离子）

Ion Name (Symbol) 离子名称（符号）	Ion Charge 电荷量
Lithium (Li) 锂离子（Li）	1+
Sodium (Na) 钠离子（Na）	1+
Potassium (K) 钾离子（K）	1+
Rubidium (Rb) 铷离子（Rb）	1+
Cesium (Cs) 铯离子（Cs）	1+
Beryllium (Be) 铍离子（Be）	2+
Magnesium (Mg) 镁离子（Mg）	2+
Calcium (Ca) 钙离子（Ca）	2+

（续表）

Ion Name (Symbol) 离子名称（符号）	Ion Charge 电荷量
Strontium (Sr) 锶离子（Sr）	2+
Barium (Ba) 钡离子（Ba）	2+
Aluminum (Al) 铝离子（Al）	3+

6. Common Anions（常见阴离子）

Element Name (Symbol) 元素名称（符号）	Ion Name (Symbol) 离子名称（符号）	Ion Charge 电荷量
Fluorine (F) 氟（F）	Fluoride 氟离子	1−
Chlorine (Cl) 氯（Cl）	Chloride 氯离子	1−
Bromine (Br) 溴（Br）	Bromide 溴离子	1−
Iodine (I) 碘（I）	Iodide 碘离子	1−
Oxygen (O) 氧（O）	Oxide 氧离子	2−
Sulfur (S) 硫（S）	Sulfide 硫离子	2−
Nitrogen (N) 氮（N）	Nitride 氮离子	3−

7. Common Polyatomic Ions（常见多原子离子）

Ion Name 离子名称	Ion Formula 化学式	Ion Name 离子名称	Ion Formula 化学式
Carbonate 碳酸根离子	CO_3^{2-}	Nitrite 亚硝酸根离子	NO_2^-
Chlorate 氯酸根离子	ClO_3^-	Phosphate 磷酸根离子	PO_4^{3-}
Cyanide 氰离子	CN^-	Phosphite 亚磷酸根离子	PO_3^{3-}
Hydroxide 氢氧根离子	OH^-	Sulfate 硫酸根离子	SO_4^{2-}
Nitrate 硝酸根离子	NO_3^-	Sulfite 亚硫酸根离子	SO_3^{2-}

8. Prefixes for Naming Covalent Compounds（多元共价化合物的命名前缀）

Number of Atoms 原子数量	Prefix 前缀	Number of Atoms 原子数量	Prefix 前缀
1	Mono 一	6	Hexa 六
2	Di 二	7	Hepta 七
3	Tri 三	8	Octa 八
4	Tetra 四	9	Nona 九
5	Penta 五	10	Deca 十

9. Types of Chemical Reactions（化学反应类型）

Type of Reaction 反应类型	Generalized Formula 通用化学式	Specific Example 具体例子
Combustion 燃烧反应	$HC + O_2 \rightarrow H_2O + CO_2$	$2C_2H_6 + 7O_2 \rightarrow 6H_2O + 4CO_2$
Synthesis 化合反应	$A + B \rightarrow AB$	$2Na + Cl_2 \rightarrow 2NaCl$
Decomposition 分解反应	$AB \rightarrow A + B$	$2H_2O \rightarrow 2H_2 + O_2$
Single replacement 置换反应	$A + BC \rightarrow AC + B$	$2Al + 3CuCl_2 \rightarrow 3Cu + 2AlCl_3$
Double replacement 复分解反应	$AX + BY \rightarrow AY + BX$	$Pb(NO_3)_2 + K_2CrO_4 \rightarrow PbCrO_4 + 2KNO_3$

10. The Effects of Change on Equilibrium in a Reversible Reaction, Le Châtelier's Principle（可逆反应中条件改变对化学平衡的影响，勒夏特列原理）

Condition 条件	Effect 效应
Temperature 温度	Increasing temperature favors the reaction that absorbs energy (endothermic). 增加温度，平衡向热量减少（吸收热量）的方向移动。
Pressure 压强	Increasing pressure favors the reaction that produces less gas. 增加压强，平衡向压强减小（减少气体生成）的方向移动。
Concentration 浓度	Increasing concentration of one substance favors the reaction that produces less of that substance. 增加某一反应物的浓度，平衡向该反应物浓度减小的方向移动。

11. Common Acids (常见的酸)

Acid 酸	Formula 化学式	Strength 强度
Hydrochloric (muriatic) acid 氯酸	HCl	Strong 强
Nitric acid 硝酸	HNO_3	Strong 强
Sulfuric acid 硫酸	H_2SO_4	Strong 强
Acetic acid 乙酸（醋酸）	CH_3COOH	Weak 弱
Citric acid 柠檬酸	$C_6H_8O_7$	Weak 弱
Formic 甲酸	HCOOH	Weak 弱

12. Common Bases (常见的碱)

Base 碱	Formula 化学式	Strength 强度
Potassium hydroxide (potash) 氢氧化钾	KOH	Strong 强
Sodium hydroxide (lye) 氢氧化钠	NaOH	Strong 强
Calcium hydroxide (lime) 氢氧化钙	$Ca(OH)_2$	Strong 强
Ammonia 氨水	NH_3	Weak 弱

13. pH Scale (pH 值)

Strong Acids ← More Acidic ← Weak Acids 强酸→酸性增加→弱酸								Neutral 中性	Weak Bases → More Basic → Strong Bases 弱碱→碱性增加→强碱					
0	1	2	3	4	5	6		7	8	9	10	11	12	13	14

附录 II
医疗卫生翻译中难译的非专业词汇

1. care：照顾；照料；（医疗）服务，医护

The aim of our hospital is to provide the best care possible. 本院的宗旨是提供最佳的医疗服务。

2. caregiver[1] / care giver：看护者；照料者

It is nearly always women who are the primary care givers. 妇女往往扮演初级看护者的角色。

The role of caregiver in this society is often taken on by women. 这个社会中，看护通常由女子来担任。

From caregiver to cared-for, from cared-for to caregiver, our relationship had come full circle. 她已从关爱者变为受照顾者，我则从受照顾者变为关爱者，我们的关系倒了个个儿。

3. health：健康；卫生；保健

He has a bee in his bonnet about health foods. 他对保健食品有自己的一套奇怪的看法。

Smoking is harmful to one's health. 吸烟对健康有害。

His pale face suggests bad health. 他面色苍白，说明他身体不好。

The report notes that several states now employ dental health directors. 报告指出，好几个州聘请了口腔卫生总监。

health preservation：养生

4. health care / healthcare：医疗，医护

health care / healthcare professionals：医护人员
the cause of health care：医疗卫生事业
health care / healthcare facility：医疗机构

---

[1] Collins Cobuild 词典将其解释为：A caregiver is someone who is responsible for looking after another person, for example, a person who is disabled, ill, or very young.

health care / healthcare provider：医疗服务提供方（供方），医疗卫生服务提供者

5. 关于医生身份

physician：医师（尤其指内科医生）

practitioner：开业的医师（执业医师，在中国，"执业医师"也被翻译成 health practitioner）

general practitioner: 全科医师

6. practice[1] (v.)：执业

In Belgium only qualified doctors may practice alternative medicine. 在比利时，只有合格的医生才可以开展替代医疗。

He was born in Hong Kong where he subsequently practiced as a physician until his retirement. 他出生于香港，后来在香港做内科医生，直至退休。

Does he still practice? 他还在执业吗？

An art historian and collector, he was also a practicing doctor. 他是历史学家、收藏家，还是执业医生。

practice[2] (n.)：活动

the practice of internal medicine：内科的医疗活动

I eventually realized I had to change my attitude toward medical practice. 我最后发现自己需要改变对医疗的看法。

If doctors find indecent behavior of their colleagues in their (clinical) practice, will they report? 医生在（临床）医疗活动 / 工作中发现同事的不良行为，会报告吗？

practice[3] (n.)：地点

The new doctor's practice was miles away from where I lived. 这位新医生的执业场所（如果根据上下文能够证实这位医生开设的是私人诊所，更好的翻译是"诊所"）离我的住地好几英里远。

If doctors find indecent behavior at their practice, will they report? 医生在工作场所发现不良行为，会报告吗？

7. well-being: 康乐；安宁；福利

Author and psychotherapist Gael Lindenfield shows how pressing the right buttons can

---

[1] Collins Cobuild 词典将其解释为：Someone who practices medicine or law works as a doctor or a lawyer.

[2] Collins Cobuild 词典将其解释为：The work done by doctors and lawyers is referred to as the practice of medicine and law. People's religious activities are referred to as the practice of a religion.

[3] Collins Cobuild 词典将其解释为：A doctor's or lawyer's practice is his or her business, often shared with other doctors or lawyers.

make a lasting contribution to your child's well-being. 作家兼心理治疗学家盖尔·林登费尔德揭示了下列可能对孩子的健康成长具有持久影响的正确方法。

For a parent who has concerns about their son or daughter's mental well-being, the experience of seeking information can be very frustrating. 那些关注子女心理健康的父母在寻求信息的路上可能会深受打击。

Until a couple of years ago there had been little research into the happiness and well-being of children born through artificial insemination. 几年前还没有对人工授精孩子生活是否幸福的调查。

World Health Organization's definition on health: "Health is not only the absence of infirmity and disease but also a state of physical, mental and social well-being." 世界卫生组织关于健康的定义:"健康乃是一种在身体上、精神上的完满状态,以及良好的适应力,而不仅仅是没有疾病和衰弱的状态。"

附录 III
常见医学词汇英汉对照

1. 学科、学院和专业

anatomy：解剖
basic medicine：基础医学
bio-chemistry：生化
clinical medicine：临床医学
genetics：遗传
medical humanities：医学人文
nursing：护理
pathology：病理
pathophysiology：病生理
pharmaceutical science：药学
physiology：生理
preventive medicine：预防医学 [1]
primary care：初级保健
public health：公共卫生
social medicine：社会医学
toxicology：毒理

2. 常见专业科室和专科医师

dental department; dentist：牙科
department of andrology; andrologist：男科
department of anesthesia; anesthetist：麻醉科
department of cardiac/thoracic surgery; surgeon[2]：心胸外科
department of ENT (ear, nose and throat); ENT doctor：耳鼻喉科
department of gynecology; gynecologist：妇科
department of internal medicine; physician：内科

---

1 注意区分 defensive medicine，这个短语指医生为了免于患者的控告而小心行医。
2 cardiologist 往往指心内科医生。

department of mental health; psychiatrist（精神医学专家）[1]：精神科
department of neurology; neurologist：神经外科
department of obstetrics; obstetrician：产科
department of oncology; oncologist：肿瘤科
department of ophthalmology; ophthalmologist：眼科
department of orthopedics; orthopedist：骨科
department of otolaryngology; otolaryngologist：五官科
department of pediatrics; pediatrician：儿科
department of pharmacy; pharmacist：药剂科
department of stomatology; stomatologist：口腔科
department of surgery; surgeon：外科
department of traditional Chinese medicine (TCM)[2]：中医科
department of urology; urologist：泌尿科
respiratory department; pulmologist：呼吸科
test lab; assayer（化验员）：检验科

3. 部分科室常见词汇

1）妇产科
delivery：生产
delivery room：产房
gestation：妊娠
infant mortality：婴儿死亡率
maternal mortality：孕产妇死亡率
midwife：助产士
midwifery：助产学
neonate：新生儿
obstructive delivery：难产
postpartum hemorrhage：产后出血
pregnant and lying-in women：孕产妇
shoulder distortion：肩难产

2）呼吸科
acute respiratory infection：急性呼吸道感染
bronch / bronchial catarrh / bronchitis / chest cold：支气管炎
chronic obstructive pulmonary disease (COPD)：慢性阻塞性肺炎（慢阻肺）

1　注意区分心理医生（psychologist）。
2　国外医学界有时把各种民族医学统称为 alternative medicine（替代医学）。

dispnea：呼吸困难

emphysema：肺气肿

phlegm：痰

pneumonia：肺炎

smoking cessation：戒烟

tracheitis：气管炎

3）神经科

acetylcholine：乙酰胆碱

appendices supraspheoidalis / appendix cerebri / appendix suprasphenoidalis / disipidin / glandula basilaris / HY / hypophysis cerebri / master gland / pituitarium / pituitary appendage / pituitary body / pituitary gland / somatic center：垂体

brain stem / brainstem / caudex encephali / encephalic trunk / truncus encephalicus：脑干

central nerve system：中枢神经系统

cerebell-/cerebello-/cerebellum/encephalion/epencephal/epencephalon/micrencephalon/opisthencephalon/parencephalon：小脑

cerebr-/cerebra/cerebro-/cerebrum：大脑

dopamine：多巴胺

hemi-/hemisphere：半球

lobus temporalis / temporal lobe / TL：颞叶

mid-brain/mesocerebrum：中脑

NA / nucleus accumbens septi / nucleus accumbens septum：伏隔核

neron：神经元

peripheral nerve：周围神经

spine：脊柱

synapse/synapsis：突触

ventral tegmental area：腹侧被盖区

4. 部分传染性疾病

bird flu / avian influenza：禽流感

epilepsy：癫痫

HIV/AIDS：艾滋病

influenza/flu：流感

leprosy：麻风病

mad cow disease：疯牛病 = bovine spongiform encephalopathy (BSE)：牛海绵状脑炎

malaria：疟疾

polio：脊髓灰质炎

tuberculosis (TB)：肺结核

5. 药学

activity：活性
agonist：激动剂
antagonist：拮抗剂
capsule：胶囊
drop：滴剂
drug for external use：外用药
duration of administration：给药持续时间
form：剂型
generic drug：非专利药[1]
intravenous drop-in / injection：注射剂
lot：批次
medicine for oral administration / medicine for oral use：内服药
oral：口服
OTC (over the counter) medicine：非处方药
patent drug：专利药
pill：丸
prescriptive medicine：处方药
route of administration：给药途径
subcutaneous：皮下
tablet：片剂
transdermal：透皮

6. 医药公司

Abbott Laboratories (ABT)：雅培制药
Astra Zeneca (AZN)：阿斯利康
Bayer：拜耳
Bristol-Myers Squibb：百时美施贵宝
Elly Lilly：礼来
Glaxo Smith Kleine (GSK)：葛兰素史克
Johnson & Johnson：强生
Lundbeck：灵北
Mead Johnson Nutrition：美赞臣
Medtronic (MDT)：美敦力
Merck：默克

---

[1] 又称仿制药，还可用 me-too drug 来表达。

Merck Sharp & Dohme (MSD)：默沙东

Novartis：诺华

Novo Nordisk：诺和诺得

Pfizer：辉瑞

Schering-Plough：先灵葆雅

Sino-America Tianjin Smith Kline & French Laboratories (TSKF)：中美史克

Wyeth：惠氏

Xi'an-Janssen：西安杨森

7. 器官的英文和拉丁文词根及举例

breast/mammo-/masto-：乳房；mammitis/mastitis：乳腺炎

esophagus/esophago-：食道；gastroesophageal reflux disease (GERD)：胃食管反流

heart/cardia-：心；cardiology：心脏外科

intestine/entero-：小肠；enteritis：肠炎

kidney/nephro-：肾；nephritis：肾炎

liver/hepa-：肝；hepatitis：肝炎；hepatitis A：甲肝；hepatitis B：乙肝

lung：肺；pulmo/pneumo-：呼吸的；pulmonary/pneumonic：肺部的；呼吸的

pancreas/pancreato-：胰腺；pancreatitis：胰腺炎

penis/phallo-：阴茎；phalloplasty：阴茎成形术

spine/spino-：脊柱；spinal bifida：脊柱裂

spleen/spleno-：脾脏；splenopexy：脾固定术

stomach/gastro-：胃；gastric acid：胃酸

urethra/urethro-：尿道；urethritis：尿道炎

vagina/colp-：阴道；vaginitis/colpitis：阴道炎

vessel/vascul-：血管；vascular disease：血管病

8. 颜色英文和拉丁文词根及举例

black/melan-：黑；melanoma：黑色素瘤

blue/cyan-：青；紫；cyanosis：发绀

green/chloro-：绿；chloromycetin：氯霉素

red/erthy-：红；erythrocyte：红细胞

white/leuco-：无色；褪色；白；leucocyte：白细胞

yellow/xano-：黄；xanthoma：黄瘤

9. 常用前缀和后缀及举例

1）前缀

ante-：前；antenatal test：产前检查

brady-：慢；bradycardia：心动过缓

dys-：困难；dysuria：排尿困难；dyspnea：呼吸困难

endo-：内；endoscopy：内窥镜

ex-：外；excretion：分泌

mega-/megalo-：大；megalocardia：心脏肥大

micro-/mini-：小；microphallus：小阴茎

post-：后；postnatal care：产后护理

tachy-：快；tachycardia：心动过速

2）后缀

-ia：状态；病（态）；alexia：失读症

-itis：炎症；pancreatitis：胰腺炎

-osis：异常；cyanosis：发绀

-rrhea：溢出，流出；diarrhea：腹泻；hemorrhage：流血

参考文献

邓大好，王燕．2022．医学英语翻译与写作教程．重庆：重庆大学出版社．

郭莉萍．2020．医学词汇学习手册：第3版．北京：协和医科大学出版社．

洪班信．2004．医学英语常用词辞典．北京：人民卫生出版社．

洪班信．2005a．医学英语汉译英1 500句．北京：北京大学医学出版社．

洪班信．2005b．英语医学术语的特征．北京：北京大学医学出版社．

洪班信．2006．医学英语常用介词搭配．北京：北京大学医学出版社．

洪班信．2007．医学英语句子的结构特征．北京：北京大学医学出版社．

Des Moines University. 2022. Medical terminology course. *DMU*. Retrieved November 10, 2022, from DMU website.

附录 IV

国家卫生健康委员会[1]及其内设机构名称汉英对照

1. 办公厅（General Office）

秘书处（总值班室）: Division of Secretariat (General Duty Office)
综合处: General Office
研究室: Research Office
督查室: Inspection Office
文档处: Division of Documentation and Archives
政务信息处: Division of Government Affairs
联络处: Division of Liaison
信访处: Division of Complaints and Appeal
保密安全处: Division of Confidentiality

2. 人事司（Department of Personnel）

综合处: General Office
干部处: Division of Personnel
监督教育处: Division of Supervision and Education
专业人才管理处: Division of Health Professionals Management
劳动工资处: Division of Labor and Salary

3. 规划发展与信息化司（Department of Planning and Information）

综合处: General Office
发展规划处: Division of Planning
建设装备处: Division of Construction and Equipment
大数据办公室（事业统计处）: Office of Big Data (Division of Healthcare Statistics)
爱国卫生工作办公室: Office of Patriotic Heath Campaign

1　其英文为 National Health Commission，前身为国家卫生与计划生育委员会（National Commission of Health and Family Planning），国家卫生与计划生育委员会前身为卫生部（Ministry of Health）。

4. 财务司（Department of Finance）

办公室：General Office
经济管理处：Division of Economic Management
预算管理处：Division of Budget Management
资产装备处：Division of Property and Equipment
审计评价处：Division of Auditing and Assessment
乡村振兴处：Division of Rural Revitalization
机关财务处：Division of Accounting

5. 法规司（Department of Law and Legislation）

综合处（行政复议处）：General Office (Division of Administrative Review)
立法处：Division of Legislation
法制审核处：Division of Law and Auditing
标准处：Division of Standards

6. 体制改革司（Department of Healthcare Reform）

综合协调处：General Office
政策研究处：Division of Policy Research
督导评价处：Division of Supervision and Assessment
公立医院改革处：Division of Public Hospital Reform

7. 医政司（Department of Medical Administration）

综合处：General Office
医疗资源处：Division of Medical Resources
医疗机构处：Division of Medical Institution
医疗管理处：Division of Medical Management
医疗质量与评价处：Division of Medical Quality and Assessment
护理与康复处：Division of Nursing and Recovery

8. 基层卫生健康司（Department of Primary Health）

综合处：General Office
运行评价处：Division of Operation and Assessment
家庭医生处：Division of Family Doctors
基本公共卫生处：Division of Basic Public Health

9. 医疗应急司（Health Emergency Response Office / Public Health Emergency Command Center）

综合处（行风处）：General Office (Division of Code of Conducts)

医疗应急管理处：Division of Health Emergency Response Management
医疗应急指导处：Division of Health Emergency Response Guidance
公共卫生医疗管理处：Division of Public Health Management
医疗卫生安全和血液管理处：Division of Health Security and Blood Management
医疗监督处：Division of Health Supervision

10. 科技教育司（Department of Health Science, Technology and Education）

综合处：General Office
重大专项处：Division of Major Project
规划评估处：Division of Planning and Assessment
生物安全一处：Division Ⅰ of Biosecurity
生物安全二处：Division Ⅱ of Biosecurity
医学教育处：Division of Medical Education

11. 药物政策与基本药物制度司（Department of Drug Policy and Essential Medicine）

综合处：General Office
药物政策处：Division of Drug Policy
药品目录管理处：Division of Drug List Management
药品供应保障协调处：Division of Drug Supply Security Coordination
药品使用管理处：Division of Drug Use Management

12. 食品安全标准与监测评估司（Department of Food Safety Standards, Risk Surveillance and Assessment）

综合处：General Office
食品安全标准管理处：Division of Food Safety Standards Management
食品安全风险监测与评估处：Division of Food Safety, Risk Surveillance and Assessment
食品营养处：Division of Food Nutrition

13. 老龄健康司（Department of Ageing and Health）

综合协调处：Division of Coordination
健康服务处：Division of Healthcare Services
医养结合处：Division of Integrated Eldercare Services with Medical Care

14. 妇幼健康司（Department of Maternal and Child Health）

综合处：General Office
妇女卫生处：Division of Women's Health
儿童卫生处：Division of Children's Health
出生缺陷防治处：Division of Birth Defect Prevention

15. 职业健康司（Department of Occupational Health）

综合处：General Office
预防处：Division of Disease Prevention
技术服务管理处：Division of Technical Service and Management
职业病管理处：Division of Occupational Disease Management

16. 人口监测与家庭发展司（Department of Population Surveillance and Family Development）

综合处：General Office
政策协调处：Division of Policy Coordination
监测评估处：Division of Surveillance and Assessment
家庭发展指导处：Division of Family Development and Guidance

17. 宣传司（Department of Publicity）

综合处：General Office
新闻网络处：Division of News Network
宣传处：Division of Publicity
健康促进处：Division of Health Improvement

18. 国际合作司（港澳台办公室）（Department of International Cooperation / Office of Hong Kong, Macao & Taiwan Affairs）

综合处：General Office
国际组织处：Division of International Organizations
欧美处：Division of European and American Affairs
亚太处：Division of Asian-Pacific Affairs
非洲处（援外处）：Division of African Affairs (Division of Medical Aid to Developing Countries)
港澳台处：Division of Hong Kong, Macao and Taiwan Affairs

19. 保健局（Bureau of Healthcare）

综合处：General Office
保健一处：Division I of Healthcare
保健二处：Division II of Healthcare
预防处：Division of Disease Prevention
财务处：Division of Finance

20. 机关党委（党组巡视工作领导小组办公室）（CPC Committee of NHC）

办公室（宣传、行业党建处）：General Office (Division of Publicity and Party Building)

纪委办公室：Office of the Discipline Inspection Commission
巡视工作处：Division of Inspection
组织处：Division of Organization
群工处（统战处）：Division of Mass Work (Division of United Fronts)

21. 离退休干部局（Bureau of Retired Officials）

综合处：General Office
组织处：Division of Organization
生活处：Division of Living
健康处：Division of Health
服务处：Division of Service

附录V
中国疾病预防控制中心[1]及其内设机构名称汉英对照

1. 中心机关（Functional Departments）

   办公室：Office of General Administration
   人事处：Office of Human Resources
   政策规划研究室：Office of Policy and Planning Research
   财务处：Office of Finance
   科技处：Office of Science and Technology
   教育培训处（研究生院）：Office of Education and Training (Graduate School)
   外事处（港澳台办公室）：Office of International Cooperation (Office of Hong Kong, Macao and Taiwan Affairs)
   实验室管理处：Office of Laboratory Management
   网络和信息安全管理处：Office of Network and Information Security Management
   资产管理处：Office of Asset Management
   基建处：Office of Infrastructure Construction
   审计处：Office of Internal Audit
   学术出版管理处：Office of Academic Publishing
   党委办公室：Office of CPC Committee
   纪委办公室（监察室）：Office of Discipline Inspection
   群团工作处：Office of Public Organizations
   离退休干部处：Office of Retired Staff Services
   保卫处：Office of Security
   后勤运营管理中心：Center for Logistics Operation and Management
   实验动物中心：Laboratory Animal Center
   健康传播中心（12320卫生热线管理中心办公室）：Health Communication Center (12320 Health Hotline Management Center Office)

---

[1] 其英文为 Chinese Center for Disease Control and Prevention。

附录 V 中国疾病预防控制中心及其内设机构名称汉英对照

信息中心：Information Center
卫生标准处：Office of Health Standards
流行病学办公室（爱国卫生工作技术指导处）：Office of Epidemiology (Technical Guidance Office for Patriotic Health Work)
全球公共卫生中心：Center for Global Public Health
卫生应急中心：Public Health Emergency Center
传染病管理处：Division of Infectious Diseases
免疫规划中心：Center for Immunization Planning
结核病预防控制中心：Center for Tuberculosis Control and Prevention
公共卫生管理处：Office of Public Health Management
慢病和老龄健康管理处：Office of Chronic Diseases and Ageing Health Management
控烟办公室：Tobacco Control Office

2. 中心直属单位（Affiliated Institutes）

传染病预防控制所：National Institute for Communicable Disease Control and Prevention
病毒病预防控制所：National Institute for Viral Disease Control and Prevention
寄生虫病预防控制所：National Institute of Parasitic Diseases
性病艾滋病预防控制中心：National Center for AIDS/STD Control and Prevention
慢性非传染性疾病预防控制中心：National Center for Chronic and Noncommunicable Disease Control and Prevention
营养与健康所：National Institute for Nutrition and Health
环境与健康相关产品安全所：National Institute of Environmental Health
职业卫生与中毒控制所：National Institute for Occupational Health and Poison Control
辐射防护与核安全医学所：National Institute for Radiological Protection
农村改水技术指导中心：National Center for Rural Water Supply Technical Guidance
妇幼保健中心：National Center for Women and Children's Health

3. 挂靠单位（Attached Institutions）

麻风病控制中心：National Center for Leprosy Control
老年保健中心：National Center for Older Adult Health Care
精神卫生中心：Mental Health Center
儿少 / 学校卫生中心：National Center for Child and Adolescent/School Health
鼠疫布氏菌病预防控制基地：Brucellosis and Plague Prevention and Control Base
结核病防治临床中心：Clinical Center for Tuberculosis Control
性病控制中心：National Center for STD Control
地方病控制中心：National Center for Endemic Disease Control

4. 相关协会（Related Associations）

中国卫生信息学会公共卫生信息专委会：Committee of Public Health Information Management, Chinese Health Information Association

中国性病艾滋病防治协会：Chinese Association of STD and AIDS Prevention and Control

中国营养学会：Chinese Nutrition Society

中国肝炎防治基金会：Chinese Foundation for Hepatitis Prevention and Control

中华预防医学会预防医学信息专委会：Committee of Preventive Medical Information Management, Chinese Preventive Medicine Association

附录 VI 国家医疗保障局[1]及其内设机构名称汉英对照

办公室：General Office
规划财务和法规司：Department of Planning, Finance, and Regulations
待遇保障司：Department of Benefit and Security
医药服务管理司：Department of Medical Service Management
医药价格和招标采购司：Department of Pharmaceutical Price and Bidding Procurement
基金监管司：Department of Fund Supervision
机关党委（人事司）：Party Committee (Department of Personnel)

1　其英文为 National Healthcare Security Administration。

附录VII 国家药品监督管理局[1]及其内设机构名称汉英对照

1. **综合和规划财务司**（Department of Comprehensive Affairs, Planning, and Finance Affairs）

   综合处（信访办）: Division of General Affairs (Office of Public Complaints and Proposals)
   秘书一处: Division of Secretariat Ⅰ
   秘书二处（应急办）: Division of Secretariat Ⅱ (Office of Emergency Management)
   文电保密处: Division of Documentation, Communication and Confidentiality
   督察处: Division of Superintendence
   新闻舆情处: Division of Media and Survey (Office of Media)
   规划处: Division of Planning
   预算审计处: Division of Budget and Audit
   财务处: Division of Finance
   政策法规司: Department of Policies and Regulations
   综合处: Division of General Affairs

2. **政策研究处**（Division of Policy Research）

   法规处: Division of Regulations
   执法监督处: Division of Enforcement Supervision

3. **药品注册管理司（中药民族药监督管理司）**（Department of Drug Registration / Department of TCMs and Ethno-Medicines Regulation）

   综合处（药品改革办公室）: Division of General Affairs (Office of Drug Regulation Reform)
   药物研究处: Division of Drug Research
   中药民族药处: Division of Traditional Chinese Medicines and Ethno-Medicines
   化学药品处: Division of Chemical Drugs

---

[1] 其英文为 National Medical Products Administration。

生物制品处: Division of Biological Products

4. 药品监督管理司（Department of Drug Regulation）

综合处（经营指导处）: Division of General Affairs (Division of Distribution Guidance)
监管一处: Division of Supervision Ⅰ
监管二处: Division of Supervision Ⅱ
监管三处: Division of Supervision Ⅲ
监管四处: Division of Regulation Ⅳ
药物警戒处: Division of Pharmacovigilance

5. 医疗器械注册管理司（Department of Medical Device Registration）

综合处: Division of General Affairs
注册一处: Division of Registration Ⅰ
注册二处: Division of Registration Ⅱ
注册研究处: Division of Registration Research

6. 医疗器械监督管理司（Department of Medical Device Regulation）

综合处: Division of General Affairs
监管一处: Division of Supervision Ⅰ
监管二处: Division of Supervision Ⅱ
监测抽验处: Division of Monitoring, Sampling and Testing

7. 化妆品监督管理司（Department of Cosmetics Regulation）

综合处: Division of General Affairs
监管一处: Division of Supervision Ⅰ
监管二处: Division of Supervision Ⅱ

8. 科技和国际合作司（港澳台办公室）（Department of Science, Technology and International Cooperation / Office of Hong Kong, Macao, and Taiwan Affairs）

综合处（港澳台处）: Division of General Affairs (Division of Hong Kong, Macao and Taiwan Affairs)
科技处: Division of Science and Technology
国际组织处: Division of International Organizations
双边合作处: Division of Bilateral Cooperation

9. 人事司（Department of Human Resources）

综合处: Division of General Affairs (Division of Training)

干部一处: Division of Personnel Ⅰ

干部二处（工资处）: Division of Personnel Ⅱ (Division of Salary)

干部监督处: Division of Personnel Supervision

10. 机关党委（Party Committee）

办公室（统战群工部）: Office of General Affairs (Department of United Front and Mass Organization Work)

组织宣传部（精神文明办公室）: Department of Organization and Publicity (Office of Public Etiquette and Ethical Standards)

纪律检查室: Division of Discipline Inspection

巡视办: Party Disciplinary Inspection Office

11. 离退休干部局（Bureau of Retired Officials）

综合处: Division of General Affairs

组织宣传处（党委纪委办公室）: Division of Organization and Publicity (Office of the Party Committee and Commission for Discipline Inspection)

生活服务处: Division of Social Care

附录VIII
常见药物英汉对照[1]

以下为常见药物。本部分表格"Samples（举例）"一栏列举了常见药物的化学名（括号内英文）及商品名（括号外英文）。同一个药物往往有多个厂家生产，因此会有多个商品名，此处仅列举其中较为常见的一个。提供此栏信息的目的是便于学习者通过国外药品的常见商品名来判断其化学成分。此内容仅用于科普及医学翻译学习，如有任何关于服药的问题，请咨询专业医师。

Category 类别	In Plain English 日常英文表达法	They Are Used for? 用途	Examples 举例
analgesics 镇痛剂	pain pills 止痛药	headaches, muscle aches and pains 治疗头痛、肌肉酸痛	Aleve (naproxen)：*（萘普生） Aspirin (acetylsalicylic acid)：阿司匹林（乙酰水杨酸） Celebrex (celecoxib)：西乐葆（塞来昔布） Codeine (codeine phosphate)：可待因（磷酸可待因） Motrin (ibuprofen)：美林（布洛芬） Tylenol (acetaminophen)：泰诺（对乙酰氨基酚）
antacids 抗酸剂	indigestion pills 消化不良药	heartburn 缓解烧心	Prevacid (lansoprazole)：普托平（兰索拉唑） Prilosec (omeprazole)：皮洛萨克（奥美拉唑） Tums (calcium carbonate)：*（碳酸钙） Zantac (ranitidine)：善胃得（雷尼替丁）
antiarthritics 抗关节炎风湿病药	rheumatism pills 风湿药	rheumatoid arthritis 治疗类风湿性关节炎	Aleve (naproxin)：*（萘普生） Aspirin (acetylsalicylic acid)：阿司匹林（乙酰水杨酸） Celebrex (celecoxib)：西乐葆（塞来昔布） Humira (adalimumab)：修美乐（阿达木单抗） Remicade (infliximab)：英夫利昔（英夫利昔单抗）

---

[1] 选编自 Des Moines University 的"Medical Terminology"网页内容。*表示暂无接受度较高的中文译名。

（续表）

Category 类别	In Plain English 日常英文表达法	They Are Used for? 用途	Examples 举例
antibiotics 抗生素	bug killers 杀虫剂	microbial infections 治疗微生物感染	Amoxil (amoxicillin)：阿莫仙（阿莫西林） Erythrocin (Erythromycin)：*（红霉素） Keflex (cephalexin)：凯复力（头孢氨苄） Pen-Vee (penicillin)：青霉素V钾（青霉素） Septra (sulfamethoxazole)：*（磺胺甲恶唑） Vibramycin (doxycycline)：辉瑞公司产盐酸多西环素胶囊商品名（多西环素）
anticoagulants 抗凝剂	blood thinners 血液稀释剂	prevent blood clots 防止血栓	Coumadin (warfarin)：施贵宝公司产华法林钠片商品名（华法林） Heparin：肝素[1] Plavix (clopidogrel)：波立维（氯吡格雷）
anticonvulsants 抗癫痫药	epilepsy drugs 癫痫药物	prevent seizures 预防癫痫发作	Dilantin (phenytoin)，大仑丁，癫能停（苯妥英） Phenobarbital：苯巴比妥[2] Neurontin (gabapentin)：镇顽癫（加巴喷丁）
antihistamines 抗组胺药	cold and flu pills 感冒和流感药	stop the runny nose, wheezing and itchiness 阻止流鼻涕、鼻塞和刺痒	Allegra (fexofenadine)：艾来（非索非那定） Benadryl (diphenhydramine)：苯那君（苯海拉明） Claritin (loratadine)：开瑞坦（氯雷他定）
antihyperlipidemics 降血脂药	cholesterol pills 胆固醇药（降脂药的一种）	lower cholesterol levels 降低胆固醇水平	Lipitor (atorvastatin)：立普妥（阿托伐他汀） Niaspan (niacin)：*（烟酸） Pravachol (pravastatin)：普拉固（普伐他汀） Questran (cholestyramine)：贵舒醇（消胆胺） Zocor (simvastatin)：维妥力（辛伐他汀）
antihypertensives 降压药	blood pressure pills 降压药	lower high blood pressure 降低高血压	Norvasc (amlodipine besylate)：络活喜（苯磺酸氨氯地平） Captopen (captopril)：*（卡托普利） Inderal (propranolol)：恩特来（普萘洛尔） Lotensin (benazepril)：*（贝那普利） Tenormin (atenolol)：天诺敏，特诺敏（阿替洛尔） Zestril (lisinopril)：捷赐瑞（利辛普利）

---

1 常见商品名较多，此处不举例。
2 常见商品名较多，此处不举例。

（续表）

Category 类别	In Plain English 日常英文表达法	They Are Used for? 用途	Examples 举例
cardiac drugs 心脏用药	heart medicine 心脏药物	treat abnormal heart rhythms, heart failure, angina pain 治疗心律异常、心力衰竭、心绞痛	Cardizem (diltiazem)：凯帝心（地尔硫卓） Cordarone (amiodarone)：脏得乐（胺碘酮） Inderal (propranolol)：恩特来锭（普萘洛尔） Lanoxin (digoxin)：隆我心锭（地高辛） Nitrostat (nitroglycerin)：耐较咛（硝化甘油）
diuretics 利尿剂	water pills 利尿剂	lower high blood pressure, treat congestive heart failure 降低高血压，治疗充血性心力衰竭	Hydrodiuril (hydrochlorothiazide)：*（氢氯噻嗪） Lasix (furosemide)：来适泄锭（呋塞米）
erectile dysfunction drugs 勃起功能障碍药	man's best friend 勃起功能障碍药	impotency 治疗阳痿	Cialis (tadalafil)：西力士（他达拉非） Levitra (vardenafil)：艾力达（伐地那非） Viagra (sildenafil)：万艾可（西地那非）
hypnotics 催眠药	sleeping pills 安眠药	insomnia 治疗失眠	Ambien (zolpidemtartrate)：思诺思（酒石酸唑吡坦） Lunesta (eszopiclone)：文飞（右佐匹克隆） Sonata (zaleplon)：索纳塔（扎勒普隆）
hypoglycemic agents 降糖药	diabetic drugs 降糖药物	lower high blood sugar 降低血糖浓度	Diabeta (glyburide)：博山（格列本脲） Glucophage (metformin)：格华止（二甲双胍） Glucotrol (glipizide)：灭特尼（格列吡嗪） Insulin (insulin)：胰岛素（胰岛素）
osteoporosis therapy 骨质疏松药	mom's bone pills 骨质疏松药	strengthen bones 强化骨骼	Actonel (risendronate)：*（利塞膦酸钠） Boniva (ibandronate)：邦罗力（伊班膦酸） Fosamax (alendronate)：福善美（阿仑膦酸盐）
tranquilizers 镇静剂	downers 镇静剂	relieve anxiety 缓解焦虑	Valium (diazepam)：安定（地西泮） Xanax (alprazolam)：佳静安定（阿普唑仑）